# ADAMS

## AN AMERICAN DYNASTY

FRANCIS RUSSELL was born on January 12, 1910. He graduated cum laude from Bowdoin College in 1933 and received a Master of Arts degree from Harvard in 1937. During World War II he was a captain in the Black Watch Royal Canadian Highlanders, later serving as a political intelligence officer for in the British Occupation Zone in post-war Germany. Russell's books include the controversial study of President Warren Harding's life, *The Shadow of Blooming Grove,* as well as *Tragedy in Dedham, The Making of A Nation, A City in Terror,* and *Sacco & Vanzetti: The Case Resolved.* Russell received Guggenheim Fellowships in 1964 and 1965, was the recipient of the Edgar Ward of the Mystery Writers of America in 1962, and was the recipient of the Friendship Award of the Federal Republic of Germany. Russell was a director of the Goethe Society of New England, a Fellow of the Society of American Historians, a member of the Black Watch Association, and the Boston Authors' Club. Russell died on March 20, 1989

# ADAMS

## AN AMERICAN DYNASTY

CASTLE BOOKS

*This edition published in 2005 by*
Castle Books ®
A division of Book Sales, Inc.
114 Northfield Avenue
Edison, NJ 08837

Copyright © 1976 American Heritage Inc.

Published by arrangement with
Ibooks, Inc.
24 West 25th Street, 11th Floor
New York, NY 10010

ISBN-13: 978-0-7858-1882-3
ISBN-10: 0-7858-1882-0

Printed in the United States of America

# CONTENTS

The Adams Family—A Genealogy
iv

Chapter 1: John Adams—The Colonial Lawyer
1

Chapter 2: John Adams—The Revolutionist
44

Chapter 3: John Adams—The Statesman
79

Chapter 4: John Quincy Adams—The Diplomat
144

Chapter 5: John Quincy Adams—Old Man Eloquent
186

Chapter 6: Charles Francis Adams—Voice of Honor
246

Chapter 7: Charles and Henry Adams—The Historians
302

Chapter 8: Brooks Adams and the Continuing Dynasty
354

**HENRY ADAMS**
*(ca. 1583-1646)*
*Farmer, of Barton*
*St. David, Somerset;*
*came to Massachusetts*
*in 1638*

**JOSEPH ADAMS**
*(1626-1694)*
*Farmer, town selectman*

**JOSEPH ADAMS**
*(1654-1737)*
*Farmer, town selectman*

**JOHN ADAMS**
*(1691-1761)*
*Farmer, church deacon*

**JOHN ADAMS**
*(1735-1826)*
*Second President of*
*the United States*

*Above: An engraving of a Gilbert Stuart portrait of John Adams*
*and various seals used by John and John Quincy Adams.*

**JOHN QUINCY ADAMS**
*(1833-1894)*
*Political leader,*
*gentleman farmer*

**CHARLES FRANCIS ADAMS**
*(1866-1954)*
*Banker, yachtsman,*
*Secretary of the Navy, 1929-1933*

**ABIGAIL ADAMS (HOMANS)**
*(1879-1974)*
*Writer*

**CHARLES FRANCIS ADAMS**
*(1910 —)*
*Former Board Chairman*
*of Raytheon*

**GEORGE CASPAR HOMANS**
*(1910 —)*
*Professor of Sociology*
*at Harvard*

*Showing the descent of the more notable members*

**ABIGAIL SMITH ADAMS**
*(1744-1818)*

**JOHN QUINCY ADAMS**
*(1767-1848)*
*Sixth President of
the United States*

**CHARLES FRANCIS ADAMS**
*(1807-1886)*
*U.S. Minister at
London, 1861-1868*

**CHARLES FRANCIS ADAMS, JR.**
*(1835-1915)*
*Railroad executive
and historian*

**HENRY ADAMS**
*(1838-1918)*
*Writer and
historian*

**BROOKS ADAMS**
*(1848-1927)*
*Writer and
historian*

**JOHN ADAMS**
*(1875-1964)*
*Historian and
investment counselor*

**JOHN QUINCY ADAMS**
*(1907 —)*
*Architect*

**THOMAS BOYLSTON ADAMS**
*(1910—)*
*Former President of the
Massachusetts Historical Society*

**FREDERICK OGDEN ADAMS**
*(1912 —)*
*Landscapist*

# 1

## John Adams

### THE COLONIAL LAWYER

**A**S SECOND President of the United States, John Adams in his single term has been overshadowed by both his predecessor and successor. Yet this chubby, opinionated New Englander, stubborn and egotistical, was truly a Founding Father, one of the handful of men without whom it would be impossible to imagine later America. Washington, reserved and aloof, even while President, became a symbol, a presence sufficient to chill the hand of anyone presumptuous enough to slap him on the back. The Father of his Country stood apart from ordinary humanity. Adams was all too obviously human, from his outer appearance to his tactlessly assertive manner, cranky, jealous, yet with a razor-sharp intellect and a keen awareness of his own weaknesses. An English diplomat considered him the most ungracious man he had ever encountered. Benjamin Franklin thought him "always an honest man, often a wise one, but sometimes in some things absolutely out of his senses." The three-branched system of American constitutional government with its built-in system of checks and balances owes more to him perhaps than to any other one man. Though he was equally opposed by Jefferson's democratic and

Hamilton's aristocratic extremists, he did establish governmental precedents at a time when it was a question whether the American experiment could survive. In later times his views appear more solidly correct than Jefferson's Rousseauistic fancies of the goodness of natural man or Hamilton's feeling of the people as a great beast. The somewhat unprepossessing little man was more intelligent than Washington and far more learned, more rational than Jefferson in regard to human nature, a political figure to whom his country would remain permanently indebted.

In 1823 in the piety of his old age Adams erected a monument in his native Quincy, Massachusetts, to his first American ancestor, Henry Adams, who in 1638 left old England for the new. In the words of John, Henry's great-great-grandson, this obscure farmer "took his flight from the Dragon persecution." The inscription was more a feeling of what ought to be than an established fact, as indeed was the long pedigree produced by the next generation of Adamses to demonstrate their descent from an ancient Gloucestershire baronial family. Later and more professional genealogists would determine that the first American Adams was born in the little village of Barton St. David in Somerset, among the Polden Hills just seven miles southeast of Glastonbury. His father and grandfather had been tenant farmers there before him, not independent yeomen but leaseholders of the lord of the manor, raising sheep and cattle and living in simple thatch-roofed stone cottages.

Henry, the third-generation copyholder and founder of America's most durable dynasty, remains a dim figure, illuminated only briefly by a few crabbed lines in court and parish records. It is known that he was born about 1583, that his people had lived in Barton St. David for over a century, and that at the age of twenty-six he married the twenty-two-year-old Edith Squire, the daughter of the blacksmith of neighboring Charlton Mackrell. In the next twenty-one years Edith bore her husband nine surviving children—eight boys and a girl—a surprising total in that day of high infant mortality. No doubt there were other children who did not survive. For some reason the Adamses between 1614 and 1622 moved to the adjoining parish of Kingweston. From there Henry and Edith left England for America. Why they left, what they hoped for, how they felt on turning their backs on the land of their inheritance remains supposition and conjecture. Like most emigrants their motives were uncertain even to themselves, a mixture of piety, shrewdness, ambition, restlessness, resentment, and hope. In the first half of the seventeenth century English migration was part of the time-spirit, an uneasy impulse accentuated by hard times that brought soaring prices in lands and rents and ever more exacting taxes. Between 1620 and 1640 some sixty-five thousand Englishmen sailed away to the West Indies or the American continent.

Henry Adams may have been one of these restless men, unable to own land and eager to go where land was almost for the asking. There is no sign that the dragon persecution had troubled him in his remote village. For the most part the parishoners of Barton St. David seemed unaffected by the lapping waves of dissent. Marriages, baptisms, and funerals took place for the Adamses as they always had, in the accepted tradition, under the curious octagonal tower of St. David's Church. But in adjoining Dorset—with Somerset and Devon a stronghold of Puritanism—the Reverend John White of Dorchester, a Puritan moderate remaining within the established Church, had stirred many a yeoman and farmer to consider leaving the timeworn paths of his ancestors. In 1623 White organized the Dorchester Adventurers to aid both non-conformists and loyal churchmen in the settling of New England. Then in 1628 the Adventurers were absorbed by the Massachusetts Bay Company which secured a liberal charter for its colonists. From 1629 to 1640 about twenty-five thousand Englishmen, mostly so-called Puritans, left their homeland for New England. Among the early migrants was Edith Adams's younger sister, Ann, married to Aquila Purchase, a master of Trinity School, Dorchester. The

Purchases sailed from England in 1633. Aquila either died on the voyage or shortly afterward. His widow remained in New England, being granted four acres of land in the new Dorchester. In 1637 she married a widower, Thomas Oliver of Boston.

Five years after the Purchases, the Adamses finally sailed. With them were eight of their nine children; their sons Henry, Thomas, Samuel, Peter, John, Joseph, and Edward and their one daughter, Ursula. Their third son, Jonathan, would remain behind for another dozen years. Accompanying them on the voyage was Margaret Shepherd, another of Edith's four sisters, with her husband, John.

As the head of a family of ten and on payment of three shillings an acre, Henry was granted forty acres at Mount Wollaston, six miles south of Boston, where the genial royalist Thomas Morton a decade before had established his ephemeral Puritan-defying Merry Mount. In 1640 Mount Wollaston became part of Braintree (later Quincy). By the time Henry received his acres the initial land clearing had been made, the first roads laid out, a school set up, and a First Church established. More influential Mount Wollaston settlers like Edmund Quincy and William Hutchinson, the husband of the irritatingly heretical Anne, were granted as much as five hundred acres each by the Massachusetts legislature, the General Court. Henry Adams contented himself with his forty.

He lived a mere eight years after setting foot on American soil, farming his acres, brewing beer in a shed next to his house, caring for his children, and acquiring a respectable minimum of posses-sions. When he died in October, 1646, at the age of sixty-three, an inventory of his estate valued his property at £75. This included a two-room house with its barn, three beds, two chests, "some auld bookes," pewter plates, a silver spoon, a frying pan, a "spitt & trivett & gridyron," a warming pan, tools, lumber, a cow and heifer, pigs, and corn. The books—it was out of the ordinary for a New England farmer to own more than the Bible—were to be di-vided among his children. His house and other possessions went to his wife "so Longe as shee liveth unmarried." When five years later Edith married John Fussell of adjoining Weymouth, the house reverted to Ursula and the two youngest sons, Joseph and Edward. Through some private agreement Joseph secured his father's farm. There he lived out the rest of his life, the sole Adams to remain in Quincy.

The second Henry Adams, one of the founders of Medfield, Massachusetts, was joined there by his remarried mother and by his brothers Peter and Edward. Jonathan, when he finally came over from England in 1651, also settled in Medfield. Most of the village went up in flames in 1676 when the Indians raided it in King Philip's War. During the attack Henry was killed on his own doorstep. Thomas moved to Concord, then became one of the founders of Chelmsford where he was followed by John who erected a mill there. Ursula, four times widowed, lived respectively in Charlestown, Watertown, Dorchester, and Roxbury.

The names of seven of the nine Adams children were to prove as ephemeral as those of their fellow voyagers, persisting on slate gravestones if at all. Only John and Joseph established enduring Adams lines. John, on his arrival in America, was apprenticed to a Cambridge millwright, and after serving his seven years continued in that trade. The businessman of the family, his affairs took him to England in 1650. Returning the following year with his brother Jonathan, he settled in the Menotomy section of Cambridge where his descendants remained until the next century when they moved to New Hampshire. In the latter part of the nineteenth century these farming Adamses evolved into traders and financiers allied and related to the Morgans, and as Episcopalian churchwardens, became stalwarts in the establishment their ancestor Henry had forsaken.

Though it would not be evident for another three generations, the extraordinary quality of the Adams blood that would make that family unique in American history derived from the seventh son, Joseph. His own life passed as obscurely as that of his father. He farmed and occasionally brewed. That he was respected is apparent in his serving for a time as a town selectman and as surveyor of highways. The most noteworthy thing about him was that he had twelve children, ten of whom survived infancy. Building on his father's modest means he left an estate of nearly £350.

The Adams historical line was passed on through Joseph's namesake and second son, and to a lesser extent through his sixth son, John, a sea captain whose grandson Samuel would turn out to be the redoubtable political dictator of Boston. The second Joseph passed his life in Quincy, much as his father before him, as a farmer and occasional maltster, a selectman, and briefly a constable. He married three times and had eleven children. His second wife, Hannah Bass, by whom he had eight children, was the granddaughter of Deacon Samuel Bass and also a descendant of John and Priscilla Alden, whose posthumous fame would have to wait on Longfellow. In marrying a deacon's daughter Joseph had married up, his rise manifest when he sent their first child (his first son), also a Joseph, to Harvard to become a clergyman, thus beginning the Adamses' long connection with the Puritan college. The middle Joseph died in 1737.

Harvard, however, was not yet to provide the sequential background for the Adamses. All unknowingly the bearer of the family tradition was now the younger son, John. An industrious young man, he followed the shoemaker's trade in the winter months when he was not farming. Several times he was chosen selectman, he became a lieutenant in a militia company commanded by Colonel John Quincy, and as a mark of his heightened importance in the rustic community he was for many years deacon of the First Church. In 1720 he left the Adams homestead and bought the four-room, two-story cottage of James Penneman with "six acres of orchard and arable land" near Penn's Hill in north Braintree. Not until 1734 when he was forty-four did he finally marry, choosing as his bride the twenty-six-year-old Susanna Boylston of a Brookline family far more noted than his own. A year after his marriage his son John was born. Unlike the earlier prolific generations, Deacon John had only three children, John, Peter Boylston, and Elihu.

In 1744 he bought the property adjoining his own for £500, a house only a few yards from his earlier acquired homestead and much like it in size and shape. With it went nine and one-half acres. From this time on, the two places were run as one, known as the Penn's Hill Farm. The second house he rented to his niece Ann and her husband, Dr. Elisha Savil, leaving it in his will to his son John. The homestead itself he left to Peter. He died in 1761, and his widow continued to live there until she married a Lieutenant John Hall in 1766.

In the century between Henry's arrival in Braintree and the birth of his great-great-grandson John, the Adams family followed the placid, plodding ways of their English forebears, respected and increasingly honored within the village and scarcely known outside. Boston, though clearly visible from Penn's Hill, might as well have been as distant as London for the Adamses. They remained unconcerned by the turbulent growth of the provincial capital, the rise of a wealthy merchant class, the agitation against the Navigation Acts, the loss of the province's charter, the insurrection against Governor Edmund Andros, the fife and drum of recruiters summoning up volunteers for the wars against the French, and Boston's vice-regal aspect under the royal governors. On their Braintree farm they were content to follow Hesiod's ancient admonition "to plough and plant and set one's house in order." Nothing more. Then with Deacon John's son and namesake some mutation altered and transformed the placid Adams stock, perhaps, as John Adams himself thought, through the admixture of Boylston blood or from the age gap between father and mother (common among extraordinary children) or by some inexplicable biological twist. With John, born in 1735, the history of the Adams family as a dynasty begins.

Eighty-nine years after John's birth his son, Secretary of State John Quincy Adams, shortly to be President, spent an autumn afternoon wandering among the tombstones of his ancestors in the Quincy graveyard, then wrote in his diary: "Four generations of whom very little more is known than is recorded upon these stones. There are three succeeding generations of us now living. Pass another century, and we shall all be mouldering in the same dust, or resolved into the same elements. Who then of our posterity shall visit this yard? And what shall he read engraved upon the stones?"

That John Adams had the mark of destiny on him was not apparent in his childhood. Small and sturdy, he was no early book-worm but an outdoor boy wandering with other boys across the familiar rolling and wooded countryside with the bluish haze of Great Blue Hill as a background, and in the foreground, as seen from Penn's Hill, the harbor and the sea. His closest friends were Edmund and Samuel Quincy, the sons of that great man of Brain-tree, Colonel John Quincy, and John Hancock, the minister's son. They played their games, whittled toy boats, flew kites, rolled hoops, explored the long marshes of the sinuous Neponset River. The Town Brook ran through the Adams farm to the Town Landing where the boys could see the scows arriving from Fore River. With awed curiosity they watched the derelict survivors of the Ponka-poag tribe as they came each year to fish in the Neponset, so different from the legendary warriors of King Philip's War, and yet Indians with all that the sinister name implied. Country boys learned to handle firearms early, and hunting soon became John's greatest joy. With his fowling piece he tramped the woods picking off unwary squirrels, rabbits, and woodchucks, and even the wary crow by imitating its caw. As he grew more skilled he shot quail, woodcock, and the wild turkey. In a scow concealed by reeds he lay in wait in the Neponset marshes for the ducks and geese as they flew south. Later, he admitted that shooting gave him a delight that he never felt "for any other business, study or amusement."

Three years before his birth the inhabitants of Braintree had taxed themselves both literally and figuratively by building a new meeting-house. Deacon Adams's pew, placed prominently just to the left of the pulpit, demonstrated his position in the church and the community. The structure of Calvinism remained far more rigid in the villages than in the towns. Church services absorbed most of Sunday with morning and afternoon services and sermons of traditionally interminable length. The boys sat in the gallery where they were given to whispering and shuffling until brought to order by the tithingman. From that vantage point the older ones cast covert eyes at the girls in their Sunday best. John's eyes were as wayward as any. From the age of ten he sensed the charm of burgeoning young ladies. In his adolescence his bright good looks attracted girls even as he was attracted to them. As he admitted in his autobiography, he was "of an amorous disposition." Yet somehow he was always able to keep his disposition under control. However he may have felt in his hot youth, in the dying embers of his old age he was glad he had restrained his "natural temperament," and he found it "consolatory beyond all expression" that he had not given in to the varieties of "libertinism" available in rural Braintree.

He first attended the one-room school for the Braintree children of all ages, run by Dame Belcher in the stern tradition of *The New England Primer*. As one of the brightest boys he became the teacher's early favorite. From there he entered the local Latin School, a staple of most Puritan-derived communities, as the first step toward college and the clergy. Again the boy found himself in a one-room school, run this time by one Joseph Cleverly, whose name belied the fact, for he was a failed schoolmaster, a Harvard graduate come down in the world, uninspired, uninspiring. For a country boy impatient of desk confinement and seeing himself as one more in a line of farmers, such a school was a bore and the study of Latin the most onerous of tasks. John showed no early love of books or learning. Only mathematics moved his fancy. He grew to hate school. Nevertheless Deacon Adams was determined to send his eldest boy to Harvard and if possible make a clergyman of him. What did his son want to be then, the exasperated deacon asked in one heart-to-heart talk. "A farmer," the boy replied to his dismayed parent.

Next morning as a practical demonstration of what it meant to be a farmer, the deacon took his son to Penny Ferry where they spent a sweltering day in swamp muck, tormented by flies and mosquitoes, cutting reeds for thatch. That evening the father asked his son if he was satisfied with being a farmer. "I like it very well Sir," the boy replied. "Ay but I don't like it so well," was his father's irritated retort, "so you shall go to School today."

Stubbornly the boy insisted that he preferred "Creek Thatch" to going to school. Long afterward he recalled the scene in his autobiography: "You know said my father I have set my heart upon your Education at Colledge and why will you not comply with my desire. Sir I dont like my Schoolmaster. He is so negligent and so cross that I can never learn any thing under him. If you will be so good as to perswade Mr. Marsh to take me, I will apply myself to my Studies as closely as my nature will admit, and go to Colledge as soon as I can be prepared. Next Morning the first I heard was John I have perswaded Mr. Marsh to take you, and you must go to school there to day. This Mr. Marsh was a Son of our former Minister of that name, who kept a private Boarding School but two doors from my Fathers. To this School I went, where I was kindly treated, and I began to study in Earnest."

Before then John had often played truant, hiding in the

marshes with his fowling piece to shoot ducks and geese. Now he put aside the fowling piece for books and in a little over a year was ready for the "Examination of Candidates for Admission" to Harvard.

On an overcast morning in the late summer of 1750 he rode to Cambridge. "Terrified at the Thought of introducing myself to such great Men as the President and fellows of a Colledge," he recalled, "I at first resolved to return home: but foreseeing the Grief of my father and apprehending he would not only be offended with me, but my Master too whom I sincerely loved, I arroused my self, and collected Resolution enough to proceed."

In his boyish awkwardness he now had to face President Holyoke and the Harvard tutors, sternly aloof in all the formality of gown and wig. After a few preliminary questions one of the tutors, Joseph Mayhew, a plump amiable man, handed the boy a page of English to translate into Latin. One glance told Adams it was beyond his thin knowledge, and he was overcome with a sinking sense of failure. But the good-natured Mayhew, noting his dismay, called him to his study and said encouragingly: "There Child, is a dictionary, there a Gramar, and there Paper, Pen and Ink, and you may take your own time." Fortified by the tools so gratuitously provided, Adams sat down at the desk with revived confidence. "The Latin was soon made, I was declared Admitted and a Theme given me to write on in the Vacation. I was as light when I came home as I had been heavy when I went: my Master was well pleased and my parents very happy. I spent the Vacation not very profitably chiefly in reading Magazines."

A few weeks later young Adams again left Braintree for Cambridge in a much more buoyant frame of mind as a Harvard freshman. The college under President Holyoke, like Massachusetts itself in the mid-eighteenth century, had been breaking away from the earlier rigidities of Calvinism. Though himself a clergyman, Holyoke was a religious liberal, firm in his faith as a clergyman yet tolerant for his time, one of Harvard's notable reformist presidents. No longer was Harvard in its second century a forcing house for Congregational ministers. Holyoke enlarged the Puritan college's horizons, softened its doctrinal rigidities. For president and tutors the truths of the Christian religion stood beyond doubt, but within that premise Harvard students were inducted into the body of knowledge, ancient and modern, that educated men were expected to absorb.

To those of a later day the college of Adams's time would seem rigid enough. All students followed the same course. Freshmen studied Greek and Latin, logic, rhetoric, and physics. Sophomores continued this curriculum except that they replaced physics by natural philosophy (as science was then called). Junior sophisters added metaphysics and geography, while seniors besides reviewing their previous studies undertook mathematics and philosophy. The day opened at six o'clock with prayers. Breakfast followed—a meager parceling of "bread, biscuit and milk"—and classes began at eight with a lecture. The rest of the morning was devoted to study and recitations in the subject of the lecture. Lunch was at noon, followed by more study and recitations. Evening prayers were at five, and supper at seven thirty. From then until nine, students were free to do as they pleased. Saturday was devoted to the study of theology under President Holyoke. Church attendance on Sunday was, of course, compulsory.

Removed from their ancestral pieties, a medieval license prevailed among the Cambridge students in spite of the efforts of tutors and president to control it. Undergraduates were repeatedly disciplined for "abominable lasciviousness," for firing off pistols, skating on the Charles without permission, cutting up at prayers, and profaning the Sabbath. In short, like students elsewhere, they roistered and wenched and drank. Drunken students even rolled logs down the stairs by Tutor Mayhew's study windows, broke open his cellar, and stole his beer and brandy. Others put snakes in Tutor Flynt's room. Adams's old Braintree friends, John Hancock and Samuel Quincy, were degraded and fined for getting a Negro slave drunk.

John Adams, though given to the normal amount of coltish pranks, never went so far. He did on occasion drink rum, punch, and flip, and he chewed tobacco. On entering he was ranked fourteenth in a class of twenty-four, graded as was the college custom according to his social level. Even this level, in his son's opinion, was due to the social weight of his mother's family. Yet, if he had been rated according to scholarship, he would at graduation have ranked among the first three of his class.

Friendship, sport, and the company of young ladies engrossed him. Yet as his Harvard years progressed he "soon perceived a growing Curiosity, a Love of Books and a fondness for Study, which dissipated all my Inclination for Sports, and even for the Society of the Ladies. I read forever, but without much method, and with very little choice. I got my Lessons regularly and performed my recitations without Censure. Mathematicks and natural Phylosophy attracted the most of my Attention." What he should do on graduating remained undefined although his parents had hoped to see him a clergyman. In 1755, at his Harvard Commencement, that rowdy, bibulous week-long carnival that drew in relatives, friends, countryfolk from miles around, as well as pedlars, pitchmen, bawds, and merrymakers, he took part in a Latin disputation at the formal exercises in the meetinghouse. Among those present was a Worcester clergyman, Thaddeus Maccarty, who had been commissioned to find a new schoolmaster. After listening to Senior Sophister Adams, he at once engaged him.

To the short, plump young Harvard graduate with the clear blue eyes, just the trace of a double chin, and a somewhat angular nose above a cupid's bow mouth, Worcester sunk in its bowl of hills was a town of limited horizons. At twenty John Adams was eager to be somebody in the world. Teaching "little runtlings" in a one-room school seemed a dead end, a grubby way of earning a living. "Hope has left me," he wrote his cousin and Harvard classmate Nathan Webb after a few weeks. His school was an affliction that, if he continued in his post, "would make a base weed and ignoble shrub of me."

Habit, which can make the intolerable at least durable, relieved him of some of his tedium and much of his impatience. Recalling his own grim schooldays with Cleverly, he strove to arouse his pupils' interests and stimulate any love of learning they might have. In time he came to enjoy himself. "The World," he noted in his diary, "affords no greater Pleasure" than to "fire the new born soul with a noble ardor. . . . Let others waste the bloom of Life, at the Card or billard Table, among rakes and fools, and when their minds are sufficiently fretted with losses, and inflamed by Wine, ramble through the Streets, assaulting innocent People, breaking Windows or debauching young Girls. I envy not their exalted happiness. I had rather sit in school and consider which of my pupils will turn out in his future Life, a Hero, and which a rake, which a phylosopher, and which a parasite, than change breasts with them, tho possest of 20 lac'd wast coats and £1000 a year. Methinks I hear you say, this is odd talk for J. Adams."

Worcester on second view turned out to be not as dreary as it had initially seemed. As a stopover on the way to New York the town managed to make contact with the larger world. Along its high road the redcoats passed in all the pageantry of war, marching north against the French and the Indians; the gay and winning Brigadier Lord Howe on the way to his death before Ticonderoga; Amherst's soldiery, the kilted Highlanders striding to the drone of bagpipes. Seeing them, the young teacher wondered if the great seat of empire might not in time be shifted to America once the French threat was removed.

As a Harvard graduate, entitled to put an "esq." after his name, a schoolmaster respectably related to the Boylstons, Adams was readily accepted into the small Worcester coterie that controlled and dominated the town. Colonel John Chandler, the local social leader, welcomed him to his hospitable house where he found himself in the company of the Reverend Maccarty, James Putnam, the town's leading lawyer, and Dr. Nahum Willard, a physician whose two sons would become John's close friends and whose wife would even attempt to wean him from chewing tobacco. Less staid, more adventurous, was the handful of advanced thinkers, Deists, and radicals with whom he liked to mingle in talk and debate about politics and religion. His diary, which he had begun at Harvard and which he would continue for the next thirty years, is full of references to his struggles with theodicy as well as to his good resolutions and subsequent backslidings from self-imposed discipline. He worried about his daydreaming, his sharp tongue, the hours he wasted. "Vanity, I am sensible," he noted, "is my cardinal Vice and cardinal Folly."

Although he had rejected the Calvinistic rigidities of the Braintree meetinghouse, he could not follow his more extreme friends to Deism where God became the Great Clockmaker remote from and indifferent to His own creation. Though he had rejected much, he could not reject the belief in a personal God, in a life beyond this life, in Christianity as the source of all morality.

The why of the universe and the problem of his own destiny in this world remained his two preoccupations. A few months' teaching convinced him, if such convincing was necessary, that he was not cut out to follow that career. His parents' wish to see him a minister he now knew was impossible. For a time he contemplated medicine, and boarded with the Willards while he considered such a future. Meanwhile, his fussy self-doubts burden the pages of his diary. "Oh!" he writes, "that I could wear out of my mind every mean and base affectation, conquer my natural Pride and Self Conceit, expect no more defference from my fellows than I deserve, acquire that meekness, and humility, which are the sure marks and Characters of a great and generous Soul, and subdue every unworthy Passion and treat all men as I wish to be treated by all. How happy should I then be, in the favour and good will of all honest men, and the sure prospect of a happy immortality!" "What," he asks himself, "is the proper business of mankind in this life?" For him, he decided, it would be the law.

It was a gradually developed decision. During his first year of teaching he took the cynical view that a lawyer "often foments more quarrels than he composes—and enriches himself at the expense of impoverishing others more honest and deserving than himself." Nevertheless, as other professional possibilities paled, he found that the law attracted him more and more. Whenever he could, he attended court sessions, listening with fascination to the lawyers' deft verbal thrusts. Finally he asked Putnam to take him on as an apprentice. Putnam amiably agreed, asking only $100 as a fee, to be paid "when convenient." For the next two years Adams, while teaching school during the day, read assiduously in Putnam's library "all the most essential Law Books." Between teaching, studying, and attending court sessions he eventually undermined his health. He set down in his autobiography that "the Physicians told me that close Application to a School and to Studies by night and by Day had thickened and corrupted the whole Mass of my blood and Juices, and that I must have recourse to a Milk Diet. . . . I . . . renounced all Meat and Spirits and lived upon Bread and milk, Vegetables and water. I found my head more at Ease and thought I pursued my Studies to more Advantage. . . . I pursued this course for Eighteen months, six or seven of which passed at my fathers house. . . . My excellent Father at last by his tender Advice at sometimes and a little good humoured ridicule at others converted me again to . . . meat and more comforting Drink, but in both of these I was extreamly sparing for many Years after. . . ."

In the autumn of 1758 his period with Putnam was over. His

parents asked him to live with them, since there had never been a lawyer in the neighborhood of Braintree. Yet they felt they must warn him that "the Town of Boston was full of Lawyers and many of them of established Characters for long Experience, great Abilities and extensive Fame, who might be jealous of such a Novelty as a Lawyer in the Country part of their County." At the age of fifteen he had left his birthplace. Now at twenty-three he was returning, but not to make his way in that cantankerous community. "These dirty and riduculous Litigations," he wrote angrily, "have been multiplied in this Town, till the very Earth groans and the stones cry out. The Town is become infamous for them throughout the County. I have absolutely heard it used as a Proverb in several Parts of the Province, 'as litigious as Braintree.' And this Multiplicity is owing to the Multiplicity of Petty foggers. . . ." His native town would always remain for him, in the Horatian phrase, the corner of the earth that smiled above all other places, but it was no corner in which to establish a law practice. To Boston he turned instinctively.

It was a bold choice for a would-be lawyer of modest means and family. For there were dozens of young lawyers starting out in Boston equipped with the connections, wealth, and influence that Adams lacked. The recognized leaders of the Boston bar were Jeremiah Gridley, a man of "great Learning, great parts and majestic Manner," Masonic Grand Master, and a militia colonel; Oxenbridge Thacher, who had turned from the ministry to law, a thin frail man of warmth and sympathy whose brilliance was masked by his unassuming manner; the gruff, one-legged Benjamin Prat, a mechanic's son who had made his way against all handicaps; and James Otis, Jr., ranked by Putnam as Boston's first lawyer, a man of passionate and heedless brilliance that verged on and sometimes carried over into madness, whose hurried nasal voice could captivate and compel other men. Brashly Adams determined to appeal to all four for advice and possible assistance.

One October morning he arrived at Gridley's. How should he best proceed to the practice of law, he asked the older man. "Get sworn," Gridley told him abruptly. Yet he was sufficiently impressed by this awkward-mannered beginner to offer to present him to the Superior Court. Finally he gave him the crusty advice to pursue the study of law rather than the gain of it, and not to marry early. That afternoon Gridley took him to a court session where he listened to the lawyers' arguments. In the evening Adams called at Thacher's and spent several hours drinking tea and discussing everything from original sin and the nature of the universe to law. But his reception at Prat's the following morning was frosty. When the crippled lawyer asked him if he had been sworn at the Worcester court and if he had a letter from Putnam, he had to reply that he did not. Those were the two essential steps, Prat told him by way of a curt dismissal. By contrast Adams's reception that evening by the younger James Otis was cordial and extended. In time Otis would become Adams's mentor and friend, the greatest man in Adams's later opinion, except for Washington, that he had ever known. At their first meeting Otis "with great Ease and familiarity promised me to join the Bar in recommending me to the Court."

Back in Braintree Adams whiled away his days before the opening of court not in study but in trivial amusements and the lighter farm chores that were for him a diversion. His diary bears the burden of this split between what he felt he ought to do and what he actually did, between his ambitions and his natural instincts. He reproached himself with the example of a more diligent young neighbor whose thoughts were *not* "employed on Songs and Girls, nor his time on flutes, fiddles, Concerts and Card Tables. He will make something." John Adams asked himself: "What am I doing? Shall I sleep away my whole 70 Years. No by every Thing I swear I will renounce the Contemplative, and betake myself to an active roving Life by Sea or Land, or else I will attempt some uncommon unexpected Enterprize in Law. Let me lay the Plan and arouse Spirit enough to push boldly. I swear I will push myself into Business. I will watch my Opportunity, to speak in Court, and will strike with surprize—surprize Bench, Bar, Jury, Auditors and all. Activity, Boldness, Forwardness, will draw attention."

The new-fledged lawyer now needed nothing but clients. Yet these were not easy to come by, nor was he always willing to prepare for them. "Return to your Study," he admonished himself, "and bend your whole soul to the Institutes of the Law, and the Reports of Cases, that have been adjudged by the Rules, in the Institutes. Let no trifling Diversion or amuzement or Company decoy you from your Books, i.e. let no Girl, no Gun, no Cards, no flutes, no Violins, no Dress, no Tobacco, no Laziness decoy you from your Books. (By the Way, Laziness, Languor, Inattention, are my Bane, am too lazy to rise early and make a fire, and when my fire is made, at 10 o'clock my Passion for knowledge, fame, fortune or any good, is too languid, to make me apply with Spirit to my Books. And by Reason of my Inattention my mind is liable to be called off from Law, by a Girl, a Pipe, a Poem, a Love Letter, a Spectator, a Play, &tc.)"

His first case was a typical village wrangle over a stray horse, and he lost it by drawing a defective writ, to the profane rage of his client and his own enduring dismay. While he was attempting to build up a practice of sorts within his narrow limits, great events were impinging on the North American continent. In the summer of 1759 Amherst occupied Fort Ticonderoga and in September Wolfe's soldiers captured Quebec, for all practical purposes bringing to an end the intermittent wars against French Canada that had been spread over the previous three quarters of a century. Then in 1760 George II died. The end of the war and of the French threat and the accession of a new King brought a shift in the relations between England and her colonies.

To the King's first minister, William Pitt, it seemed only

reasonable to expect financial assistance from America for the war just fought and for the still-active European war effort. No new laws would be needed, merely a stricter enforcement of already existing customs and shipping regulations. During the decades of war against the French these regulations had been suspended or simply disregarded by wealthy merchants and shippers. The accession of George III was followed by a tightening up of customs duties and the reintroduction of Writs of Assistance, or general search warrants, giving customs officials the right to inspect warehouses or houses for smuggled goods. Such writs were of unquestioned legality in England and in common use there. Before 1760 they had been issued to eight Massachusetts customs officers without arousing controversy. But in 1760 a suit was brought against their use by a disaffected customs official in collaboration with the younger James Otis on behalf of merchants seeking immunity from prosecution for customs violations.

Some time before this suit was brought before the Court, Chief Justice Samuel Sewall of Massachusetts died, and Governor Francis Bernard appointed Lieutenant Governor Thomas Hutchinson to succeed him. Hutchinson, though a judge of probate and ex-officio a member of the Governor's Council, was not a professional lawyer and did not solicit the justiceship for which he was, nevertheless, well qualified. The plurality of offices, for which he was later reproached, was commonplace in the colonies and brought him no financial benefits. A member of a close-knit family with an accumulation of high offices, he was at this point in his career generally respected throughout the colony. For thirty years he had skillfully and devotedly served Massachusetts as agent in all external affairs. For almost two decades he had been the leading figure in the popular Governor William Shirley's administration. Temperate, reserved, lacking all ostentation, devoted to the well-being of America as an integral part of the empire, he hesitated for some weeks to accept the proferred post.

At the same time, the younger James Otis was determined that the post should go to his own father, militia colonel James Otis, a veteran of the Barnstable and Plymouth bars, Speaker of the House and former attorney general, who with all the fervor of a self-made man yearned to see himself in the scarlet of a judge. Governor Shirley some years before had promised the next Court vacancy to Colonel Otis and the colonel had come to feel it was his right. When the younger Otis approached Hutchinson on his father's behalf, the lieutenant governor praised the colonel but said he would have to think it over, an indication of his own hesitancy that Otis took for a promise. But Governor Bernard thought that his appointment would be inadvisable, partly at least because of the instability of Otis's son, who as deputy advocate-general of the Vice-admiralty Court had shown marked reluctance to prosecute violations of the Navigation Acts.

Hutchinson's appointment, though it stirred up those who feared stricter application of the customs law, caused no protest. As his most recent biographer, Bernard Bailyn, admitted, it "infused new energy and efficiency into the work of the superior court and helped strengthen law enforcement in general throughout the province." Young Otis, however, was furious. A few days before, he had stormed into the governor's office and told Bernard that if his father was not appointed judge, he would set the whole province in flame.

Although the late Chief Justice Sewall himself was without formal legal training and had come straight to the bench from his position as tutor and librarian at Harvard, John Adams viewed the appointment of nonlawyer Hutchinson with a resentment equal to Otis's. The ambitious young lawyer considered it outrageous that a layman should be advanced over members of the bar. To him it seemed a personal as well as a professional affront. Obsessively suspicious—a deep and persistent quality of the Adams character—he saw Hutchinson's elevation as a conspiracy of corrupt forces secretly contriving to block the advance of uninfluential but honest and able men like himself.

In the matter of the Writs of Assistance it would have fallen to young Otis to argue the Crown's case before the five justices of the Superior Court, but Otis resigned his official office to become with Oxenbridge Thacher attorney for the protesting merchants. Adams's old mentor, Jeremiah Gridley, became attorney for the Crown.

Court was held in the sedate court chamber of the Town House under full-length portraits of Charles II and James II. Every lawyer in town was present, from Benjamin Prat—shortly to become chief justice of New York—to John Adams in wig and gown, the youngest lawyer present, sitting at a table with pen, paper, and an ink pot. Gridley began by arguing soberly that colonial customs officials possessed the same statutory powers enjoyed by customs officials in England. The Superior Court was authorized to issue Writs of Assistance in America. This was clearly the law. Thacher attempted to refute Gridley on points of law, arguing from precedent, but the weight of precedent and authority was clearly against him. Both men argued from the point of view of the law as it existed. Otis, when he began to speak, set the argument on another plane.

Gridley and Thacher were sober eighteenth-century rationalists. In Otis the romanticism of the next century was already apparent. To the Crown's cold logic he replied with words of flame, searing to the emotions if not to the reason. He spoke in all his eloquence for three hours, skipping from the classics to common law, history, even the Bible. Adams, spellbound to the point of forgetting to take notes, was reminded of Cicero. Acts of Parliament, Otis argued, that conflicted with the unwritten British Constitution or even more broadly with "natural equity" were of no effect. "All precedents are under the control of the principles of law." This was the substance of his argument of natural rights as he paraphrased

Coke's dogma that "a man's house is his castle." What the principles of law were, what natural equity was, remained as impossible to define as the "fairness" to which a United States Supreme Court chief justice would appeal two hundred years later. But such questions did not intrude on those carried away by Otis's oratory. As an old man, Adams recalled that incandescent hour in the Town House: "Near the fire were seated five judges, with Lieutenant Governor Hutchinson at their head as chief justice, all in their fresh robes of scarlet English cloth, in their broad bands, and immense judicial wigs and against them James Otis, a flame of fire! With the promptitude of classical allusions, a depth of research . . . a profusion of legal authorities, a prophetic glare of his eyes into futurity, and a rapid torrent of impetuous eloquence, he hurried away all before him. . . . Every man of [a] crowded audience appeared to me to go away, as I did, ready to take up arms against writs of assistance. . . . Then and there the child Independence was born."

In May of that same year Deacon John died of influenza during one of those periodic epidemics that swept the land. His widow inherited a third of his estate. To Peter Boylston went the Adams homestead. Elihu received a farm in neighboring Randolph. John, because he had already been given a "liberal education," received the smallest share, the farmhouse a few yards from the homestead.

With this property, however, he became a citizen in his own right in the community, a freeholder, a taxpayer, entitled to speak and vote at Town Meeting, eligible for office. Promptly—too promptly for his liking—he was elected to the nonpaying post of surveyor of highways with the choice either of accepting or paying a fine. "They might as well have chosen any Boy in School," was his disgruntled observation, "for I knew nothing of the Business: but since they had chosen me, at a venture, I would accept it in the same manner and find out my Duty as I could. Accordingly I went to ploughing and ditching and blowing Rocks upon Penn's

Hill, and building an entire new Bridge of Stone ... but the next Spring brought down a flood, that threw my Bridge all into Ruins. ... The blame fell upon the Workmen not upon me, for all agreed that I had executed my Office with impartiality, Diligence and Spirit."

In November, after three years of practice in the inferior courts of the province, he and Sam Quincy in black gowns with white bands and with powdered wigs were sworn as barristers before the Superior Court. Determined as ever to succeed, he felt he had not come very far in those three years with his footling cases derived from neighborhood malice, his occasional filing of writs and drawing up of wills, all in such petty contrast to the large legal affairs of Boston across the bay.

For him the year was most notable for his meeting with Abigail Smith, the sharp-eyed, sharp-tongued sprightly seventeen-year-old daughter of the Reverend William Smith of nearby Weymouth. Though fragile in body, Abigail had a robust mind, witty, engaging, at times impish. Already she had read Shakespeare, Molière, "the poets," Locke, the *Spectator*, the available classics, philosophy. John thought her the best-educated woman he had ever met. His cold blue eyes warmed to her. She in turn was taken with this ruddy, short-necked lawyer, so voluble, who gave his opinions with such abrupt gusto on everything from literature and law to religion and society.

Abigail's mother, a Quincy, was not so taken with the moody, stiff-mannered suitor, part lawyer, part farmer, and of no particular family. She had hoped for someone more on the Quincy level. Nevertheless, whatever her doubts, she made no formal objection to her daughter's choice. Abigail and John became engaged, but for all his impatience they would not marry for another three years. Whatever free time he could muster he spent with her. Though they lived only four miles apart they wrote each other constantly, in the century's arch tradition giving each other classical pen names, in their case Diana and Lysander. When in August, 1763, the sitting of the Superior Court kept John a few extra days in Boston he wrote impatiently: "Could my Horse have helped me to Weymouth, Braintree would not have held me, last Night.—I lay, in the well known Chamber, and dreamed, I saw a Lady, tripping it over the Hills, on Weymouth shore, Spreading Light and Beauty and Glory, all around her."

The six weeks that he had to stay in quarantine after being inoculated for smallpox seemed unendurable to them both. "Tomorrow makes the 14th Day," Abigail wrote. "How many more are to come? I dare not trust myself with the thought. Adieu. Let me hear from you by Mr. Ayers, and excuse this very bad writing, if you had mended my pen it would have been better, once more adieu. Gold and Silver have I none, but such as I have, give I unto thee—." His case proved a relatively mild one, and in a few days she was writing him teasingly in reply to his list of symptoms and medicaments that she was disappointed pointed his purgations had not made him a more sociable creature, to say nothing of his other faults.

With Adams's tactlessness he answered by setting forth a list of her "faults." She is "extreamly negligent, in attending so little to Cards . . . that noble and elegant Diversion." The effect on her "of a Country Life and Education, I mean a certain Modesty, sensibility, Bashfulness . . . enkindles Blushes forsooth at every Violation of Decency, in Company, and lays a most insupportable Constraint on the freedom of Behaviour." Thirdly, she "could never yet be prevail'd upon to learn to sing." Fourthly, "you very often hang your Head like a Bulrush. You do not sit, erected as you ought." Another fault is "that of sitting with the Leggs across. This ruins the figure and the Air, this injures the Health." The last imperfection "is that of Walking, with the Toes bending inward . . . commonly called Parrot-toed."

"I thank you for your Catalogue," she replied with genial mockery, "but must confess I was so hardned as to read over most of my Faults with as much pleasure as any other person would have read their perfections. And Lysander must excuse me if I still persist in some of them. . . . Especially may I avoid that Freedom of Behaviour which according to the plan given, consists in Violations of Decency. . . ." As for singing, she would have corrected it "if I had not a voice as harsh as the screech of a peacock." The fourth fault "shall be rectified, tho not with any hopes of being lookd on as a Beauty. . . . The 5th fault, will endeavour to amend of it, but you know I think that a gentleman has no business to concern himself about the Leggs of a Lady. . . . The sixth and last can be cured only by a Dancing School."

For all her light mockery, John was the man she had chosen and, as she admitted, she would rather have the smallpox by inoculation ten times than endure another such separation. Their letters expanded. She threatened to travel over for a look at him through the window. Finally he emerged from sick bay undamaged except for slightly loosened teeth. After spending the golden days of that summer together, they were married at last in October, 1764.

Though Adams had married for love, he had also married into a family of more influence and culture than his own, and in so doing he raised his own status. Through the Quincy tribe, more important cases soon came his way. He and Abigail took up their lives in the house he had inherited next to the Adams homestead.

The period from the death of Deacon Adams to his elder son's marriage marked a notable decline in the popularity and reputation of Lieutenant Governor Hutchinson. Otis attacked the lieutenant governor week after week, planting and nurturing the suspicion that Hutchinson—devoted as he was to the empire—was deeply corrupt, concerned chiefly with furthering the interests of himself and his large family at the expense of his fellow Americans. The mercantilist and populist opposition were all too ready to view Hutchinson as being willing to sacrifice colonial liberties for the sake of the royal prerogative. Massachusetts debtors—always more numerous than creditors—had never forgiven him for earlier successfully leading the province away from cheap paper money. Those swayed by Otis's appeal to natural law in his Writs of Assistance argument held the chief justice as the cold embodiment of formal law. The writs became the more resented as they were enforced, eleven of them being issued between 1761 and the spring of 1765.

Opinion, however intemperate and irrational, swung against Hutchinson and his politically entrenched family. The over-expansion of the war years that had brought prosperity to merchant, farmer, and laborer, came to an end with the signing of the peace treaty between France and England, and was followed by a harsh decade-long depression that saw the bankruptcies of a number of wealthy merchants and on a lower level jobless artisans walking the streets. Hutchinson and the ineffectual Governor Bernard became the convenient scapegoats for hard times. Feeling against Hutchinson came to a head in the agitation over the Stamp Act.

The war's end left England with a heavy debt and burdensome taxes. Lord Bute, the prime minister and the King's favorite, and Secretary of State George Grenville determined to raise money from the—in the British view—lightly taxed colonists. Shallow men of limited outlook, they acted with casual unconcern over American sensibilities or reactions. Pitt remarked acidly of Grenville that the saving of a penny's worth of candle meant more to him than the preservation of the empire. In 1764 Parliament passed the Sugar Act, the first act designed expressly to raise revenue in the colonies. With its economically unfeasible duty on molasses and its general tightening up of shipping regulations it would, if strictly enforced, have ruined the thriving New England molasses-rum trade as well as the carrying trade itself. The act was generally evaded. However, the Stamp Act, passed the following year, seemed evasionproof. It required the purchase of prestamped paper at prices ranging from a few pennies up to £10 for an encompassing class of documents: the various papers used in court proceedings, ship clearances, bonds, mortgages, indentures, leases, appointments to public office, contracts, bills of sale, and even advertisements in newspapers, college diplomas, playing cards (a shilling a pack), and dice (ten shillings a pair).

Before the act was passed Hutchinson wrote to England in formal protest, pointing out that the English government had long ago conceded to the colonies the right to make their own laws and tax themselves; that the Americans were not represented in Parliament; that the colonies were not indebted to the government for their settlement and development; that England's natural profit from the colonies, which would be endangered by such a tax, was far greater than any such tax would yield. Nevertheless, when the heads of the Whig "popular party" in the Massachusetts legislature prepared a remonstrance against the tax, Hutchinson as the presiding officer of the Governor's Council toned it down before it was dispatched to England. Other colonies sent over far more intemperate petitions, and when Parliament passed the Stamp Act the lieutenant governor's restraint seemed ill rewarded. The popular party leaders now turned on Hutchinson, and Otis and Adams accused him of treachery. Otis swore that the whole idea of the Stamp Act had been hatched by Hutchinson and Bernard and that he knew the very house and the very room in Boston in which this had taken place.

Hutchinson's reputation was further defiled when in March, 1765, he delivered a charge to the grand jury in which he spoke of its need to bring perpetrators of "riots, routs and unlawful assemblies" to justice. (This was the first of eight charges that Hutchinson made during his ten years as chief justice, encompassed in speeches in which he expressed his basic thoughts on government and laws.) He was particularly concerned by the need for juries to keep their deliberations private and to protect the identity of public-spirited citizens who came forward to testify in confidence—all of which increased still further the growing resentment against him. John Adams wrote with obsessive anger that the chief justice's "constant endeavor" had been "to discountenance the odium in which informers are held" and "in fine spun, spick and span, spruce, nice, pretty, easy warbling declamations to grand inquests to render the characters of informers honorable and respectable."

After the first flurry over the Stamp Act, it seemed briefly as if the colonists would resign themselves to accepting the distasteful measure before it went into effect in November. To make the tax more palatable the British government planned to appoint colonials as stamp-tax distributors. Among the prominent Americans who applied was Benjamin Franklin. In Boston this remunerative post was offered to Andrew Oliver, secretary of the province and Hutchinson's brother-in-law and fellow councilor.

The "alarm bell" against the Stamp Act was sounded on May 29, 1765, by Patrick Henry in a fiery speech to the Virginia House of Burgesses that was followed by the passage of the Virginia Resolutions denying the right of the British government to lay taxes and impositions on the colonies. Henry's position seemed at first so extreme that even Otis considered it treasonable, but the resolutions set off a chain reaction of Stamp Act opposition among the colonies that reached its peak in Massachusetts. In Boston a secret group known as the Loyal Nine under the thumb of Samuel Adams determined on physical resistance to the act.

Sam Adams, thirteen years older than his second cousin John, had busied himself—to the detriment of his personal affairs—with little but politics since his graduation from Harvard in 1740. He had gone through the modest fortune his father had left him, had failed in the paternal brewing business, and had shown little inclination to earn a living elsewhere. A hail-fellow-well-met as he strolled along the narrow Boston streets in his shabby red suit, he was a familiar figure in Boston taverns where he was known as Sam the Publican. His father, Deacon Samuel Adams, had been a charter member of the "Caucas Clubb" an association of shopkeepers, mechanics, and shipyard workers that managed through its belligerent solidarity to obtain a tight grip on the Town Meeting and town offices. Son Sam, through the caucus, would make himself Boston's first ward boss and later its political "dictator." Not until he was thirty-one, however, did he achieve his first remunerative job by getting himself elected town scavenger. Three years later he was elected collector of taxes. Indifferently casual to money, Sam the official showed himself not only negligent in collecting taxes but equally careless in handling the sums he had collected. Whenever he found himself short of money he put his hand in the public till, always intending to pay back but somehow never getting round to it. After eight years in office he was short the then staggering sum of £7,000. Yet, when this was made public, and a prison term for embezzlement hung over his head, Boston's Town Meeting enthusiastically endorsed him for another term. In 1765 he officially entered politics through his election by the Town Meeting to the Massachusetts House of Representatives. Closely allied with Otis in his attacks on Hutchinson, he then became deeply involved in the agitation against the Stamp Act.

"A fierce and sober type of the seventeenth-century covenanter," the Anglo-Irish historian William Lecky called him, "poor, simple, ostentatiously austere and indomitably courageous . . . hating with a fierce hatred monarchy, the English Church, and all privileged classes and all who were invested with dignity and rank."

Though riotous mobs were commonplace in eighteenth-century cities, Boston had become notorious in America for civic disorder, a warning example to staider towns and to the countryside. Three times in the 1740s the mob rose, in 1747 taking over the streets for three days in a riot over the impressment of American seamen by the royal navy. North End and South End gangs clashed annually in the Pope's Day celebration, an offshoot of Guy Fawkes Day, in which each gang carted an effigy of the Pope on a large wagon and attempted to capture that of its rival. In this local saturnalia liquor flowed, heads were broken, and sometimes lives lost. It was the inspiration of Sam Adams and the Loyal Nine to unite the two mobs and turn their aimless turbulence to political ends. From then on they took the name and formed the nucleus of the "Sons of Liberty," a phrase first used to describe the dissenting Americans by the Whig Colonel Isaac Barré in a House of Commons speech opposing the Stamp Act.

On the fourteenth of August the Sons of Liberty made their first overt move by hanging an effigy of Andrew Oliver and a large boot—to represent Lord Bute—on a huge elm tree in central Boston that would be known henceforth as the Liberty Tree. That evening the mob, shouting "Liberty, Property and no Stamps!" and with the effigy in tow, proceeded to Oliver's elegant town house, broke down the doors, and forced their way in. His garden was "torn in Pieces," John Adams noted with capitalized shock, "his House broken open, his furniture destroyed and his whole family thrown into Confusion and Terror." Yet, Adams found himself wondering, was not Hutchinson really to blame? "Has not his Honour the Lieutenant Governor discovered to the People in innumerable Instances, a very ambitious and avaricious Disposition? Has he not grasped four of the most important offices in the Province into his own Hands? Has not his Brother in Law Oliver another of the greatest Places in Government? Is not a Brother of the Secretary, a Judge of the Superiour Court? Has not that Brother a son in the House? Has not the secretary a son in the House, who is also a Judge in one of the Counties? Did not that son marry the Daughter of another of the Judges of the Superiour Court? Has not the Lieutenant Governor a Brother, a Judge of the Pleas in Boston? and a Namesake and near Relation who is another Judge? Has not the Lieutenant Governor a near Relation who is Register of his own Court of Probate, and Deputy Secretary? Has he not another near Relation who is Clerk of the House of Representatives? ... Is not this amazing ascendancy of one Family, Foundation sufficient on which to erect a Tyranny? Is it not enough to excite Jealousies among the People?"

Oliver was so intimidated by the mob's visit that he agreed next day to submit his resignation to London at once. Twelve days later it was Hutchinson's turn, a raucous crowd, mostly Sons of Liberty, roaring down to his pilastered North End mansion that flaunted its loyalty by displaying a carving of the crown of England over each lintel. Hutchinson was dining with his wife and children when he heard the shouts and howls of the approaching cudgel-boys, and barely escaped with his life. "The hellish crew fell upon my house with the rage of devils," he wrote afterward, "and in a moment with axes split the door and entered." Until amost morning they plundered and gutted the house, destroying what they could not take away—china, rugs, hangings, clocks, furniture, family portraits, until nothing remained but the bare walls and the floor. They ripped out the wainscoting, cut down the fruit trees in the orchard, and even demolished the cupola, then on leaving carried away silver and money and Hutchinson's private papers, including the unfinished manuscript of his *History of the Massachusetts-Bay* which they strewed in the gutter.

Hutchinson's plight stirred up not only sympathy but resolutions in his favor from the more respectable inhabitants, and even Sam Adams repudiated the "high-handed Enormity" that he had helped perpetrate. However, he then concocted the fable that papers found in Hutchinson's house proved him responsible for the Stamp Act.

The sack of the Hutchinson mansion was a sudden gust that

nevertheless showed which way the wind trended. The Stamp Act rapidly developed into one of those intensely emotional issues that transcend reason. Trade regulations and indirect taxes had been accepted for generations. Why a direct tax should suddenly become tyranny defied logic. At most times taxes have lacked the general assent of those who pay them—otherwise there would be few taxes. But Otis's phrase "taxation without representation is tyranny" became a flaming slogan to stir the colonists to a unity they had not sensed before. Applying as it did to all, the Stamp Tax stood out in strident obviousness, particularly arousing the lawyers, who had replaced clergymen as the most articulate and persuasive members of the community. "There is not a family between Canada and Pensacola," Hutchinson wrote, "that has not heard the name of the Stamp Act and but very few . . . but what have some formidable apprehensions of it." And he told of a friend whose servant refused to go out to the barn on a dark night because he was afraid of the Stamp Act. The people, Hutchinson concluded, "Run distracted . . . absolutely without the use of reason."

Astute Americans like Franklin now hastened to reject all previous thought of becoming tax distributors. In December the unfortunate Andrew Oliver was compelled by the Sons of Liberty to appear before the Liberty Tree in a pouring rain and resign his office as stamp distributor designate. Some months before that the radical leaders of the Massachusetts House of Representatives invited the other colonial assemblies to consult together on "the acts of parliament for laying duties and taxes on the colonies." Eight assemblies accepted, and in October the Stamp Act Congress convened in New York City.

"The Year 1765," Adams wrote in his diary, "has been the most remarkable Year of my Life. . . . In Every Colony, from Georgia to New-Hampshire inclusively, the Stamp Distributors and Inspectors have been compelled, by the unconquerable Rage of the People, to renounce their offices. Such and so universal has been the Resentment of the People, that every Man who has dared to speak in favour of the Stamps, or to soften the detestation in which they are held, how great so ever his Abilities and Virtues had been esteemed before, or whatever his fortune, Connections and Influence had been, has been seen to sink into universal Contempt and Ignominy.

"The People, even to the lowest Ranks, have become more attentive to their Liberties, more inquisitive about them, and more determined to defend them than they were ever before. . . ."

Earlier that same year Adams had been asked by Gridley to join a law club meeting "for the study of Law and oratory." There were only four members, Sam Fitch and Joseph Dudley making up the additional two. Gridley told Adams confidentially that he had been looking for promising young men who would in the future support the "Honour and Dignity of the Bar." He had decided to bring Adams "into Practice, the first Practice," something he could easily do merely by recommending him. One of the aims of the club was to have its members publish articles of distinction in the newspapers, and with this in mind Adams undertook to write a "Dissertation on Canon and Feudal Law." It appeared in the Boston *Gazette* at the height of the Stamp Act agitation. In spite of its title, the essay was a tract for the times rather than a scholarly treatise, a passionate, eloquent, and highly accurate account of the development of *"Rights* derived from the great Legislator of the Universe." Unsigned as was then customary, it stirred up much speculation as to who the author was, and it was even reprinted in England. Whatever the public might think, the inner circle of Boston lawyers knew well enough that the author was Gridley's protégé. Adams had made his mark in the town.

As the year waned, and the time came for the Stamp Act to go into effect, trade stagnated, the courts were suspended, and the Custom House closed. If it was impossible to distribute stamps, it seemed equally impossible to function without them. How long, Adams asked himself, would Massachusetts remain in this "languid Condition?" His law business had shrunk away. As he noted gloomily, it had been a month since he had drawn a writ, and he feared for the welfare of his family, now increased by his daughter Abigail, born in June.

"Thirty Years of my Life are passed in Preparation for Business," he wrote. "I have had Poverty to struggle with—Envy and Jealousy and Malice of Enemies to encounter—no Friends, or but few to assist me, so that I have groped in dark Obscurity, till of late, and had but just become known, and gained a small degree of Reputation, when this execrable Project was set on foot for my Ruin as well as that of America in General, and of Great Britain."

These obsessively gloomy thoughts were relieved by a Boston constable who arrived to notify him that he, along with Gridley and Otis, had been requested by the town to appear before the governor in council "in Support of their Memorial, praying that the Courts of Law in this Province may be opened." Although Adams felt that he held up his end awkwardly, his appearance with Gridley and Otis before Hutchinson was, he realized, of "Service to my Business and Interest." He would now be drawn more and more to Boston, expanding his acquaintanceship among all the social groups, from cousin Samuel and the Sons of Liberty to his more remote cousin, the opulent merchant and friend of Hutchinson, Nicholas Boylston.

Adams argued before Hutchinson that a law could not require what was impossible, that it was impossible to procure stamp papers, and to close the courts because of the lack of stamps would serve no practical purpose. Hutchinson replied that the council was unable to instruct the courts. In some cases the lower courts did open, but the Superior Court remained closed. "The Times are terrible," Adams noted, "and made so at present by Hutch[inson]."

The winter of 1766 was hard and cold. Adams, growing in

reputation, was elected one of Braintree's four selectmen. Though it was an unpaid job, often requiring a delicate balancing between factions, he noted approvingly that it would increase his connections with people. In January came news of Pitt's eloquent speech against the Stamp Act. Then, following a change of ministry in London, the act itself was repealed although word did not reach Boston until May. The news was greeted with cannon fire, the ringing of church bells, displays of fireworks, and on Boston Common the raising of "an Obelisk very beautifully Decorated." "Repeal," Adams observed, "hushed into silence almost every popular Clamour." What remained was the lesson, taken well to heart by Sam Adams and the Sons of Liberty, of how readily a mob could be manipulated for political ends to coerce an inert majority. The new legislature showed a purge of many of those who had stood by governor and council. Sam Adams was chosen clerk, the mercurial Otis speaker.

The reopened courts bustled with cases. John Adams now decided to concern himself chiefly with his practice, his duties as selectman, his family, and his farm. In July Abigail gave birth to a boy whom they named John Quincy after his maternal grandfather. "I am amazingly changed," Adams wrote to an old friend "since the Stamp Act is repealed . . . I am at perfect ease about politics. I care not a shilling who is in and who is out."

His ease lasted only the few months until Parliament passed the revenue acts sponsored by the shallow, casual Charles Townshend, chancellor of the exchequer. Townshend, with little understanding of the American scene, glibly proposed an import tax on paper, painter's lead, glass, and tea, a measure which he maintained would "lay a foundation for such taxation as might in time ease this Country of a considerable burden." In addition, Parliament revised the system of Vice-admiralty Courts and established a five-man American Board of Commissioners of Customs. News of the Townshend Acts soon shattered the Massachusetts calm.

At a Boston Town Meeting in October, called to protest the Townshend impositions, the citizens, with Otis as moderator, voted not to import or use any of the duted articles and sent a circular letter to the other colonies seeking their support. Adams was as yet more angered than involved, but whenever he went to Boston he made a point of conferring with Cousin Sam and Otis. The large town attracted him intellectually as well as financially, and though he loved Braintree and feared for his health in the rancid atmosphere of Boston, he finally moved there with his family early in 1768, renting a "White House" on Brattle Square. In his diary he continued his conscience-probing debates. He asked himself whether he was more concerned with money and power, prestige and importance, or the welfare of his country. Then, as if on the rebound, he wondered whether his present course as a lawyer riding circuit across the rutted Massachusetts roads would lead him to any of those things.

Adams arrived in Boston at a time when the legislature and Governor Bernard were at bitter odds and the agitation against the Townshend Acts and the newly arrived customs commissioners was sharpening. At the instigation of Samuel Adams, over a hundred well-known merchants, with varying degrees of enthusiasm as Sam breathed down their necks, signed nonimportation pledges. The radicals attacked Bernard in pamphlets and newspapers, while the Sons of Liberty paraded ostentatiously past the Town House and the Custom House. Frightened by repeated mob threats, the customs commissioners appealed to England for troops to protect them. Bernard did not dare affront the Sons of Liberty by making such a request himself, though privately he longed to see redcoats march up the street.

Following the appeal of the intimidated officials, the frigate *Romney* arrived from Halifax. Under the protection of her guns, customs officers seized John Hancock's sloop *Liberty* for landing contraband wine. Hancock, the wealthiest man in the colony, was the principal financial supporter of the Sons of Liberty. He had started out in life as a poor boy. Then his rich, childless uncle took him in hand, sent him to Harvard, after his graduation made him a junior partner in his business, and on dying left him his £70,000 estate. An openhanded, superficial young man, Hancock lacked any deep convictions but loved display and courted popularity. His lawyers, Otis and Thacher, first brought him into close contact with the "patriot" opposition. He was flattered when they asked him to become a candidate for representative to the General Court and was delighted to find himself one of the four elected at the Boston Town Meeting. Afterward, Samuel Adams, on running into his cousin John on the street near Hancock's elegant Beacon Hill mansion, remarked that "this town has done a wise thing today, they have made that young man's fortune its own!"

The seizure of the *Liberty* touched off another night of rioting. A mob of "sturdy boys and negroes" attacked those customs officials they could lay hands on and stoned the houses of those they could not. The terrified commissioners sought safety aboard the *Romney*. Meanwhile, once the official wheels had been set in motion, Hancock stood to lose not only his sloop but most of his fortune in subsequent fines.

It was a season of sullen resentment for Boston, with high prices, artisans out of work, and rumors current after the *Liberty* riot that British troops might soon arrive—everything the fault of the British government and its colonial adherents, if Sam Adams and the Sons of Liberty were to be believed. Hutchinson thought his fellow townsmen looked more "soure and discontented" than he had ever seen them. The Sons of Liberty hoisted a barrel of turpentine on top of the post that crowned Beacon Hill, and Sam Adams declared that lighting it would bring thirty thousand countrymen to Boston "with their knapsacks and bayonets fixed." Rumor gave way to actuality when on October 1, 1768, two regiments, the Fourteenth and the Twenty-ninth, landed from Halifax. In spite of Sam's brave words, "all the threatenings of Opposition vanished" as the red-coats marched up King Street with "Drums beating, Fifes playing, and Colours flying." In November they were augmented by two regiments dispatched from Ireland.

John Adams was riding circuit when the first troops landed. On his return he found that one regiment had taken to drilling in Brattle Square almost in front of his window, and he woke each morning to the sound of the "Spirit Stirring Drum and Earpiercing fife." Not long after his return he received a visit from his close friend Jonathan Sewall who was preparing to resign as advocate general of the Court of Admiralty. Sewall came bubbling over with the offer of Governor Bernard to appoint Adams in his place. For the thirty-three-year-old lawyer it was a flattering offer. Yet he was well aware that it was not just a compliment to his talents but a plan as well to separate those talents from the Sam Adams-Otis faction. He wanted none of it. Sewall told him Bernard was well aware of his political principles; it was his talents the governor wanted. But Adams could not be tempted. His law practice was growing and he was coming to be looked on as one of Boston's half dozen foremost lawyers.

This was clear when Hancock now asked him to defend him in the affair of the *Liberty*, the most important case at the time in the whole country. As attorney general, Jonathan Sewall was called on to undertake the prosecution. The case dragged on for most of the winter of 1768–69, being finally withdrawn by the Crown attorneys. Adams was "weary and disgusted with the Court, the Officers of the Crown, the Cause, and even with the tyrannical Bell that dongled me out of my House every Morning." A few months after this impasse he and Otis were retained by four sailors charged with murdering a British naval lieutenant who had led a party aboard their brig in an attempt to impress some of them into the King's navy. Since Otis was in one of his "unlucid intervals," most of the defense burden fell on Adams. Sewall was again the Crown prosecutor. It was indeed a sensational event that stirred the whole community, drawing more auditors than any previous Boston trial. The twenty-man special Court of Admiralty included Governor Bernard, Lieutenant Governor Hutchinson, Adams's Harvard classmate Governor John Wentworth of New Hampshire, and Judge of Admiralty Robert Auchmuty. But before Adams could present his final argument, Hutchinson asked for an adjournment, and when the court reopened announced that the lieutenant's death was justifiable homicide and hence no crime at all. Though happy at his clients' acquittal, Adams with his inately suspicious nature saw the verdict as motivated more by fear than justice.

There was much to fear in the growing tension in Boston's narrow streets. Two British regiments had been withdrawn, but the Fourteenth and the Twenty-ninth remained, and the soldiers—themselves for the most part the scrapings of society—were subjected to daily insults and challenges from street urchins, cudgel boys, and the more belligerent artisans. Fights and brawls became common. The redcoats were there as policemen, and as such became highly vulnerable hate objects. And, however challenged by street rowdies, the soldiers were legally barred from retaliation. As the inhabitants of Boston well knew, troops could not be used to put down civil disturbances except when specifically requested to do so by the civilian authorities. But when unrest threatened and Bernard or Hutchinson appealed to the council as the authorized authority, that now radical-dominated body always refused permission for the soldiers to act. Any action they might take even in their own defense would be subject to the judgment of a local court and a local jury, and the Sons of Liberty and their ilk had become convinced that the military would never dare move.

Samuel Adams continued privately to cherish his long-range goal of breaking the tie with England and establishing in America a republic resembling the ancient Sparta he had read about in *Plutarch's Lives*. Protests against the seizure of the *Liberty* and the

Townshend Acts and the forcing of merchants to sign nonimportation agreements were all means to his larger end, and as a tool he had the formidable Boston mob. "Certain busy Characters," John Adams noted, were seeking "to inkindle an immortal hatred . . . between the Inhabitants of the lower Class and the Soldiers," egging them on to "Quarrels, Rencounters and Combats." To Lieutenant Colonel William Dalrymple, commanding the Fourteenth, it was clear that authority in Boston was at a very low ebb. The brooding crisis waited only on the event, and that would not be long in coming. There were signs enough along the way. Soldiers and ropemakers roughhoused each other on sight. The Sons of Liberty tarred and feathered George Gailer, a crewman aboard the *Liberty*, whom they suspected of having "informed" on his ship. A mob chased John Mein, the pugnacious loyalist printer, through the streets until he finally took refuge with the Main Guard. On February 22, 1770, another mob attacked the house of Ebenezer Richardson, an earlier customs informer. Richardson, a pugnacious man, responded to the stones hurtling through his window by leveling a musket at his tormentors and discharging it. By chance he hit an eleven-year-old street urchin who died a few hours later. Sam Adams saw to it that the boy's funeral was one of the largest ever held in America, a long protest march through the snow.

The inevitable climactic confrontation between soldiers and civilians finally came the night of March 5, a chilly moonlit evening with a foot of packed snow on the ground. Down King Street from the Town House, Private Hugh White of the Twenty-ninth walked his solitary post. Captain of the day was the Irish-born, forty-year-old Thomas Preston whom even the radicals considered "a sober honest man, and a good officer." Ropemakers and soldiers had earlier been brawling again, and a number of civilians were seen skulking about town in the moonlight with sticks and cudgels. As White stood near his sentry box a group of apprentices began to mock and jeer at him until finally he lost his temper and knocked one of them to the ground with his musket butt. The apprentice's cries soon drew a crowd. Somewhere a church bell began tolling. Voices shouted, "Fire!" White became a target for snowballs, chunks of ice, and lumps of coal. Frightened, he retreated to the Custom House steps, pounding on the door and trying in vain to get in, while the rapidly growing crowd began to shout "Kill him! Kill him!" and dared him to fire.

Those that pressed into King Street, John Adams later called a "motley rabble of saucy boys, negroes, molattoes, Irish teagues and outlandish jack tarrs." Whatever they were, they threatened to overwhelm the lone redcoat. With White's life in danger, Captain Preston led out a relief party from the Main Guard of a corporal and six privates. Marching in file with empty muskets, they forced their way through the throng at bayonet point to reach White, but the crowd was by now so large and threatening that they could not return. Forming a convex line behind Preston, the soldiers proceeded to load. Catcalls, jeers, a shower of missiles and shouts of "Damn you, you dare not fire," "Fire and be damned!" taunted them. As the foremost surged forward, the soldiers forced them back with bayonets. Preston's arm was almost broken by the blow from a cudgel. Some of the soldiers' faces were bloodied. Private Hugh Montgomery, knocked into the gutter by a club, scrambled to his feet, seized his musket, shouted out "damn you, fire!" and pulled the trigger. Though the shot hit no one, it was a signal. Preston gave no command, but the other soldiers began a sporadic firing. Samuel Gray, a ropemaker, was the first to fall, a bullet shattering his skull. Also dead in the snow were apprentice Samuel Maverick, sailor James Caldwell, and a huge dusky man in the front rank who had been shouting and brandishing a club—an Indian or a mulatto who called himself Michael Johnson, but whose name was later determined to be Crispus Attucks. Several others were wounded, the Irish breeches-maker Patrick Carr mortally. Fully aware of the implications of the dead men lying in the snow, Captain Preston in a rage demanded to know why his men had fired. They answered that they had heard the word "fire" and thought he had given the order.

During all the tumult in King Street, John Adams was meeting with friends at a club in the South End. It had been a melancholy winter for him, marked by the death of his year-old daughter, Susanna, a loss he would nurse in his heart for years and that would not be assuaged by the birth of a son, Charles, that spring. When the club members heard the alarm bells ringing, they started out for the town. "In the Street We were informed that British Soldiers had fired on the Inhabitants, killed some and wounded others near the Town house." By the time Adams, hurrying home to his pregnant, ailing wife, arrived at the Town House, King Street was quiet again although lined by grenadiers in their peaked bear-skin caps. As he reached Brattle Square, he found a company of soldiers drawn up, "with their Musquets all shouldered and their Bayonetts all fixed." To reach his door he had only a "very narrow Space" past the soldiers but he pursued his way "without taking the least notice of them, or they of me, any more than if they had been marble Statues."

# 2

# *John Adams*

## THE REVOLUTIONIST

**W**HILE HE was growing up, Adams had taken for granted that he was a transplanted Englishman with an Englishman's rights under the Crown. Unlike his cousin Sam, he was no doctrinaire republican, no leveler. Yet he remained as convinced as Sam that Hutchinson and a corrupt clique were engaged in a conspiracy against American liberties. And the logic of independence kept pressing in on him. How could the colonists be represented in a Parliament three thousand miles away? Even though American members might be admitted, their numbers would be too small to have any effect. If representation was practically impossible, what was the conclusion? He still hesitated to draw it distinctly. Though by Sam Adams's standards he was a moderate, he remained sympathetic to the radicals' point of view if not to their methods. Occasionally he attended a meeting of the Sons of Liberty, even being present at a bibulous spread in Dorchester to mark the Sons' fourth anniversary. Yet on the way home he wondered whether he should have gone, and then concluded rather lamely that "many might suspect, that I was not hearty in the Cause, if I had been absent."

Long after Adams had gone to bed on the night of the King Street shootings, Hutchinson—acting governor since Bernard's departure for England in August—met in the Town House with justices of the peace to hold a court of inquiry. Before morning they issued warrants for Preston and the eight soldiers, who were thereupon jailed to await trial. A mood of turbulence shook the town. Sam Adams, "the Matchiavel of Chaos," had already dubbed the incident the Horrid Massacre. He seemed in complete command, haranguing a huge meeting at Faneuil Hall, demanding the immediate removal of all redcoats. Councilors and selectmen begged Hutchinson to give the order.

Sam turned the "martyrs'" funeral into a tremendous political demonstration, while Paul Revere perpetuated the legend with a grossly inaccurate engraving that would fix the image of the Horrid Massacre in all the colonies: the lined-up redcoats at the command of their sword-flourishing officer firing on harmless civilians. In the agitated weeks after the Massacre the Sons of Liberty, controlling Boston, tarred and feathered an occasional recalcitrant to prove their power. Meanwhile, the trial of Preston and his soldiers lay in the offing. Solicitor General Samuel Quincy, John Adams's boyhood playmate, was appointed special prosecutor, but the radicals feared his loyalist temperament and insisted on the additional appointment of the radically inclined Robert Treat Paine. Thirty years later John Adams was to recall how the day after the shootings the loyalist merchant James Forrest, known locally as the Irish Infant, came to his office in tears begging him to undertake Preston's defense since no other Boston lawyer would do so. Adams in accepting replied loftily that counsel ought to be the last thing an accused lacked in a free country. It was not quite the whole story. Josiah Quincy, the brilliant cross-eyed radical brother of the conservative solicitor general, who had at first turned down Preston's emissary, was advised to undertake the defense by Sam Adams, Hancock, and the Sons of Liberty leaders.

They undoubtedly gave the same advice to John Adams. Given the inflamed state of Boston opinion, Sam and his friends could not conceive of a jury acquitting Preston and his soldiers. Sure of the verdict, they were willing to let the defense have the best lawyers available so that no one could later claim the trial was unfair. Nor would sound Whigs like Adams and Quincy be likely to turn the hearings into a general attack on the Sons of Liberty.

Hutchinson, hoping for a calmer and more judicious atmosphere, succeeded in postponing the trial to the autumn session of the Superior Court. Even then there was difficulty in selecting a jury, the defense challenging so many prospects that the list was finally exhausted, with five jurors still to be picked. Sheriffs in such circumstances had the right to collar spectators or even passers-by and press them into jury duty as talesmen. At this critical point Sam Adams's guard must have been down, for somehow the wealthy loyalist merchant Gilbert Deblois managed to get himself on the jury, along with four other conservatives sympathetic to Preston. At the start of the trial it was clear to the knowing that this jury would never convict. Yet even a radical jury would have been hard-put to convict Preston on the facts that were brought out. Adams became convinced of his client's innocence and that of the soldiers as well. It was his private opinion that Hutchinson was the real culprit in summoning troops to Boston in the first place. Preston, it was clear, had not given the order to fire. His soldiers had been menaced by a mob—Adams emphasized the word "mob"—to the peril of their lives. Skillfully he developed the facts, though his summing up was scarcely needed for the predisposed jury to bring in its verdict of innocent.

Undertaking the defense of the eight soldiers a few weeks later, Adams and Quincy took great care to see that none of the jurors were from mob-dominated Boston. The two defense lawyers had a certain falling-out, as Quincy wished to make much of the general threats and abuse to which the soldiers had long been subject, while Adams, refusing to put the whole town in a bad light, would go no further than to condemn the King Street mob. He was still able to argue effectively that the provocation to which the soldiers had been subjected reduced the charge against them from murder to manslaughter. Most devastating to the prosecution was the deathbed testimony of the rioter Patrick Carr who admitted that the soldiers had fired in self-defense and said he did not blame the man, whoever he was, who had shot him. Adams laid much of the blame for the shootings on Crispus Attucks "to whose mad behaviour, in all probability, the general carnage of that night is chiefly to be ascribed."

The prosecution was unable to bring out that any of the soldiers but Montgomery and Private Matthew Kilroy had fired their muskets. These two the jury found guilty of manslaughter; the other six were freed. By pleading "benefit of clergy" and reading from the Scripture, the two escaped further penalties after being branded on the thumb, a minor barbarism that still made Adams wince. Some of his fellow townsmen volubly disapproved of the vigor of Adams's defense efforts. He remained convinced—this being an essential part of his character—that he had done the right thing, and he continued to insist that "the Verdict of the Jury was exactly right."

The Sons of Liberty, however, bore him no grudge, for in a special Town Meeting in June they elected him as one of Boston's four representatives to the legislature. Yet, for all the flattery of his selection, he felt dubious about taking up politics again. In his hypochondria he had once more adopted a diet of toast and milk and wondered whether his feeble health could stand up to public life. He had more legal business than any man in the province. Should he throw away such bright prospects out of a sense of public duty? When he asked Abigail about it she burst into tears.

Following the Massacre, Hutchinson removed the General Court to rural Cambridge beyond the "dangerous influence" of the Boston mob. John Adams, after suppressing his doubts and being sworn in as a legislator, was appointed with his cousin Sam to a committee to carry to the acting governor the Massachusetts Assembly's objections to being moved. Hutchinson refused to allow the legislators to return to Boston, even though in the course of the summer he was twice more waited on by the committee. Sam and Otis as the most vociferous leaders of the opposition urged John to take his turn haranguing Town Meetings on "misconduct of British colonial officials," but this rabble-rousing he declined. Troubled by Abigails' ill health as well as his own, he longed for the quiet of his farm. Finally, early in 1771 he decided to move back to Braintree while keeping his office in Boston.

With the ending of the Massacre trial, and as the year 1770 ebbed, the passions that had flared up after the killings were to all appearances dying down. Hutchinson considered the province calmer than it had been four or five years before, and he noted "a surprising change in the temper of the people." Public opinion had in fact grown weary of constant agitation, and there was a noticeable lack of support for the radicals.

A month after the Massacre, Parliament, on the petition of London merchants affected by American nonimportation agreements, repealed the Townshend Acts except for the duty on tea which the new prime minister, Lord North, against more prudent counsel, insisted on retaining as a token of parliamentary authority. Yet, at the beginning, this compromise seemed generally acceptable across the ocean. Commerce with the colonies revived, as did the tea trade. By mid-autumn the great protest movement against the Townshend Acts was over. Even John Hancock in the years 1771 and 1772 brought over forty-five thousand pounds of dutied tea to Boston.

In March, Hutchinson publicly took the oath of office as governor. Through the judicious use of patronage he hoped to bring order to the Massachusetts political scene and put the radicals in their diminished place. Many Massachusetts towns sent their best wishes for his inaugural. None came from John Adams. With Hutchinson governor, his brother-in-law, Andrew Oliver—brother of Chief Justice Peter Oliver—became lieutenant governor. Nathaniel Rogers, a nephew, succeeded Andrew as province secretary. Adams felt depressed, filled with a sense of futility and defeat, and more than ever aware of what he considered his failing health.

Sixteen months after moving to Braintree the ever restless Adams came back to Boston, his family increased by a third son, Thomas Boylston. The months in Braintree, he felt, had taught him how better to live in a city. He determined to avoid politics, Town Meetings, and all the other public activities that had so consumed his time previously. As his thirty-seventh birthday neared, he reflected on the melancholy fact that more than half his life was probably over. "What an Atom, an Animalcule I am!" he lamented, "—The Remainder of my Days I shall rather decline, in Sense, Spirit, and Activity. My Season for acquiring Knowledge is past. And Yet I have my own and my Childrens Fortunes to make. My boyish Habits, and Airs are not yet worn off."

Toward the end of 1772 his cousin Sam on behalf of the town's standing committee invited him to make the annual Massacre Day address. He declined. It was, he told Sam, an odd request for one who had helped free the redcoats. Besides he was too ailing, too old, and he had decided to give up politics for good.

When, however, his friends put him up for a seat in the Governor's Council, he could not bring himself to decline a second time. The councilors were elected by the assembly from its own members, so Adams first had to get himself elected to the legislature. Again he was in politics. Again he was dubious. "What will be expected of me? What will be required of me?" he asked himself. He need not have been concerned, for even though elected to and chosen councilor by the assembly, he was still subject to Governor Hutchinson's approval, and the governor would have none of him because of "the very conspicuous part Mr. Adams had taken in opposition."

Hutchinson's period of calm was of short duration, lasting only until the news spread that his salary was henceforth to be paid by the Crown rather than by the assembly. When it was subsequently learned that judges would also be paid by the Crown, local indignation boiled over. With the judges under royal control it was easy for Sam Adams and the Sons of Liberty to rouse men's fears and anger over what they considered a threat to their liberties. The governor's involved and learned explanations to the assembly as to the relations of the province and the mother country had little countereffect. Then in 1773 dark rumors began to circulate about a hidden scandal in which Hutchinson was involved that would soon be made public. The rumors were given substance in a pamphlet containing carefully edited extracts from letters written by Hutchinson and four of his relatives to an English political acquaintance at the end of the sixties, letters in which—the readers were told on the title page—would be found "the fatal source of the confusion and bloodshed in which this province especially has been involved and which threatened total destruction to the liberties of all *America*."

The letters had been stolen, and Benjamin Franklin as London agent for the Massachusetts House of Representatives had got hold of them and sent them to America. In them Hutchinson had written little that he had not said publicly a number of times, but in his informal correspondence he had let himself go freely and sharply about the disorders, the activities of various radical leaders, and the state of politics in passages that, taken out of context, could and would be used devastatingly against him. In one letter, referring to the province and the colonies, he had used the fatal phrase "there must be an abridgement of what are called English liberties." To the Massachusetts Assembly he had earlier explained that just by the nature of geography it was "impossible that the rights of English subjects should be the same, in every respect, in all parts of the dominions." But the radicals brandished the "abridgement" phrase to prove that Hutchinson's goal was to destroy all American liberties. For every man who read the letters there were dozens who merely heard about them.

Hutchinson's letters destroyed him politically. The Massachusetts House petitioned the Privy Council to have him impeached and removed from office. In Philadelphia and Princeton he was burned in effigy. To John Adams he appeared a "vile serpent" whose dominating impulses were "ambition and revenge." Adams's old friend Jonathan Sewall, writing under the name of Philalethes, published seven well-argued essays in explanation and defense of Hutchinson's letters, but though they were reasonable and logical, they had little effect on inflamed public opinion.

Passions scarcely had time to cool before a new crisis was on hand that would culminate in the Boston Tea Party, the seminal event for the American Revolution. For three years American importers had paid their Townshend duties on tea, and Americans had continued to drink the almost universal beverage without giving much heed to the tax. In any case, much of the tea they drank had been smuggled in from Holland, since high English duties made Dutch tea cheaper, and large-scale smuggling was easy. Then in 1773 the East India Company found itself in financial difficulties with a surplus of some eighteen million pounds of tea. Under the law the company could sell its tea only at wholesale auctions in London, but Parliament now gave the company permission to export directly abroad, while at the same time granting a remission of the ninepence-a-pound internal tea duty. The company directors then decided to send seventeen hundred chests of tea to four American ports. In October the British ship *Eleanor* and the American-owned *Dartmouth* and the brigs *Beaver* and *William* set sail for Boston. No one in England expected any difficulties, for at current prices the tea even with its threepence duty would be cheaper than the smuggled Dutch tea.

The first active opposition to the tea shipments appeared in New York and Philadelphia. Merchants objected to the East India Company's monopoly, and many engaged in smuggling from Holland saw their livelihood threatened by cheap legal English tea. The Sons of Liberty, frustrated in their attempts to stop importations of duties tea, seized these new shipments as an unrivaled propaganda opportunity. But feeling was at first languid in Boston, and John Adams admitted later that if resistance had not started elsewhere the town would probably have accepted the tea, duty and all. The first summons of the Sons of Liberty—issued while the tea ships were still in mid-ocean—for townsmen to meet in protest at the Liberty Tree brought a scant response. At about the same time the Boston Committee of Correspondence sent out a circular letter to the other Massachusetts towns calling their attention to the tea plan. By the time the *Dartmouth*, the first to arrive, had anchored in the harbor on Sunday, November 28, with 114 chests of tea aboard, merchants—among them Hutchinson's sons—who were to accept the tea had already received threats and one of them had had his house windows smashed. A ship lying at anchor under the protection of British guns was an easily grasped symbol, and resentment rose like a flood, spreading from the radicals to the moderates. Next day notices were posted all over Boston addressed to "Friends! Brethren! Countrymen! The House of Destruction or Manly Opposition to the Machinations of Tyranny stares you in the Face," and calling for a meeting at Faneuil Hall.

Again, as at the time of the Stamp Act, church bells tolled, and agitated crowds gathered. Sam Adams and his friends prepared to take full advantage of the lapses of a blundering English government. And as in all such crises, emotion outstripped reason. In his autobiography, John Adams, in a coldly realistic appraisal of public sentiment, had remarked that "the poor People themselves who by secret manoeuvres are excited to insurrection are seldom aware of the purposes for which they are set in motion: or of the Consequences which may happen to themselves: and when once heated and in full Career, they can neither manage themselves, nor be regulated by others."

The radicals managed to persuade most of the moderates that the tea must be returned to England, for once it was landed and the duty paid, any protest would be a lost cause. To their demands that the *Dartmouth* return to England, Hutchinson replied that a seventy-year-old provincial law prevented him from issuing passes to vessels not cleared by customs. He stood firm against any concessions. If the duty was not paid by December 17, the customs officers could then legally seize the cargo and land the tea, which the consignees could then claim on payment of the duty.

Three weeks of protest and agitation followed. Sam Adams through his emissaries continued to demand the tea's removal. Governor Hutchinson continued his refusal. Meanwhile the *Dartmouth* had docked at Griffin's Wharf, watched by an armed guard of radicals to be sure that the tea was not landed. On the morning of December 16, the day before the customs officers could legally seize the *Dartmouth's* cargo, a large crowd assembled in the Old South Meeting House to debate what action to take. In spite of rain and cold, several thousand men came in from the country districts to join those milling in the streets. By mid-afternoon over seven thousand had gathered in and near the Old South. Sam Adams, Josiah Quincy, and others warmed them with oratory to counteract the bone-chilling weather. The meeting summoned Francis Rotch, the twenty-three-year-old son of the *Dartmouth's* owner, Joseph Rotch, to take his vessel away. Young Rotch explained that he could not, whereupon he was dispatched to make a last appeal to the governor, then in the safer surroundings of his country place in Milton, seven miles away. Hutchinson still refused to grant a pass to the *Dartmouth*, explaining again that it would be a violation of the Acts of Trade.

It was nearly dark when Rotch returned to the stuffy candlelit hall to tell those present of the governor's final refusal. Would Rotch nevertheless return his vessel to England? He could not, he told them, for that would be his ruin. Did he plan to unload the tea? Only, he said, if ordered to by authorities, and then solely to protect himself. At this point Sam Adams stood up melodramatically to announce that "this meeting can do nothing more to save the country." As if on signal a war whoop sounded in the gallery, echoed by a small group in the doorway made up as Indians. At once the meeting broke up with shouts of "The harbor, a teaport tonight!" "Griffin's Wharf!" "The Mohawks are coming!" Led by the "Indians," the crowd surged down to the waterfront where the *Dartmouth* and *Eleanor* lay tied up near the brig *Beaver*. While lookouts kept watch, the "Indians" seized control of the three vessels. For the next three hours, unmolested, they hauled 340 heavy tea chests from the holds and dumped them overboard. Some ninety thousand pounds of tea worth about £9,000 spilled into the water.

During the crisis week John Adams had been attending Plymouth court and did not get back to Boston until the morning after the Tea Party. He learned the news from Abigail. Then for the first time in three months he turned to his diary: "Last Night," he wrote, "3 Cargoes of Bohea Tea were emptied into the Sea. This Morning a Man of War sails.

"This is the most magnificent Movement of all. There is a Dignity, a Majesty, a Sublimity, in this last Effort of the Patriots, that I greatly admire. The People should never rise, without doing something to be remembered—something notable And striking. This Destruction of the Tea is so bold, so daring, so firm, intrepid and inflexible, and it must have so important Consequences, and so lasting, that I cant but consider it as an Epocha in History. . . .

The Question is whether the Destruction of this Tea was necessary? I apprehend it was absolutely and indispensably so."

Yet he could not help but wonder how the King and ministry would take this defiant act. "Will they resent it? will they dare to resent it? will they punish Us? How? By quartering Troops upon Us?—by annulling our Charter?—by laying on more duties? By restraining our Trade? By Sacrifice of Individuals, or how." Then, as the weeks slipped by and the excitement of the Tea Party subsided, as jokes circulated about all the fish caught in the harbor having the flavor of Bohea, he began to wonder if the event had been all that decisive. He doubted if there was spirit enough on either side to settle the issue of American grievances versus parliamentary authority, and he predicted that the impasse would outlast his lifetime.

Whoever conceived the Tea Party, it had been a stroke of genius to disguise the tea-dumpers as Indians, transforming what might have seemed one more riot to a symbolic act. Approval went far beyond radical circles, and the local mood was jubilant. Hutchinson wrote that "the people seem regardless of all consequences." Loyalists as well as the Sons of Liberty recognized that the event had given colonial America a new sense of unity.

In England the reaction was one of general outrage. "The clamour against the proceeding is high and general," Franklin wrote in urging Bostonians to compensate the East India Company for its loss. Having seen the British government back down on the Stamp Act and the Townshend duties, the American opposition thought the colonists need merely stand firm again to get their own way, little suspecting what was being prepared in London. Parliament first passed the Port Bill to bar Boston from any shipping except coasters carrying in fuel and provisions. The Custom House was to be transferred to Plymouth and the seat of provincial government to Salem, and the act was to remain in force until full restitution had been made. This act was followed by the Massachusetts Government Bill.

Under it the King took over the appointment of members of the Governor's Council. Superior Court judges were to hold office at his pleasure. Other judges could be removed by the governor, who was also empowered to appoint or remove county sheriffs. These in turn were to select jurors. Only one Town Meeting a year would be allowed, and that for the election of officers. Special Town Meetings could be called only with permission of the governor. "We are now to establish our authority or give it up entirely," Lord North announced at the end of the parliamentary debates, little realizing how his actions would bring the Americans together in a unity of opposition. Even Hutchinson was dismayed at the severity of the measures. Much to his relief he was at last replaced by General Thomas Gage, the well-liked British commander in chief for North America.

Gage's popularity was not enhanced by the arrival in Boston of four regiments of infantry and three of artillery. Tents dotted the Common and the town echoed to the fife and drum and to parade commands. Boston became occupied territory, its wharves and waterfront idle, thousands out of work. Indignation and sympathy swept through the other colonies. From as far away as South Carolina came gifts of grain, flour, livestock, fish, rice, and money. A contribution even arrived from London well-wishers. From New York came the suggestion that committees of correspondence meet to establish grounds for the redress of American grievances. On June 17 the Massachusetts Assembly adopted a resolution calling for a Continental Congress. When Gage heard what was going on in the assembly he sent the province secretary to dissolve it, but he was too late to prevent the vote. Delegates picked for the prospective Congress were Samuel and John Adams, James Bowdoin, Thomas Cushing, and Robert Treat Paine.

By the end of August all the colonies but Georgia had chosen delegates for a Continental Congress to be held on September 6 in Carpenters' Hall, Philadelphia. Adams was flattered to be chosen as a delegate, yet, characteristically, he complained about his health, grumbled over the effect on his business, and lamented his inadequate education. "I feel myself unequal to this Business," he admitted. "A more extensive Knowledge of the Realm, the Colonies, and of Commerce, as well as of Law and Policy, is necessary, than I am Master of."

The six weeks between his selection and his departure he spent in Maine on the circuit of the Superior Court. He found the time irksome and was distressed by the prevalence of Tory sentiment, particularly among lawyers and clergymen. At Falmouth above Portland he met his old friend Jonathan Sewall whom he cared for "as his own soul" despite their political differences. The Tory Sewall tried to persuade him not to be a delegate, not to destroy his career by defying the irresistible power of Britain. Adams told him that it was his unalterable determination to survive or perish with his country. But when the two left to go their disparate paths, Adams had to admit to himself that their parting was "the sharpest thorn on which I ever set my foot."

On August 10 Adams and the other Massachusetts delegates— with the exception of Bowdoin, who declined to serve—left for Philadelphia, a leisurely journey of much entertainment and hospitality, for to many the Massachusetts group had become heroes of resistance. Few of the fifty-six delegates from the twelve colonies arriving in Philadelphia were certain what permanent relations they wanted with England, but a complete separation was something most did not entertain, and while enumerating their grievances they still declared themselves loyal subjects of George III. John and Sam Adams were appointed to a committee to discuss the basic rights of the colonists. The delegates finally adopted a Declaration of Rights and Grievances in which they asserted the rights to which they considered they were entitled "by the immutable laws of nature, the principles of the English Constitution and the several charters of the compacts." They called for a repeal of the Coercive Acts, the Quebec Act, and several other laws deemed unconstitutional, and demanded that the colonies be returned to the freedom from interference that they had enjoyed before 1763.

Mingling in a more diverse and sophisticated society than he had yet experienced, Adams took constant notes on what he saw and heard. For him the Congress was a rare opportunity to observe not only the intriguing "mystery of politics" but the secrets of human nature, the motivations of men. One Sunday he happened to drop in at a "Romish Chappell" and to his Puritan surprise found himself much moved by the beauty of the service. "The Scenery and the Musick is so callculated to take in Mankind" that he wondered the Reformation ever succeeded. "The Paintings, the Bells, the Candles, the Gold and Silver. Our Saviour on the Cross over the Altar, at full Length, and all his Wounds a bleeding. The Chanting is exquisitely soft and sweet."

As the Philadelphia weeks slipped by, he was at times overborne by the ennui, the "nibbling and quibbling" of debates, and he felt himself surrounded by "Trimmers and Timeservers." "I am wearied to Death with the Life I lead," he wrote Abigail. "The Business of the Congress is tedious, beyond Expression. This Assembly is like no other that ever existed. Every Man in it is a great Man—an orator, a Critick, a statesman, and therefore every Man upon every Question must shew his oratory, his Criticism, and his Political Abilities."

After the passage of the Declaration of Rights and Grievances, a committee that included Adams and Patrick Henry began work on a "humble petition to His Majesty." Meanwhile, the Congress adopted Articles of Association summarizing American grievances and declaring that imports from Great Britain should be banned by November, and that if within a year Parliament did not repeal the objectionable statutes all exports from America to Great Britain and her possessions would cease.

There were unexpected delays in preparing the petition to the King, "the address to the people of Great Britain and the memorial to the inhabitants of British America," but when the documents were at last completed Congress adjourned, prepared to meet in May if Parliament had not by then taken action satisfactory to the colonists. Adams left "in a very great Rain, from the happy, the peacefull, the elegant, the hospitable, and polite City of Phyladelphia." "We live, my dear Soul," he had written Abigail earlier, "in an age of tryal. What will be the Consequence I do not know." But he and most of the delegates did feel that in the face of united colonial firmness Britain must yield or face commercial ruin.

On his return to Massachusetts Adams found local militia units and minutemen preparing for immediate action as in the times of the Indian wars. Hay-foot, straw-foot volunteers went stumbling through their drill on every village green. By now the Sons of Liberty controlled the countryside, effectively intimidating the disorganized loyalists, who in Adams's opinion numbered about a third of the population. More prominent Tories were taking refuge in Boston, just as more prominent Whigs were leaving the garrisoned town. Those in the smaller towns and villages who opposed royal authority had been organizing ammuniton dumps and supply depots. The King's writ no longer extended beyond Boston.

That winter was the mildest within memory. Life in Massachusetts went on with an eighteenth-century casualness incomprehensible to future generations. General Gage knew exactly where the militia and minutemen had set up ammunition dumps, and they in turn learned of his orders almost as soon as he had issued them. After drilling troops mornings on the Common, the young and elegant Colonel Lord Percy would often drop in to have breakfast with John Hancock's pert fiancée, Dorothy Quincy, and Hancock's Aunt Lydia. Hancock and Sam Adams remained in Boston and even held a Boston Massacre Anniversary meeting in March, attended by a scattering of British officers in uniform who were given front-row seats.

John Adams was elected to the Massachusetts Provincial Congress which met in Cambridge, an assembly that did little more than vote to enlist twelve thousand minutemen. He spent most of the winter writing replies under the name of Novanglus to the skillful Tory pamphleteer Massachusettensis, arguing at length on constitutional grounds for colonial resistance. Massachusettensis had charged that the Whigs were using the pretense of rights to seek complete political independence. Adams insisted even in that cumulating spring that the American colonists owed their fealty and allegiance to King George "whom God long preserve and prosper." But Parliament, he continued to insist, had no authority over America.

He was at work on his Novanglus papers when April 19, 1775, the day of Lexington and Concord, overtook him. British troops marching to Concord to confiscate ammunition fired on minutemen at Lexington Common. A bloodier confrontation occurred at Concord's North Bridge. Then the redcoats on their way back from Concord were routed by American farmers and militiamen firing from behind stone walls. As the shots echoed on that day of bloodshed and death, those colonials opposing the redcoats were no longer discontented subjects of George III. They had become Americans. So it seemed to John Adams who was in Braintree when he heard the news. For him any fealty and allegiance to the King had now come to an end. Three days later he rode to Cambridge to see the embryo American army gathering there. The men lacked uniforms, equipment, or even rations. Living in huts and lean-tos on Cambridge Common, they scoured the neighborhood for food. Their officers, whom they had elected, they called by their first names. High spirits made up for lack of military discipline, the new soldiers boasting to Adams that they would drive the British into Boston Harbor.

The Second Continental Congress was scheduled to meet in a few weeks. Delayed by a bout of illness, Adams left for Philadelphia some days after the other Massachusetts delegates. He was pleased with his reception along the way. "Our Prospect of a Union of the Colonies," he wrote Abigail, "is promising indeed. Never was there such a Spirit. Yet I feel anxious, because, there is always more Smoke than Fire—more Noise than Musick." His health remained precarious as ever and by the time he reached Philadelphia his eyes were so inflamed that he at first could scarcely read or write.

The most famous addition to the Second Congress delegates and the oldest among them was Dr. Benjamin Franklin, back from London. George Washington, in the handsome buff and blue uniform of a militia colonel, again represented Virginia. At the opening the Massachusetts delegates presented a letter from their provincial congress asking approval for what would be, in effect, an independent America. Adams in a passionate speech urged that now that the sword had been drawn, it was time to throw away the scabbard. The people of every colony should set up their own government under their own authority. To most of the delegates the New Englander's demands were still far too radical. Adams noted "horror, terror, and detestation" on the faces of the more conservative delegates as he spoke. His motion was at once tabled.

The Congress's most pressing problem was to provide for the army at Cambridge, supply its basic needs, and appoint a commander in chief. Several candidates for commander were available: the elderly Massachusetts militia colonel Artemus Ward; Charles Lee, gnomish former English lieutenant colonel and future traitor; and John Hancock, president of the Congress, who flattered himself on his talent for things military. But to Adams all others were dwarfed by the towering figure of Washington. "I am determined," he told his cousin Sam, "to make a direct motion that Congress should adopt the army before Boston, and appoint Colonel Washington in command of it." As soon as the delegates were called to order Adams told them they must select a commander to take charge before the embryo army disintegrated. He had in mind, he said, a man present, splendidly equipped for the office. At this Hancock beamed. But when Adams "came to describe Washington for the Commander, I never remarked a more sudden and sinking Change of Countenance. Mortification and resentment were expressed as forcibly as his Face could exhibit them. Mr. Samuel Adams Seconded the Motion and that did not soften the Presidents Phisiognomy at all." Washington was elected unanimously, while Ward and Lee were named second and third in command.

When the new generals rode out of the city, accompanied by the Philadelphia Light Horse and militia officers in glittering new uniforms while bands played, drums beat, and fifes squealed, the pudgy civilian Adams felt himself stirred by martial ardor. "Such is the Pride and Pomp of War," he complained to himself afterward in the privacy of his boardinghouse bedroom. "I, poor Creature, worn out with scribbling, for my Bread and my Liberty, low in Spirits and weak in Health, must leave others to wear Laurells which I have Sown; others, to eat the Bread which I have earned—a Common Case."

He was still in Philadelphia when the Battle of Bunker Hill took place, the first large-scale engagement between British regulars and American volunteers. It took three bloody assaults for the redcoats to dislodge the Americans from the high ground of Charlestown where they had fortified themselves, with almost half the British soldiers becoming casualties. On that hot June morning as the British ships began firing in advance of the troop landing, Abigail and her eight-year-old Johnny, the boy who would one day be the sixth President of the United States, hurried to Penn's Hill. From the knoll they could hear the slam and crash of the cannon and see the smoke of burning Charlestown billow up into the serene air. Braintree might even be next! "I shall tarry here till tis thought unsafe by my Friends," she later wrote her husband, "and then I have secured myself a retreat at your Brothers who had kindly offerd me part of his house."

Adams, anxiously awaiting news from Boston and Braintree, realized with dismay that many of the Philadelphia delegates still hoped to settle their differences with the mother country while remaining within the British empire. He could no longer be one of them. Congress adjourned for August and Adams arrived home exhausted in mind and body. He slept for sixteen hours, then rose refreshed to spend a day wandering "all alone, through the fields, groves, meadows . . . of peaceful happy Braintree." By way of recognition the Massachusetts Provincial Congress elected him to the functionless council and named him chief justice of the as yet nonexistent Supreme Court. The month's end saw him with his cousin Sam again on the road to Philadelphia. There it was the same story again: talk, talk, talk, while Washington's army besieging Boston remained unpaid and ill-supplied. Congress, lacking precedents, continued uncertain of itself, uncertain still whether to take more aggressive action against England or make further attempts at a reconciliation. For many delegates, as Adams wrote to General Gates, the thought of complete independence remained "an hobgoblin, of so frightful mien, that it would throw a delicate person into fits." Only by a narrow margin did the delegates finally approve a measure sponsored by Adams to commission vessels and privateers to prey on British shipping, an act that Adams considered to be the beginning of an American navy. Then, in an unwonted burst of energy, the Congress voted to provide for an army of twenty thousand men.

To the wary delegates Adams argued eloquently that since Great Britain had made war on the colonies, they were no longer colonies but states. As such they must form their own governments. The thought of people creating their government was still to many a distressing thought. What would you have, they asked him dubiously. He advocated the familiar triad of the executive, the legislative, and the judicial, as had already been represented by governors, colonial assemblies, and justices. The three branches of government should be equal and balanced in order to check the tendency in all government to turn into tyranny. There should be a house of commons chosen by properly qualified voters, a council chosen by the house members, and a governor selected by house and council. Each branch should be independent, yet capable of vetoing the other branches. In brief, a prudent system of restraints and balances. The most difficult part in this mighty contest would be for Americans "to contrive some method for the colonies to glide insensibly from under the old government into a peaceable and contented submission to the new one."

What haunted Adams was the fear of "the leveling spirit," the unbridled democracy that through a single-branch legislature would use the "will of the people" to enforce tyranny. His conclusion was that "there is no good government but what is republican . . . because the only definition of a republic is an empire of laws, not of men!" Universal suffrage he would always view as the suffrage of the irresponsible. In America where land was so easy to acquire, a small property qualification, not too rigorously enforced against men of character, represented stability, sobriety. So it had been in Massachusetts. In May, 1776, when James Sullivan as a member of the Massachusetts Assembly engaged in constituting a new government turned to him for advice, Adams counseled against changing the property-based franchise. Once it was altered "new claims will arise; women will demand a vote; lads from twelve to twenty-one will think their rights not closely enough attended to; and every man who has not a farthing will demand an equal voice with any other, in all the acts of state." In his darker moments he even wondered if there was enough civic virtue to support a republican form of government.

Early in December he was granted leave to return home and by

Christmas found himself where he was happiest, with his own family among his Braintree hills. After Christmas he visited General Washington at his Cambridge headquarters. As the weeks slipped by in the familiar surroundings, he was seized again by his notion to retire from politics, and he petitioned the provincial assembly to replace him as a delegate. The Massachusetts legislators refused to consider his petition. He was in their opinion irreplaceable, skilled in the ways of politics, learned in the affairs of the Congress. In any case, since there was no prospect of reestablishing a Superior Court, since law business was at a standstill, and since he was too old and too much a civilian to take up a career as an army officer, he had little practical choice but to continue as a public man or withdraw to Braintree as a dirt farmer. Delegate, then, he must remain.

After dining with Washington, he set off on the road to Philadelphia in the hard winter season. At Framingham he admired the cannon that Henry Knox had brought down from Fort Ticonderoga, so recently captured by Ethan Allen. His journey was a cold one, through blizzards, over frozen ground suddenly turned to mire by winter rain, with the usual grubby discomfort of taverns alleviated somewhat by the comfort of fireside talk. He found his fellow delegates dejected by the season, uncertain as to the future, lacking most of their initial enthusiasm. News of Montgomery's and Arnold's disastrous attack on Quebec city had depressed them greatly.

Their flagging spirits were revived by a pamphlet written by a pock-marked, bottle-nosed English emigrant, the doctrinaire radical Thomas Paine. His *Common Sense*, a ringing denunciation of King and Parliament that in blunt, unforgettable phrases demanded a complete break with England, would prove one of the most influential documents in American history. In his passionate appeal for independence Paine reached out beyond the delegates to the ordinary American, the farmer, the artisan, the laborer, the indentured servant, stirring them as nothing before had. Many attributed the pamphlet to Adams. Like his cousin Sam, he was delighted by its eloquence, its enthusiasm for the cause even if, unlike Sam, he was dubious about its politics and its philosophy. What he feared most was Paine's leveling spirit, with its end result, the omnipotent, tyrannous democratic assembly.

As the winter ebbed, the Ticonderoga cannon were brought to Boston. General Howe, commanding the British troops, had neglected to seize and fortify Dorchester Hill overlooking the town. On the night of March 2 Washington sent four thousand men with 370 teams of horses to occupy the hill. Belatedly, the British batteries across the bay opened fire, but by morning the Americans had erected a system of breastworks and cannon emplacements that made the British position in Boston untenable, and this with the loss of only a single man. The roar of the American and British batteries shook the Braintree house and rattled the windows. Abigail wrote that "the Cannon continued firing and my Heart Beat pace with them all night." Two weeks later the British garrison and as many loyalists as could find passage abandoned Boston. At sunrise on March 17 Abigail hurried to her Penn's Hill lookout with Johnny and little Nabby. Scattered across the bay they could see the largest fleet ever assembled in America, some 170 ships, their bare masts and spars like a forest. Then as the three watched, the crews began to hoist canvas, and the ships under full sail glided down the roads and toward the outer harbor.

While the British forces were preparing to leave Boston and Adams anxiously awaited news from Braintree, Congress discussed throwing open American ports to European vessels and creating an American navy. The issue of independence kept coming up, to the discomfort of many of the Southern aristocrats. A rumor was widespread that British commissioners were on their way over to effect a reconciliation. Adams dismissed this hope as "airy fairy," but it persisted. On April 3, he wrote in his diary: "great Things were done. The Naval System made great Progress." Three days later he noted with satisfaction that Congress "opened the Ports and sett our Commerce at Liberty." He warned Abigail, however, that this was still not independence, and to Gates he wrote that they had been waging half a war and were now waging three quarters of one.

Independence shone on the horizon, for some a great light in the East, for others a will-o'-the-wisp. The Pennsylvania and New York delegates insisted that they were bound by their assemblies to resist any move to separate them from the mother country. John Dickinson, who in his earlier *Letters of a Pennsylvania Farmer* had so eloquently attacked the Townshend duties and who had been Adams's intimate in the First Congress, had become in the Second Congress one of the most outspoken advocates of reconciliation with England. Every packet overseas brought word that the commissioners with their reconciliation proposals might be expected daily. Some of the more conservative members of the Congress spread the story that Adams was pushing for independence to assure himself of the chief-justiceship in Massachusetts. When Richard Henry Lee proposed that the assemblies of the "United Colonies" be entrusted to form their own government, Adams added a much stronger preamble demanding that "the Exercise of every kind of Authority under the said Crown should be totally suppressed, and all the Powers of Government exerted under the Authority of the People of the Colonies."

On May 15, over the objections of Dickinson and the New Yorkers, the resolve and preamble were passed by the majority. "Great Britain," he wrote Abigail, "has at last driven America to the last Step, a compleat Seperation from her, a total absolute Independence, not only of her Parliament but of her Crown. . . . I have Reasons to believe that no Colony, which shall assume a Government under the People, will give it up. There is something very unnatural and odious in a Government 1000 Leagues off. An whole Government of our own Choice, managed by Persons whom We love, revere and can confide in, has charms in it for which Men will fight."

Yet in spite of the May 15 resolution, which he considered the most important ever taken in America, many delegates continued to drag their feet along the independence road. For all Adams's urging they hesitated, those from the middle states showing themselves particularly balky. Finally on June 10 Congress resolved to postpone the matter of independence until July.

In the ensuing weeks, demand for independence grew. It was a feeling more marked on the artisan level and among the disaffected and disinherited than among the professional and upperclass groups from which the delegates were drawn. Congress met again on July 1. Before the Declaration of Independence prepared by Jefferson, Adams, and the others could be accepted, the resolution favoring independence, which had been hanging fire for the past two months, had still to be approved; and there remained those who refused to approve. Dickinson, as the leader of the opposition, spoke so eloquently against severing the English tie that when he finished there was a long and awkward silence. No one seemed ready to answer him, until finally John Adams stood up. Plump, rubicund, awkward, he had neither the presence nor the voice of an orator, as he himself readily admitted. His facts, however, were marshalled with the exactness of a proposition in geometry. Step by step in relentless nasal tones he traced the development of the quarrel with England, the legal implications, the deepening crisis leading to the armed challenge, the efforts at reconciliation, and the present inevitability of independence. It was perhaps the greatest speech in his career. Yet it was not enough. On adjournment, New York, Pennsylvania, Delaware, and South Carolina were still not ready to face the actuality of independence. The whole debate had been "an idle mispence of time," Adams wrote a friend a few hours later. "Nothing was said but what had been repeated and hackneyed in that room before, a hundred times for six months past."

A long night of talk, persuasion, and maneuverings followed. Through it all ran a feeling of inevitability, so that even those who had been dubious felt themselves carried away in the emotional current. Adams, moving from delegate to delegate and group to group, grew convinced that the resolution would pass the next day, perhaps almost unanimously. July 2 turned rainy. Congress whiled away the damp morning. The moment of decision came after lunch. A shift was already apparent before the voting. South Carolina had given in. Dickinson had agreed not to take his seat, leaving a Pennsylvania majority for independence. Then at the last minute a mud-streaked delegate arrived posthaste from Delaware bringing instructions to change that small state's vote. So, with New York alone abstaining, the delegates of twelve former colonies resolved on independence.

"Yesterday," Adams wrote Abigail, "the greatest Question was decided, which ever was debated in America, and a greater perhaps, never was or will be decided among Men. . . . I am surprised at the Suddenness, as well as Greatness of this Revolution. Britain has been fill'd with Folly, and America with Wisdom, at least this is my Judgment.—Time must determine. It is the Will of Heaven, that the two Countries should be sundered forever." But, he concluded somberly, "the People will have unbounded Power. And the People are extreamly addicted to Corruption and Venality, as well as the Great.—I am not without Apprehensions from this Quarter. But I must submit all my Hopes and Fears, to an overruling Providence, in which, unfashionable as the Faith may be, I firmly believe."

July 2 he set down as destined to be the most memorable date in America's history. "It ought to be commemorated," he noted, "as the Day of Deliverance by solemn Acts of Devotion to God Almighty. . . . solemnized with Pomp and Parade, with Shews,

Games, Sports, Guns, Bells, Bonfires and Illuminations from one End of this Continent to the other from this Time forward forever more."

Right as he was in substance, Adams was wrong in his date, for the national holiday stemmed from the actual signing of the Declaration of Independence two days later. Paragraph by paragraph the delegates went through the document, altering a phrase here, another there, the most notable being the deletion of a long paragraph, out of deference to Georgia and South Carolina, censuring the Crown for allowing the importation of slaves. The Declaration was quickly approved, with this time only John Dickinson as the solitary holdout.

Four days later the Declaration was published. "The Bells rung all Day, and almost all Night," Adams wrote. "Even the chimes chimed away!" He sent the news to Abigail by the first post. She was delighted. "Nor," she replied, "am I a little Gratified when I reflect that a person so nearly connected with me has had the honour of being a principal actor in laying a foundation for [the country's] future Greatness." On the eighteenth of July she was in Boston, going "with a Multitude into Kings Street to hear the proclamation for independance read and proclamed. Some Feild pieces with the Train were brought there, the troops appeard under Arms and all the inhabitants assembled there. When Col. Crafts read from the Belcona of the State House the Proclamation, great attention was given to every word. As soon as he ended, the cry from the Belcona, was God Save our American States and the 3 cheers which rended the air, the Bells rang, the privateers fired, the forts and Batteries, the cannon were discharged, the platoons followed and every face appeard joyfull. . . . After dinner the kings arms were taken down from the State House and every vestage of him from every place in which it appeard and burnt in King Street. Thus ends royall Authority in this State and all the people shall say Amen."

Burdened with duties as delegate from Massachusetts and his ever more arduous and encompassing duties as chairman of the Board of War and Ordnance, Adams was up at four every morning and usually it was not until ten or later at night that he could stumble bleary-eyed into bed. Not for months had he even had the time to take a walk. "I will not say that I expect to run distracted," he confided to Abigail, "to grow melancholly, to drop in an Apoplexy, or fall into a Consumption, but I do say, it is little less than a Miracle that one or other of these Misfortunes has not befallen me before now." He longed for his home and the "bracing native air" of Braintree. He worried about his farm, his family, his vanished law practice, his diminishing assets, his current expenses which were more than the sum granted him by the Massachusetts legislature. "Let me have my Farm, Family and Goose Quil," he wrote, "and all the Honours and Offices this World has to bestow, may go to those who deserve them better, and desire them more. . . ."

Faced with a makeshift army lacking the most basic necessities, Adams occupied himself to exhaustion with organization, logistics, discipline, recruitment, bounties, pay, the quarrels of senior officers, the clamor of the unqualified for commissions, grossly profiteering army contractors. Somehow he had to conjure up rations, medical and hospital supplies, uniforms, weapons, even powder and flint. Procurement was not his direct responsibility, but it became his direct problem, even as Congress printed more paper money whose value declined by 10 percent a month. One of his chief concerns was to enlist a regular army for the war's duration to replace the native short-term militia. And there was the problem of discipline in an army where privates called officers by their first names and considered military obedience a survival of British rule. Adams recalled that the greatness of republican Rome had been built on the discipline of her legions. "The American Army," he wrote, "will stand or fall ... according as it adheres to or deviates from the same discipline. ..."

Matters grew even worse with Washington's defeat by General William Howe on Long Island and the British sweep of New York. New England troops in that engagement had cut and run, while the officers refused to discipline their troops. Sickness was rife, desertion common. "The cowardice of New England men has put my philosophy to the trial!" Adams exclaimed. Only after Washington had entrenched his forces at Harlem Heights did Adams finally receive a leave of absence. In mid-October, after almost a year's interlude, he set out for his beloved Braintree.

To that quiet backwater beyond the mainstream of events, news trickled in belatedly as from another world. Washington's army withdrew to White Plains, then continued its ragged retreat into Jersey, followed by the saturnine General Howe. Forts Washington and Lee on either side of the Hudson fell to the British along with several thousand American prisoners and quantities of materiel. Ten thousand British and Hessian soldiers were only thirty miles from Philadelphia, and on December 12 Congress moved to Baltimore. Adams's favorite commander, General Lee, was captured in his dressing gown by a British patrol. It was for the Americans the darkest moment of the war. Many of Washington's ill-shod, ill-equipped, ill-fed men were waiting only until the first of the year when their enlistments would be up. Militiamen were deserting in droves. A more aggressive British general might have ended the campaign then and there, but Howe suspended operations and retired to New York for the winter leaving behind him a chain of posts from Staten Island to Princeton.

However depressed he might be by the news from outside, Adams renewed himself in the familiar domestic routine with his wife and four children. When the weather held, he looked to all the details of his farm, strode over his fields under the glazed shadow of the Blue Hills. On stormy days he worked at his desk in the little room that was his library-office and that by now overflowed with books. He re-established his ties with friends and relatives and called on Boston's political figures, among whom he now loomed large. Then at the turn of the year came the sudden exultant news of Washington's triumph over the Hessian garrison at Trenton, that desperately successful gamble being followed by the battle at Princeton where he had thrown Cornwallis's hastily summoned forces off balance before withdrawing to winter quarters at Morristown. It was at last an American victory, minor perhaps in itself, but for Adams a turning point in the war. Shortly after the New Year he set off on horseback for Baltimore, a "hard and rough ride" in the worst weather he had ever experienced. Crossing the Catskills, he thought of Hannibal crossing the Alps. "The Highlands are a grand Sight," he told Abigail, "a range of vast Mountains, which seem to be rolling like a tumbling Sea."

Not until February 1 did he arrive in Baltimore, but he found the city despite its muddy littered streets a "very pretty Town." Congress seemed to him more spirited and determined than ever. In a burst of energy the delegates had set up Boards of War, Ordnance, Navy, and Treasury, with a Chamber of Commerce, all to be made up of men not members of Congress. As Congress continued to authorize the printing of more paper money, and the inevitable inflation followed, Adams became more and more concerned with public finances. The only way to deal with the printing-press money, he felt, was to "draw in some that is already out, and devise Means effectually to support the Credit of the Rest." Taxes and bonds would provide the remedy. But he was now to experience the innate reluctance of parliamentary governments to levy enough taxes to pay for a war. As for bonds he knew that investors would not be attracted at less than 6 percent interest, and Congress would offer only 4 percent. "I tremble for the consequences of this determination," he wrote forebodingly. Inflation seemed to him as grave a threat as simon-pure democracy.

Between his duties as a delegate and his concern for military affairs he scarcely had time to sleep. His eyes troubled him, and, increasingly near-sighted, he had to resort to spectacles. Although he had never served, he felt that the chief-justiceship of Massachusetts was too much for him, and he resigned. "I could not be, at the same Time in Maryland and Massachusetts Bay," he told Abigail, "which was Reason enough for the Measure, if I had no other, but I have many more and much stronger. I have not Health enough, and never shall have to discharge such a Trust. I can but just keep myself alive, and in tollerable Spirits when I am master of my own Time and Course of Life. But this is not all. I am not formal and ceremonious enough for such a stiff Situation."

By the middle of February Congress moved back to Philadelphia, a very different city now, for half the inhabitants had fled, leaving behind chiefly the neutral Quakers, "as dull as Beatles," from whom in Adams's opinion "neither good is to be expected nor Evil to be apprehended." Beset by the inflation, he found even the most modest lodgings beyond his means, and he had no money left to send to Abigail. He was troubled by the laggard support from his own state, the scanty enlistments, the renewed Tory activity, and he could not get out of his mind the cowardice of the New Englanders at Long Island. His frustrations at the Board of War grew. Congress ignored his advice. The generals failed to give him essential information. He had done his best to build up an army, and he was appalled by the deaths, caused more by sickness and neglect than by combat.

At the end of March the first good news from abroad arrived. The American commissioners to France appointed earlier by Congress—Benjamin Franklin, Silas Deane, and Arthur Lee—had been welcomed there more warmly than anyone had dared hope. Now the French government had agreed to lend three million livres to the Americans without interest for the duration of the war. "All Europe," Adams wrote, "wish us well, excepting only Portugal and Russia. . . . Patience and perseverance will carry us through this mighty enterprise. . . ."

To his disgust, Congress thrust aside the vital issue of the Articles of Confederation, which would define the form that the new government should take, to debate about what gifts should be sent to the ladies of the French court. "Narragansett Pacing Mares," he wrote Abigail, "Mooses, Wood ducks, Flying Squirrells, Redwinged Black birds, Cramberries, and Rattlesnakes have all been thought of. Is this not a pretty Employment for great Statesmen as we think ourselves to be?" Congress's pressing problem was again the raising of money. Once more Congress fell back on the printing press and the inflation continued, accelerating as inflations do.

April found Adams stodgy from lack of exercise, suffering from sore eyes and a cold he could not shake. With the renewed spring weather he took to getting up at four in the morning for an hour's ride before sunrise on his little mare. "The Charms of the Morning at this Hour, are irresistable," he wrote. "The Streakes of Glory dawning in the East: the freshness and Purity in the Air, the bright blue of the sky, the sweet Warblings of a great Variety of Birds intermingling with the martial Clarions of an hundred Cocks now within my Hearing, all conspire to chear the Spirits. . . . I shall be on Horseback in a few Minutes, and then I shall enjoy the Morning, in more Perfection." Summer brought with it sunnier prospects. Even as privateers took their toll of British shipping, arms and equipment were arriving from France for the army that was at last taking shape. Adams was convinced that in spite of all difficulties the struggle against England would succeed. Yet his own personal life seemed fragmented. "This Day compleats Six Months since I left you," he told Abigail. "I am wasted and exhausted in Mind and Body, with incessant Application to Business, but if I can possibly endure it, will hold out the Year. It is nonsense to dance backwards and forwards. After this Year I shall take my Leave. . . . Next Year compleats Three Years, that I have been devoted to the Servitude of Liberty. A slavery it has been to me, whatever the World may think of it."

In August, after much indecision, Howe finally landed his forces at Elk River preparatory to an advance on Philadelphia. Adams was blithely optimistic that Washington, though outnumbered three to two, would drive the English back to Chesapeake Bay. But Washington's forces in straight combat were still not a match for the British regulars, and after a stiff battle before the city he withdrew south, abandoning Philadelphia to the enemy. Adams noted sadly in his diary: "The Prospect is chilling, on every Side. Gloomy, dark, melancholly, and dispiriting. When and where will the light spring up? Shall We have good News from Europe? Shall We hear of a Blow struck by Gates? Is there a Possibility that Washington should beat How? . . . From whence is our Deliverance to come? Or is it not to come?Is Philadelphia to be lost? If lost, is the Cause lost? No—the Cause is not lost—but it may be hurt."

Congress moved to Lancaster, but Adams was scarcely settled there when word came of Burgoyne's surrender of his entire army at Saratoga, the first defeat in the field of a major British force. When "Gentleman Johnny" Burgoyne had started on his march from Canada with the intent of splitting New England from the other colonies, even the unmilitary Adams had seen the folly of it, predicting that the British general was preparing his own destruction. Now his prediction had come true! The news of Burgoyne's surrender lifted him "up to the stars." It gave him even greater satisfaction to know that this had been a victory of New Englanders. On October 25 Abigail rode to Boston for the victory celebration. It was a special day, for her as well, her thirteenth wedding anniversary. "May future Generations rise up and call you

Blessed," she wrote John, "and the present behave worthy of the blessings you are Labouring to secure to them."

On November 3 official word of Burgoyne's surrender was delivered to Congress. Four days later John and Samuel Adams received leave of absence to visit their families. But before they left, reports arrived censuring the American commissioner in Paris, Silas Deane. Before his appointment as commissioner, Deane had been a secret agent for Congress, collecting supplies through a dummy trading company. But he had been accused of using his position for his own private profit. As Adams was about to mount his horse for the long ride home his fellow Massachusetts delegate, shrewd Elbridge Gerry, came out in the courtyard to tell him confidentially that Deane had been a disgrace to the country. Gerry wanted him recalled at once and replaced by Adams. Whatever Deane's lapses, Adams protested that he had no wish to replace him, that he knew little French and less of France, and that his one aim at this point was to retire to private life.

He decided not to serve again as a delegate to Congress. After a brief relaxation at home he began to pick up the loose ends of his law practice. He had gone to Portsmouth, New Hampshire, on an important case when he learned that Congress had appointed him to replace Deane. Should he accept? His patriotism, subtly reinforced by his vanity, urged him to do so. In the end he decided to leave the decision to Abigail. She had been unable to restrain her curiosity when the letter of notification arrived and had opened it at once. He must have sensed her decision in advance. She would of course have him go.

Adams was all too conscious of his lack of experience and training, the burdens he would have to leave to Abigail, the perils of a winter voyage across a sea patrolled by the enemy. He spent the weeks before embarkation in tending to the details of his farm and his Boston house. In his spare time he tried to renew his thin knowledge of French with the aid of a grammar. He decided to take ten-year-old Johnny with him, along with his servant, Joseph Stevens. Meanwhile Abigail took charge of the practical arrangements. Somehow she managed to scrape together £100 in silver currency. As food for the voyage she collected six chickens, "two fat sheep," fresh meat, fourteen dozen eggs, five bushels of corn, a barrel of apples, thirty pounds of sugar, two pounds of tea and chocolate, two bottles of mustard, a box of wafers, and pepper. In addition she provided twenty-five quills for John's pen, a dozen clay pipes, and two pounds of tobacco. A ten-gallon keg of rum, six dozen small barrels of cider, three dozen bottles of Madeira, thirty bottles of port, and an unspecified additional quantity of rum would seem to have been sufficient to keep passengers and crew light-headed and light-hearted all across the Atlantic!

On February 14, 1778, Adams and Johnny and the servant Stevens drove in a sleigh to Mount Wollaston where they met the captain of the frigate *Boston* lying offshore. It was a raw day with a high wind, the spray blowing up from the sea like hail. On the way to the landing they stopped at the house of John Spear to pick up the sailors manning the barge to take them aboard. Spear's wife, a gaunt, witchlike woman given to prophecies, was a distant relative of the Adamses. She predicted a stormy voyage. "Mr. Adams," she warned her remote cousin, "you are going to embark under very threatening Signs. The Heavens frown, the Clouds roll, the hollow Winds howl, the Waves of the Sea roar upon the Beech." And with that ominous forecast, father and son embarked. As the *Boston* weighed anchor, Adams standing wistfully on deck could see Penn's Hill under its white blanket where Abigail stood watching, and beyond Penn's Hill the violet-shadowed saddleback range of the Blue Hills.

DRAFTING THE DECLARATION OF INDEPENDENCE.
THE COMMITTEE—FRANKLIN, JEFFERSON, ADAMS, LIVINGSTON AND SHERMAN.

In an engraving of Alonzo Chappel's painting, *Drafting the Declaration of Independence*, Benjamin Franklin, Thomas Jefferson, Robert Livingston, John Adams, and Roger Sherman, from left to right, work at creating what would prove to be one of the greatest documents in history. *National Archives*

This engraving of John Adams is based on a portrait by John Singleton
Copley painted in 1783, the year the Treaty of Paris was signed. Adams
had become the colonies' strongest advocate for independence after an
evening of treasonous conversation with his cousin Samuel on New Year's
Eve, 1772. He would later serve as vice president in both administrations
of President George Washington and later succeed him as the second
president. Adams worked with John Jay and Benjamin Franklin in Paris
from 1782-1784 to negotiate the end of the Revolutionary War and, even
more important, the recognition of the United States as a sovereign nation.
The Treaty of Paris, signed on September 3, 1783, guaranteed official
recognition the United States of America by Spain, France, the
Netherlands, and most notably, by Great Britain. *Library of Congress*

The revolutionary leader Samuel Adams, cousin to John Adams, is depicted in a painting by John Singleton Copley, who was considered the foremost artist in colonial America. By the time he was forty, Samuel Adams had parlayed a Harvard education, a tidy inheritance, and a decent malt business into complete ruin. But he also discovered a sixth sense for public opinion, and by organizing the Sons of Liberty in 1765 he made himself one of the foremost early leaders of the fight for American independence. *Library of Congress*

A 1799 engraving of John Adams shows him surrounded by the seals of the sixteen states at the time of his presidency. Beneath each is a listing of the number of Federal legislators and the state's population. At the top of the illustration an eagle grasps in its claws an olive branch, an arrow, and a banner containing the words, "Millions for our defence not a cent for tribute," a reference to the notorious XYZ Affair. In 1796 French boats had seized more than 300 American merchant ships. The American envoys Elbridge Gerry, Charles Pinckney, and John Marshall traveled to Paris to discuss a diplomatic solution to the hostility, but three French agents, referred to later as X, Y, and Z, demanded a substantial bribe to open negotiations. Pickney's outraged reply, "Not a sixpence, Sir!" became the basis for a famous rallying cry for American military strength. *Library of Congress*

President John Adams wrote this message to the United States Senate on July 2, 1789, recommending that George Washington be promoted to Lieutenant General. The text reads: "Gentlemen of the Senate: I nominate George Washington of Mount Vernon to be Lieutenant General and Commander in Chief of all the Armies raised or to be raised in the United States. [signed] John Adams". Washington would be the first person in the new republic to hold this rank. *National Archives*

John Quincy Adams was the first president to have his photograph taken. He was also the first person to follow his father (John Adams) to the presidency, and the only president to take a seat in the House of Representatives after his term at the White House. *Mathew Brady Studio/Library of Congress*

Soon after leaving the White House, in 1829, John Quincy Adams ran for and was elected to the House of Representatives. In 1846 he suffered a paralytic stroke. He returned to the House four months later, where the whole chamber rose and did him homage, but he was at his desk in February 1848 when he had another stroke. *Death of John Quincy Adams* is a Currier and Ives lithograph of John Quincy Adams's passing in the Speaker's Room of the Capitol on February 21, 1848. *Library of Congress*

FREE SOIL. FREE LABOR. FREE SPEECH

MARTIN VAN BUREN    CHARLES F. ADAMS

GRAND DEMOCRATIC FREE SOIL BANNER.

A lithograph by Currier and Ives from a daguerreotype by John Plumbe shows Free Soil Party candidates Martin Van Buren and Charles Francis Adams in the presidential race of 1849. Adams knew he didn't have a chance when he ran for Vice President as a Free-Soiler, but he and Van Buren, the head of the ticket, felt they should take a stand against the expansion of slavery into the territories—a position that neither the Whigs nor the Democrats would adopt. *Library of Congress*

# 3

## *John Adams*

**N**EVER BEFORE had Adams ventured beyond the farther reaches of Boston Harbor. Scarcely out of sight of land, he endured the ominous excitement of being pursued by British men-of-war, until the *Boston* finally managed to give them the slip. "It would have been more eligible for me to be killed on board the Boston or sunk to the bottom in her, than to be taken Prisoner," Adams concluded afterward. His escape was followed by a storm as violent as anything predicted by his eccentric cousin. "To describe the Ocean, the Waves, the Winds, The Ship, her motions, rollings, pitches, Wringings and Agonies, The Sailors, their countenances, language and behaviour, is impossible." Laid low by seasickness it took him several clear days before he could muster enough strength to crawl on deck and huddle under a blanket. "The Life I lead was a dull Scaene to me," he recalled a generation later in his autobiography, "—No Business, no Pleasure, no Reading, no Study. Our little World was all wet and damp. There was nothing I could eat or drink, without nauseating. We had no Spirits for Conversation, nor any thing about which to converse. We saw nothing but Sky, Clouds and Sea, and then Seas, Clouds and Skies.

I had heard often of Learning a Language, as English or French for example, on a Passage: but I believe very little of any thing was ever learned at Sea." With the return of balmier weather he and Johnny resumed their study of French, the voyage enlivened by their ship's capture of a smaller British privateer.

After more than five weeks at sea the *Boston* finally made landfall on the Spanish coast, then moved slowly against headwinds to the Gironde estuary in France and up the Garonne River to Bordeaux. For the provincial lawyer, the first of his line in six generations to recross the Atlantic, the ordered French landscape with its patina of centuries was strangely moving. As his ship coasted slowly up the river he could see a thousand years of history along the banks—neat fields bounded by hedgerows, country houses framed by ancient trees, churches, convents, a countryside rooted in the past, in time-edged contrast to the raw land of New England with its sudden seasons.

The American agent, John Bondfield, met him at Bordeaux and introduced him to his first French city while elucidating the tribulations of the commission, the bitter animosity between Lee and Deane, the foibles of the pleasure-loving Franklin. Adams was astonished by the warmth of his Bordeaux reception, not yet realizing that much of it was the result of his being mistaken for his cousin Sam, notorious throughout Europe for his twisting of the British lion's tail. In Paris it became clearer to him after the question was debated in the press—and even across the Channel in London—whether or not he was the famous Adams, and it was finally decided that although he was an Adams he was not *the* Adams. "I am inclined to think," he wrote once he was settled in Paris, "that all parties, both in France and England—Whiggs and Tories in England, the Friends of Franklin, Deane, and Lee, in France, differing in many other Things, agreed in this—that I was not the fameux Adams."

He lodged first with Franklin, a none-too-satisfactory temporary arrangement. In his youth Adams had revered the scientist-philosopher from Philadelphia, but his association with him in the Second Continental Congress had given him dubious second thoughts that would expand in Paris. The moralistic New Englander could not but look askance at the elderly, indolent freethinker whose life seemed "an endless round of social events," whose love affairs were still common gossip, who preferred the court and the theater, food and women, and the talk of wits to any desk routine. Franklin in marten-skin cap and Quaker dress, posing as the Rousseauistic natural man—the pose that had made him the rage of Paris—blinded Adams to the success of the other's personal diplomacy, which had been primarily responsible for France's declaring war on England.

Adams found the affairs of the commissioners in a bewildering tangle. Franklin had been too occupied with his private life to concern himself with the commission's day-to-day routine. Lee's nature, innately suspicious, had become corroded by his antagonisms to Franklin and the absent Deane. The real burden of the commission was therefore left to Adams, not only vital matters of supply but such routine concerns as passports, clearances for American vessels, provisions for American prisoners in British hands, and so on. A vast and disorganized amount of paper work had accumulated in regard to Congress and its newly established departments. "I found that the Business of our Commission would never be done, unless I did it," Adams wrote. "My two Colleagues would agree in nothing. The Life of Dr. Franklin was a Scene of continual discipation. I could never obtain the favour of his Company in a morning before Breakfast which would have been the most convenient time to read over the Letters and papers. . . . It was late when he breakfasted, and as soon as Breakfast was over, a crowd of Carriages came to his Levee or if you like the term better to his Lodgings with all Sorts of People; some Phylosophers, Accademicians and Economists; some of his small tribe of humble friends in a literary Way whom he employed to translate some of his ancient Compositions . . . ; but by far the greater part were Women and Children, come to have the honour to see the great Franklin, and to have the pleasure of telling Stories about his Simplicity, his bald head and scattering strait hairs, among their Acquaintances. These Visitors occupied all the time commonly, till it was time to dress and to go to Dinner. . . . Mr. Franklin kept a horn book always in his Pockett in which he minuted all his invitations to dinner, and Mr. Lee said it was the only thing in which he was punctual."

While Franklin played and Lee sulked, Adams sat at his desk trying to bring some order to the commission's chaotic affairs while abstaining from the social life that seemed the chief concern of the other two. Deane, he discovered, had left no records to account for the vast business he had conducted. Agents, with his approval, had drawn large sums of money without submitting vouchers or even orders. The commissioners had no control over the funds for which they were held responsible. What his country had received as an equivalent, Adams was never able to determine.

Shortly after his arrival in Paris, Adams, with Franklin and Lee, dined with Turgot, the French minister of finance. Adams was astonished not only by the splendor of Turgot's residence but by the men and women he met there whose names and titles echoed through history. The house, the library, the formal gardens, made Boston's finest mansions seem raw and almost mean, and Adams could not help but reflect on the destiny that had taken him from his weather-scored Braintree cottage to the circle of the court of France. His first official visit was to the Count de Vergennes, the foreign minister, an aristocratic diplomat, like most professionals skilled at masking his thoughts behind an inscrutable urbanity. The Frenchman formed no liking for the graceless Yankee with the habit of blurting out what he thought and with a face that betrayed him even when he chose to remain silent. In turn, Adams never really trusted Vergennes.

In spite of the burden of his work Adams soon became acclimated to Paris. His narrow New England personality expanded. He wrote Abigail, who had heard disquieting rumors that the *Boston* had been captured and taken to Portsmouth, that "after all the Fatigues and Dangers of my Voyage, and Journey, I am here in Health. . . . The Reception I have met, in this Kingdom," he continued, "has been as friendly, as polite, and as respectfull as was possible. It is the universal Opinion of the People here, of all Ranks, that a Friendship between France and America, is the Interest of both Countries. . . . The Delights of France are innumerable. The Politeness, the Elegance, the Softness, the Delicacy, is extreme. In short stern and hauty Republican as I am, I cannot help loving these People, for their earnest Desire, and Assiduity to please. It would be futile to attempt descriptions of this Country especially of Paris and Versailles. The public Buildings and Gardens, the Paintings, Sculpture, architecture, Musick, &c. of these Cities have already filed many Volumes. The Richness, the Magnificence, and Splendor, is beyond all Description. This magnificence is not confined to public Buildings such as Churches, Hospitals, Schools, &c. but extends to private Houses, to Furniture, Equipage, Dress, and especially to Entertainments." Yet, he concluded with a trace of selfrighteousness, "I receive but little Pleasure in beholding all these Things, because I cannot but consider them as Bagatelles, introduced, by Time and Luxury in Exchange for the great Qualities and hardy manly Virtues of the human Heart. I cannot help suspecting that the more Elegance, the less Virtue in all Times and Countries. . . . All the Luxury that I desire in this World is the Company of my dearest Friend, and my Children, and such Friends as they delight in, which I have sanguine Hopes, I shall, after a few Years enjoy in Peace."

He had sent Johnny to an academy at Passy, and the boy, soon far more proficient in French than his father, visited him on weekends. Meanwhile, Adams's labors did not keep him as desk-bound as he sometimes pretended. He was of course presented to the King, a plump, cheerful man of twenty-four. He developed a taste for the theater, and gradually his ears grew accustomed to the quick Gallic syllables. In company, as at the theater, he began to recognize phrases, then whole sentences. He worked hard at learning French, and as his ear and tongue improved he observed that Franklin, who prided himself on his fluency, was not only given to grammatical lapses, but his pronunciation was "very inaccurate."

There was much in Paris to surprise a Puritan-derived New Englander; the easy gaiety of French Sundays, the casualness of French amours. Adams was astonished at the freedom with which the great men of France displayed their mistresses and even more astonished to discover that these women had been picked not for their beauty, but for their wit and intelligence. Impressive to him too were the women presiding over brilliant salons. France itself continued to grow on him. In contrast to the rugged Massachusetts landscape it seemed a great garden. Abigail, in far-off Braintree, continued to manage the farm and care for the children, finding each day much like the next. It had been a relief to her to learn her husband had arrived safely, but she was somewhat annoyed that he did not subsequently write more to her. Meanwhile, she struggled with her own immediate problems. Money was scarce, taxes heavy, the price of goods had doubled, and there were no farm laborers to be had.

As Adams delved into the affairs of the commission and worked out the details of a French treaty, he became more and more convinced that for all the costs, Congress was getting little in return. A single envoy with a few clerks, he thought, would be more efficient than three commissioners. Writing to his cousin Sam he suggested that all commissioners be removed except for one in France and one in Spain. Franklin with his popularity would be the inevitable choice as sole French commissioner, provided that negligent man was given no control over money matters. But even though it meant his own recall, Adams insisted one commissioner alone was enough.

With the treaty agreement between the French and Americans, with Burgoyne's disaster at Saratoga, and with American waters patrolled by the French fleet, Adams had hoped that England would make peace. Instead, it seemed by the autumn of 1778 that the stubborn British government was determined to expand the war. Adams felt dismayed. News from New England was discouraging. The Tories were still numerous and increasingly active. Safe behind the theater of war, a class of new-rich traders, contractors, and currency manipulators had sprung up. "Fellows who would have cleaned my shoes five years ago have amassed fortunes and are riding in chariots," James Warren wrote him from Boston. "Were you to be set down here . . . you would think you was upon enchanted Ground in a world turned topsy turvey."

The winter was mild in France. On the day after Christmas Adams and Johnny strolled through the evening streets to view the illuminations celebrating the birth of the Queen's daughter, Maria Theresa Charlotte. "Splendid indeed," he wrote Abigail. "My little Friend who was with me will write you a Description of it. The Military school, the Hospital of Invalids and the Palace of Bourbon, were beautiful and sublime indeed, as much so as an Illumination can be. I could scarcely have conceived that an Illumination could have such an Effect. I suppose the Expence of this is a Million of Livres. As much as I respect this Country, particularly the King and Royal Family I could not help reflecting how many Families, in another Country would this Tallow make happy for Life, how many Privateers would this Tallow fit out, for chasing away the Jerseymen and making Reprisals on Messrs. Les

Anglois.—But Taste will have its Way in this Country." Shortly after New Year's he heard that Congress was about to make Franklin minister to the French court and that he himself was to be relieved. Grateful, he wrote his wife that he would soon be home, even as he planned passage on the next available man-of-war sailing for America.

With his French interlude drawing to a close, Adams found himself increasingly converted to what at first had seemed an utterly alien way of life. Although his Puritan nature still reacted against the ostentation of the court, he thought the Parisians the happiest people in the world. Everything, from the manner of living to the cuisine, had a charm that only British prejudice could reject. With theater entertainments, good company, and good books, he needed only to have his family with him in a time of peace to be completely happy in France.

Meanwhile the New England winter had been bitter. Even Boston Harbor froze over. "How lonely are my days?" Abigail wrote in her isolation. "How solitary are my Nights? Secluded from all Society but my two Little Boys, and my domesticks, by the Mountains of snow which surround me I could almost fancy myself in Greenland. We have had four of the coldest Days I ever knew, and they were followed by the severest snow storm I ever remember, the wind blowing like a Hurricane for 15 or 20 hours renderd it impossible for Man or Beast to live abroad, and has blocked up the roads so that they are impassible." Deane, now back in America and with scant regard for Congress, was vitriolically attacking his detractors in the newspapers. Adams in a fury denounced Deane to Franklin. In the midst of this controversy news came that Franklin had been made sole plenipotentiary. Adams went at once to Versailles to take leave of Vergennes, holding a long conversation in French in "which I found I could talk as fast as I pleased." With carefully measured courtesy the foreign minister expressed his esteem, adding that the King had been particularly satisfied with Adams's wise and prudent conduct.

Leaving France was also for Adams a time for personal stock-taking. Looking at himself in the mirror, as if he were someone else, he saw weakness of character in the reflected face where he would have liked to see the virtuous sternness of a Roman senator, the reserve of a stoic. "By my Physical Constitution, I am but an ordinary Man," he noted regretfully, observing his over-plump florid features. "When I look in the Glass, my Eye, my Forehead, my Brow, my Cheeks, my Lips, all betray this Relaxation. Yet some great Events, some cutting Expressions, some mean (*Scandals*) Hypocrisies, have at Times, thrown this Assemblage of Sloth, Sleep, and littleness into a Rage a little like a Lion. Yet it is not the Lion— there is Extravagance and Distraction in it, that still betrays the same Weakness."

Not until June 18, 1779, did he and Johnny sail from L'Orient aboard the French frigate *La Sensible*. Also aboard were the new minister plenipotentiary to the United States, the Chevalier de la Luzerne, and his secretary, François de Barbé-Marbois. For Adams it was a delightful voyage. He talked for hours with the two diplomats. Johnny gave them English lessons, they reading aloud from Blackstone's *Discourses*, he correcting every word, syllable, and letter of their pronunciation. The Frenchmen asked Adams many questions about America and its leaders, and he answered them with characteristically indiscreet frankness. Particularly were they curious about his views on the revered Dr. Franklin. "It is universally believed in France, England and all Europe," he told them bluntly, "that his Electric Wand has accomplished all this Revolution but nothing is more groundless. He has [done] very little. It is believed that he made all the American Constitutions, and their Confederation. But he made neither. He did not even make the Constitution of Pensylvania, bad as it is."

How the smallness of Braintree affected Adams after the largeness of Paris, he never said. There was beyond all else the joy of seeing Abigail and the children again. Yet even as his eyes grew attuned to his native landscape, his thoughts carried him overseas. The cherished daydream of retiring to his Braintree acres had lost any immediacy. Some day, perhaps—but before then, he had his role to play in the world of affairs. Of that he was certain. He wrote a long and careful report to Congress on the European situation. Spain in June had entered the war against England on Vergennes's promise to aid in recovering Gibraltar and the Floridas. Prussia and the United Netherlands might be next. Great Britain was becoming isolated; to Adams's mind a great tree that had been girdled. As for the Dutch Republic, so similar to America in manners, religion, and even constitution, Adams felt that Congress should send a minister there, a man of "consummate Prudence" with "a Caution and Discretion that will be Proof against any Tryal." And though he did not say so outright, he implied that he was such a man. He was angered when Congress failed to thank him for his services or appoint him to a new post, and infuriated when he discovered he was among the commissioners and agents censured for squabbling and partisanship. Writing to his congressional friends, he demanded a copy of the charges against him.

Meanwhile, Congress with somewhat premature optimism was debating the question of appointing a minister to negotiate a treaty of peace and a treaty of commerce with Great Britain, and after a certain amount of political jockeying selected Adams. He insisted stubbornly that he first wanted the details of the "Complaints and Evidences" against him. Elbridge Gerry, a member of Congress from Massachusetts, pointed out that his appointment was in effect a rejection of all such charges. Though agreeing to accept, Adams replied realistically: "I suspect that I shall go to France and live there without much Negotiation with England for some time. . . . My request is that in case there should be no Business to do as a

Negotiator with England, and in case you should send to Holland or Prussia, that you will employ me to one of those places."

During the three months that he spent at home he was chosen to represent Braintree in a convention to draw up a constitution for Massachusetts. When the convention met he was selected, along with Sam Adams and James Bowdoin, to draft the new constitution. The actual drafting was his work alone. In it he embodied his long-meditated system of checks and balances against a headstrong democracy: a separation of the legislative, executive, and judicial powers; a bicameral legislature, with election to the upper house restricted to property owners; representatives to the lower house to be elected from each corporate town. The Massachusetts constitution would greatly influence ensuing state constitutions and would indeed shadow the Constitution of the United States.

For some time before Adams sailed again for France he and Abigail talked over whether she should go with him. In the end it did not seem feasible. Since Congress did not provide for families, the expenses would be far too heavy. And then there was the matter of the children. Adams thought optimistically that the separation would not be too long, that six months or a year should see a treaty of peace, to be followed shortly by a commercial treaty. The second week in November, 1779, he left for Boston where, following Luzerne's instructions, *La Sensible* was waiting for him. This time he took ten-year-old Charles with him as well as Johnny (now thirteen), his servant Joseph Stevens, and a personal secretary, John Thaxter.

So empty did the Braintree house seem to Abigail after they had left that she could not swallow a bite of food. Desperate in her loneliness, she decided to follow them to Boston for one last glimpse before *La Sensible* sailed, "tho my Heart would suffer again the cruel torture of Seperation." By the time she arrived they had gone aboard and she could see no more than the masts and spars of the ship offshore.

From shipboard John wrote her that he hoped it would be the last separation they should suffer from each other for any length of time. Little could he guess as he watched his homeland slip below the horizon that it would be nine years before he saw Penn's Hill again. A heavy mid-Atlantic storm caused a leak in the frigate that kept two pumps going night and day. Fearing for his ship, the captain headed for the near port of Ferrol, Spain. Rather than wait for another ship to carry him comfortably to Nantes or Brest, the impatient Adams set out across the Pyrenees with his party in three ramshackle calèches drawn by mules. It was a miserable journey in the winter discomfort of primitive Spain, and by the time they arrived, weary, damp, and flea-bitten, at the French border, they had all come down with severe colds. There at least they were able to exchange the calèches for an easy-riding post chaise and reached Paris early in February after an overland journey of more than twelve hundred miles. As quickly as possible Adams went with Deane and Franklin to Versailles to see Vergennes.

Not only did the foreign minister resent the voluble and assertive American, but he distrusted him as well, suspecting unjustly that Adams was ready to come to terms with the English behind French backs. Vergennes decided that he must put the other in his place, reducing if not eliminating the powers given him. Yet so suavely did he receive Adams that the American was convinced of his good will. "I never heard the French Ministry so frank, so explicit," he wrote Congress, "so decided . . . in the Course of this Conversation in their declarations to pursue the War with vigour and afford effectual Aid to the United States." Vergennes asked Adams to conceal his commission for the time and above all to keep it from being known in London. Secretly he set about to undermine Adams's authority. Only slowly did the American come to realize that the Frenchman's good will was a myth, that his real intentions were to keep "Us embroiled with England as much, and as long as possible, even after a Peace."

Spain was now allied with France, while Holland, Sweden, and Denmark had joined Russia in a policy of armed neutrality. The English government in its isolation began to consider new plans for reconciliation. Adams warned an English correspondent that any such plans short of complete independence for America, or with the idea of separating America from her allies, were "visionary and delusive, disingenuous, corrupt and wicked." He passed much of each day now writing letters since, with any English treaty in abeyance, there was little else for him to do. Weekends he spent with his boys, taking them to see the King's gardens and Versailles, trying out their French, in which they were far more fluent than he. For all his pleasure in Paris, he now saw the city in more somber tones. "There is every Thing here," he wrote Abigail, "that can inform the Understanding or refine the Taste, and indeed one would think that could purify the Heart. Yet it must be remembered there is every thing here too, which can seduce, betray, deceive, deprave, corrupt and debauch it."

He was beset, too, with many problems, having had to assume debts without any certainty that Congress would be able to pay them. When Congress at last took up the problem of inflation by issuing new currency to be exchanged for the old at the rate of one dollar to forty, Vergennes, seeing the debt to France scaled down by this slight of hand from $200 million to $5 million, was outraged. French merchants, he pointed out, who had accepted paper money for vitally needed commodities found themselves expropriated. Adams replied testily that most of the merchants had acquired their money at a discount, and that in any case Congress intended to pay them off with the equivalent value of their goods at the time of sale. He followed this with a five-thousand-word monograph on international finance in which he concluded that private French creditors did not deserve much sympathy since all merchants were profiteers. Vergennes's retort, after a week's silence, was snubbing: "Details in which you have thought proper to enter have not yet changed my sentiments; but I think that all further discussion between us on this subject will be needless."

For six months Adams, at Vergennes's request, had kept his English mission secret, but with more and more impatience. Now he wrote the French minister that the time had come for a "frank and decent communication of my full powers." Vergennes was and remained convinced that any such premature disclosure might encourage the British in their efforts to detach the Americans from the French alliance. He replied icily that the time for Adams to communicate his plenipotentiary power to the British had not yet come. "I pray you, and in the name of the King request you," he concluded, "to communicate your letter and my answer to the United States, and to suspend, until you shall have received orders from them, all measures with regard to the English ministry."

Undaunted, Adams continued his epistolary stream. "I am determined to omit no opportunity of communicating my sentiments to Your Excellency upon everything that appears to me to be of importance to the common cause," he told Vergennes. The French minister wanted no more unsolicited advice. "I think it my duty to inform you," he wrote back, "that Mr. Franklin being the sole person who has letters of credence to the King from the United States, it is with him only that I ought and can treat of matters which concern them, and particularly of that which is the subject of your observation." Nor did the King "stand in need of your solicitations to induce him to interest himself in the affairs of the United States." Vergennes refused to enter into any more discussions with Adams or even to answer his letters.

Franklin wrote to Congress: "Mr. Adams has given offense to the court here by some sentiments and expressions contained in several of his letters written to the Count de Vergennes. I mention this with reluctance. . . . It is true that Mr. Adams' proper business is elsewhere; but the time not being come for that business, and having nothing else here wherewith to employ himself, he seems to have endeavored supplying what he may suppose my negotiations defective in."

Feeling himself rebuffed, superfluous in Paris, Adams turned his attention to the United Netherlands. He had felt for some time that if their high mightinesses, the States-General of the United Province, could be persuaded to recognize the United States, and Dutch bankers to grant America loans, it would do much to lessen his country's dependence on France. And since the first American minister to Holland, Henry Laurens, had been captured by the British en route there, Adams let his friends in Congress know that he considered himself eminently qualified for the post. At the end of July, 1780, taking his two boys with him from their Passy school, he left for Amsterdam. At first the sturdy bourgeois virtues of the Dutch attracted him, their order and industry, the cleanliness of their cities. Later, harassed and frustrated by their elusiveness, he came to consider them as money grubbers, servants of Mammon.

In September Congress notified Adams of his additional assignment as interim representative to Holland. This was made more permanent five months later when he was made minister plenipotentiary to negotiate a treaty. Always a stickler for form, he rented a large and handsome mansion that he felt comported with his dignity as a representative of republican America. He also acquired a carriage and coachman, and—what certainly would have astonished his Braintree neighbors—servants in deep blue livery with scarlet piping. Johnny he now enrolled at the University of Leyden, one of the best in Europe, he assured himself.

That December, England, as a result of many disputes over shipping, declared war on Holland, and Adams was hopeful that this would speed his recognition as minister. Yet months passed without any decision by the States-General. Dutch merchants, dismayed at British raids on their ships, wanted peace. Nor were their high mightinesses ready to jeopardize a desirable accommodation with England by recognizing the representative of a revolted colony.

Adams traveled diligently from city to city, cultivating influential Dutchmen and making lists of friends of America and of those willing to lend money to the United States. Congress, in anticipation of a loan, had prematurely drawn bills on Adams in Amsterdam. To his mortification he was forced to forward these protested bills to Franklin in Paris. Fortunately Franklin had just received an additional six million livres from the French King with which he was able to pay off the overdrafts.

While their high mightinesses and hereditary stadholder, the Prince of Orange, were temporizing about receiving an American minister, Vergennes in the early summer of 1781 sent for Adams to discuss articles of peace proposed by the courts of Russia and Germany. Adams took little hope from such proposals. He approved of a suggested year's truce and direct negotiations between Great Britain and the United States, but he wanted no mediation through European nations that might compromise American independence. So he informed Vergennes, nor could he resist following this up with renewed letters of advice. Meanwhile, in America Luzerne was doing his best to undercut Adams, persuading Congress that Adams should be instructed to "take no steps without the approbation of His Majesty," that is to say Vergennes. Congress depended on French gold, French ships, and even French soldiers, and faced with an empty treasury, resentful, poorly equipped troops, and dissatisfied officers, was in no mood to antagonize France. Adams was instructed to endeavor to make the French sensible of "how much we rely upon His Majesty's influence for the effectual support in everything that may be necessary for the present security or future prosperity of the United States." Then Congress replaced the one-man peace commission by a commission of five that included Adams, Jay, Franklin, Jefferson, and Henry Laurens, while revoking Adams's commission to negotiate an English commercial treaty.

Only partially recovered from a fever, Adams was preparing to leave for The Hague when he learned of Congress's summary action. "I am a Sheep and . . . I have been fleeced," he wrote a friend plaintively. Even as Congress demoted Adams it appointed his friend, Francis Dana, former secretary of the legation in Paris, as minister plenipotentiary to Russia, in the hope of obtaining recognition of the United States by the Empress Catherine. Since French was the language of the Russian court, and Dana did not speak it, he needed an interpreter. After much thought Adams decided to let the now bilingual Johnny go to St. Petersburg as Dana's private secretary.

At The Hague Adams continued to press the Dutch for recognition of American independence. "They are afraid of everybody," he complained, "afraid of France, afraid of America, England, Russia and the northern Powers." The mood changed with startling abruptness when the news came of Cornwallis's surrender of his army to the Americans on October 19, 1781. Here indeed was "the world turned upside down," the great military victory that Adams had almost despaired of. Although negotiations would drag on for another two years, Cornwallis's surrender ended the war for all practical purposes. This was as clear to the Dutch as to anyone else, and in April, 1782, their high mightinesses resolved to accept Adams "in the quality of envoy of the United States of North America" and grant him an audience.

Nothing but his patient and persevering efforts, Adams rightly felt, had prevented the United Provinces from going over to the English. "One thing, thank God, is certain," he congratulated himself, "I have planted the American Standard at the Hague. There let it wave and fly in triumph over . . . British pride. I shall look down upon the Flagstaff with pleasure from the other World." At a reception given by the diplomatic corps Adams was at last officially presented to his colleagues. Bowing to him, the Spanish minister remarked: "You, sir, have struck the greatest blow in all Europe. It is the best blow that has ever been struck in the American cause."

After the fall of Lord North in England, the agents of the new Shelburne ministry arrived in Paris to discuss peace with the American commissioners, and with Vergennes's approval first talked informally with Franklin. Adams had grown increasingly resentful of the curtailment of his original commission, and with his resentment his suspicion and dislike of Franklin grew. "I knew he had conceived an irreconcilable Hatred of me," he wrote years later, "and that he had propagated and would continue to propagate Prejudices, if nothing worse, against me in America from one end of it to the other." The newly appointed secretary of foreign affairs, Robert Livingston, Adams considered a partisan of Franklin and Vergennes and warned him that America's policy must be based on its own interests and not on instructions from the French foreign minister.

Now that Adams had been officially recognized in the Netherlands, there was little for him to do in The Hague but wait for their high mightinesses to conclude the treaty. Periodically he was overcome by homesickness and waves of depression. He missed Johnny and decided he must have the boy back from St. Petersburg. Most of all he missed Abigail. "Oh when shall I see my dearest Friend," he wrote her. "—All in good Time. My dear blue Hills, ye are the most sublime object in my Imagination. At your reverend Foot, will I spend my old Age, if any, in a calm philosophical Retrospect upon the turbulent scaenes of Politicks and War. I shall recollect Amsterdam, Leyden and the Hague with more Emotion than Philadelphia or Paris." Yet, whatever his protestations, his dark temporary moods, his so often expressed wish to retire to his Braintree acres, he could not resist the lure of power. The intricacies of diplomacy intrigued him, his pride swelled each time he squeezed his pudgy figure into his diplomatic uniform—the blue and buff of a Continental officer—his vanity (however he might privately belittle it) expanded in the thought of himself, the Braintree country boy, dealing as an equal with the leaders of nations. Beyond his own concerns he had a glowing vision of his country, the nation-to-be, its forests cleared, its plains one vast garden, a colossus of a hundred million inhabitants, a great new force in the world for the benefit of mankind.

Whatever her pride in her husband, Abigail felt her isolation more and more. "May I come to you, with our daughter, in the Spring," she asked him, "provided you are likely to continue abroad. . . . Remember that to render your situation more agreable I fear neither the Enemy nor old Neptune, but then you must give me full assureance of your intire approbation of my request." Tentatively he agreed. If he was not to return home he wanted his wife with him. However until he could determine how long he would be staying, she had better remain in Braintree.

After the signing of the Dutch treaty, he left for Paris where Jay had already joined Franklin to begin negotiations with the British (Jefferson was still in America, and Laurens in British custody). Adams still regarded Franklin, the fallen idol of his youth, with profound distrust, feeling that the old man would do his best to drive a wedge between the other two. He was appalled at the instruction from Congress to govern himself ultimately by the advice and opinion of the French ministry. Before he did that, he announced, he would resign, and he was relieved to find that both Jay and Franklin considered the instructions improper and had decided to ignore them. His meeting with Franklin went off better than he had expected, the old man showing himself more concerned about his country than about his personal feelings. Jay, in any case, was on Adams's side. Like Lee before him he did not like the French, considering them not a "moral people," and he suspected that Vergennes was out to rob the United States of fisheries, Western lands, and the right of navigation of the Mississippi River.

The British negotiators proved unexpectedly conciliatory. "We can never be such damned Sots as to think of differing again with you," one of them remarked to Adams. "Why, in truth," Adams replied with some asperity, "I have never been able to comprehend the Reason why you ever thought of differing with Us." There were questions of debts owed by American merchants, debts that many merchants now claimed had been cancelled by the war; the question of compensation to Tories and the counter-questions of destruction done by British soldiery and of the property—including slaves—taken away in the evacuation of the South; questions of fishing rights off Newfoundland and of the limits of the Western boundaries, on neither of which Adams was prepared to concede an inch. As to the question of the debts, Franklin maintained this was up to the individual states. Adams, however, felt that just debts should be recovered, and Jay and Franklin "gradually fell into this opinion." Anxious to come to terms, the British were willing to make concessions, and agreement was reached more easily than the Americans had anticipated. Vergennes was furious at the American commissioners' failure to consult with him, and for this he blamed Adams. Deane's supporters and the pro-French party in Congress took up the argument that the commission had not followed its instructions. Adams's old sense of persecution was instantly aroused. He was convinced that Franklin would get all the credit for the treaty, whereas he would be censured for disregarding orders. "I am weary, disgusted, affronted and disappointed," he wrote. Congress had dishonored itself by surrendering its sovereignty into Vergennes's hands. "Blush! blush! ye guilty Records! blush and perish! It is Glory to have broken such infamous orders."

From time to time Adams might daydream of retiring, fancy himself on his New World Sabine farm, but his assertive ambition ever and again thrust such notions aside. His own insecurity, the insecurity of the self-made man, demanded assurance, recognition, place. What he now wanted with burning inner intensity once the English treaty was settled, was to be the first minister of the United States to Great Britain, a position that he was convinced he deserved above all others and that he feared would go to Franklin. Obsessed by the thought, he wrote Livingston, setting forth the qualities that a minister to the Court of St. James's should have: a classical education, knowledge of ancient and modern history, philosophy and ethics, Roman civil law, and the laws of England and the United States. Such a man should be mature but not too old, upright, of an independent spirit, one who would set his country's interests above any private ambition. Adams was obviously such a man, Franklin as obviously was not!

Vergennes with the fatalism that is the mark of a good diplomat was willing to accept the preliminary treaty as a *fait accompli.* Adams nevertheless continued to regard him and the French court with morbid suspicion. In shoulder-shrugging mockery Franklin wrote to Livingston that "the instances he [Adams] supposes of their ill will to us . . . I take to be as imaginary as I know his fancies to be that Count de Vergennes and myself are continually plotting against him." That was indeed what Adams believed.

Abigail across the ocean watched the wartime boom collapse while she scraped together money to pay the taxes. She sold to her neighbors various trinkets her husband sent her from overseas, made her own and her children's clothes, and got along with "only two domesticks." The news beyond Braintree was dismaying. More merchants and traders, she thought, would be ruined by the peace than by the war. In Philadelphia, Pennsylvania soldiers mutinied and besieged Congress in the State House. Congress itself seemed penniless and impotent, and Abigail wondered if anarchy and disorder were to succeed the Revolution. Charles, who had returned out of homesickness after his brother had gone to St. Petersburg, was now almost old enough to enter college, but his mother was fearful of Harvard's corrupting environment.

On her wedding anniversary she wrote her husband sadly, "Do you not recollect that Eighteen years have run their anual circuit, since we pledged our mutual Faith to each other, and the Hymeneal torch was Lighted at the Alter of Love. . . . I recollect the untitled Man to whom I gave my Heart. . . . Who shall give me back Time? Who shall compensate to me those *years* I cannot recall? How dearly have I paid for a titled Husband; should I wish you less wise, that I might enjoy more happiness? I cannot find that in my Heart." Somehow she managed to scrimp together $200 in hard cash with which she bought seven acres at the foot of Penn's Hill. John was delighted with the fine grove that he had admired since he was a boy. He wanted to return home, perhaps serve for a time in Congress or even the Massachusetts legislature. Abigail had heard him sound such a modest note many times before. She knew he was sincere, but she also recognized the unquenchable ambition underlying such protestations. The rumors current that he might soon be appointed ambassador to England left her profoundly troubled. "What ever lustre in the Eyes of some People there may be in the Feather of being the first Minister to England," she wrote her friend Mercy Warren, "you, Madam, will surely see that his Situation is more to be pitied than envied."

Negotiations dragged on in London over the final treaty while Adams and the others cooled their heels in Paris. The less occupied he was, the more he longed for his wife and daughter. Finally, in September, 1783, the treaty was signed. Shortly afterward word came that Adams and Franklin and Jay—all together or any one of them—had been appointed to negotiate an English commercial treaty. Knowing he would now have to stay in Europe at least until spring, Adams instructed Abigail and Nabby to leave the boys with relations and join him. As soon as he should hear of her arrival he would "fly with Post Horses to receive you at last, and if the Ballon should be carried to such Perfection in the mean time as to give Mankind a safe Navigation of the air, I will fly in one of them at the Rate of thirty knots an hour."

Later in the month Adams came down again with his Dutch fever. In spite of vigorous bleedings by his physician he recovered fairly rapidly. As soon as his health picked up, he determined to see England. Congress might not in the end send a minister there, or might send someone else, but in any case he wanted a glimpse of the land of his ancestors. His attitude toward England remained that of a young man who had been driven to leave the paternal roof but who later in the independence of his manhood came to realize his affection for what he had left. England had been the enemy, the oppressor with whom—he had once written—America could never be friends. Yet of all countries it was, even unseen, the one he admired most; the mother country, Shakespeare's island, source of his blood, his speech, his thought. English institutions, the common law he so revered, English literature, were as much his as any born Englishman's, as were the time-encrusted names the homesick New England settlers had given to their new settlements. Whatever he might have said of England, it was to him no foreign country.

After a violently rough Channel crossing he saw the cliffs of Dover looming up ahead of him, and in spite of seasickness he had a feeling of coming home. In London he found rooms overlooking the Thames at the Adelphi Hotel in the Strand, outrageously expensive yet not unlike what he had been used to in America. Through young John Singleton Copley, whom he had known in Boston before the Revolution, he got tickets from Lord Mansfield to hear the King's speech at the opening of Parliament. "Standing in the lobby of the house of lords, surrounded by a hundred of the first people of the kingdom, Sir Francis Molineux, the gentleman usher of the black rod, appeared suddenly in the room with his long staff, and roared out with a very loud voice—

*'Where is Mr. Adams, Lord Mansfield's friend!'* I frankly avowed myself Lord Mansfield's friend, and was politely conducted by Sir Francis to my place. A gentleman said to me next day, 'how short a time has passed since I heard that same Lord Mansfield say in that same house of lords, "my Lords, if you do not kill him, he will kill you." ' "

Still not in the best of health, Adams, after a short stay in London, set out for Bath to take the waters. He had scarcely arrived before he was summoned back to Holland to negotiate a loan against the threatened collapse of American credit.

Abigail and Nabby finally sailed in June, 1784, taking their own provisions, including a milk cow. With them went Abigail's maid, Esther Field, and John Briesler, a husbandman to whom Abigail had once intended to rent a farm. It was a rough voyage in cramped quarters, with food prepared, wrote Abigail, by "a great, dirty, lazy negro, with no more knowledge of cookery than a savage." A northeaster off Newfoundland so battered the ship that the cow died. When at last Abigail saw the gulls dipping above the waves, she knew the voyage must be almost over. "am I so near the land of my forefathers?" she asked. "& am I, gracious Heaven; there to meet, the Dear long absent partner of my Heart? how many, how various, how complicated my Sensations!"

Once settled in London at Osborne's New Family Hotel, Abigail found the urbane Georgian city much to her liking. She was pleased with what she saw of the London style of entertaining although the informality of women's dress surprised her. Old American friends, settled in London, at once came to call: Torys like the Hallowells; John's cousin, Ward Boylston, transformed into a London dandy; young Winslow Warren, son of James and Mercy Warren. John had commissioned Winslow to search in the Herald's Office in London for a titled Somerset Adams—a quest that would preoccupy later generations of Adamses. Winslow could find no armigerous relations but suggested that John adopt the arms of any Adams he pleased since people had become much more indifferent to such matters than formerly. Following this somewhat cynical advice, Adams took the Quincy arms for his bookplate.

When toward the end of July Adams at The Hague learned of his family's arrival he exclaimed that the news made him twenty years younger. Since he was daily anticipating being called to Paris by the other commissioners, he was forced to send Johnny to London in his place. The boy to whom Abigail had bid goodbye on that bitter winter day was now a handsome and self-possessed young man. Seeing Johnny and Nabby together, Abigail wrote her sister, Mary Cranch, that if she were not their mother she would say "a likelier Pair you will seldom see in a Summer's day."

Having received word that Jefferson had at last joined the other commissioners in Passy, Adams decided to go first to London to take his family to France with him. After a three-day journey he was at last reunited with his Abigail, a meeting that somehow made up for almost a decade's absence. Next day they set off for France. But that country, unlike England, seemed to Abigail an alien land. She was appalled by the rural poverty, the wretched peasant huts that she saw from her coach. Paris, where they stayed a few days, she thought the dirtiest and smelliest place she had ever visited. Some of the buildings and squares were impressive, but most of the streets were narrow and littered, the shops and houses far from elegant. Boston was much better, even as London was better than Boston.

Adams had rented the estate of the Count de Roualt bordering on the Bois de Boulogne and about a mile from Passy, a mansion of halls and salons and some thirty bedrooms. To run such an establishment, as Abigail discovered, required a corps of domestics. There seemed to be a servant for every small function. To polish the red-tiled floors one man, stripped to the waist, did nothing but whirl about with brushes strapped to his feet. She thought her own

servants a swarm of lazy incompetents more concerned with pil-
fering than with any domestic duties, and she much resented being
dunned for tips by other people's servants.

Abigail, if one can judge by her letters, fancied herself the austere Roman matron, a Cornelia whose jewels were her children.
Yet before long even her prim New England nature began to yield
to the graceful spell of French social customs. She soon delighted
in the theater, although on her first visit to the ballet she was
shocked by the female dancers with what seemed to her their wan-
ton display of legs, drawers, and garters.

Adams conferred daily with Franklin and Jefferson, and sometimes Abigail entertained them at Auteuil. In spite of her husband's
dislike of the old man and her own knowledge of his easy immorality, she was not wholly impervious to Franklin's charm. Adams regarded Jefferson as an old friend, and as the three worked
amiably on the drafts of proposed commercial treaties with the
various European nations his rancor against Franklin abated. He
thought the old man was more gracious than at any time since he
had known him.

An isolationist faction in Congress was pressing for the elimination of all ministers and ambassadors in Europe. It distressed
Adams, for he was all too aware how many affairs needed to be
settled and how necessary it was to have someone in authority to
conduct the negotiations and conclude the agreements. It was
particularly so in England where mercantile debts, frontier posts,
and the status of the Tories still hung fire. Yet only with slow reluctance did Congress finally agree to the need of having a minister to England. Even after such an agreement, it was by no
means certain that Adams would get the post. A number of congressional delegates disliked him, among them the partisans of
Franklin and Deane. They objected that he was too vain and too
headstrong, although in the end they were forced to admit that he
was qualified and that no one else approached him in experience

and effectiveness. Early in February nine of the eleven state del-egations present in Congress endorsed him as the first American minister to the Court of St. James's.

Elbridge Gerry forwarded the details of the attack on Adams prior to his confirmation, and the news took away much of his joy and satisfaction in the prize he had so coveted. To relieve his feelings he wrote a long disquisition on vanity which he planned to send to Gerry but then changed his mind. Franklin, he wrote in this suppressed essay, who pretended to be free from vanity, was in his heart "the vainest Man and the falsest Character I have ever met with in life." Before moving on to London he sent Johnny back home to continue his studies at Harvard.

Though they spent only a few months at Auteuil, the Adamses were saddened when the time came for them to go. John had grown attached to his rural surroundings as well as to Jefferson's company. Abigail was depressed at the thought of leaving a place to which she knew she would never return. She had even become fond of the servants who, as the Adams carriage drew away, stood on the steps and wept.

There were many in England, as Adams would soon discover, who bore him enduring enmity as one of the authors of the American troubles. The *Public Advertiser* greeted him on his London arrival as "His Excellency John Adams (honest John Adams), the ambassador of America," adding: "An Ambassador from America! Good heavens, what a sound! . . . Tis hard to say which can excite indignation most, the insolence of those who appoint the char-acter, or the meanness of those who receive it." Exiled Tories spread the rumor that Adams would never be received by the King.

As soon as Adams was settled in his hotel he called on the secretary of state for foreign affairs, who notified him that he would be presented to the King the following Wednesday. In prep-aration he carefully rehearsed his speech. He was ready to tell the King that he thought himself "more fortunate than all my Fellow

Citizens in having the distinguished honor to be the first to stand in your Majesty's Royal Presence in a Diplomatic Character." He hoped to be instrumental in restoring "the old good Nature and the old good Humour between People who, tho' seperated by the ocean and under different Governments, have the same Language, a Similar Religion, and kindred Blood."

Adams was very nervous when he woke on the day of his presentation. Abigail got him ready, listened to his speech, checked his appearance—his new coat, his silk breeches and silk stockings, his sword, his sash, his silver-buckled shoes, his wig, his gloves. Then the foreign secretary arrived in his coach to take him to the antechamber of the court, "the Room very full of Lords & Bishops and all Sorts of Courtiers, as well as the next Room, the King's Bed Chamber." From there Adams was escorted to the King's closet. Following strict court etiquette he bowed at the door, again when he was halfway into the room, and finally as he stood before the King. Both men appeared ill at ease, the King agitated, Adams suffering from stage fright. Oddly enough they were much alike, short, stubborn, choleric men—Farmer George and Farmer John—moral, well meaning, tactless, and lovers of their country. In time they would recognize their similar natures and even come to like one another. George's voice trembled as he replied to the other's well-rehearsed address, saying he was very glad that the choice had fallen on Adams to be first minister from the United States. Then, measuring his words slowly, almost haltingly, he added, "I will be very frank with you. I was the last to consent to the Seperation; but the Seperation having been made, and having become inevitable, I have always said, as I say now, that I would be the first to meet the friendship of the United States as an independent power. The moment I see such Sentiments and Language as yours prevail, and a disposition to give this Country the preference, that Moment I shall say, let the Circumstances of Language, Religion, and Blood have their natural and full operation." Then after a few more words he bowed to signify that the audience was at an end. Adams walked backward, with as much grace as he could muster, bowed again at the door, and was led by the master of ceremonies "through all the appartments down to my Carriage. Several Stages of Servants, Gentlemen Porters and Under Porters, roaring out like Thunder as I went along, 'Mr. Adams's servants, Mr. Adams Carriage!' "

In later appearances at court Adams took pleasure in talking to, and more often listening to, the King, who had the facility for small talk that the American did not possess. George, although ready to welcome Adams, could not bring himself to extend a welcome to Jefferson, the man who had written the diatribe against him in the Declaration of Independence. Some time later, when Adams appeared at court with his visiting colleague, the King turned his back on that hated face.

For his London residence Adams rented a spacious house on Grosvenor Square facing Lord North's town house, which prompted Abigail's witticism that she was still "opposite" to him. She was discouraged to find that she needed an even larger staff than in her Auteuil mansion, a situation made worse by the niggardly sums Congress allowed its ambassador. Adams's frugality grew to be a joke among the members of the diplomatic corps. Nevertheless the Grosvenor Square house soon became the center of the American colony in London, frequented by painters, scientists, merchants, émigrés, and Tory refugees down on their luck. Much to his joy Adams after fifteen years again met Jonathan Sewall, whose loyalty to the Crown had brought him exile and a marginal existence in London. The two friends spent an evening of talk together, losing track of time completely. Political differences had failed to break the bond between them. Yet Sewall was sharply aware of Adams's limitations. "He is not qualifyed by nature or education to shine in Courts," the exile wrote, "his abilities are, undoubtedly quite equal to the mechanical parts of his business as ambassador;

but this is not enough—he cant dance, drink, game, flatter, promise, dress, swear with the gentlemen, & talk small talk & flirt with the Ladys—in short he has none of the essential *arts* or *ornaments* which constitute a courtier—there are thousands who with a tenth part of his understanding, & without a spark of his honesty, would distance him infinitely in any Court in Europe."

Adams's ambassadorial problems, though they made no great demands on his time, seemed infuriatingly prolonged: frontier posts still in British hands; unpaid compensation for slaves and other confiscated American property; restrictions on American trade and shipping, as in the West Indies; the old problem of prewar debts; the fate of American vessels captured since the armistice; and finally the intricacies of the commercial treaty. As an American, Adams was not generally popular in London. Never one to shrug off insults, he was particularly stung by the barbs in the British press. London journalists referred to him as a penny pincher, a proscribed rebel, a commercial agent, a bumpkin lawyer. In Grosvenor Square he often thought back to the lost simplicities of Braintree, and he was delighted when he was able to purchase a few stony acres next to his farm. "My view," he wrote, "is to lay fast hold of the town of Braintree and embrace it with both my arms and all my might. There to live—there to die—there to lay my bones and there to plant one of my sons in the profession of the Law and the practice of Agriculture like his father."

Reports from across the sea were troubling him more and more. So weak and ineffectual had the federal government become that many wondered if it could survive. Washington described it as "a shadow without substance." In Massachusetts the former Continental captain Daniel Shays led a rebellion of farmers and debtors in what was essentially a populist revolt. Although Shays's Rebellion turned out to be no more than a few winter skirmishes between irate indebted farmers and reluctant militiamen, it seemed to Adams to foreshadow the radical democratic rising he had feared. Men of thought like Noah Webster had even come to believe that a limited monarchy was preferable to such rampant republicanism. Washington at Mount Vernon was "mortified beyond expression" when he viewed "the clouds that have spread over the brightest morn that ever dawned upon any country." Adams thought that the people's just or even imaginary complaints of grievances should not be discouraged. He was deeply troubled, though, by noisy radical agitation for the abolition of senates and governors, for a division of property and for the cancellation of debts. Retiring to his upstairs library he began what he planned to be a curative work on the nature and science of government. As he later explained:

"In 1780 when I arrived in France, I carried a printed copy of the report of the Grand Committee of the Massachusetts Convention, which I had drawn up; and this became an object of speculation, Mr. Turgot . . . and others admired Mr. Franklin's [Pennsylvania] constitution and reprobated mine. Mr. Turgot, in a letter to Dr. Price . . . censured the American constitution as adopting three branches in imitation of the constitution of Great Britain. The intention was to celebrate Franklin's constitution and condemn mine. I understood it and undertook to defend my constitution, and it cost me three volumes.

". . . I never thought of writing till the Assembly of Notables in France had commenced a revolution . . . who I knew would establish a government in one assembly, and that I knew would involve France and all Europe in all the horrors we have seen, carnage and desolation, for fifty, perhaps a hundred years.

"At the same time, every western wind brought us news of town and county meetings in Massachusetts adopting Mr. Turgot's ideas, condemning my constitution, reprobating the office of governor and the assembly of the Senate as expensive, useless, pernicious, and not only proposing to toss them off, but rising in rebellion against them.

"In this situation I was determined to wash my hands of the blood that was about to be shed in France, Europe, and America, and show to the world that neither my sentiments nor actions should have any share in countenancing or encouraging any such pernicious, destructive and fatal schemes. In this view I wrote my defense of the American constitutions. I had only the Massachusetts constitution in view, and such others as agreed with it in the distribution of the legislative power into three branches, in separating the executive from the legislative power, and the judiciary power from both."

Hastily written, poorly organized, his first volume appeared under the ponderous title *A Defense of the Constitutions of Government of the United States of America against the attack of M. Turgot, in his letter to Dr. Price, dated the twenty-second of March, 1778.* More an anthology than an original work, three quarters of it consisting of quotations from other authors ancient and modern, it has been described as "a morbid anatomy of a hundred dead republics." For all that, it became a minor best seller in the United States, and Adams claimed that in the Constitutional Convention it "dissipated the vapors of Franklin's foggy System, demolished Hamilton's airy Castles and united the Convention in the plan they finally adopted." He may have exaggerated, but it was used there as a reference book, and many speakers quoted from it.

Restive in London, where his official duties had become minimal, he determined now to return home. He notified John Jay, the new American Secretary of State, that he would not accept a renewal of his commission even if Congress voted it, and in a private letter to Jay he begged him to arrange matters so that he could leave as soon as possible. He was pleased by the news of the coming Constitutional Convention which he hoped and trusted would preserve the foundering Union. After completing a second volume of his *Defense*, he and Abigail took a holiday trip through southern and western England. At Winchester, Abigail noted the tomb of the Sieur de Quincy, first Earl of Winchester. John was certain that the Braintree Quincys were descendants of the earl and did his best to trace the line. The resolutely republican Abigail thought that it was of little consequence, since all people could trace their descent from Adam.

Through the autumn and winter of 1787 Adams worked on a third volume of his *Defense*, a work which his enemies would maliciously misinterpret as advocating monarchy. Starting from Plato's premise that democracy, the untrammeled, unleashed will of the people, was the worst of all governments, Adams pointed out the danger that any elected Executive might turn into a people's tribune. It would, to his mind, be better to make magistrates and Senators hereditary than to have civil tumult, with brawling annual elections and bribed partisans fighting in the streets. He insisted that he was a republican on principle. Nevertheless, Kings were preferable to chaos. Thinking no doubt of Tom Paine, he added that he had no wish to overthrow monarchies for the sake of theoretical republics.

While he was completing his *Defense*, Adams arranged with his American agent to purchase the Vassall house in Braintree, a large country house second only to that of Colonel Quincy's and formerly occupied by a wealthy Tory family that had fled during the Revolution. It was a house he had much admired in his boyhood. Both he and Abigail had a sentimental affection for the Braintree homestead. "My little cottage," Abigail had written in May, "encompassed with my friends, has more Charms for me than the drawing-room of St. James, where studied Civility and disguised Coldness cover malignant Hearts." Yet for all its charms it was no longer adequate, not large enough to begin to contain all the furniture, pictures, silver, and books they had acquired, not commensurate with the dignity of Adams's present position in the world. Even Abigail knew they could never go back to such peasant simplicity.

Adams's last months in England were brightened by the news that the national convention, called after Shays's Rebellion, had drawn up a new federal Constitution. Although he realized it was vastly preferable to the Articles of Confederation, he wished that it had given more power to the President and less to the Senate. He particularly objected to the Senate's right to approve executive appointments. "A result of accommodation cannot be supposed to reach the ideas of perfection of any one," he wrote finally, "but the Conception of such an idea, the deliberate union of so great and various a people in such a plan, is without all partiality or prejudice, . . . the greatest single effort of national deliberation that the world has ever seen." Europe, as he prepared to leave it, was drifting toward some tumultuous unknown. Prussian troops had occupied Holland. Lafayette and others were attempting to set limits to the power of the French Crown, an effort which had so far resulted merely in the unloosing of street mobs. Adams doubted that republics would work in Europe since the common people were not yet ready for self-government. He was glad to be going home. Presenting himself to the King for leave-taking, this time without nervousness, he assured His Majesty of the friendly disposition of his country, thanked him for his protection and civilities, and extended his best wishes to the "Royal Family, Subjects, and Dominions." The King replied affably in kind, wishing Adams "a safe and pleasant voyage and much comfort with your family and friends," then chatted informally about the Adams family.

Before leaving London Adams learned to his dismay that only six states had ratified the new Constitution, and New York so far had refused even to participate. He and Abigail sailed on the *Lucretia*, an American ship bound for Boston, on April 20, 1788. Abigail decided that she had seen enough of the world and that she would never care to cross the ocean again. "I do not think the four years I have past abroad the pleasantest part of my life, tis Domestick happiness & rural felicity in the Bosom of my native Land, that has charms for me," she concluded, "yet I do not regret that I made this excursion Since it has only more attached me to America." On the long voyage Adams walked the deck, a corpulent figure, fifty-four years old but aged before his time, palsied, wheezy, his teeth and eyesight failing. With time on his hands he let his mind dwell on the decade that was past, the changes, those who had died, the current uneasy state of his country, the old enmities he would now face again. Yet he hoped more than he doubted.

Abigail had earlier sent over instructions as to what should be done to the new house: the color of paint, the wallpapers, the repairs, a new ell. But when the Adamses arrived, the work was still incomplete, with neither kitchen nor barn ready. Distance too had lent its enchantment. The house that Abigail remembered as a mansion now seemed after Auteuil and Grosvenor Square "like a wren's house." Their furniture came chipped and scarred and had to be unpacked in the garret. While Abigail did her best to bring some order out of the confusion, John slipped away and bought six cows.

In his years abroad Adams had talked of Braintree, dreamed of Braintree, his birthright. Yet coming from the larger world he found it difficult at first to adjust himself to the actuality of his limited surroundings. The legend of Cincinnatus going back to plough his native acres had somehow lost its appeal. He grew morose, self-pitying, seeing himself as an old man, alienated, without the means to support his old age. Nabby, married to Adams's former secretary in the London legation, Colonel William Stephens Smith, wrote him encouragingly from New York that he would either be the next governor of Massachusetts or the first Vice President of the United States. His friend Dr. Benjamin Rush assured him that his labors for his country had been only a beginning. Adams knew that with John Hancock entrenched as governor of Massachusetts he had no chance for that office, nor did he wish to be one of the new United States Senators. The vice-presidency would and could be the only fitting reward for his services to his country. Alexander Hamilton as nominal head of the Federalists reluctantly agreed to support Adams—whom he privately referred to as the Duke of Braintree—since he needed the support of the New England Federalists. At the same time he secretly contrived to whittle down Adams's vote and diminish his political influence. Washington received all 69 electoral votes; Adams only 34. So offended was Adams by what he considered a deliberate affront that he contemplated resigning.

In the ten months between Adams's return to Braintree and the official notification of his election as Vice President he had assimilated himself once more to his native earth. Europe receded in his mind to a static memory. Engrossed in his new estate, he supervised his hired hands and laborers in all weather as they cleared pastures, built fences, planted trees, and gardened. With the possessive passion of a country squire he longed for more land, more fields, more livestock. This would be his last anchorage, no matter what office he might hold. After his election when he entered Boston and the church bells rang and the crowds lining King Street cheered and waved their hats, he found it the proudest moment of his life.

He arrived in New York, the Provisional Capital, a few days before Washington made his solemn and ceremonial entry, and was sworn in as Vice President. No one was certain how to act in the new circumstances. There were no set forms, no precedents, no protocol, no established etiquette. James Madison, as the leader of the House of Representatives, wrote to Jefferson in Paris that "we are in a wilderness, without a single footstep to guide us."

Convinced as he was that ceremony was essential to create

respect for government, Adams spent his early weeks in the Senate drawing up what he considered dignified forms. From his larger experience of European courts he felt impelled to lecture the Senators as if he were a schoolmaster, unaware of the resentment he caused. With the Court of St. James's still vivid in his mind he laid down how many times a messenger from the Senate must bow on entering the House with a bill, and was chagrined when the Representatives rejected all bowing. His suggestion that the sergeant at arms be called the "Usher of the Black Rod" was similarly dismissed. The chief thorn in his side was the belligerently crude Senator William Maclay of Pennsylvania. The six-foot-three Maclay was a lawyer, frontier surveyor, soldier, Indian commissioner, and large landowner. A radical democrat in a predominantly Federalist gathering, he felt he was serving with "a set of vipers" most of whom "cared for nothing else but . . . the creation of a new monarchy in America." Adams referred in the Senate chamber to Washington's Inaugural Address as "his most gracious speech." Maclay at once challenged the phrase as being the same that was placed before the King of England's speeches, and moved that it be stricken out. The Vice President was upset and surprised that anyone should object to a phrase taken from the practice of a government under which Americans had formerly lived long and happily. Maclay replied that everything related to that government was odious. He saw Adams's formal expression as "the first step of the ladder in the ascent to royalty."

There followed a debate on what the President's title should be. Adams privately favored "His Majesty." A committee on titles toyed with "Excellency," "His Most Benign Highness," "High Mightiness," "Elective Majesty," and "Elective Highness" before settling on "His Highness, the President of the United States of America, and Protector of the Rights of the Same." Maclay wanted nothing more than the Constitution's designation of "President of the United States of America." This was most distressing to Adams who told the Senators that heads of fire companies and cricket clubs were called "President." For forty minutes he spoke passionately from the chair in favor of "His Highness," asking finally: "What will the common people of foreign countries—what will the sailors and soldiers say, 'George Washington, President of the United States?' They will despise him *to all eternity*. This is all nonsense to the philosopher," he admitted, "but so is all government whatever." Maclay retorted that it made no difference what foreign sailors and soldiers thought. "Perhaps the less they think, or have occasion to think of us, the better."

The House of Representatives, under the leadership of James Madison, who had already declined the appendage of "Honorable," eliminated all extraordinary titles, leaving Washington—somewhat to his regret—as simply "Mr. President." Delighted at the austere outcome, Maclay in mockery took to calling the Pennsylvania Congressmen "Your Highnesses of the House," while they in turn designated him "Your Highness of the Senate." Adams they labeled "His Rotundity."

Maclay continued to resent Adams, even though within a month the latter had so far informalized himself as to give up wearing the sword he had worn when he first presided. The Pennsylvania Senator carried over his mockery of the Vice President into his private journal. On May 11 he observed: "He takes on him to school the members from the chair. . . . Instead of that sedate, easy air which I would have him possess, he will look on one side, then on the other, then down on the knees of his breeches, then dimple his visage with the most silly kind of half smile. . . . God forgive me for the vile thought, but I can not help thinking of a monkey just put into breeches when I saw him betray such evident marks of self-conceit."

For eight years Adams presided as Vice President, an office he came to consider one of the most insignificant ever conceived. It was particularly galling for him to have to listen in silence day after day to the gabble of lesser men. Nevertheless, and in spite of the Maclays, he managed to establish a certain decorum in the Senate. Sitting in a plain chair behind a green-fringed table, he rapped sharply with his silver pencil case to call any Senator to order while another was speaking. The sedate atmosphere of the Senate was in marked contrast to the casual disorder of the House of Representatives downstairs where Congressmen wore their hats and read newspapers during debates, or chatted with their neighbors.

Adams was overcome at times by dark moods in which he thought himself outside the mainstream of events, and time and again he longed to be back in Quincy. (In 1792 North Braintree in a dispute over school funds broke away from Braintree to become the independent township of Quincy.) His eyes troubled him, the tremor of his hands increased, his nerves were on edge, and he was convinced that time was running out for him. Because of inflamed gums he had to have the rest of his teeth extracted, and the contours of his face changed. In the summer of 1792 he left off wearing his wig, more as a matter of comfort than because wigs were going out of fashion. But the exposure left him so bald and wrinkled that many of his friends did not recognize him.

His two terms as Vice President marked eight years of tumultuous American history, of the organization of the first cabinet and the Supreme Court, of crises with warring England and Revolutionary France, of domestic stability brought about by Secretary of the Treasury Hamilton's brilliant reestablishment of the public credit, and at the same time of an increasing virulence of party politics as Secretary of State Jefferson's Antifederalists—later Republicans—organized in opposition to the Hamiltonian Federalists. For all the limitations of his office, Vice President Adams was seen more and more as Washington's heir apparent, but he was also subject to criticism from the growing Antifederalist opposition as an indirect way of attacking the unassailable Washington. Yet in his early vice-presidential years he had no desire to succeed Washington, was not even sure he would live that long. When in the spring of 1790 Washington came down with influenza and was thought to be dying, Adams was aghast. No one, he well knew, could replace that father-figure, and he pictured himself as Washington's successor presiding over the disintegration of the Union. Relieved as he was by Washington's recovery, he was much troubled by the partisan violence of the coming mid-term elections and again wondered if it might not be better in the interest of civic order to extend the terms of Senators from six years to twelve or twenty or thirty or even for life. He also felt that if presidential elections should become scenes of bloodshed and riot it might be necessary to preserve liberty by calling a national convention to elect a hereditary President.

During the first Congress there was much dispute as to the site of the new Capital. New York, Philadelphia, Baltimore, Wilmington, Germantown, and the falls of the Delaware were all considered. On a Senate motion to stay two more years in New York, Adams broke a tie by voting against it. Congress then decided that at the close of the session the Capital would be shifted to Philadelphia for a ten-year period, and then moved permanently to a ten-mile-square "Grand Columbian Federal City" to be built on the banks of the Potomac.

While Adams was in New York he had rented a pleasant if rundown house on Richmond Hill overlooking the Hudson, where Abigail joined him. In Philadelphia they first lived at Bush Hill, a house several miles away, before moving to the town itself. But before her husband's first term was out Abigail had found the climate and temper of Philadelphia too much for her health and had retired to Quincy, leaving Adams to bachelor quarters during the congressional sessions. Weekly she wrote him tender, witty, informative letters that he found far more entertaining than all the speeches he had to listen to in the Senate. She recounted the details of the farm, the rain that had at last filled the drying wells, a lamb with mumps that needed to have its throat rubbed daily with goose grease, tree trunks that had been tarred in vain against slugs and caterpillars, the flourishing stands of hay. He in return sent her instructions about planting and rotating, lamented his lot for the hundredth time, and promised to return to his acres for good. His bachelor life became routine. Following a hearty New England breakfast he read the newspapers, smoked a "segar," then took a brisk walk in the formal gardens of the State House. After presiding over the Senate he usually spent the evening reading state papers, visiting friends, or writing letters.

The outbreak of the French Revolution, the storming of the Bastille, and the drafting of a new constitution by the Estates was as disturbing news to him as it was cheering to the Jeffersonian Republicans. Though he believed some reformation was long overdue in France, he maintained that unless the French created a proper balance between their legislative, executive, and judicial branches they would have neither laws nor liberty nor lives. Brooding over the Revolution's sanguinary momentum he began a series of essays, *Discourses on Davila*, that appeared in the Federalist Pennsylvania *Gazette*.

Davila, a sixteenth-century Italian historian, had written of the French civil wars of that period, and Adams's discourses were an extended commentary on the Italian's work. Adams compared those civil wars to the French Revolution and predicted that the latter would end in disaster, as the former had, for want of a balanced government. He reminded his readers that American peace and security depended on the balance of the three branches of government as set forth in the Constitution. In his parallel, Adams tried to refute the popular dogma that men were equal and perfectible, and he again explained why he considered titles, forms, and formalities a necessary adjunct of government. At once the Republicans denounced him as an enemy of the rights of man and

of republican government, a monarchist, a champion of aristocracy, the quondam revolutionary who had been seduced by his
years in European courts.

Adams was dismayed and discouraged by the furor his *Discourses* caused, and with the savagery of the attacks on him his
old sense of persecution overbore him. Among other effects the
*Discourses* created a breach between himself and Jefferson. Not
long after they had appeared in print, a copy of Paine's *Rights of
Man*—answering Burke's attack on the French Revolution, and as
yet unpublished in America—was shown to Jefferson before being
sent on to the printer. Jefferson appended a few comments of his
own which the printer without informing him used as a foreword.
He had written that he was extremely pleased to find that the
pamphlet would be reprinted in America and "that something is
at length to be publicly said against the political heresies which
have sprung up among us." Everyone understood he meant the
Davila discourses. John Quincy, just starting his law career, rushed
to defend his father under the pen name of Publicola. Jefferson,
though he assumed Adams himself to be Publicola, wrote his old
friend apologetically that he had never intended to have his comments made public. Adams thanked him and added that he himself
was not Publicola. Though both men were ostensibly reconciled,
their friendship had been marred, and they would gradually drift
apart until they came to see each other as enemies. Jefferson was
delighted to have the French discard their monarchy and said that
rather than have the Revolution fail he would prefer to see half
the earth desolated. Adams on the contrary deplored the Revolution and was disgusted by the arrest of Louis XVI. The King's
execution appalled him. Danton, Robespierre, Marat, and the rest
he considered furies.

Washington could of course have a second term without opposition, but it was well known that his personal preference was
to retire to Mount Vernon. Though Adams was completely loyal

to Washington, he had no intention of stepping aside for Jefferson to assume the presidency by default. As the election of 1792 neared, the struggle between Hamilton and Jefferson, of the Federalists representing the well-to-do, the well-born, the educated, the mercantilists, and centralists, against the Republican sons of the Sons of Liberty and the newly enfranchised lower classes linked incongrouously with Southern aristocrats fearing a strong central government, grew more intense.

Whatever his inner reluctance, Washington came to feel that the stability of the country required him to serve another term. The Antifederalists, unable to oust Adams, resolved to replace him by Governor George Clinton of New York. Disgruntled by the rising political rancor, Adams at the end of the congressional session returned to his farm where he remained all the summer and autumn. Hamilton, as leader of the Federalists, begged him to return to Philadelphia, pointing out that to remain in Quincy would be an admission of defeat, a yielding to his enemies. Adams refused to budge, claiming that he had not recovered from "brake-bone fever," and that Abigail's health as well as his own kept him at home. Not until November did he leave for New York and Philadelphia.

In spite of all their efforts the Antifederalists were not able to defeat him, but they did manage to make conspicuous gains in Congress. Republicans, infatuated with the French Revolution, even took to displaying miniature guillotines at their banquets, with the implication that heads would one day roll in America. In Boston admirers of the French Revolution called one another Citizen and Citizeness. Citizen John Hancock and Citizen Sam Adams embraced in public to great applause. Even Washington was no longer sacrosanct, the more rabid Republicans now denouncing him, as Abigail recounted, as "an Ape of Royalty; Mrs. Washington abused for her drawing-rooms; their celebration of Birthdays sneered at; himself insulted. . . . They compare him to a Hyena and a Crocodile. The President has not been accustomed to such language, and his feelings will be wounded, I presume."

France having declared war on England, Washington shortly after his second inaugural issued a Proclamation of Neutrality. A month later the bumptious Citizen Edmond Charles Genêt arrived as minister of the French Republic in a ship with a liberty cap lashed to the masthead. Genêt demanded recognition of his new government and fulfillment of the 1778 treaty, which would have brought the United States into the war as a French ally. Washington delayed receiving Genêt, maintaining that the treaty applied only to a defensive war. Adams, while refusing to take a public stand, privately urged delay, pointing out that treaties were made on the assumption that the state of things in both countries would remain nearly the same. During the spring and summer, while Genêt toured the country rallying the Republicans to him and challenging Congress to judge between Washington and himself, Adams observed the uproar from his quiet corner of Quincy, taking his own satisfaction no doubt when Washington finally lost patience with Genêt's insolence and demanded his recall. When Genêt's Jacobin successor finally arrived and demanded the other's arrest and deportation to France, Washington relented enough to grant the brash young man political asylum.

The most critical event in Washington's second term was not tension with France or the Antifederalists but the possibility of war with England. In their desperate struggle with France the English showed, and would continue to show, little incidental regard for American rights or American sensibilities. British warships swooped down on neutral vessels bringing supplies to, or products from, the French West Indies. On secret Orders in Council the royal navy seized more than 230 unarmed and unsuspecting American ships engaged in the West Indian trade. Americans were outraged, and the Francophiles clamored for war. Adams grew deeply troubled. Watching the war spirit spread without being able to check it or speak out against it, he found his situation as disagreeable as any he had experienced. He knew that his country, lacking an army and navy and with foreign and domestic debts still unpaid, was in no condition to go to war. Nevertheless, in April, 1794, the House of Representatives passed and sent to the Senate a nonintercourse bill prohibiting all commerce with Great Britain. Its passage would almost certainly have brought on hostilities and when the vote in the Senate came out a tie Adams cast the deciding vote against the measure. To the fury of the Republicans, Washington then sent Jay to London to open negotiations over American differences with England, and to Adams's relief war was for the time averted.

Adams's moment of greatest joy and satisfaction as presiding officer came just before the end of the session when the Senate received a message that the President of the United States had nominated John Quincy Adams to be resident minister of the United States at The Hague. Putting politics aside as the session closed, the Senators unanimously advised and consented, and Adams set out afterward by stage for Quincy in better spirits than he had known for months.

By the year's end Jay, following Hamilton's instructions, had succeeded in completing a treaty with England that adjusted matters of commerce, boundaries, treatment of returning Tories, prewar debts, and such matters. In the interest of peace both sides had made concessions, but it was particularly galling to Americans that Jay had glossed over the impressment of American seamen and seizure of American vessels, long a thorny issue. Washington reluctantly accepted the treaty, calling the Senate into special session to ratify it. Republicans in anger accused Jay of selling out his country. In city after city he was burned in effigy. So bitter was the reaction that there was talk of dissolving the Union. Adams, who had predicted a ten-year life for the new Constitution, now began to wonder if it would last eight. "I sometimes think that I am laboring in vain and spending my life for naught," he wrote gloomily, "in a fruitless endeavor to pursue a Union that, being detested on both sides, cannot last." In the next regular session of Congress, however, the Senate again approved the treaty and it was expected that the House after some grumbling would vote the funds to carry it out. Instead the debate bogged down in rancor and recrimination. Finally the Boston Federalist Fisher Ames in the most telling speech of his career broke the back of the opposition. The measure passed by one vote, it being cast by House chairman Frederick Muhlenberg who was promptly stabbed by his fanatical Republican brother-in-law.

Adams considered Jay's treaty for all its imperfections far better than going to war, but his old resentment flared up again against King George, "the mad idiot who will never recover," the "blunderer by nature." As the third presidential election year approached, the Vice President and those close to the President were aware that Washington was this time determined to retire. Adams had long been recognized as the next in Federalist succession. It was a thought that he had earlier tried to deny to himself, but it had grown on him, his ambition thrusting through his denials. Once he became convinced that Washington would retire, he wrote Abigail, "Either we must enter upon ardors more trying than ever yet experienced; or retire to Quincy, farmers for life." Jefferson, having left the cabinet because of his differences with Hamilton, had withdrawn to his Monticello plantation. He remained, however, the leader of the Republican Antifederalist opposition. His assertion that he had no ambition to govern men was one that Adams declined to accept. Certain Southerners hinted that they were willing to accept Adams as Vice President if the Northern Federalists would support Jefferson for President. That, Adams announced angrily, he would never do.

Long before Washington made his Farewell Address to the nation—written mostly by Madison and Hamilton—in September,

1796, Adams knew beyond doubt that he would be the choice of the Federalists to succeed him. To emerge from the lassitude of the vice-presidency stirred his blood and revived him. With the prospect of the presidency before him he shook off the weight of years. Though his hands still trembled, he felt bold and strong.

The Farewell Address was, in Fisher Ames's words, "a signal, like dropping a hat, for the party racers to start." South Carolina's Thomas Pinckney, soldier, lawyer, and diplomat who negotiated the popular treaty with Spain, was the Federalist choice for Vice President. Jefferson was the inevitable presidential choice of the Republicans, with Aaron Burr as his running mate. Adams refused to take an active part in the political campaign, remaining on his farm like Cincinnatus waiting for his country's call—a role he again fancied for himself. He walked across his fields, bronzed in the harvest, took the familiar path to Penn's Hill to look out over the harbor. Sundays he went to two services at the meetinghouse. "The Christian Religion," he observed in his diary, "is, above all the Religions that ever prevailed or existed in ancient or modern Times, The Religion of Wisdom, Virtue, Equity, and Humanity, let the Blackguard Paine say what he will. It is Resignation to God, it is Goodness itself to Man." Meanwhile, the Republicans leveled their verbal brickbats at him, ridiculing him for what they felt was his endorsement of the rich and the well-born. Throughout Massachusetts Republican radicals nailed handbills to gateposts and doors and fences denouncing Adams as an aristocrat and a royalist.

The North still remained a Federalist stronghold, and for a time there seemed no real doubt about the election's outcome. Hamilton, as leader of the party, publicly urged Federalist electors to support Adams and Pinckney with the "great object of excluding Jefferson." But secretly he planned to draw enough votes from Adams, whose stubborn personality he disliked, to elect the more pliable Pinckney. With his connivance eight Federalist South

Carolina electors agreed to cast combined votes for Pinckney and Jefferson. When this leaked out, eighteen New England electors let it be known that they would switch their second votes from Pinckney to various minor candidates. For some time the election seemed to hang in the balance. In the end Adams was elected with 71 votes, while Jefferson with 69 votes—ten more than Pinckney received—became Vice President. Earlier Adams had predicted that it would create a "dangerous Crisis in publick affairs if the President and Vice President should be in opposite Boxes." That was what he as President-elect was now faced with.

As Inauguration Day neared, a general feeling of good will for the new President was apparent. Even the Republicans shared it. When for a time it had seemed that there might be a tie vote in the Electoral College, Jefferson instructed Madison that if the election was to be decided in the House of Representatives preference be given to Adams as his senior from the commencement of their public life. Adams was touched by Jefferson's friendly gesture. Hamilton, he never forgave. In his fixed opinion, Washington's Secretary of the Treasury was a haughty, conniving hypocrite, as debauched as Franklin, "the bastard brat of a Scotch peddler."

For his inaugural Adams bought a new coach, liveries for his coachman and footmen, and a pearl-colored broadcloth suit for himself. On Inauguration Day, as legislators and officials gathered in the House of Representatives, all eyes were on the outgoing rather than the incoming President. Washington walked to Congress alone, dressed in plain civilian black. There was spontaneous applause as his tall, dignified figure crossed the threshold of the House. Jefferson on his arrival received only slightly less applause. Adams arrived in his new carriage, without outriders and drawn by only two horses, in contrast to the six to which Washington was accustomed. He wore a sword with his grey suit and carried his cockaded hat. Slowly he walked to the Speaker's dias and sat down, with Jefferson on his right and Washington two seats away.

Washington seated there seemed indeed the Father of his Country and many shed tears at the sight of his stern yet tranquil face. Adams noted the tears, though—as he wrote afterward to the absent Abigail—"whether it was from grief or joy, whether from the loss of their beloved President, or the accession of an unbeloved one, or from the Novelty of the thing . . . I know not." He had spent a wakeful, uneasy night, and as he stepped forward to take the oath of office from the chief justice, he was noticeably pale, although he managed to conceal the trembling of his hands. After the oath, he stepped forward to deliver his Inaugural Address, a moderate and conciliatory speech—the Federalist die-hards would find it far too conciliatory—in which he expressed the wish to reconcile "various political opinions . . . and virtuous men of all parties and denominations." He then returned to his chair, sat for a moment in silence as the applause welled about him, then stood, bowed, and walked out of the room. Washington beckoned Jefferson to follow, but the new Vice President did not think it proper to precede Washington. Only after Washington beckoned more imperiously did he obey. The others waited for the ex-President, and closed in on him when he started for the door. Recalling Washington's stern features, Adams thought that he seemed to be saying: "Ay! I am fairly out and you fairly in! See which of us will be happiest."

Abigail remained in Quincy until some order could be reintroduced to the vacant presidential mansion. Only a few sticks of battered furniture had been left behind. Adams complained that there was not a chair fit to sit on or a bed to sleep in. The servants in the interlude before his arrival had staged a drunken party from which they had not wholly recovered. In the midst of this domestic chaos, a 110 pound cheese shaped like a cartwheel arrived as a present from the state of Rhode Island. Adams wondered if he could not perhaps survive on it when his money ran out. Prices had tripled and quadrupled in the last four years. "I expect to be obliged to resign in six months because I can't live," he wrote Abigail. She had had the Quincy arms painted on her carriage door. When Adams heard of this he winced at what he knew would be the reaction of the Republicans and ordered her to have the device removed at once.

Never during the next four years did Adams's enemies let him forget that he was "president by three votes." The crucial event of his administration was to be an undeclared war with Revolutionary France—then in its Directory stage. That he, through skill and patience, kept it from becoming a declared war was one of his prouder accomplishments. The French government, angry at the American refusal to honor the earlier treaty of assistance and at the ratifying of the Jay treaty, and offended at parts of Adams's Inaugural Address, refused to receive Pinckney as the new American minister. As an added insult, Pinckney was ordered to leave French soil. French frigates seized American vessels in the West Indies, and French captains were ordered to hang American sailors captured on British ships. Any American ship with so much as a British handkerchief aboard was subject to confiscation without compensation.

Reacting to their challenge, Adams summoned a special session of Congress, and over the rising opposition of Jefferson's Republicans, called for the arming of merchant vessels and the enlarging of the navy. Then as if to emphasize his aim of preserving peace and friendship with all nations, he sent Pinckney, Gerry, and John Marshall to Paris on a conciliatory mission. Far from welcoming the American ministers, the Directory at first refused to receive them, and for several weeks they cooled their heels in government anterooms until at last they were granted a single brief and unofficial interview with the minister of foreign affairs, the wily, insinuating cripple, Charles Maurice de Talleyrand-Perigord. Then, when it seemed that their mission had failed, they unexpectedly received visits from three of Talleyrand's agents—later publicized as X, Y, and Z in President Adams's report to Congress. The three anonymities suggested that, in spite of the corruption of the United States government, the Directory would receive the American envoys on payment of a pocket token of twelve million livres to Talleyrand personally, plus fifty thousand sterling and the promise of a large loan from the United States.

For Talleyrand, known ironically as the Incorruptible, a bribe was a normal and necessary preliminary to negotiations, the more so to him because as the former freethinking Bishop of Autun he had lost his fortune in the Revolution. The Americans were outraged. "It is no, no; not a sixpence!" Pinckney told X, who had brought the demand. After several futile months the Americans broke off talks with X, Y, and Z and demanded their passports.

On first hearing of the XYZ demands and the treatment of his envoys, Adams thought that a declaration of war was called for to preserve the national honor. But calmer second thoughts prevailed, and he held back the actual XYZ dispatches from Congress. His message of March, 1797, was relatively mild, for he merely requested measures to protect the American coast and authorization to arm American merchantmen. Jefferson, nevertheless, thought any such actions an affront to France and considered the message "insane." Congress, with Republicans leading the outcry, then demanded the publication of the actual XYZ dispatches. Adams led them to the trap and let them fall in.

The disclosure of the dispatch contents was like a bomb set off in Congress. Even Jefferson had to admit that the dispatches had produced such a shock among the Republicans as had not been seen since independence. Reaction throughout the country was even sharper than in Congress as Americans responded in a fervor of indignant patriotism. "Millions for defense but not one cent for tribute!"—a phrase coined by an imaginative newspaperman— became a national toast. Federalists were transformed overnight to champions of American rights against foreign insolence, and

"*Ça Ira*," the marching song of the French Revolution sung and whistled in every American town, vanished in thin air. Joseph Hopkinson, composer of "Hail Columbia," was happy to note that "American tunes and American sentiments have driven off those execrable French murder shouts which not long since tortured our ears in ... every lane and alley in the United States." Red-white-blue French cockades disappeared like the Revolutionary tunes, and "Gallic devotees" still bold enough to sport such hat badges had them snatched off. Rumor had it that French agents with traitorous native accomplices were planning to burn Philadelphia and slaughter its inhabitants. All foreigners became suspect. President Adams, having long been reconciled to his lack of appeal, discovered to his surprise and pleasure that he had suddenly become popular. A few months earlier he could appear in the Capital "without receiving the slightest mark of attention." Now he was cheered in the streets, and when he went to the theater audiences applauded "the eagle-eyed and undaunted Adams." Attestations of loyalty poured in on him from all sides.

The Directory, its armies by now the most formidable in Europe, continued its overseas challenge unabated. From the West Indies, French picaroons beat up and down the Atlantic coast—often within sight of land—ready to capture American merchantmen. Some thirty thousand French agents within the United States did their best to rally the discomposed Republicans and Francophiles against the Adams administration. One result of this quasi war was the passage by Congress in June and July, 1798, of three laws known as the Alien and Sedition Acts to deal with what they considered an internal conspiracy. The first law extended the period of residence required for citizenship from five to fourteen years. The second, an "act concerning aliens," passed a week later, allowed the President to arrest or deport enemy aliens. It would not go into effect unless there was an actual declaration of war or imminence of invasion. However, under its mere threat thousands of French agents hurriedly took passage home. The final bill, the Sedition Act, prescribed heavy fines and imprisonment for anyone "who shall be writing, printing, or speaking, threaten any person holding an office under the government, with damage to his character, person or estate." The acts were to stay in effect for two years.

In the eyes of later liberal historians the Alien and Sedition Acts would remain an unforgivable black mark against the second President and his administration. Yet though Adams approved of them—as did Washington from his retirement—they were not sponsored by him. And a more careful examination shows them to be much more justified and much less harsh than their reputation would have them. Under the second act no alien could be deported even in wartime *unless* he held enemy citizenship. As for the Sedition Act, it was less harsh than the law of libel derived from English common law, for, in the latter, truth was no defense if the intent of an alleged libel could be proved to be malicious. Under the Sedition Act truth *was* a defense no matter how malicious the author's intent, and lack of truth excusable if the motive was honest.

In the latter part of Washington's administration and under the Adams presidency the party press had reached a degree of billingsgate scarcely comprehensible to later generations. A writer in the Boston *Chronicle* stated that Adams and his son John Quincy had received $80,000 in graft over a two-year period. A Republican editor referred to the President as the "old, querulous, bald, blind, crippled toothless Adams." The much less thick-skinned Washington had not been spared in his last years, having been labeled "treacherous," "mischievous," and "inefficient," and derided for "his stately journeys through the American continent in search of personal incense."

After the passage of the Sedition Act a number of Republican editors, skilled in such invective, were forced to shut up shop. But there were only ten prosecutions, the most celebrated—or notorious—being that of Congressman Matthew Lyon of Vermont, called the Spitting Lyon after an altercation in the House of Representatives during which he spat in the face of Connecticut's Roger Griswold. Charged with having published libelous statements against President Adams, Lyon was fined a $1,000 and sentenced to four months in jail, a sentence that merely succeeded in making the Republican Lyon a martyr, since he was re-elected to Congress from his cell. Though Federalist spite was apparent in the Alien and Sedition Acts, one can hardly hold the requirement of truth in political statements to be unwarranted during a *de facto* war. Jefferson considered the acts unconstitutional, a step toward monarchy. Yet he felt that individual states had the right to take such action, and when he was President he was quite willing to instigate a suit against a Federalist editor whom he accused of libeling him.

Talleyrand, realizing that for France to go to war with the United States would be playing into the hands of England, now became more conciliatory and revoked the decrees authorizing depredations against American shipping. Nelson's destruction of the French fleet in the Battle of the Nile in August made an accommodation with the Americans even more essential. Adams thought that whether or not his country negotiated with France, "vigorous preparations for war will be alike indispensible." Congress speeded up rearmament, created a Navy Department, authorized a fifty-ship navy, and to prepare against a possible French invasion voted to create an additional army of ten thousand men supplemented by a provisional army of fifty thousand.

Adams's tentative conciliatory attitude to France was continually opposed by the Hamiltonian die-hards who saw war with France as a means of throttling their political opponents. Hamilton considered the President "a mere old woman and unfit for a President," and even thought of persuading Washington to come out of retirement to run against Adams in 1800.

In the second half of his administration Adams found himself caught between the Hamiltonian Federalists and Jefferson's reviving Republicans. As the French threat receded, the Republicans were able to capitalize on opposition to the Alien and Sedition Acts and resentment of new taxes—particularly a property tax— that rearmament had made necessary. The President spent the summer of 1799 in Quincy in a brooding, suspicious mood intensified by Abigail's ill health. Friends who visited him found him morose, snappish, at times openly discourteous. When the time came for him to return to Philadelphia, Abigail was not well enough to go with him. In October the thirty-fifth anniversary of his wedding found him underway, lonely and alone in Trenton. "Few pairs can recollect so long a Union," he wrote her lovingly.

Long before 1800 the Republicans had launched a lively grassroots campaign to defeat Adams, with barbecues, rallies, and newspaper ventures to arouse their followers. Since Washington had died in December, 1799, the Hamiltonian Federalists looked elsewhere for a candidate to replace Adams. In an early state election Aaron Burr and his "Little Band" managed to win control of New York, which meant that New York's electors, chosen by the legislature, would be Republicans. Adams, after enduring much, finally ousted two pro-Hamilton members of his cabinet, Secretary of War James McHenry and Secretary of State Timothy Pickering, whom he had inherited from Washington. Hamilton then prepared a letter entitled "the Public Conduct and Character of John Adams" in which he described the President as a person of "disgusting egotism," "distempered jealousy," and "vanity without bounds." Though Hamilton intended to use the letter privately to discredit Adams among the Federalist leaders, he was less than dismayed when Burr got hold of a copy and made it public. "Pickeronian" Federalists attacked the President as vindictively as they did Jefferson. Adams was becoming a man without a party. Abigail sensed that he would not be reelected. He himself came to admit he would probably be defeated, even though his vanity could not bear the thought.

Republicans in the election year circulated a story that Adams had planned to marry one of his sons to a daughter of George III and establish a dynasty that would reunite America and England. Only when Washington visited him three times, the last time in his Revolutionary uniform, and threatened to run him through with his sword did he—according to the tale—give up this cherished scheme. Another story, Adams found amusing enough to relay to his friend and former law student William Tudor. "If nothing flew on Eagles Wings as Said or done by me, but what had really been said or done, I should have less to complain of," he wrote Tudor. "Among a million of Reports, one was circulated far and wide and believed by thousands, that General Pinckney had imported from England four pretty Girls two of them for my use and two for his own. Now I declare upon my honor, if this be true Gen. Pinckney has kept them all four to himself and cheated me of my two." The poison-tongued Republican journalist James Callender warned that Adams was out to make himself King of America. Callender liked to refer to Washington and Adams as the monarchs at Mount Vernon and Braintree. Federalists managed to give almost as good as they got. Jefferson was portrayed as an atheist, a libertine who had children by his own female slaves, a vivisectionist, an "intellectual voluptuary," a man whose election would bring down "the just vengeance of insulted heaven."

Adams was convinced that if the election were lost it would be because of divisions among the Federalists. "For myself," he wrote, "age, infirmities, family misfortunes have conspired with the unreasonable conduct of Jacobins and insolent Federalists to make me too indifferent to whatever can happen." He spent the summer of 1800 as usual in Quincy and in September made his way to the new raw Federal City on the Potomac to which the government was moving and which was now to be called the City of Washington in the District of Columbia. As yet the city with its sweeping vistas and great boulevards was little more than a plan on paper drawn up by the French engineer Major Pierre L'Enfant. A half-completed Capitol, a few neoclassical buildings, set down in a bleak landscape of reddish mud, formed the background for Washington's three thousand inhabitants. "Houses scattered over a space of ten miles, and trees and stumps in plenty," Abigail noted when she arrived a few weeks after her husband "with a castle of a House—so I found it. The Presidents House. This House is twice as large as our meeting House . . . built for ages to come. The establishment necessary is a tax which cannot be born by the present sallery. No body can form an Idea of it but those who come into it: Not one room or chamber is finished of the whole. It is habitable by fires in every part, thirteen of which we are obliged to keep daily, or sleep in wet and damp places." The unfinished East Room she at least found useful for drying the family wash. Gouverneur Morris, after picking his way through the mire of unpaved streets, remarked that the new Federal City might be all right for the future but that he was not posterity. In Adams's fourth annual message to Congress at the end of November he asked God's special blessing on the new city: "May this territory be the residence of virtue and happiness! In this city, may that piety and virtue, that wisdom and magnanimity, that constancy and self-government which adorned the great character whose name it bears be forever held in veneration! Here, and throughout our country, may simple manners, pure morals, and true religion, flourish forever!"

Two weeks later, the Electoral Colleges assembled in each state. It was clear that the election would be close. After the votes of thirteen of the sixteen states were announced, the tally stood 65 for Adams to 58 for Jefferson. If Adams could capture the eight votes of South Carolina, where Federalist sentiment was strong, he would win his re-election. But the Republicans with brisk underhand promises of patronage managed to swing the state to Jefferson and

Burr. "The consequence to us personally is that we retire from public Life," Abigail wrote to her youngest son Thomas Boylston: "for myself and family I have few regrets, at my age and with my bodily infirmities I shall be happier at Quincy. neither my habits, or my education or inclinations have led me to an expensive stile of living, so on that score I have little to mourn over; if I did not rise with Dignity, I can at least fall with ease: which is the more difficult task."

Adams's public humiliation was dwarfed by the almost simultaneous news of his son Charles's death. The gayest of his children, the promising young lawyer, had fallen away, drifted downward, ended his life as a wastrel and a drunkard. "Oh! that I had died for him," Adams cried out in his grief, "if that would have relieved him from his faults as well as his disease."

Following their rigid instructions all the Republican electors gave their second votes to Burr, with the result that he and Jefferson were tied and the election had to be settled in the House of Representatives, where each state had a single vote. Disgruntled Federalists planned to throw their votes to Burr, but were dissuaded by Hamilton who considered Burr "the most unfit and dangerous man of the community." Jefferson was at least honorable. It took thirty-six ballots in the House, though, to give Jefferson the required majority, the Spitting Lyon of Vermont having the satisfaction of casting the deciding vote.

In his remaining weeks in office Adams brooded over the election results, which he realistically attributed to Federalist dissension. Beyond this he could not grasp that his eighteenth-century belief in reason and hierarchic order had given way to Jefferson's nineteenth-century trust in instinct and individual judgment. The election, for all its narrowness, was in Jefferson's words "as real a revolution in the principles of our government as that of 1776."

Adams was as troubled by his future as by the election. What would he do back in Quincy, he asked. "Something I must do or

Ennui will rain upon me in Bucketts. . . . Will Books and Farms answer the End?" He had even thought of going back to the bar, but "I have forgotten all my Law and lost my organs of Speech, and besides that I have given my books away." To Thomas Boylston, who wrote him full of grief and affection, he replied: "Be not concerned for me. I feel my shoulders relieved from a burthen. The short remainder of my days will be the happiest of my life." The more practical Abigail wondered how they would make out financially.

In the final session of the expiring Congress, on February 13, 1801, the Federalist majority passed a national judiciary reform bill that among other things created twenty-three new Federal judgeships. Adams at once submitted his nominees to the Senate. In his last weeks he filled a number of other Federal posts. Republican detractors had it that he spent half his last night in office signing commissions for a host of Federalist placements. Regardless of the date of the new jurists' appointments, they were labeled the Duke of Braintree's Midnight Judges. In actuality Adams signed the appointments of only three judges on his last evening, despite the myth. But he did not stay to see Jefferson inaugurated. Early in the morning, hurt and angry, he left the President's Palace, and his coach was rattling on the road north by the time his successor was sworn in.

Adams was sixty-four years old when he left Washington, and the "short remainder" of his days was destined to last another quarter of a century. In his Quincy retirement his mind went back again and again to the causes of his defeat, and always he saw as his nemesis the dark and insidious intriguer Hamilton. Jefferson, who at once forced a bill through the new Congress to get rid of the Adams-appointed judges, he was sure he could never forgive. During the first months at Quincy he was up at dawn to work with the men on his acres, restoring both his physical and mental self in the farm routine. Then as his spirits recovered, he left most of the manual labor to his hired hands. Sometimes he rode for miles along the shore, or walked over the familiar paths in the Blue Hills. Much of his time he spent in reading and writing, although the tremor of his hands made guiding a pen difficult. The house filled with children and grandchildren and finally great-grandchildren, and though—as Abigail noted—he grew testier with age, he was happy to have them near him.

Although his palsy increased and his speech became hardly intelligible, his hearing held up and his eyesight grew no worse. He could read adequately with spectacles, and his mind remained as clear as ever. Time enough he had now to think and write about politics, history, philosophy, religion, the future of his country. John Quincy suggested that he write his autobiography, a task he started on several times but never completed. He reread the classics, explored the branches of philosophy. With renewed serenity he turned to old relationships that had been strained by politics. His most active and eager correspondent was now his old friend Dr. Benjamin Rush, who had strayed for a time into the Republican fold. The correspondence between the two men became the most engrossing intellectual satisfaction of each. They discussed politics, the various political leaders, the deification of Washington (of which they both disapproved), and even their dreams.

For Adams, growing old in seagirt Quincy, the years seemed to accelerate. Jefferson's second administration followed so quickly on the first that the ex-President could not believe four years had elapsed. Again he saw his country caught in the titanic struggle between the two great adversaries England and France, but this time it was England, mistress of the seas after Trafalgar, that bore down harder on the Americans, the royal navy harassing American ships, searching American vessels, and impressing sailors suspected of being deserters. As tension with England built up, Jefferson countered with a Nonimportation Act and, when this proved ineffectual, an embargo that closed the great ports of Boston, New

York, Philadelphia, and Baltimore and left their ships rotting at the docks and their workers idle in the streets. In New England the disgruntled Federalists were talking of seceding to form a Northern confederacy. It was all as Adams had foreseen, predicted. America without a powerful navy and adequate army would be at the mercy of any predatory belligerent, and Jefferson had let the army and navy crumble away.

Throughout the Jefferson and Madison administrations, as Adams observed Europe under the despotic grip of Napoleon, he had gloomy moments of wondering if he himself did not share the blame for the horrors of Revolutionary France, the wreck of Europe, and the carnage that had culminated in Napoleon's campaigns. Perhaps Burke had been right after all, perhaps all the eighteenth-century revolutions in the name of popular and representative government had merely paved the way for a new despotism. "Have I not been employed in mischief all my days?" he asked Dr. Rush plaintively in August, 1811. "Did not the American revolution produce the French revolution? And did not the French revolution produce all the calamities and Desolations to the human Race and the whole Globe ever since? I meant well, however. My conscience was clear as a crystal glass, without a scruple or a doubt. I was borne along by an irresistible sense of Duty. God prospered our labors, and, awful, dreadful, and deplorable as the consequences have been, I cannot but hope that the ultimate good of the World, of the human Race, and of our beloved Country, is intended and will be accomplished by it."

When British intransigence finally brought on the War of 1812, Adams was full of scorn for the New England Federalists who opposed "Mr. Madison's War" and who plotted secession. Though the war was brief and inconsequent, he was proud of his country's response, of the early naval victories, of Madison's demonstration that a President could still declare war without being thrown from his chair. The ex-President came to see Madison's administration, "notwithstanding all the errors, blunders, confusion, distractions, disasters, and factions with which it has been tormented, as the most glorious period of the history of the United States."

It had long been Dr. Rush's aim, as a mutual friend, to bring the two old Revolutionary leaders, Adams and Jefferson, together in their old age, and he sounded out both of them on a number of occasions. Adams admitted that he had never thought of Jefferson as a personal enemy and that he had forgiven the ancient injuries. Still, he could see no point in exchanging letters, maintaining he had nothing to say to him. Nevertheless, a few days later he sent "two Pieces of Homespun lately produced in this quarter" to Monticello while wishing its master "many happy New Years." Jefferson replied cordially, setting off a correspondence that would continue with deepening satisfaction for both until their deaths. "You and I ought not to die before we have explained ourselves to each other," Adams wrote.

During his remaining Quincy years, Adams was made president of the American Academy of Arts and Sciences and of the Massachusetts Society for Promoting Agriculture. His membership on the Board of Visitors for the professorship of natural history at Harvard took him to Cambridge once a month. The years slipped by. As to most men who live beyond the appointed Biblical span, his last years were laced with tragedy. In the spring of 1813 Rush died, his old, constant, unshaken friend. His beloved Nabby, after a long and unfortunate marriage to a pretentious drifter, came home to Quincy to die of cancer. Other members of the Adams clan, other friends, were disappearing. Thomas Boylston's infant daughter died nearby in the very same room Adams had been born in, and the old man, looking down at the tiny body, wondered why he was still living. Thomas himself, lawyer, judge, and failed local politician, took to the bottle in his middle years, going off on drunken sorties that lasted for days and from which he would return to threaten his wife and abuse his children. His nephew

Charles, who had come to hate his uncle, nevertheless thought his shrewish aunt greatly responsible for her husband's degeneration. Old John tried to mask his own heartbreak by an acceptance of fate, viewing his son's decline as a check to family hubris.

In October, 1818, Abigail suffered a stroke, lingered on a few weeks, and then died. Adams was stunned by her death. He had always assumed that she would outlive him. With her gone, he felt he had nothing to wait for but his own death. Jefferson wrote him with touching tenderness. "While you live," Adams replied, "I seem to have a bank at Montecello on which I can draw for a Letter of Friendship and entertainment when I please." Whatever his personal grief, he looked on his country's future with renewed optimism. "I am not tormented with the fear of death," he wrote a friend in the spring of 1821. "We shall leave the world with many consolations; it is better than we found it—superstition, persecution, and bigotry are somewhat abated, governments are a little ameliorated, science and literature are greatly improved and more widely spread. Our country has brilliant and exhilarating prospects before it, instead of that solemn gloom in which many of the former parts of our lives have been obscured."

The following summer West Point cadets, two hundred of them being in Boston, marched out to Quincy and past the Adams house with flags flying and bands playing. The old man stood on the porch to review them, then watched them drill in the field across the road. Afterward he spoke to them in the courtyard, telling them Washington should be their model and their ideal. His little speech was followed by a cold buffet. The band under a great chestnut tree on the lawn played "Adams and Liberty" and other patriotic airs while the old President beat time to the music. Finally the cadets filed past, each one shaking his gnarled and trembling hand. It was his last public appearance. From then on he was confined to his bedroom and the easy chair in his study. He could write only with great pain and had to "borrow hands" to carry on his correspondence. John Quincy had spoken of himself writing his father's biography, and with this in mind he began to sort out trunks and boxes filled with his papers.

In the autumn of 1824, on a farewell visit to America, Lafayette, the last military hero of the Revolution, came to see Adams in Quincy. It was an awkward meeting. Publicly the old President said he was delighted, but privately he remarked, that it was not the Lafayette he remembered. Lafayette in turn later observed sadly that Adams was not the John Adams he had once known. The greatest triumph of Adams's life and its final vindication came almost at its end with the election of his son to the presidency. John Quincy, as Monroe's Secretary of State, and General Andrew Jackson were the leading candidates. Though Adams admired Jackson, he felt he could not compare with his son. Jackson, while he received a plurality of the votes, lacked a majority, and the election went to the House of Representatives. Not until February, 1825, was it finally decided, after Henry Clay had persuaded the Kentucky Congressmen to give their state vote to Adams, electing him by a majority of one. Jefferson wrote at once to congratulate his old friend. Adams answered that every line from Monticello gave him a glow of pleasure. "I look back with rapture to those golden days when Virginia and Massachusetts lived and acted together like a band of brothers," he concluded.

There was no possibility of Adams's going to his son's inaugural. Even a trip to Boston was now out of the question. Yet, scarcely able to move from his bedroom to his study, he lingered on into 1826. When a committee to celebrate the fiftieth anniversary of independence in Boston invited him to be present, he had to decline although he did give them the toast for the day: "Independence Forever!" Would he add anything, they asked him. "Not a word," he replied. On the Fourth of July, as the bands played and the militia and the Ancient and Honorable Artillery Company passed in review on Boston Common, as Josiah Quincy,

Sr., "the Boston Cicero," rehearsed his oration for the day, John Adams lay dying in Quincy. He slept through the morning, then woke at noon. A granddaughter told him it was the Fourth of July. "It is a great day. It is a good day," he replied. An hour later he roused himself to mutter indistinctly, "Thomas Jefferson still survives." By a strange twist of fate that would come to seem for many an awesome sign of providence, Jefferson had died on that same day, several hours earlier. Adams did not speak again. At six in the evening, run down like an old watch—as he himself had phrased it—his heart ceased to beat.

# 4

# *John Quincy Adams*

## THE DIPLOMAT

L IKE MOST self-made men, John Adams wanted greater advantages and wider horizons for his children than he himself had had. As he explained to Abigail when he was a commissioner in Paris: "I must study Politicks and War, that my sons may have liberty to study Mathematicks and Philosophy. My sons ought to study Mathematics and Philosophy, Geography, natural History and naval Architecture, navigation, Commerce and Agriculture, in order to give their children a right to study Painting, Poetry, Musick, Architecture, Statuary, Tapestry and Porcelaine." The intent became true to a remarkable degree, and it was realized initially in his son John Quincy. "Few of our great statesmen have had an individuality as marked," Allan Nevins wrote of John Quincy Adams; "perhaps no other has combined so many anfractuosities, humors and prejudices with so much ability, liberality and high rectitude of character."

At the age when John Adams was roaming the Blue Hills or shooting wildfowl in the marshy estuary of the Neponset with no greater goal than to be a farmer in the homely rusticity of Braintree, his son was being formed by the most sophisticated city in

Europe. The mere fact that the boy became bilingual in Paris set him apart from most of his countrymen, gave him the gift of another tongue without which one's own tongue is never wholly comprehensible. More graceful, better looking, more self-assured, and at an early age far more knowledgeable than his father, he stayed the devoted and accommodating son with no sign of even youthful rebellion.

Born on July 11, 1767, he was named John Quincy after his maternal great-grandfather who died on his christening day. His first cohesive memory was of being taken to Boston in 1770 on the eve of the Boston Massacre and seeing an illuminated transparency. At six he wrote his first letter, to his cousin Elizabeth Cranch: "i thank you for your last letter I have had it in my mind to write you this long time but afairs of much leess importance has prevented me i have made But veray little proviciancy in reading . . . to much of my time in play ere is a great Deal of room for me to grow better." John Adams, so often away on legal journeyings, admonished his wife: "Let us therefore my dear Partner, from that Affection which we feel for our lovely Babes, apply ourselves by every Way, we can, to the Cultivation of our Farm. Let Frugality, And Industry, be our Virtues, if they are not of any others. And above all laws of this Life let our ardent Anxiety be, to mould the Minds and Manners of our Children." The eight-year-old boy, who had watched the smoke curl up from the Battle of Bunker Hill, who had cowered in bed in fear of attack by a British landing party, who a year later had seen the last white sail vanish as the British ships left Boston Harbor, was and would remain—whatever his larger horizons—a child of the Revolution and a child of his century. Johnny was not sent to the town school but was tutored by his father's law clerks until the course of the Revolution called them away. His mother supervised his further progress, listening to his daily readings. She taught him to declaim one of her favorite poems, William Collins's "How Sleep the Brave," and every morning before he got out of bed he would recite the Lord's Prayer and then Collins's two stirring verses.

John Adams, away in Philadelphia, had consoling plans for his boys. Johnny would develop a taste for literature and for business, Tommy would be a physician like his great-grandfather, while Charles needed merely to be good and useful. The father's absences reinforced the Puritan sense of duty in his small eldest son. "I have been trying ever since you went away to learn to write you a letter," the boy wrote. "I shall make poor work of it, but Sir Mamma says you will accept my endeavours, and that my Duty to you may be expressed in poor writing as well as good. I hope I grow a better Boy and that you will have no occasion to be ashamed of me when you return. Mr. Thaxter says I learn my Books very well—he is a very good Master. I read my Books to Mamma. We all long to see you; I am Sir your Dutiful Son." John Quincy loved books, the more imaginative the better, among them a much abridged *Arabian Nights* and Abigail's Shakespeare volumes. However, *Paradise Lost*—that favorite poem of his parents—proved too much for him, though he tried it twice. To ease his way through that formidable epic he took to smoking as he read, acquiring a permanent taste for tobacco though none for Milton.

Johnny was preparing to enter Governor Dummer Academy in Byfield, Massachusetts, when he learned that John Adams had been appointed commissioner to replace Silas Deane in Paris. He begged and finally persuaded his father to take him along. Eager for the adventure of crossing the Atlantic and for the sight of Europe so vaguely but deliciously apprehended through books, he was ready, in his mother's words, to enter "the world in which he is to live."

On the voyage over, Johnny began to pick up French from a French army surgeon aboard who was charmed, as were most adults, by the precocious boy. From the captain he learned the names of all the sails and how to use the mariner's compass. Once in Paris and enrolled at Passy Academy he followed a strict schedule—up at six in the morning, with studies going on till eight thirty in the evening, and interrupted only by meals and a brief recreation period. Weekends he spent with his father who soon discovered to his mortification that his son absorbed more French in a day than he could in a week. Johnny remained a serious, prematurely old little boy. "We are Sent into this World for Some end," he wrote his brother Charles; "it is our duty to discover by Close study what this end is & when we once discover it to pursue it with unconquerable perseverance." Passy Academy was expensive, and Adams soon found that Johnny's education was costing him more than he could afford. Although he took much pleasure in his son's company he had to admit to Abigail that he would not have brought him if he had known the expense.

After his brief return to the United States in 1779, Adams planned to take Charles back to France with him and leave Johnny at home to prepare himself for Harvard. But Abigail insisted that the older boy go too, since Europe would be far more important for his education. When Adams was shifted from Paris to the Netherlands in 1780, he enrolled his two boys in a Latin School in Amsterdam. But the usually docile and adaptable Johnny, set in a lower form because he could not speak Dutch, hated the school. Soon the rector was complaining about the American pupil's impertinence and disobedience. Adams then withdrew both boys, placed them with an American studying medicine in Leyden, and had them tutored in Latin and Greek. The next year the Rector Magnificus admitted Johnny to the University of Leyden where he might have stayed had he not been requested to accompany Francis Dana on his mission to Russia. Deficient in French—the language of the Russian court—Dana took him to St. Petersburg as his secretary-interpreter.

It took two months of overland travel in the summer of 1781 for Dana and Johnny to reach the Russian capital. They passed through Berlin, in the process of being renewed by Frederick the Great, then across Russia and north over the Russian steppes. "There is nothing very remarkable on Dantsic, Konigsberg, or Riga;" he wrote his father, "in coming to this last we pass'd thro' Courland. . . . All the Farmers are in the most abject slavery, they are bought and sold like so many beasts, and are sometimes even chang'd for dogs or horses. Their masters have even the right of life and death over them, and if they kill one of them they are only obliged to pay a trifling fine; they may buy themselves but their masters in general take care not to let them grow rich enough for that; if any body buys land there he must buy all the slaves that are *upon it*." Peter's Italianate city on the Neva, though still unfinished, struck the two Americans as one of the handsomest they had seen. But Dana made little progress in obtaining Catherine's recognition of his country, since the Empress wanted no quarrel with England.

For the fourteen-year-old boy in this imperial city, education was a problem. There were no schools or academies, and the few tutors available charged such exorbitant fees that Adams when he heard about the cost considered bringing his son back. Johnny explained that the nobility sent their children abroad to study, and that there were no schools for the others. He studied on his own, doing more desultory reading than studying. He remained in St. Petersburg fifteen months, until his father sent for him. Then by slow stages, with an Italian friend, Count Greco, he made his way back through Scandinavia, hindered much by bad weather and frozen harbors. He was five months underway before he finally reached Amsterdam where he stayed with John Dumas, an agent of Franklin's, until his father's arrival in July. Adams had been out of touch with the boy during that return journey and had notified French and Dutch consuls all along the Baltic. "Received a Letter from my Son John, dated at Gottenburgh the 1. of Feb.," he wrote in his diary. "This Letter gave me great Joy, it is the first I have received from him since he left Petersbourg, and the first News I have had of him since the Beginning of December when he was at Stockholm.—I have suffered extream Anxiety on his Account." Abigail finally heard from her son after a two-year silence. She was glad to learn that he was well and back with his father but advised him to return home and enter Harvard.

When Abigail with Nabby finally did arrive in England, Adams wrote from The Hague: "Your Letter of the 23d has made me the happiest Man upon Earth. I am twenty Years Younger than I was Yesterday. It is a cruel Mortification that I cannot go to meet you in London, but there are a Variety of Reasons decisive against it, which I will communicate with you here. Meanwhile I send you a Son who is the greatest Traveller of his age, and without partiality, I think as promising and manly a youth as is in the whole World." John had left his mother as an eleven-year-old boy. He returned a self-possessed young man of seventeen, with a delicate, intelligent face, finely modeled nose, and luminous eyes. As Abigail told her sister of the meeting: "I drew back not really believing my Eyes—till he cried out, Oh my Mamma! and my Dear Sister. Nothing but the Eyes at first sight appeared what he once was. His appearance is that of a Man, and in his Countanance the most perfect good humour."

During that summer of 1784 at Auteuil Johnny got to know his sister again. They had much in common, they discovered. Johnny often found himself in the company of Jefferson and Lafayette, both of whom considered him charming and intelligent. John Adams's appointment to the Court of St. James's left his son with the decision whether to stay in London as his father's secretary or to return to Massachusetts and a course of study at Harvard. The thought of going back to a schoolboy routine after seven years of adult freedom in Europe dismayed him. But his Adams common sense told him he had better take the plunge, and while his family was preparing to move to England, he sailed for America.

His reception at New York was a poor preparation for Cambridge, for on landing he was greeted as an adult, almost a celebrity, a diplomatic courier, the bearer of pertinent information. Richard Henry Lee, president of the Continental Congress, insisted on housing him during his stay in New York. A few days after his arrival in Braintree the European sophisticate, with a certain condescension, made his way to Cambridge to request admission to Harvard as a junior. He was somewhat deflated when President Joseph Willard declined to consider him until he had made up his deficiencies in the classics. The next few months he spent in the poky town of Haverhill where he boarded in the cramped household of his clergyman uncle, John Shaw, who tutored him. Finally, the following March, President Willard, four tutors, three professors, and the librarian examined him in Latin, Greek, Watts's *Logic*, and Locke's *Essay on Human Understanding.* He himself was all too aware of his mediocre performance. Nevertheless, President Willard, after hearing his translation of a few Latin lines, told him he was admitted.

John Quincy spent fifteen months at Harvard before receiving his bachelor's degree in the summer of 1787. After St. Petersburg, Paris, Versailles, London, and The Hague, Cambridge seemed a primitive backwater, the students bumpkins, the tutors ignoramuses, and the president a man deserving of scant respect. Johnny held himself apart, a deliberate stranger, writing his mother that he did nothing but study. Noticing how pale and drawn he had come to look, how often he complained of migraines, his Aunt Mary Cranch insisted that he see the family doctor, Cotton Tufts, who advised him to take more exercise and improve his diet. Contemptuous of the college, he even neglected his appearance. The two Cranch girls, his cousins, dropping in on him in his room at

Hollis Hall, found him unkempt, wearing a soiled gown, his fingernails black, his uncombed hair greasy about his shoulders, the room itself littered and filthy. Though he took no part in the diversions of the other students, he recorded their pranks and scrapes and rebellions in his diary, usually with sympathy. Harvard was indeed a crude and uncivilized milieu, and student conduct often outrageous. John Quincy recorded that one of his classmates when drunk collared a tutor, cursed him out, and threw a handful of gravel in his face—for which he was degraded to the bottom of his class and forced to read a confession. John Quincy considered the punishment much too severe. During Shays's Rebellion he spoke on the relationship between equality and liberty, like his father defending the Platonic assertion that democracy was the greatest tyranny and maintaining that the rebellion proved again that too much equality meant less liberty.

He graduated with his cousin Billy Cranch. Aunt Mary spent a week preparing for their joint senior spread, to which all relatives and friends were invited, providing two shoulders of beef à la mode, four boiled hams, six tongues, and a plum cake that required twenty-four pounds of flour, as well as an ample supply of porter, cider, punch, and wine. John Quincy, who ranked second among the fifty-one awarded their degrees, delivered one of the two English orations. He was chagrined, however, when the pro-Shays Boston *Centinel* remarked on his performance that "the publick expectations from this gentleman, being the son of an Ambassador, the favourite of the officers of the College, and having enjoyed the highest advantages of European instruction were greatly inflated."

Harvard was a deflating experience for the returned exile, though later he came to think it had reduced his opinion of himself to a more realistic level and saved him from early ruin. Law seemed to be his future, although he could muster no great enthusiasm for it. A month after his graduation he rode fifty miles north to arrange to read for the next three years with the noted Newburyport lawyer Theophilus Parsons. The prospect of the isolated and inbred little seaport at the mouth of the Merrimack River dismayed him as he recorded gloomily in his diary that in three weeks he would be an inhabitant of the place.

Parsons had several other law students in his office whom he charged $100 each for their apprenticeship. He expected them to put in an eight-hour day at the office and then go home to four hours of additional study. "Quiet" and "tedious" were the two adjectives young Adams used most frequently to describe his Newburyport years. Outwardly resigned to his meager world, he developed unconscious symptoms of revolt that a later age would consider psychosomatic—dizzy spells, blinding headaches, constant colds, sour stomach, sore eyes, insomnia, and troubled dreams when he did sleep. Beyond his work he met a few young men in the town, spent the occasional Saturday night in a tavern, and suffered the subsequent hang-over that kept him from church the following morning. The sight of a pretty girl inevitably cheered him. But for the most part he remained depressed. The future seemed dark and "the bubble reputation" deceitful. He admitted that he kept his diary just for the pleasure of complaining. His vacations revived him, but as soon as he returned to Newburyport his health gave way.

In the summer of 1788 when his parents returned from England he rode at once to Braintree to see them and stayed on to help them get settled in their new home. There on July 11 he reached his majority. As he wryly recorded it: "This day completes my twenty first year. It emancipates me from the yoke of parental authority, which I never felt, and places me upon my own feet, which have not strength enough to support me. I continue therefore still in a state of dependence. One third of the period of my professional studies has also now elapsed; and two years more will settle me, should life and health continue: in a situation where all my expectations are to center. I feel sometimes a strong desire to know what my circumstances will be in seven years from this: but I must acknowledge I believe my happiness would rather be injured than improved by the information."

Shortly after his return to Newburyport he broke down completely. Returning to Braintree he tramped the fields, rode horseback, worked outdoors on the farm, yet failed to shake his depression or insomnia. He went back to Newburyport but was able to stay only a few weeks before he had a relapse. This time he remained in Braintree over the winter, spending his days in riding, skating, shooting, desultory reading, and visiting. When his father finally left for New York to take the oath as Vice President, John Quincy went back to Newburyport and this time he stayed. His relatives and friends all advised him to take life and the law a little less seriously. Following their advice, he spent more time in the small social world of Newburyport, dancing, flirting, writing verses—some agreeable, some less so—in the manner of Pope, to local young ladies and composing one long poem, "A Vision," meant to express his quest for female loveliness. By June he was much improved.

When two years of his apprenticeship were over, he visited his parents in New York, mixing in the wider social life of that more urbane town and observing the first functionings of the new government. In November, 1789, President Washington passed through Newburyport, and it fell to John Quincy to write the welcoming address. To his mother's annoyance he fell in love with the blonde, blue-eyed Mary Frazier, who was destined to die young and whom he would ever after wistfully remember. In his final Newburyport winter he was laid up with influenza, and his recovery left him torpid. With the coming of spring he began to think more of his future. He wanted to be independent, no longer a burden to his parents. But, once a lawyer, where should he set up practice? Newburyport had enough lawyers, even if one could

stand the small-town atmosphere. Braintree needed no more lawyers than his cousin Billy Cranch. For a New England Adams,
Boston seemed the only choice left. In July, 1790, he received his
master's degree from Harvard—a mere formality then—and that
same year was admitted to practice at the bar.

In August he opened a small office on Court Street and sat
there among his books waiting for clients who showed no great
eagerness to appear. To while away the time he read Cicero, Tac-
itus, Burke, Clarendon, and Hume. Deep and disturbing thoughts
of the blonde Mary still came between him and the printed page.
In October he tried his first case. Handicapped by only three hours'
notice, opposed by the clever young Harrison Gray Otis, he trembled and stammered as he addressed the court. His bad health had
followed him from Newburyport, a condition which the realistic
Abigail attributed to impatience and the lack of any real legal
practice. She thought he would improve physically and mentally
if he had some money, and persuaded her husband to send him
£25 a quarter. With the law making so little demands on his time,
he diverted himself with desultory card games, assemblies, and
visits. He read much romantic poetry, copying stanzas into the
pages of his diary, which otherwise remained almost blank. Finally
he took himself in hand and set out to collect books and newspaper
articles for a work on national government. The appearance of *The
Rights of Man* gave him an opportunity to organize his thoughts
and his material in answer to Paine's pamphlet with his Publicola
essays in the *Columbian Centinel*. These he prepared with much
care, since he realized he was confronting one of the fieriest po-
lemicists of the day. Publicola's challenge to Paine caused a furor
on both sides of the Atlantic. The pieces were reprinted in England,
and Paine even had them published in France in order to refute
them. Though John Quincy was at first upset by the turbulent
reaction, he had the satisfaction of knowing that, young as he was,
he had gained attention at a national and international level.

Whether a well- or ill-kept secret, Publicola did little for John Quincy's law business. Living in Boston, often staying in Quincy, he took a small part in his native town's politics, even serving on the committee to incorporate the northern part of Quincy as Braintree. But his experience with the Braintree Town Meeting, the much-vaunted grass-roots democracy, gave him sobering second thoughts. At one meeting, he told his brother Tom, the seven hundred members present looked as if they had been gathered from all the country's jails. For him this crude voting bloc was a confirmation of his distrust of and contempt for unrestrained democracy. His own personal life remained frustrated and frustrating. He ate too much and began to put on weight. He drank too much and suffered hang-overs. There are enigmatic references in his diary to casual encounters on the Common, followed by promises of reform and application to work. At least he was earning enough so that he could write his father to say that he no longer needed an allowance.

After Washington's Proclamation of Neutrality, in 1793, John Quincy published another series of essays, this time under the name of the Roman general Marcellus, in which he argued at length for American neutrality in the war between France and England and for disregard of the old treaty with France. The arrival of the cocky and insolent Genêt and his exuberant welcome by the democratic-republican societies so outraged the young Adams that he wrote a third series of essays, this time taking the pen name of Columbus. The articles were widely circulated, read by Washington—who was told who the author was—by cabinet members, and Congressmen, and they did much to counteract the uncritical enthusiasm with which Genêt had been first received. Secretary of State Edmund Randolph now hinted to the Vice President that there might be the possibility of sending his son on a diplomatic mission to Holland. Adams wrote Abigail the tentative good news, told her to have John Quincy ready to leave at once for Philadelphia, then ended with the prudent warning that the Senate might not approve.

In the wake of Randolph's hint, President Washington formally appointed, and the Senate unanimously consented to, John Quincy Adams as minister resident to The Hague. "This intelligence was very unexpected," John Quincy noted in his diary, "and indeed surprising. I had laid down as a principle, that I never would solicit for any public office whatever, and from this determination no necessity has hitherto compelled me to swerve." In Philadelphia on his twenty-eighth birthday he received his commission from the Secretary of State.

Most of the summer he spent in Braintree impatiently waiting for instructions. In preparation for his mission he read through the six folio volumes of his father's European dispatches to Congress during his European negotiations. John Adams thought a three-year diplomatic mission would be a good preparation for a future political career. During the long summer weeks John Quincy developed second thoughts. The post might not be a preparation for anything. What would an embryo law practice amount to after a three-year interruption? And he recalled his sense of alienation on his earlier return from Europe. Would he not come back again with a foreign disposition, a stranger in his own land? When his instructions finally arrived he was chagrined to discover that his mission would be essentially financial, a matter of obtaining an $800,000 loan from the Dutch to ransom Americans held captive by the Algerians. Beyond that he was to keep a daily memorandum and a letter of progress. He was to travel to The Hague by way of London in order to deliver important dispatches to John Jay, then negotiating the treaty of his name with the British. His brother Tom would accompany him as his secretary.

John Quincy and Tom sailed from Boston in the *Alfred*, an unsteady, leaky vessel with a captain so incompetent that the voyage might have ended in disaster had it not been for the unusually calm weather during the twenty-eight-day crossing. But the English landscape in the first touch of autumn was as "enchantingly beautiful" as John Quincy had ever seen it. In London Jay welcomed him as a professional diplomat, going over the treaty with him in detail. Jay was not happy with his treaty but felt he could do no better; that whatever its defects it was much preferable to war. The other shared his view, convinced that the United States would suffer far less from the treaty terms than from the most successful war.

By the time of his arrival, the Netherlands was in a state of disintegration. Revolutionary France had given Europe its first taste of total mobilization, and French mass armies were spreading out all over Europe, into Catalonia, northern Italy, Germany, and the Low Countries. Only the autumn rains had kept the French general Pichegru from taking Amsterdam. The weak Stadholder William V, the Prince of Orange, was as unpopular as he was ineffectual. An undisciplined British army under the incompetent Duke of York had proved for the Dutch an ally worse than the enemy. Many Dutchmen, spearheaded by the Patriotic party, were ready to welcome the well-disciplined French soldiers as liberators. Men sported tricolor cockades openly on the streets of Amsterdam and The Hague. "The Carmagnole song, and the Marseilles hymn, were everywhere singing."

John Quincy, from his Hague observation post, thought that the fall of the government was inevitable and was surprised at how little the people seemed to care. A cold spell froze the ground across which the French troops were able to march unopposed into Amsterdam. The English forces withdrew; the Prince of Orange abandoned his country. Under French auspices the Patriotic party dissolved the old forms and set up the Batavian Republic. Adams's instructions were to go along with any new constitution the people might choose as long as the Netherlands remained independent, but if the country lapsed into a dependency of France his mission was to terminate. Regularly he sent his formal reports to Randolph and frequent letters to his father crammed with observations and comments.

Through the spring and summer the American minister observed the progress of the French occupation with increasing distaste. Initial Dutch enthusiasm soon gave way to dismay as the French made clear their demands: the Batavian Republic to declare war on England, pay the costs of the occupying army, accept the increasingly worthless French currency, and pay a huge indemnity. Adams warned his government that France intended to draw the United States into a war with Great Britain, and that any such war would result in the total destruction of American commerce.

Randolph welcomed John Quincy's succinct, well-organized dispatches. As for the reticent Washington, he indulged in what would be for him high praise when he wrote that the "American Minister at The Hague had been very regular and intelligent in his correspondence." Vice President Adams could not restrain his joy and pride in his brilliant son.

In October John Quincy received orders from Randolph to leave at once for London where he would find documents and directions awaiting him. That the trip concerned Jay's treaty he knew, but no more than that. Leaving his brother Tom in charge of the ministry, he set out for England in the worst of weather. By the time he arrived most of his instructions, concerned chiefly with Jay's treaty, had become obsolete. The American minister, Thomas Pinckney, being away, Adams took over the discussion of British-American differences with Secretary of State Lord Grenville, whom he distrusted as he did most British officials. Shortly after his arrival he was presented at court, but unlike his father he remained unimpressed. The Queen asked him whether he was any relation to the Mr. Adams who had been there some years ago. The King inquired as to whether American winters were not more severe than in England. That ended their talk.

Late in April John Quincy received permission from the Secretary of State to return to The Hague. He stayed on in England, however, because of his growing interest in Louisa Catherine Johnson, one of the seven daughters of the American consul in London. Over the winter Adams had been an attentive visitor at the Johnson house. Though he was attracted to the rather shy Louisa he kept his feelings well under control. Prim and not as pretty as her older sisters, she nevertheless came to seem to him, for all that she was ten years younger than he, a suitable if rational choice. He told his mother that he thought it was time for him to have a family.

When he left for Holland in May, he was engaged. It was a choice more of the head than the heart. He showed no great eagerness to plunge into matrimony. Louisa, in love and tormented by uncertainty, begged him to marry her right away. He explained that conditions in the Netherlands were too turbulent. After the country settled down, he would send for her. She would have to reckon on an indefinite engagement that might last anywhere from one to seven years. Personal affairs must be secondary. His overriding concerns in Holland were political, his greatest fear that French influence might force his country into war with England. To his brother Charles he wrote that such a war at such a time would dissolve the Union. Meanwhile, he marked time in The Hague under the French occupation.

In June of 1796 he received a commission as minister plenipotentiary to Portugal, a rise in rank unanimously approved by the Senate. Washington had made the appointment on his own, and it had been as much of a surprise to John Adams as to his son. Abigail, while delighted with her son's advance, remained troubled about his fiancée. He must remember, she warned him, that the girl was ten years younger than he was, had never been in the United States, and was unused to American ways. He replied that his choice was irrevocably made. To Louisa he wrote that their separation would probably last only a year now. Then he might return to the United States to practice law, perhaps settle in one of the Southern states, where legal prospects were more encouraging. He continued to remain vague as to any marriage plans; he did not know when he would leave Holland or even if he would get to London at all before going on to Portugal. "If the most ardent wishes of my heart could give me a conveyance, the wings of the wind would loiter in comparison with its rapidity," he wrote sententiously. But his actions showed otherwise. He could view a long wait with equanimity. Louisa, restless and loving, brooded until she was almost ill. Sometimes she wrote him in a hot burst of despair. He then coldly reproached her for her lack of self-control.

John and Abigail had come to accept the fact that their oldest son was bound to marry and now advised him to do so before going on to Portugal. John, however, took amiss the idea of Johnny's quitting the foreign service. No President, whoever he might be, John wrote, would promote others less capable over John Quincy. When it seemed to young John that he might soon be leaving for Portugal he mentioned incidentally to Louisa that she should be ready for a sudden departure. Overjoyed, she and her mother proceeded to buy a complete wedding outfit and when it turned out that her fiancé had nothing definite in mind by that offhand remark, Louisa had the humiliation of having to lock up her finery and conceal her premature wedding preparations.

Joshua Johnson, Louisa's father, was planning to return to the United States in the spring. She wrote John Quincy that she would try to persuade her father to embark for America from Holland so that they could at least see one another. Such a brief meeting, he replied, would be consistent neither with her dignity nor his delicacy. Joshua, who was also a part owner of a shipping concern, wrote in turn to his prospective if hesitant son-in-law suggesting that the Johnsons visit The Hague with marriage in prospect. John

Quincy said bluntly that he could not marry at this time. Brooding over the rejection of the visit as if it were a rejection of herself, Louisa wrote him full of anger and frustration. He replied with chill reproach: "You say 'I should be sorry to put it in your power or in that of the world to say I wished to force myself upon any man *or into any family*'—and I feel all that you meant I should feel by this suggestion, I see the *suspicion* of your heart in which it originated, and deeply as it probes my sensibility, my bosom is protected by the clear and unhesitating consciousness that the suspicion is without any foundation.—I can say the same of the other passage where you observed that I 'appear to regret what had passed in respect to your attending me to Lisbon, and have taken an improper method of showing this regret'—.... You have in some former letters spurned at the idea of thinking yourself *honoured* by your connection with me, And you now again mention I will not say with what temper of mind, *my Dignity.* . . . My *dignity* my *Station* or my family, have no sort of concern with any subject of debate between you and me—"

In March the packet arrived containing John Quincy's recall from The Hague and his appointment to Portugal. Then his hesitancies about Louisa unexpectedly vanished and he determined to get to London and put an end to their separation. "Our difficulties are ended," Louisa wrote, forgiving and full of happiness. "The more I know you the more I admire, esteem and love you, and the greater is my inclination to do everything in my power to promote your happiness and welfare." Her enthusiasm again turned him hesitant and he warned her not to be too eager, not to expect too much. Johnson was ready to fit out one of his own ships for John Quincy and send it from Holland to England and thence to Portugal. The less than ardent suitor would have none of this, saying that it was neither his intention nor hope to have a ship sent over just for Louisa and himself.

Finally Adams arranged his own passage, landing in England

the second week in July and going directly to London where he arrived at Osborne's Hotel at five in the afternoon. Though the evening still lay ahead of him, he made no effort to see Louisa until next day. Her feelings were so bitter that only years later could she bring herself to mention them. Even after the long-parted couple were together at last, Adams seemed in no hurry to be married. Johnson suggested that he stay with them, but the young man declined. He now learned that in May President Adams had nominated, and the Senate had approved, him as minister plenipotentiary to the King of Prussia. Meanwhile, a troubled Johnson wrote him a note commenting on Adams's apparent reticence in regard to Louisa. John Quincy sensed then that he had no honorable alternative but to ask her to name the date for their marriage. He was taken aback, however, when she named the following week.

The wedding at All Hallows Church, Barking, was a small family affair, and the two-week honeymoon ended in what was for Louisa a tragedy. Joshua Johnson, swindled by his partner in the shipping business, found himself suddenly bankrupt and had to leave the country to avoid his creditors. Louisa in her wretchedness feared that everyone would think the Johnsons had deceived Adams about their foundering affairs until after the wedding. Kindly Tom Adams assured her he believed her innocent. John Quincy said nothing.

The couple left for Berlin at the end of September together with brother Tom and Louisa's maid. John Quincy's mission was to renew a treaty with Prussia and while in Berlin renegotiate another treaty with Sweden that had originally been handled by Franklin. He was not overly pleased at his new appointment. Portugal might be of less importance than Prussia, but Washington had sent him there. His father in sending him to Berlin would inevitably stir his enemies to cry nepotism. At Hamburg he learned that Frederick William II, the inconsequent successor to the great Frederick, was at the point of death. Because of the King's illness the Prussian minister of state could not receive the American's credentials. A new King would require new credentials. Fortunately the new King, the amiable if narrow-minded Frederick William, did not hold with such legalities, being eager to receive the first American minister to Prussia as soon as possible. America, that remote other world, was indeed a subject of much interest to the Prussian court.

Though the Adamses were cordially received, Louisa seldom appeared in public. Ailing, homesick, lonely, she let her cold-mannered husband make the constant round of social appearances. Rumor spread through the diplomatic corps that the never-seen Mrs. Adams was ugly, horse-faced. She herself had come to think that John Quincy was ashamed of her and did not want her at court. But by New Year's, somewhat recovered in health, she was presented to the young and beautiful Queen Louise. When it was seen that the American minister's wife was young and attractive, she was made welcome and soon became almost popular. The daughter-in-law of a President of the United States, as well as the wife of a minister, she took pride in being addressed as Your Excellency or sometimes Princess Royal. She was troubled, however, that her husband's salary, although double what he received at The Hague, forced him to live much more modestly than the ministers of other countries.

The continual round of balls, routs, and gatherings that made up court life soon wearied John Quincy. When forced to attend such events, he seemed to pay scant attention to his wife, leaving her to shift for herself as he sat at the card table or even went home early while she stayed on for supper. He complained that his life was an unprofitable one, that after a year in Berlin his sole accomplishment was to learn to read German after a fashion. Particularly annoying to him was formal court dress, and he wrote to his father suggesting that the United States adopt a diplomatic uniform, preferably plain.

Progress on the Prussian treaty turned out to be slower that Adams had anticipated. It was finally signed on his thirty-second birthday. Because of Sweden's fears of the French, no American treaty with that nation was possible. John Quincy's dispatches and letters continued as illuminating, accurate, and encompassing as ever, and nothing of importance escaped his observation and his succinct comment. For his father and his government he became the most reliable single source of European information. Little as he liked the English government, he grew almost obsessed with his hatred of France, his father's enemy. Both Adamses attributed much of the President's domestic difficulties to the partisans of Revolutionary France. John Quincy was pleased that in Berlin he saw fewer of his pro-French countrymen than he had in The Hague. For Lafayette he developed a particular distaste, commenting sourly on his disguised ambition, his propensity for intrigue, and his political immorality.

Meanwhile Louisa's poor health persisted. In two years she suffered several miscarriages. Yet she continued to participate in court socials. Queen Louise went out of her way to be gracious to her. One time noticing her pallor the Queen gave her a box of rouge, much to the disgust of John Quincy who forbade her to use it. Some months later when she surreptitiously applied a little, he washed it off.

With the signing of the treaty Adams's mission was accomplished. For a respite he took his wife on a trip to Dresden and Carlsbad. In Carlsbad, that fashionable watering place, they met many members of the nobility, to Louisa's pleasure. Two months of travel did much to improve her health. She returned pregnant. Then in December she suffered fainting spells which led to another miscarriage. Adams had begun to despair of having a family and Louisa despaired for both of them.

The remaining months that Adams passed in Berlin were more literary than diplomatic. During the winter he became engrossed in translating Wieland's long poem *Oberon*. In the summer he took Louisa on a journey through Silesia, a region not frequented by travelers and one he hoped might provide exports of Bohemian glass and flax to the United States. He spent some days in the Riesengebirge—the Giant Mountains dividing Silesia from Bohemia—even getting up at two o'clock one morning to climb to the summit of the highest peak, the Riesenkoppe (Giant's Head—about a mile high) to see the sunrise. On his descent he was so inspired that he sat down and wrote a poem describing the scenery and his emotions. Later he would write a series of letters on his Silesian travels for a Philadelphia literary journal, *The Portfolio*. He found the trip one of the pleasantest he had ever made, not the least because for two months he was out of sight and sound of the political world.

The summer had been a quiet one in Europe, but with the approaching autumn John Quincy feared the worst. War was in the offing, and the military balance was so weighted toward the French that they seemed irresistible. Events in America were moving to their own climax. Even from Berlin it was clear to him that his father's reelection was unlikely, and he wrote consolingly, begging the President not to let the rejection prey on his mind. Worried about his father's finances, he offered to put his own thin savings at the President's disposal, not realizing that his brother Charles to whom he had entrusted his money had lost much of it and had given the rest to Nabby's husband to save that feckless man from imprisonment for debt. Charles's wretched life ended that December. Tom, who had returned home some time before, wrote his unhappy brother's epitaph: "Let silence reign forever over his tomb."

On failing of reelection, President Adams considered it his duty to recall his son. His mission concluded, John Quincy spent most of the winter of 1801 in writing, including some verse which he had printed under a nom de plume in *The Portfolio*. In April,

Louisa at last gave birth to a son whom they named George Washington Adams. Ailing all winter, fearful of another miscarriage, she almost died under the ministrations of a drunken midwife who handled her so roughly that for a time she lost the use of her left leg. Since she could neither stand nor walk, the departure of the Adamses had to be delayed. When they finally left in mid-June she was so weak that she had to be carried half-fainting to the carriage. The voyage from Hamburg took fifty-eight days. Fortunately for Louisa the seas were calm. At first the baby suffered so from dysentery that his parents feared he would die, but in mid-ocean he managed to recover.

The Adamses landed at Philadelphia. Tom Adams, meeting them there, was shocked at Louisa's worn appearance. She herself thought she had not much longer to live. John Adams was so delighted to have his son once more on American soil that he offered his Quincy house as their permanent home. After a four-year absence, John Quincy was faced with the prospect of starting his career all over again. His European experiences were of no practical value in Massachusetts. He had a wife and child, a non-existent law practice, and no immediate way of earning a living. Uneasy in the crowded Quincy home, he rented a modest house in Boston at 39 Hanover Square, but since it would not be ready for several months he and his family stayed on with his father.

For Louisa the contrast between familiar Europe and unfamiliar America was overwhelming. "Had I stepped into Noah's Ark," she wrote of the Quincy house, "I do not think I could have been more utterly astonished." The clatter, the nasal Yankee accents, the clothes, the food, the dinner hour, the church services, she found primitive and alien. "I was literally and without knowing it a *fine* lady," she explained herself later. Abigail did not take to the "fine lady" at all, but fortunately the "Old Gentleman," as Louisa referred to her father-in-law, did. Louisa was too dispirited to assert herself.

When Louisa and John Quincy finally moved to Boston she had little idea how to run a house, and for all Abigail's officious efforts to instruct her she did it badly. Her husband repeatedly took her to task for her mismanagement and her extravagances. He decided that her personal maid was too much of an expense and that she herself should take complete charge of little George, though subsequent sleepless nights when the baby cried made him regret that particular economy. Since his reopened law office attracted few clients, he was more than gratified when the judge of the District Court of Massachusetts appointed him one of the new commissioners in bankruptcy. This alone would have given him a comfortable living. But a new ruling turned over control of such appointments to the President of the United States. Jefferson, when he saw the name Adams, crossed it out.

In the spring of 1802 Governor Caleb Strong appointed John Quincy a Senator to the General Court of Massachusetts, a position in which Adams himself admitted he was not able to effect much good or prevent much evil. That autumn he was the Federalist candidate for Congress from the Boston area, failing election by a mere 59 votes. Small as the margin of defeat was, he had become convinced that Federalism was doomed. Law seemed his only alternative. For all the scantiness of his practice he followed a strict routine, rising early, reading several chapters of the Bible, walking briskly to his office, filling in the rest of his time with study, an occasional oration, and "the unavoidable encroachment of dissipation." Weekends he spent with his parents in Quincy, a spot of earth that became almost a necessity for him. Louisa, for whom Quincy was anything but a necessity, used her chronic bad health as an excuse for not going.

When one of the Massachusetts seats in the United States Senate became vacant, John Quincy was among those most frequently mentioned to fill it. After much political backing and filling, the Massachusetts legislature finally elected him over Timothy

Pickering who would in turn be elected to a subsequent Senate vacancy. For Adams, as for his father, his election to the Senate was a sign that he was again on the highroad that led to a political future. As he prepared to leave for Washington, his second son was born. He named the baby John for his father, which pleased Abigail although she regretted that the namesake so little resembled his grandfather.

The Adamses left for Washington in September. Louisa was ill on the way—it was thought for a time she had yellow fever—and they had to spend some time in New York before she recovered enough to travel further. During that time the Senate met to vote on the Louisiana Purchase treaty, and when Adams reached Washington the treaty had already been ratified. Most Federalists, particularly in Massachusetts, had been opposed to the purchase of Louisiana, seeing in the acquisition of the vast new region a tipping of the power balance from the East to the West. Adams on the contrary regarded it as one of the happiest events since the adoption of the Constitution. Here began his rift with the Federalists, a rift that was in any case inevitable, since this stubbornly independent man was never one who could bring himself to accept party discipline. Later he would write: "Each Senator is a representation not of a single State, but of the whole Union. His vote is not the vote of his State, but his own individuality." Such a high-minded attitude was not generally appreciated by fellow politicians and by constituents. John Quincy kept his individuality in the Senate at the expense of his popularity. Whimsically he complained that his Senate opinions on every subject were eventually overruled; the bills he prepared seldom reached the Senate floor.

For Louisa, with her memories of London, Paris, and Berlin, unfinished Washington was as dreary as it was desolate. She and her husband stayed for a while with her married sister, Nancy Hellen, several miles from the Capitol. Money continued to be a problem to both the Adamses, one that perplexed her and made him morose. She complained that he was cold and unkind, that he should understand her wish to be with her sisters and her widowed mother. He replied that she should understand his wish to be with *his* family. At the end of the Senate sessions he went to Quincy while she stayed in Washington, partly because she disliked Quincy, partly because he felt he could not stand the expense of moving his family twice a year. Living apart they, for all their differences, missed each other, and he particularly missed his children.

In August, 1805, Senator Adams finally brought Louisa and the boys back to Quincy. They did not live in the big house but several miles away. That summer, quite unexpectedly, he was notified by Harvard that he had been appointed Nicholas Boylston Professor of Oratory and Rhetoric. Pleased as he was, he was faced with two obstacles to his acceptance. As Boylston professor he would be required to give forty weekly lectures in the course of a year. Since his duties as Senator kept him half the year in Washington, he asked if he might give two lectures a week for twenty weeks. Secondly, the religious test required for professors troubled his prickly Adams nature. The test, he told Harvard's president, must be waived, his objection being to the requirement, not to the doctrines. Harvard agreed to his conditions and he and Louisa returned to Washington, leaving the children with their grandparents.

Louisa, being once more pregnant, spent the following spring and summer in Washington. John Quincy left for Quincy in April. In mid-June he was installed as Boylston professor. His friends from Boston came in their coaches to hear his early lectures. Graceful, witty, and well-organized as these lectures were, he soon found the teaching experience itself irksome. However hard he worked preparing his lectures, he kept being troubled by the thought that he might not be fulfilling the high expectations Harvard had of him. In Washington Louisa had another miscarriage.

Depressed as ever, longing for her children, she went back to Quincy in August. The boys at first scarcely knew her, and when she and her husband took them to the smaller Quincy house, baby John howled for his grandmother. Preoccupied with his Harvard duties, John Quincy spent most of his days in Cambridge where he had rented a room. His wife accused him of neglecting the children and of not wanting her back. He explained to her with some annoyance that his time was not his own. That explanation she considered not good enough. Since she relinquished all claims to his time in the winter, she told him, she was less willing to relinquish it in the summer.

Aaron Burr's conspiracy became the scandal of the ensuing winter. Jefferson in his anger against Burr and his associates had instigated a bill in Congress that would have suspended the right of habeas corpus and gone far beyond the earlier Alien and Sedition Acts in moving the country toward a dictatorship. The bill passed the Senate but was later rejected by the House. Adams helped prepare the bill, declaring that on extraordinary occasions such a temporary extreme measure could be justified in order to preserve the government and the rights of the people. Foreign affairs continued to occupy most of his attention; the titanic struggle between England and France, with its repercussions on American trade and shipping. To the belligerents, American feelings were a side issue. In the spring of 1807 the British ship of war *Leopard* fired on and captured the American frigate *Chesapeake*, and the *Leopard*'s captain seized four American sailors who he claimed were British deserters. To the British, plagued by naval desertions and desperately in need of seamen in their war for survival, the boarding of the *Chesapeake* was a minor encounter. To Americans it seemed a national affront, to which they reacted with surging anger and defiant pride. Adams came to think that the *Chesapeake* incident started the most important period of his life. When the Republicans in Boston called for a protest meeting at the State

House, Adams was a member of the committee drafting the protest resolutions. At first the Federalists held back, reluctant to let even the impressment of seamen interfere with the lucrative if hazardous overseas trade. Nor could they forgive John Quincy his cooperation with the Republicans. The day after the meeting was his fortieth birthday; it was also the day that marked his parting with the Federalists. Though they would finally bow to popular feeling on the *Chesapeake*, they would never again consider Senator Adams one of themselves.

In August John Quincy recorded in his diary the birth of his third son. The infant first appeared to be stillborn, but after half an hour showed signs of life. Adams named the boy Charles Francis after his unfortunate brother. On his return to Washington after the child's birth, he found that news of his political apostasy had preceded him. Federalist colleagues were unforgiving. So unpopular was he that legislators hesitated to support an Adams measure even when they agreed with it. He had now come to believe that the United States could not avoid war with Great Britain no matter how ruinous the results. Jefferson's more pacifistic Embargo Act in reply to French and English blockades and counterblockades passed through Congress over the violent protests of merchants and shipping interests. American ships were to be kept in port, depriving the British of vital supplies and essential markets until they mended their ways. John Quincy thought such an embargo a diplomatic weapon and was willing to endorse it at least temporarily. Federalists considered this the final proof that he was one of Jefferson's supporters. In his diary he recorded his declining political prospects. He saw no chance of the Massachusetts Federalist legislature's reelecting him, and he began to make preparations to return to Boston as a private citizen and resume the practice of law, even though he considered himself indifferently qualified for it.

When the Republican members of Congress met to discuss the

1808 presidential election and to vote on a choice of candidates, Senator Adams was included among them. He voted with the others but did not speak. The balloting favored Secretary of State James Madison. John Quincy received one vote for Vice President. That single vote, however, succeeded in branding him in New England as a Federalist renegade.

Boston docks lay mouldering under the effects of Jefferson's embargo. No longer were the town's more proper citizens prepared to drive out to Cambridge to listen to the traitorous Senator-professor give his lectures at Harvard. Their feelings matched those of one enraged Federalist who announced that he wished to God "the noble house of Braintree had been put in a hole and a deep one too twenty years ago."

New England remained Federalism's last outpost; the Massachusetts legislature passed resolutions instructing the state's two Senators to oppose the Jefferson administration and its embargo. Senator Adams's defense of the embargo cost him personal no less than political friends. In June, 1808, as a challenge to their recalcitrant Senator, the legislators elected a wealthy merchant to replace him. Stung by this, Adams resigned before the end of his term, returned to Quincy and his garden, and devoted the rest of his time to his Harvard lectures. Outwardly he seemed calm, but inwardly he seethed. Only within the circle of his family would he drop his mask of imperturbability. Louisa wrote that her husband's restless anxiety almost drove her crazy.

Rumors were circulating in Boston that President-elect Madison had determined to make Adams his Secretary of War. John Quincy denied there was any such possibility, though the rumors were current enough for his father and his brother Tom to have heard them. The smoke of rumor did conceal some fire. Madison, a few days after his inauguration, sent for John Quincy to tell him that the Russian Czar had asked for an exchange of ministers. The President proposed to nominate Adams as minister plenipotentiary with the mission of cultivating the Czar's friendship and negotiating a maritime treaty. Though Adams's friends might consider it an exile, for him it was the welcome resumption of his interrupted career. Louisa was the last to know, being told finally by Tom. As usual, all arrangements were made without consulting her. She and baby Charles were to go, along with her sister Catherine and Nabby's eldest son, William Steuben Smith, who would serve as secretary of the legation. Two servants, Martha Godfrey and a Negro called Nelson, would accompany them. The two older boys, to Louisa's sorrow, were to be left behind. Parting was a great shock to her. When she and her family visited John and Abigail to say goodbye, she was not left alone a minute with the old man for fear that she might stir his pity enough to let her take George and John with her.

The Adams family sailed in August from Charlestown on the *Horace* for an eighty-day voyage to St. Petersburg. There was some question whether the ship would reach the Russian capital before ice closed the Baltic ports. The *Horace*'s captain wanted to stop at Kiel and let the party make the rest of the journey overland. Adams insisted that he had to reach his destination as quickly as possible, and refused to consider any intermediate port. A favoring wind brought them to the imperial city before the ice formed.

At St. Petersburg they took five primitive rooms at the Hôtel de Londres, supposedly the best in the city but built more like a fortress than a hostelry. Louisa described her room as a stone hole entered by a stone passage, and so full of rats that they snatched away the bread she kept on her bedside table for the baby.

Czar Alexander I received Adams with a cordiality that was at least in part due to his growing doubts about the Russian-French alliance. Adams had been instructed in the formalities of the presentation, which he found more embarrassing than his official business. Louisa was presented to the Empress Mother a week later. She complained that her husband went off to the palace, leaving her to face the elaborate etiquette of the presentation alone.

The life of the court in that exotic city was one of luxurious frivolity—dinners, balls, masquerades, entertainments, sleighing parties, all that idle ingenuity could invent. The Adamses, held down by their niggardly government allowance, were over-shadowed by the more opulent members of the diplomatic corps. Louisa worried that she could not afford even the dresses needed to attend the required functions, since the Empress Mother had a sharp way of commenting on gowns seen too often. Social life took up most of Adams's time, and there were moments when his Puritan nature rebelled, and he announced angrily that he would no longer lead a life of such irregularity and dissipation. Living beyond one's means was common in St. Petersburg, and Adams's means were less than any of those with whom he associated.

All Europe had changed much since his last sojourn. Then, he recalled, a sort of republican or democratic spirit was prevalent. Now "the very name of the people is everywhere buried in oblivion. . . . Jacobin grubs bursting into butterfly princes, dukes and counts . . . and an iron furrow tearing up the bowels of the nations." Adams liked the Czar, whom he described as young, handsome, and elegant in person, affable in manner, as friendly to America as Napoleon was offensively hostile. To his surprise John Quincy, though inferior in rank to an ambassador, found himself sought out at court. At the French ambassador's ball the Czar danced a polonaise with Louisa, then followed this by dancing with her sister. Catherine, handsomer and more self-possessed than Louisa, laughed and chatted with the Czar as if he were not a Czar and so intrigued him by her sprightly manner that he delayed the ambassador's supper for twenty-five minutes to continue dancing with her. That same evening Alexander observed to Adams that he had failed to recognize the American minister on the street because he looked so different without his wig. John Quincy, who detested wigs and wore one only because it was required at court functions, took the Czar's remark to mean that he could now discard the wig for all time.

Alexander undoubtedly liked the Adamses, but his cordiality was reinforced by his need for a free flow of trade between the United States and Russia, particularly since Russia was now engaged in a war with Turkey. And, while Russia as an ally of France remained officially at war with England, the French alliance was wearing thin. Adams sensed the anti-French feeling, though it was still below the surface, and he sent reports of it in cipher to the State Department. When Napoleon requested the Czar to close his ports to American ships, Alexander refused. He continued his friendly overtures to the Adamses, inviting them to events usually restricted to ambassadors.

As the year 1810 waned, Adams began to consider returning home the following year. Constantly harassed by expenses, he was embarrassed at the sorry figure he had to cut in the social life of the diplomatic corps. Though he had found an apartment, everything still cost too much. By arranging with a restaurant to supply the family meals he was at least able to dispense with a steward, a cook, two scullions, a porter, and a man to make fires. Later, without consulting his wife, he rented a house in a cheap part of town. She objected. The house she considered too small, the location too mean. Again she was pregnant and worried about her health.

The winter came early, stayed long. Not until June did the first ship arrive with mail from America. John Quincy was pleased to learn that James Monroe was now Secretary of State, a man who would be more moderate than his predecessor in regard to England. In the same post Adams was astonished to hear that he had been appointed to the Supreme Court. Though it would have made his father more than happy, he knew at once he could not accept.

His law studies had never really interested him, and his legal experience, as he well knew, was superficial. Nor did he share his father's veneration for the common law.

On July 16 he noted that he had been married fourteen years, "during which I have to bless God for the enjoyment of a portion of felicity, resulting from this relation in society, greater than falls to the generality of mankind, and far beyond anything that I have been conscious of deserving. Its greatest alloy has arisen from the delicacy of my wife's constitution, the ill health which has afflicted her much of the time, and the misfortunes she has suffered from it. Our union has not been without its trials, nor invariably without dissensions between us. . . . There are natural frailties of temper in both of us; both being quick and irascible, and mine being sometimes harsh. But she has always been a faithful and affectionate wife, and a careful, tender, indulgent, and watchful mother." Two weeks later Louisa give birth to a daughter whom John Quincy, contrary to his wife's wishes, named Louisa Catherine. The parents thought of asking Alexander to be godfather, then decided against it, fearing that this would be too monarchal for American public opinion.

The climactic year of 1812 found Adams deeply concerned over the threat of war between his country and England or France, a war in which he was convinced the United States had nothing to gain and everything to lose. He thought that if Americans would only show patience, both England and France in their need for American products and American trade would see reason. Yet by April he had become persuaded that war with England could not be avoided unless—faint possibility—the British government gave up the practice of impressment and repealed the Orders in Council that had made American ships trading at any European port the prey of the royal navy. The British foreign secretary, Lord Castlereagh, belatedly turning conciliatory on the impressment issue, announced the suspension of the Orders in Council, unaware that

Congress had already declared war on his country.

The fateful summer that marked Napoleon's invasion of Russia and the declaration of war against England by the United States, also marked Adams's forty-fifth birthday. "I am forty-five years old," he took time to note in his diary. "Two-thirds of a long life are past, and I have done nothing to distinguish it by usefulness to my country or to mankind. I have always lived with, I hope, a suitable sense of my duties in society, and with a sincere desire to perform them. But passions, indolence, weakness, and infirmity have sometimes made me swerve from my better knowledge of right and almost constantly paralyzed my efforts of good."

Meanwhile, Czar Alexander's worst fears were realized when on June 24, 1812, Napoleon with his Grand Army of half a million men—the largest the world had yet seen—crossed the Neman River. Adams remained a firsthand observer of that debacle. Scarcely had it begun, however, when his infant daughter died of dysentery after some weeks of intense suffering. Even in the midst of the invasion the Czar sent his condolences. Burying their child in an alien land, the Adamses were inconsolable. John Quincy had planned to leave Russia in the spring. Now the war prevented it. When Napoleon reached Moscow, Adams in St. Petersburg saw disaster staring the Emperor in the face. "The situation of the French army in the midst of their triumphs is absolutely desperate," he wrote. Napoleon's headlong flight with his broken army through the winter snows he thought had been unequaled since the days of Xerxes. At Kazan Cathedral he was present with the royal family at a *Te Deum* for Napoleon's defeat.

The winter was singularly cold in St. Petersburg, with seventeen consecutive days of below-zero temperatures. Adams was weary of that strange northern world that seemed cruelly empty since the death of his daughter. The American war preyed on his mind. Alexander in his need had formed an alliance with England, the erstwhile enemy. Monroe wanted to make it quite clear to the Czar that the alliance would not affect Russian relations with the United States. Alexander was nevertheless disturbed by that far-off war and told Adams he was willing to mediate. Adams replied that though England was to blame for the war, he would inform Secretary of State Monroe of the Czar's offer. Monroe was ready to accept at once and dispatched Secretary of the Treasury Albert Gallatin and Senator James Bayard to join Adams as negotiators. The British government, however, refused to consider any such mediation. When the Czar renewed his offer in November, the answer in London was still No, but this time Lord Castlereagh offered direct negotiations instead. Monroe, accepting, added Henry Clay— the American perhaps most responsible for bringing on the War of 1812—and the new minister to Sweden, Jonathan Russell, to the negotiators who were to meet with their British counterparts at Gothenburg in Sweden. As Adams prepared to leave, all St. Petersburg was celebrating the news that Paris had been taken by the allies, that Napoleon had abdicated, and that Europe was at peace.

To Adams's annoyance the Anglo-American negotiations were shifted south to Ghent in Belgium. Reluctantly making his way there, he met his four colleagues and with them rented a house and set up bachelor quarters. It was not a wholly satisfactory arrangement. The others sat round after dinner smoking and drinking wine and passing the time, quite contrary to his own abstemious habits. Clay's gambling, drinking, and casual amours he found particularly offensive. As to the negotiations, he was pessimistic. England had come out of the Napoleonic Wars the mistress of the world, and this was reflected in the arrogant demands of the British negotiators headed by Lord Gambier. Adams was particularly distressed at the news of the burning of Washington by the British, an act he considered contrary to all rules of warfare and worse than the worst excesses of the French Revolution. But almost equally distressing to John Quincy was the

Hartford Convention with its implied threat of New England's secession from the Union.

Negotiations went on for almost a year. Though Adams headed the commission, the Swiss-born Gallatin emerged as the natural leader, the most acceptable to the English contingent. The chief stumbling block in the negotiations was the British demand for a buffer zone between the United States and Canada that would include what would later become Wisconsin, Michigan, Illinois, and much of Indiana and Ohio, to be used as a reserve for Britain's Indian allies. Adams refused to consider leaving such vast territories to a few savage tribes. Americans had a natural right to the use of such land "to settle, cultivate and improve their territory." He thought the English government aimed to continue the war in order to hamper the progress and growth of its former colonies. To his father he confided that reconciling British and American pretensions "will be found more unnatural than yours and mine wandering life." Yet, when it seemed that negotiations would break down, the British suddenly showed themselves conciliatory, even anxious for peace. Partly this was due to the defeat of the British forces invading from Canada at Plattsburg, New York. But the chief impulse to a settlement was the weakened English diplomatic position before the Congress of Vienna. Faced with this, British Foreign Secretary Castlereagh wanted the American war settled once and for all.

One of the British negotiators also happened to be named Adams, though he and his American counterpart soon established that they were in no way related. John Quincy remarked that the British Adamses displayed a coat of arms with a red cross whereas the American Adamses had none other than the stars and stripes. (For all his disparagement of heraldry, John Quincy later concocted an Adams coat of arms which he quartered with the Boylston, Quincy, and Smith arms for his bookplate.) The two Adamses did not find each other compatible. On Christmas Eve, 1814, the

Peace of Ghent was signed by both sides. The Americans set aside nationalistic thoughts of conquering Canada. The British gave up any notions of seizing Maine and blocking American expansion. Impressment, no longer an issue at the war's end, was not even mentioned. Adams stubbornly insisted on the minor point of fishing rights for his New Englanders. At the end he told Lord Gambier he hoped this would be the last peace treaty needed between Great Britain and the United States. To Louisa in St. Petersburg he wrote that the day of peace was the happiest in his life.

The end of the peace mission brought out more ill-feeling among the Americans than had the mission itself. Gallatin wanted all the documents sent to London for the treaty of commerce as yet to be negotiated there. Clay insisted that such papers be sent to the State Department. As head of the mission Adams said that he would keep custody of them. Clay was furious, but Adams refused to budge. Unaware of such altercations, the principal gentlemen of the city gave a peace dinner to both missions. Olive trees in tubs decorated the hall, set off by intertwined English and American flags. "God Save the King" and "Hail, Columbia" were played alternately and incessantly all the evening. Adams, annoyed that everyone had to appear in full uniform, sat with the British negotiators between the intendant and the mayor. It fell to him to give the next to last toast: "Ghent, the city of peace," he proposed, "may be the gates of the temple of Janus, here closed, not be opened again for a century."

Adams regarded the Peace of Ghent as one of his greatest accomplishments, although in his darker moments he feared it would be no more than a truce. After his seven-month sojourn he left on January 26 for Paris, the nostalgically familiar city that he had first known thirty years before, and that in spite of revolution, war, and the overthrow of two dynasties looked little changed. He was presented to Louis XVIII, brother of the executed King whom he had seen as a boy. Inevitably the King asked him the old familiar question: Was he related to the celebrated Mr. Adams?

While Adams was spending pleasantly relaxed days sightseeing and renewing his boyish years, Napoleon escaped from Elba and began his sweep across France. Adams refused to believe the rumor that the Corsican corporal would enter Paris in a week. But within that time Bourbon notices were torn down and pictures of Napoleon and Marie Louise suddenly appeared in print-shop windows. When the rumor became a fact, Adams walked along the boulevards hoping in vain to get a glimpse of the man for whom the crowds were now shouting *"Vive l'Empereur!"* Not until the following day did John Quincy finally see Napoleon as the Emperor reviewed his troops at the Place du Carrousel. That same evening Louisa, whom he had been expecting for a week or more, arrived in her carriage. Hers had been a grim, gruesome, and astronomically expensive journey from St. Petersburg. "I quitted its gaudy loneliness without a sigh," she wrote, "except that which was wafted to the tomb of my lovely Babe." Outside Frankfurt she passed through a battlefield where thousands still lay unburied, and almost fainted from the stench and the horror. Outside Strasbourg her carriage was surrounded by the hastily improvised imperial army. The undisciplined soldiers turned threatening until an officer announced that the carriage held Americans. Even so, Louisa was forced to shout *"Vive Napoléon"* as they progressed. Little Charlie sat by his mother's side rigid with fear.

Several times in the next few days Adams managed to get a closer look at Napoleon. He saw the Emperor at the theater and wondered at the people's wild fervor. Having observed how quickly the Bourbons had lost favor, he thought the current enthusiasm for Napoleon would prove no more stable. The change of regime made little difference. Unhampered by official duties, he relaxed in the enjoyment of one of the pleasantest interludes he could remember. Secretary of State Monroe had promised on the conclusion of the peace with Britain to appoint him minister to the Court of St. James's. While waiting for his credentials, he continued to sightsee, attend the theater, and visit old acquaintances, finding the dissipations of the city as alluring as he had at twenty.

Although Adams awaited his credentials eagerly and with some impatience, his attitude toward England remained hostile, an ineradicable antipathy. Nevertheless, to follow in his father's footsteps stirred both his pride and his filial devotion. Mid-May saw him again, after eighteen years, on the road from Dover to London. Less intrigued by the landscape than his father had been, he noted the many beggars and homeless wanderers along the highway in the wake of the postwar depression. Clay and Gallatin had arrived in London two months earlier and had already laid the groundwork for a commercial treaty when Adams joined them. As usual he was faced with the problem of making ends meet. To save money he rented a house, in suburban Ealing, attractive if inconvenient. Once settled there with Louisa and Charles, he was soon joined by George and John. After such a long separation the two older boys seemed almost strangers. George at fourteen was very tall though nervous and often ailing. John, his grandfather's favorite, was small, full of energy.

In Adams's first weeks the talk in London was all of Napoleon. Would he succeed this time? Most thought he would be defeated and seek refuge in America. Three weeks after the arrival of the Adamses, Wellington overwhelmed the French Emperor at Waterloo. John Quincy took his family out that evening in their carriage to view the victory celebrations. After the splendor of the Russian displays, these seemed mean and listless, small illuminations spelling out "Wellington and Bluecher," "Victory," "GR [Georgius Rex]," "GPR [Georgius Regni Procurator]." A few bonfires. Nothing more.

Lack of his proper formal letter delayed John Quincy's presentation at court. Unlike his father he was unimpressed by the event. George III being now blind, mad, and in seclusion, Adams was

presented to Queen Charlotte. In spite of her reputation for coldness to Americans, she went out of her way to be cordial. What
he thought of her he kept to himself. He was more open in his
opinion of her son, now the Regent, whom he described as "a
Falstaff without the wit, and a Prince Henry without the com-
punctions." Much of Adams's time was taken up by ceremonial
state functions. Unfortunately he found he had little time for his
sons. They were good boys, but to their father's regret showed very
little interest in their studies.

Even in cut-rate Ealing his financial problems continued. He
was embarrassed that he could not adequately return the hospitality of the diplomatic corps or even show proper civility to his
visiting countrymen. Morosely he concluded that unless his government untied its purse-strings a little more willingly, permanent
missions could go only to men of wealth.

Adams by this time had become his country's most astute and
experienced diplomat, yet no extraordinary events or achieve-
ments marked his two years at the Court of St. James's. Initial
treaty negotiations were so difficult that at times they seemed
hopeless to the three American negotiators. The impetuous Clay
was for breaking off, Gallatin urged patience, and Adams held
aloof. Then, abruptly, the British negotiators became reasonable.
As Adams wrote his father, there were only two significant articles:
the abolition of discriminating duties, and the admission of American commercial vessels to four British settlements in the East
Indies.

By the time the treaty was signed the question of the impressment of Americans in the royal navy, the chief issue of the War
of 1812, had become academic. With the peace, unemployed and
half-starved seamen haunted the docks of the great English ports
looking for any berth. The shortage had become an over-
abundance. Remaining was the secondary problem of slaves taken
away by the British. Against all his personal inclinations Adams

found himself officially in the position of having to demand the return of all slaves who had been captured or "rescued" during the late war. Lord Liverpool, the British prime minister, made out that the return should apply only to slaves seized on the battlefield, not to those who had taken refuge with the British army and navy on the promise of freedom. Adams insisted that all property, including slaves, must be returned, and he informed the embarrassed Lord Liverpool that British officers had enticed slaves from their masters with such promises and had then resold them into slavery in the West Indies.

In September the prolonged negotiations with the foreign secretary, Lord Castlereagh, over the British refusal to allow American trade with the West Indies were broken off when Castlereagh left for Ireland to visit his father. John Quincy remarked that he wished he could visit *his* father.

John Adams in Quincy was becoming restive at his son's long absence. Further absence, the old man wrote, might make any public career in America impossible. Then, too—as he pointed out—there were the children to consider. John Quincy agreed completely. They needed parental supervision. His son George was getting of an age to be admitted to Harvard, and his father hoped he would become a scholar. A few weeks after Monroe's overwhelming victory in the 1816 presidential election, the American newspapers leaked the news that John Quincy Adams was to be recalled and named Secretary of State in the new presidential cabinet. John hoped it was true.

Though troubled by Adamsian scruples and self-doubt, John Quincy did not hesitate to accept. There were the customary finalities of office before he left England, farewell audiences with the Queen and with the Regent, a last meeting with the haughty Castlereagh. The British foreign secretary had earlier offered to mediate the dispute between the United States and Spain over the Florida boundaries. But Adams had a built-in mistrust of British goodwill. Before he left, he was faced with the problem of official gifts. The British government customarily gave each departing minister a purse of £500. Adams considered the acceptance of such a gift not only contrary to the United States Constitution but degrading in itself. He refused, much to the irritation of the master of ceremonies who saw himself done out of his customary 10 percent tip.

Adams sailed home with his family aboard the *Washington*. Europe, and England in particular, seemed through his disillusioned eyes to be increasingly antagonistic to the United States and its political power. European rulers hoped that the American Union would not last. He was determined to devote his best efforts to seeing that it did. The aim of his foreign policy would be to keep the peace; he would base his principles on union and national expansion. Such thoughts he mulled over daily on his fifty-day voyage. He had been away eight years. He would never see Europe again.

# 5

# *John Quincy Adams*

## OLD MAN ELOQUENT

NCE MORE the son returned to Quincy, the unfamiliarly familiar landscape, his home yet not his home. As soon as the carriage stopped before the homestead, his two older boys ran to their grandmother standing in the doorway. Charlie alone held back, not remembering her. All the Quincy and Adams clans, headed by Tom and his five children, gathered to welcome the exiles. How Louisa found this Noah's Ark a second time she did not say. Their stay was brief. Much to her regret, she had to leave her children behind upon going on to Washington with her husband. He had already made his plans for them without consulting her. George, his grandfather's favorite, would spend the year in Cambridge being tutored in mathematics for admission to Harvard. John and Charles were to attend the Boston Latin School. Weekends they could come to Quincy, but during the week they were to live at Dr. Thomas Welch's where their father had stayed as a young man upon coming from Newburyport.

Just before John Quincy left London he reached his fiftieth year. The graceful boy had become the graceless man, pudgy, bald, the once-delicate features coarsened by time. His nose had grown long, his chin drooped. Like his father, he suffered from watery and inflamed eyes. So afflicted was he with arthritis that at times he could scarcely hold a pen, and Louisa had to write for him. The humors of age were on him. With devastating insight he saw himself as "reserved, cold, austere and forbidding." Avoiding strong attachments for persons or things, he had few friends. He turned with obsessive bitterness against those who crossed him. Some quality in him defied popularity. The verses that he wrote all his life and that he would publish in his old age were indicative of the man—metrical exercises devoid of warmth or inner feeling:

> Nor crown, nor sceptre would I ask
> But from my country's will,
> By day, by night, to ply the task
> Her cup of bliss to fill.

Such stanzas, whatever their lyric lack, represented his strong, almost crushing sense of duty, his most fundamental characteristic, the rock on which his personality was anchored.

In Monroe's cabinet he would reach the height of his career. With natural endowments and extended training for the office, he was destined to be one of the great Secretaries of State. During a time of Federalist eclipse, when political parties themselves were on the wane in the new nation, Adams was suddenly thrust into the established presidential succession. Madison had been Jefferson's Secretary of State, Monroe had been Madison's, and now John Quincy had moved to that key position, fully conscious of its significance. He was not as conscious of how or why he, a New Englander, should take his place in the Virginia dynasty. Clay and the Westerners had bitterly opposed his appointment. But, as Monroe explained to Jefferson, if he as President should take his Secretary of State from Virginia or the South or the West, it would set the whole country north of the Delaware against his new administration. A Northern man would be the most circumspect choice and among the Northerners Adams "by his age, long experience in our foreign affairs and adoption into the republican party, seems to have superior intentions to anyone there."

Richard Rush, Secretary of State Adams's minister to England, wrote that "of the public history of Mr. Monroe's administration all that will be worth telling to posterity hitherto has been transacted through the Department of State." Adams was a nationalist and an expansionist. Monroe would have been willing to see his country's western boundaries defined by the Rocky Mountains. For Adams nothing less than the whole North American continent would suffice. As Secretary of State he was chiefly responsible for three events portentous to his country's history: the treaty with Spain extending the United States horizon to the Pacific; the acquisition of Florida; and the Monroe Doctrine with its implications of the as-yet-uncoined phrase "Manifest Destiny."

In Monroe's cabinet Adams felt most sympathetic to Secretary of War John Calhoun, the tall, blue-eyed planter from South Carolina. A Yale graduate, an 1812 War hawk, Calhoun was drawn to Adams by their common nationalism. Not at all drawn was Secretary of the Treasury William Crawford, the handsome, violently ambitious Georgian who had coveted Adams's position for himself. Initial cabinet meetings were awkward. "My office of Secretary of State," Adams wrote, "makes it the interest of all the partisans of the candidates for the next Presidency (to say no more) to decry me as much as possible in the public opinion. The most conspicuous of these candidates are Crawford . . . , Clay, the Speaker of the House of Representatives, and De Witt Clinton, Governor of New York. Clay expected himself to have been Secretary of State, and he and all his creatures were disappointed by my appointment. He is therefore coming out as the head of a new opposition in Congress to Mr. Monroe's administration, and he makes no scruples of giving the tone to all his party in running me down."

The new Secretary of State came thoroughly prepared for the issues he would have to face. What, Monroe asked, should be done about Spain's South American colonies now emerging as independent nations? Adams, who saw few parallels between the American and the South American revolutions, recommended a wary neutrality. Clay and Crawford and their supporters demanded immediate recognition of South American independence.

Adams's first act on taking over the State Department was to reorganize it in the light of his own diplomatic experience. He inherited a department in great disorder. Records had been mislaid. Accounts had not been kept. Papers were not properly filed. Most of the reorganization, even to the trivia, devolved on him. His only staff was a chief clerk. After sorting out the jumble of papers, he prepared an index for diplomatic communications and a register for consular correspondence. His instructions to American diplomats concerning their duties were on the level of distinguished state papers, trenchant and discerning generalizations to be used as guidelines in observing and judging the state of the world.

Proud as he was of his position, Adams found himself weighed down by work and responsibilities with little time even to consider his family. His social obligations were particularly annoying to him—a waste of time in his opinion. News of his boys in Quincy was often troubling. John kept sending him grumbling, poorly written letters. George neglected his studies, though his father was much relieved when in March he was somehow admitted to Harvard. Charles, whose preferred tongue was French, did well enough at Boston Latin but was homesick for Europe.

Florida remained Adams's most immediate concern. For fifteen years it had been a latent if vexing problem. As early as 1802 Pinckney had proposed that Spain sell both East and West Florida to the United States. The Louisiana Purchase had left the Spanish boundaries vague, and in 1810 United States forces had occupied western Florida. For Spain, Florida itself was of no great value. Monroe told Adams that the Spanish minister, Don Luis de Onís, had instructions to dispose of the whole region on the best terms he could get. Eastern Florida could not be defended, as the Spanish government—preoccupied with South American revolts—was well aware, and it feared that the United States might seize not only Florida but Spanish Mexico.

Before any terms could be clarified negotiations were broken off by General Andrew Jackson's precipitate military action. Border incidents between the Seminoles of Spanish Florida and the frontiersmen of lower Georgia had resulted in so much rapine and killing that Monroe finally dispatched a punitive expedition under the impetuous Jackson to teach the Indians a lesson. Though the general had orders not to molest Spaniards or Spanish forts, he paid little heed to his instructions. In a whirlwind campaign he invaded East Florida, seized the Spanish fort of St. Mark's where the Seminoles had taken refuge, hanged a number of Indians as well as two Englishmen he suspected of abetting them, then went on to capture Pensacola, which he considered the center of Indian intrigue. Deposing the Spanish governor, he appointed an American in his place. Having done this, he wrote Monroe that the whole of East Florida should be seized, and that he could do it in sixty days without involving the government.

The Spanish minister at once protested the violation of his country's sovereignty. Adams explained to him that the failure of Spanish officials to restrain the Florida Indians from butchering settler families had made it necessary for Jackson to pursue them across the border as a matter of self-defense. Although Adams privately deplored Jackson's hanging of his prisoners, publicly he defended him over the opposition of the rest of Monroe's cabinet, who considered that the general had willfully committed an unjustifiable act of aggression. Crawford and his supporters proceeded to condemn Jackson on the high ground of international law, quoting Vattel and other authorities to sustain their argument, though Crawford's impulse was political rather than legal or moral. In defending Jackson, Secretary Adams gave better than he got, justifying him by citations not only from Vattel but Grotius and Puffendorf as well. He was dismayed, however, at Jackson's reaction to his erudite defense. "Damn Grotius!" the general exclaimed. "Damn Puffendorf! Damn Vattel!—this is a mere matter between Jim Monroe and myself!"

Monroe was much troubled by the Florida dilemma. If he condoned Jackson's conduct he might be accused of starting a war. But if he censured Jackson he would not only affront public opinion—almost solidly behind the general—but give the appearance of knuckling under to Spain. He was willing to restore Pensacola to its Spanish governor, but he was prepared to yield St. Mark's only to a force strong enough to control the Indians. The Spanish problem would continue to haunt both him and his Secretary of State. Meanwhile, Jackson's Florida actions brought on a lengthy congressional investigation. Finally vindicated, he toured the Eastern cities in triumph.

Through the sultry summer Adams worked and worried himself in the State Department to the point of exhaustion. He could not sleep nights. Only at the summer's end did he manage to get away to Quincy and pass a few days with his parents "while the candles burn." The candles did not have long to burn for Abigail. In October, 1818, she came down with typhoid and died a few weeks later. Her son was stunned. Though he had lived most of his life away from her, he nevertheless needed the consoling awareness that she was still there. Her existence, he admitted, was the comfort of his life. Yet even on the day she died he was confined to his office preparing instructions for Rush and Gallatin in London to renew the Convention of 1818.

Rush and Gallatin found their British counterparts more cordial and conciliatory than they had expected. The issues were the now threadbare ones of fisheries, boundaries, and impressment. Then, during the course of the negotiations, the British foreign secretary, Lord Castlereagh, proposed that the United States join with Great Britain in abolishing the slave trade. Adams was more favorably inclined than the other members of Monroe's cabinet, yet in the end he was forced to reply that although the President considered the proposal indicative of mutual understanding, yet on constitutional grounds the United States could not accept. The Secretary of State pointed out that, beyond any constitutional question, Negroes confiscated from slave traders posed an insoluble problem since his government could neither guarantee their liberty in the slave states nor control them in the free. There also remained the old American fear of foreign interference with its shipping. Public opinion would not tolerate officers of foreign nations boarding and searching United States vessels as suspected slavers. Again Adams officially was forced into the position of acquiescing in that which he privately detested.

His years as Secretary of State saw a hardening of his personality. He became increasingly testy and suspicious. More and more, bitterness and invective crept into his diary. In spite of his more sophisticated background he was like his father in lacking assurance. Never was he wholly at ease socially. He himself noted that in company he either talked too much or too little. People, he thought, liked him better when he talked, though afterward he was often troubled by what he had said and the manner in which he had said it. Gossip unnerved him. He was distressed by the rumor current that he was to represent the Prince Regent at the christening of the British minister's daughter. The story even reached Monroe, who questioned Adams. He replied indignantly that it was a malicious fabrication of his enemies. He was hurt, moreover, that

Monroe had so little confidence in him that he could give such a story credence.

It was ironic that Adams should have been suspected of toadying to the English, for his antipathy to England was so ingrained that it verged at times on hatred. He remained far more suspicious of English intentions than did Monroe. In his negotiations with Spain he wanted no British interference. These prolonged negotiations continued to frustrate and exhaust him, forcing him to shunt aside all other State Department business. The Spanish foreign minister had broken off relations with the American minister in protest against Jackson's highhanded Florida invasion. But in January the French minister, Hyde de Neuville, let Adams know confidentially that Spain's new prime minister was at last willing to settle matters and even to consider extending the United States boundary to the western sea. For Adams the possibility of a window on the Pacific was a hope he had long cherished. When he was in St. Petersburg he had written his father that "the whole continent of North America appears to be destined by Divine Providence to be peopled by one *nation*, speaking one language, professing one general system of religious and political principles, and accustomed to one general tenor of social usages and customs." Suddenly this hope was brought a giant step nearer.

Complicated discussions and counterdiscussions between Adams and Onís followed about those vaguely defined regions west of the Rockies. Seizing the advantage of Spain's weakness, the American showed himself a tenacious, not to say relentless, negotiator. On behalf of the United States he offered $5 million for Florida. Onís held out vainly for an additional million. Finally on Washington's birthday the two diplomats put their signatures to the treaty that not only gave Florida to the United States but extended American boundaries to the Pacific. Adams, as he signed, thought the day was perhaps the most important of his life. The treaty passed unanimously in the Senate. Monroe admitted that he had expected to get no more than Florida. "The acknowledgment of a definite line of boundary to the South Sea forms a great epoch in our history," Adams congratulated himself in his diary.

Monroe's first term was a period of party dormancy known superficially as the Era of Good Feelings. Yet in its course the attitudes of North and South were polarizing. The manufacturing North wanted high tariffs. The agricultural South with its foreign commerce wanted none. But the primary issue was that of slavery. Since the Northwest Ordinance of 1787, slave and free states had been admitted to the Union in pairs. Eleven slave states balanced eleven free states. Missouri's application for statehood in 1819 just after Alabama had been admitted as a slave state threatened to upset this balance. Northerners objected to a slave Missouri. The ensuing debates dominated Congress. Adams voiced no public views on this thorny issue, but privately he expressed the thought that "never since human sentiments and human conduct were influenced by human speech was there a theme for eloquence like the free side of this question now before Congress of this Union. By what fatality does it happen that all the most eloquent orators of the body are on its slavish side? There is a great mass of cool judgment and plain sense on the side of freedom and humanity, but the ardent spirits and passions are on the side of oppression. Oh, if but one man could arise with a genius capable of comprehending, a heart capable of supporting, and an utterance capable of communicating those eternal truths that belong to this question, to lay bare in all its nakedness that outrage upon the goodness of God, human slavery."

Meanwhile, the district of Maine had separated from Massachusetts to seek admission to the Union. This gave the necessary leeway for the Missouri Compromise by which Maine would be admitted as a free and Missouri as a slave state, but slavery would be prohibited "forever" elsewhere in the Louisiana Purchase above the 36°30' parallel, Missouri's southern border. Adams took no active part in the compromise, yet the whole question shaped his political thought. He favored the compromise as the best that could be obtained while keeping the Union intact. However, he thought that "if the Union must be dissolved, slavery is precisely the question upon which it ought to break. For the present, however, this contest is laid asleep."

The relatively tranquil course of the Monroe administration was not reflected in the State Department. Adams's problems surrounded him, plagued him on all sides. The British government showed no signs of easing restrictions on West Indian trade. France was making ridiculously exaggerated claims against the United States and refused to settle reasonable ones. Portugal had its own claims, while lack of any military aid from the United States caused growing resentment among the evolving South American nations.

Overshadowing all other burdens of office for the Secretary of State was Spain's failure to ratify his treaty. Political disorder in Spain had clouded the prospect of ratification. When a new Spanish envoy, Don Francisco Vives, arrived without a treaty, Adams advised Monroe to occupy Florida. The President objected that this might bring on a war with Spain. Adams assured him that Florida could be occupied without risk and that in his opinion no other course could be taken with honor. The Secretary then wrote a sharp note to Vives expressing his surprise that the Spanish minister was not the bearer of ratification. Monroe, in deference to the political situation in Spain, recommended that any action be postponed until the next session of Congress.

So burdened by affairs was Adams in the summer of 1820 that he could not make his annual visit to Quincy. Problems with Spain, the coming census, and his projected report on weights and measures consumed all his days and most of his nights. He took to rising at three in the morning, and still the day was too short for him. The census was then one of the responsibilities of the State Department, and it fell to Adams to make preparations for the fourth census, in which much more information was being asked than in the previous three. As for his report on weights and measures, he had for the last three years devoted every hour he could spare to it. He had greatly admired the French metric system originating in the Revolution, and he hoped that it would be adopted as a model everywhere. He thought if he could persuade France, Great Britain, and the United States to agree on a single system, the other principal nations would follow suit.

The presidential election of that autumn was tranquil to the point of indifference. There was no party to oppose Monroe. In the Electoral College, however, New Hampshire's William Plumer cast a lone vote for John Quincy Adams, since he disapproved of Monroe, whose failure to balance the budget had led to a $3 million increase in the national debt. Adams was surprised and dismayed at his solitary vote because it implied disapprobation of an administration he considered basically intelligent, honest, and patriotic.

A month before Monroe's second inaugural the belated Spanish treaty arrived, at last ratified. That very same day Adams submitted his *Report on Weights and Measures*. Expanding its theme to include the philosophy, ethics, and political economy of the age of mercantilism, it would prove the most important literary accomplishment of John Quincy's life, and it met with universal approval. Old John Adams expressed his admiration but wrote that at his age its mass of historical, metaphysical, and political data was too overwhelming to read.

By 1822 it was obvious that before long all South America, from Mexico to Peru, if left to itself would break free from Spain. But there were disturbing signs that European nations were preparing to intervene to restore the old order. Monroe sent a special message to Congress declaring that Colombia, Chile, Peru, Mexico, and Río de la Plata (Argentina) had achieved such success in their revolt against Spain that they deserved to be recognized. In regard to Spain the President promised his country's perfect neutrality, however, if the struggle continued. To the protest of the Spanish minister, Secretary Adams replied that the United States felt obliged to recognize the independence of these countries, the recognition being merely an acknowledgment of existing facts that in no way hindered Spain from trying to recover the colonies. Spain, Adams thought to himself, resembled a man in a nightmare trying to raise his arm but unable to stir a muscle.

The Secretary of State had drawn up instructions for the new ministers to the South American countries with great skill, setting the tone of future political and commercial relations. Nevertheless, he was dubious about the nature of the Southern Hemisphere revolutions, wondering whether military dictators might not control the new states, whether the Pope and his cardinals might not inhibit the freedom of action of those emergent but still Catholic countries. Clay in a speech at Lexington had recently expressed the wish that all the New World nations would participate in a vast American system of improvements and commercial exchange. Adams was not quite ready for that, but he did think that the emancipation of the South American continent would open up a prospect of prosperity for all mankind in which the Western Hemisphere would take the lead.

The Russian Czar in his ukase of 1821 had ordered the closing of the Northwest Territory from Russian Alaska as far south as Vancouver Island. Adams opposed any such edict as presumption. He was willing to have the whole West Coast kept open for all commerce indefinitely. Nevertheless he insisted that the American continents were no longer open to European colonial establishment. Here, several years in advance, was the nucleus of the Monroe Doctrine.

In 1823 French troops invaded Spain in support of the capricious and incapable Ferdinand VII who had been a virtual prisoner of his own military for the previous three years. George Canning, Castlereagh's successor as England's foreign secretary, feared that France or the Holy Alliance might now attempt to reconquer the South American colonies that had been Spain's chief source of revenue and that had become one of Great Britain's most profitable trading areas. Canning threatened France with war while at the same time pointing out that his country had not formally recognized the former Spanish provinces and intended neither to appropriate them nor to tolerate any such attempt by France. Adams feared that one result of the French occupation of Spain might be that still-Spanish Cuba and Puerto Rico would be ceded to another European power, and he concluded that from their strategic location the United States on geographical, commercial, political, and even moral grounds had the right to annex them.

Concerned by the maneuverings of the Holy Alliance partners, Adams wrote at length to Richard Rush in London. From a transcendental conception that would later be labeled Manifest Destiny, Adams saw the "finger of nature" directing that the United States should establish all future settlements on the Northwest's Pacific coast. He instructed Rush to propose a 50° latitude boundary between the United States and Britain's North American possessions, but since the line ran on the 49° latitude to the Rockies, he was willing to compromise by continuing that same parallel to the Pacific.

On receiving his instructions Rush sought out Canning. Much to the American's surprise the foreign secretary asked if the United States government would consider going hand in hand in opposing any European incursion in South America. Later Canning set down his views in writing. He thought Spain could never recover her South American colonies, that their recognized independence was only a matter of time and circumstance. England did not want them but could not stand by and see them seized by any other power.

Monroe, who had consulted Jefferson and Madison, was more inclined to the British proposal than the suspicious Adams, who thought that Canning's object in seeking partnership was not to stop the Holy Alliance but to prevent the United States from acquiring some of the former Spanish-American possessions. With Cuba in mind, he was not prepared to give any such pledge. There was indeed the possibility that the Holy Alliance might invade the hemisphere, Russia taking California, Peru, and Chile; France, Buenos Aires; while Cuba would be left for Great Britain. Where would the United States be then? Adams wanted to know. Monroe suggested that if the Holy Alliance moved against South America, Britannia with her rule of the waves would defeat them. South America would then fall under British protection. Adams replied that to avoid this it was up to the United States to act quickly. He was willing to accept British naval support only where it was to the two countries' mutual interest.

From these debates and cabinet discussions the Monroe Doctrine evolved. In Monroe's first version, based on a paper given him by Adams, he had spoken out against the French incursion into Spain. Adams advocated strong protests against European interference in the Western Hemisphere, but he wanted it made equally clear that what happened in Europe was of no concern to the United States.

The Monroe Doctrine in its final form was made public in December, 1823, in Monroe's seventh annual message to Congress. In it he set forth Adams's noncolonization principle, declaring that the American continents were "henceforth not to be considered as subject for future colonization by any European powers. With the existing colonies or dependencies of any European power the United States had not interfered and did not intend to interfere."

But, he added, his country "could not view any interposition for the purpose of oppressing them, or in controlling in any other manner their destiny, by any European power, in any other light than as the manifestation of an unfriendly gesture towards the United States." The message was a bold warning to the members of the Holy Alliance, and Adams admitted that it might mean war. Nevertheless he declined to cooperate with the British because of their refusal, out of deference to the Holy Alliance, to recognize formally any South American country. Basically he did not want any cooperative venture with a land he so distrusted.

Though the Monroe Doctrine was the President's responsibility, most of the credit for it must go to his Secretary of State. The noncolonization principle was Adams's own. "That this principle . . . was disagreeable to all the principal European sovereigns I well knew," he admitted with a certain smugness, "and that those of Great Britain, France and Russia had explicitly expressed their dissent from it, notwithstanding which, I adhered to it."

Monroe's election had marked the end of the Virginia dynasty that, with the exception of John Adams's single term, had occupied the presidency since Washington's inauguration. During those years a congressional caucus of the leading party had nominated the President's choice as his successor and this had been ratified by the electors, most of whom had been chosen by their state legislatures. Now in the Era of Good Feelings, the system itself had broken down. No longer did parties contend for power, nor was there even the continuity of a Virginian succession. Party candidates had given way to individuals with their partisans. Seventeen candidates looked hopefully to the 1824 election, though by the middle of Monroe's second term they had been whittled down to five: John Quincy Adams, Henry Clay, John Calhoun, William Crawford, and Andrew Jackson. Monroe made no effort to pick his successor. Yet many thought that the President would in the end continue the tradition of endorsing his Secretary of State, and

Adams's opponents made every effort to prevent this. Ambitious as he was to become President, both for himself and for his family, Adams felt the office should come to the man. He looked on the eagerness of the other candidates with self-righteous contempt. "Do they call it aristocratic hauteur and learned arrogance?" he asked rhetorically. "Why, so be it, my worthy friends and approved good masters. It is not cringing servility, nor insatiate opportunity." His detached attitude he labeled the Macbeth Policy: "If chance will have me King; why, chance may crown me./Without my stir." Yet even Adams would eventually find it impossible to keep so tight a checkrein on his ambitions. "To suffer without feeling is not in human nature," he admitted in his diary; "and when I consider that to me alone, of all the candidates before the nation, failure of success would be equivalent to a vote of censure upon my past service, I cannot dissemble to myself that I have more at stake upon the result than any other individual in the Union."

From the perspective of Monticello Jefferson saw the choice as between Crawford and Adams, and he favored the party man Crawford. For Adams the deviously ambitious Crawford was the one candidate he most disliked and distrusted. By the summer of 1823 he saw little hope in his own candidacy. Of the others, he favored Jackson, whom he considered strong and meritorious, a President who would administer the government with integrity and disinterestedness, free from all bargains, compromises, coalitions, or corruptions. Adams had met Jackson during the Spanish negotiations and shortly after the treaty was signed had him to dinner. As further evidence of his high opinion of the impetuous general, he and Louisa gave a dinner and ball in January, 1824, to honor him on the anniversary of the Battle of New Orleans. The ball was one of the great social events of the year. Adams invited all the members of Congress except two "whose personal deportment to me has been such that I could not invite them." When

Jackson arrived resplendent in his general's uniform, Louisa took his arm and led him to the head of the table where he gallantly drank to her health.

Louisa bore up to the demands of Washington society more easily than did her husband. The burden of entertaining fell on her, and she blamed him because he never encouraged her. She held regular Tuesday socials, attended by fifty to a hundred guests, that sometimes included music and dancing. Occasionally the Adamses gave great balls, opening up their Washington house to several hundred persons. John Quincy worried continually whether enough guests would show up, whether they would have a good time, whether the affair would be a failure. Louisa was always gracious and at ease. However, in the preparations for the Jackson ball she exhausted herself, and for some time afterward she remained in seclusion, a semi-invalid. The thought of her husband's thin chances in the coming election did not disturb her. She considered that in his eight years as Secretary of State he had served his country better than anyone else. If he was not elected it would be a disgrace for the country, not for him. She dreaded the election year. Young John, now serving as his father's secretary under rather dubious circumstances, thought that John Quincy was facing the forthcoming election with amazing coolness. A poorish student at Harvard, John had seemed at last ready to graduate in 1823 when he and the entire senior class were expelled for rioting and insubordination. John Quincy tried in vain to straighten matters out with the college authorities. But not for another half century would the members of the class of 1823 receive their degrees, and then for the most part posthumously.

Adams's high hopes for his boys did not seem to be coming to very much. George, who as a promising Harvard undergraduate had beat out young Ralph Waldo Emerson for the Boylston Prize, was now eccentric, a hypochondriac, a drifter. After breaking his arm in the spring of 1823, he became convinced that he would never recover. When he finally did, he began in a desultory way to read law in Daniel Webster's office. John had been a wild young man at Cambridge with scant interest in his studies. Charlie, who was two years younger than most of his classmates when he entered Harvard, did not find the college to his taste. He stood near the bottom of his class and wanted to leave. His father insisted that he at least finish his freshman year. "If I must give up all expectation of success or distinction for you in this life," John Quincy wrote him, "preserve me from the harrowing thought of your perdition in the next!"

The summer of 1824 brought on a turbulence of presidential candidates in an atmosphere of partisan virulence. Rumors abounded. As support for Jackson, "the man of the people," swelled in the South and the West, there was casual talk of a Jackson-Adams ticket: "John Quincy Adams, who can write, and Andrew Jackson, who can fight." Crawford's health was precarious, though his supporters tried to conceal the fact. He remained secluded, almost blind after suffering what may have been stroke but was more probably an overdose of lobelia for his erysipelas. Rumor had it that he was very sick. Contrary rumors predicted that the forces of Clay and Adams would combine. Clay complained that "it seems as if every liar and calumniator in the country was at work day and night to destroy my character." He was convinced that no one would win a majority in the Electoral College.

That did indeed seem the most likely outcome. Adams as the only nonslaveholder among the candidates had the solid if unenthusiastic support of New England and probably New York. Crawford kept his hold on the South. Clay had the West, though Jackson was making inroads on both him and Crawford. When one of Calhoun's chief lieutenants defected to Jackson, Calhoun dropped out of the race, to remain the uncontested choice for Vice President.

Wearied of the Washington weather and the political distemper,

Adams left the State Department to spend September in Quincy. It was no longer a relaxing environment. Thomas Adams, living under his father's roof with his six children, had taken to drink. Periodically he disappeared, returning to behave like a "brute in his manners and a bully in his family," according to his nephew Charles. Sometimes the seventeen-year-old nephew had to sit up all night listening to his uncle's drunken ravings. Finally Charlie appealed to his grandfather, who told him stoically that this affliction was necessary to check their pride. If all the Adamses had been distinguished they would have been crushed by the envious, but now the world would pity them and its pity would destroy envy.

With the arrival of John Quincy and Louisa in Quincy, family tensions increased. George was afraid of his father, resentful of his mother. Charlie complained that his father, whom he referred to as Monsieur, failed to understand him. Next year, he reflected, "Monsieur may be driving about in the wind, scarcely knowing his future home." The same thought troubled John Quincy, who fell to wondering how he should fill his days after his probable defeat. He had bought a flour and meal concern in Washington and hoped the income from that would bring him enough to meet his general expenses. Long ago he had given up any thought of returning to his law practice. Now he would retire to his books and his thoughts.

The autumn elections ran from October 29 to November 22 as the twenty-four states individually chose their electors. The results confirmed Clay's earlier prediction. Jackson, who had received about 42 percent of the popular vote, won 99 votes in the Electoral College, to Adams's 84, Crawford's 41, and Clay's 37. Since no candidate had a majority, the names of the three highest were sent to the House of Representatives.

In the House Jackson controlled eleven states—two short of the necessary majority—while Adams held the pledges of seven, leaving Crawford and Clay with three each. Adams now had the choice of following the "will of the people" and ceding his votes to Jackson, or maneuvering to have himself elected a minority President. Whatever his reasons, he chose the latter way. To win he would need not only the support of Clay's three states but also three more. Clay confided to friends that since Crawford was ailing and Jackson was a soldier, Adams seemed a lesser evil. He finally promised to support the New Englander. Later he explained that he had decided on Adams since he could not on principle support a military man. When this news spread, there was talk that Adams had offered Clay the post of Secretary of State in return for his support. Adams's voluminous diary is for once silent. Clay was furious at the rumor. But the Jacksonites continued to maintain loudly and bitterly that a "corrupt bargain" had been struck.

The weeks before the election were a period of backstairs bargaining and dealing. Putting aside his Macbeth principle, the austere and withdrawn Adams suddenly blossomed out as a glad-hander, dropping in at boardinghouses and hotels to call on obscure Congressmen whom he scarcely knew to solicit their support. His henchmen, unbeknownst to him, went considerably further in their manipulations. When the balloting at last took place on a snowy February afternoon, he was elected on the first ballot, thirteen states voting for him—Clay's three plus three more that somehow had been lured from Jackson. In the privacy of his diary Adams admitted that the election had not taken place in "a manner satisfactory to pride or just desire; not by unequivocal suffrages of a majority of the people; with perhaps two-thirds of the whole people adverse to the actual result."

Monroe gave his last levee that evening. Lafayette, then making an extended triumphal tour of the United States, was present as the nation's guest. President-elect Adams and Vice President-elect Calhoun also attended, as did President-maker Clay. But all eyes fastened on the formidably erect figure of General Jackson making his way through the crowd with a lady on his arm. When he came face to face with Adams, he hesitated, then with self-contained courtesy extended his left hand. "How do you do, Mr. Adams?" he said. "I give you my left hand, for the right, you see, is devoted to the fair; I hope you are very well, sir." Adams could merely muster: "Very well, sir. I hope General Jackson is well."

Next day Daniel Webster and his congressional notification committee waited on Adams to inform him officially that on March 4 he would be the next President of the United States. As the President-elect listened to Webster's sonorous voice, he trembled and the sweat rolled down his face. Barely able to control his voice, he read them a prepared acceptance speech. After they had gone he wrote his father, asking for his "blessing and prayers." Old John replied: "the multitude of my thought and the intensity of my feelings are too much for a mind like mine, in its ninetieth year."

The incoming President had determined to retain Monroe's cabinet wherever possible. But Crawford, whom Monroe had once threatened with a pair of fire tongs, declined to serve. Whatever Adams may have discussed with Clay, he now explained to Monroe that he had decided to make the Kentuckian Secretary of State. His talents and services had made him worthy of the position, in Adams's opinion, and beyond that an appointment was due the West for its support in the election. Clay was in a dilemma. He wanted the State Department both for itself and for its key place in the succession. Yet if he accepted, he would be labeled an intriguer; and if he declined, he would be called a coward. Better, he decided, the intriguer label. When Jackson heard of Clay's acceptance, he burst out furiously: "So you see the *Judas* of the West has closed the contract and will receive the thirty pieces of silver! His end will be the same. Was ever such a bare-faced corruption?" Later he wrote more calmly that John Quincy Adams was not the "virtuous, able and honest man" he had supposed him to be. From that moment Old Hickory severed all relations with the two men who he believed had treacherously defeated him. For the next four years Adams and Clay would be hounded by the "corrupt bargain" accusation.

On the day of his inauguration Adams recorded in his diary that "after two successive sleepless nights, I entered upon this day with a supplication to Heaven, first for my country; secondly for myself and for those connected with my good name and fortunes. . . ." As he commenced his Inaugural Address he faltered, but regained his composure as he went along. The most noteworthy point in his address was his call for federal sponsoring of internal improvements. All too aware of his minority status, he concluded: "Less possessed of your confidence in advance than any of my predecessors, I am deeply conscious of the prospect that I shall stand more and oftener in need of your indulgence." Then he took the oath from Chief Justice John Marshall, his hand resting on a "volume of the laws."

Once installed as Secretary of State, Clay advised Adams to remove his political enemies from office at once. Adams refused. Such a purging by each new administration, he objected, would make the government a scramble for office. He told Clay he had decided as a matter of policy to renominate all those against whom there was no complaint, whatever their attitude toward him.

For the second time an Adams family had come to occupy the White House. Louisa disliked the grandiose presidential mansion with its vast state rooms, its piecemeal furniture, and its shabby living quarters. She thought it did not have the comforts "of any private mechanics family." Less sensitive to his environment than his wife, Adams soon adapted himself to the White House routine, although he found the tumult of visitors, official and otherwise, irritating and taxing to the limit of his endurance. In his diary he described his existence as more regular than at any earlier period. "It is established by custom that the President of the United States goes not abroad into any private companies; and to this usage I conform. I am, therefore, compelled to take my exercise, if at all, in the morning before breakfast. I rise usually between five and six—that is, at this time of year, from an hour and a half to two hours before the sun. I walk by the light of moon or stars, or none, about four miles, usually returning here in time to see the sun rise from the eastern chamber of the House. I then make my fire, and read three chapters of the Bible, with Scott's and Hewlett's Commentaries. Read papers till nine. Breakfast, and from nine to five P.M. receive a succession of visitors, sometimes without intermission—very seldom with an interval of half an hour—never such as to enable me to undertake any business requiring attention. From five to half-past six we dine; after which I pass about four hours in my chamber alone, writing in this diary, or reading papers upon some public business—excepting when occasionally interrupted by a visitor. Between eleven and twelve I retire to bed, to rise again at five or six the next morning."

As Secretary of State one of his great joys in the warm weather had been to swim naked in the Potomac, and as President he continued his early morning dips, usually with John and his valet Antoine. One morning, however, while they were crossing the river in a canoe a squall upset them, and the President, still in his clothes, was barely able to make the shore. Then a week later while he was swimming, a party of draggers recovered the body of a man who had been drowned the night before. Looking at the corpse, Adams decided that he had better give up his morning swim.

Charles was to graduate from Harvard in June but his low academic standing excluded him from any part in the commencement exercises and he begged his father to let him come to Washington before then. His father replied sourly that Charles would do well to be as far away from Cambridge as possible on that inglorious day and added that it was about time he decided on a profession. Louisa wrote with a mother's warmheartedness, urging her boy to come as soon as possible since Lafayette was about to pay them a visit and she wanted Charles's help in entertaining him and his son, George Washington Lafayette.

The Frenchman's stay turned out to be a trial for all the Adamses. John and Charlie had to give up their rooms to the Lafayettes, Charlie found George Washington dull and Lafayette himself irritating. The Revolutionary hero preferred talking to listening. "Tired of him," Charlie wrote to his grandfather, adding that "you may think these sentiments very degenerate, my dear grandfather, in a descendant of yours, but I advise you, we of the third generation look with more impartial eyes on *all* the actors of the revolution, and are apt to think that we have overpaid one hero."

Later in the summer Adams returned to Quincy to a jubilant reception. Crowds gathered to applaud wherever he passed. Nor did he quite sense the thin crust of his popularity. At Quincy he was preoccupied again with his boys. Charles he decided to educate in the law. George distressed him most, a restless and unhappy young man, without aim or purpose. Louisa was ill during most of the journey back to Washington. The renewed prospect of the bleak, badly furnished President's House depressed her, and she was convinced she could never feel at home there.

In December Adams delivered his first State of the Union message to Congress. For a minority President it was a singular address, a reversion to Federalism in its demand for a strong national government. "Liberty is power," he told the legislators, and he warned them of being "palsied by the will of our constituents." He asked for an enlarged system of internal improvements to be paid for by surplus revenues; a network of national highways and canals to bind all sections of the country together; a Department of the Interior to assist in conserving and developing the public domain; exploration of the Pacific Northwest; a national university, such as Washington had recommended; a national observatory to emulate the many European "lighthouses of the skies"; a naval academy; a uniform militia law; a national bankruptcy law; improved patent laws; and a standard system of weights and measures.

Congress turned a deaf ear. Many of his listeners resented his references to the advances made by European countries, and his enemies prepared to warm up the old accusations of the Adams family weakness for monarchies. His demand for internal improvements came at a time when Southerners were beginning to realize the dangers to their "peculiar institution" from increasing national control. Jefferson from his retirement thought that a number of the Adams proposals were unconstitutional. The phrase "lighthouses of the skies" became a derisive by-word, one that his enemies were never to let him forget.

On New Year's Day, 1826, several thousand persons attended Adams's first presidential open house. Both he and Louisa thought the ensuing winter much pleasanter and quieter than they had expected. Yet the outward calm of peace and prosperity was deceiving. Adams stood alone. He had no one he could count on in the House or Senate, and Congress paid no heed to his program. Under the leadership of the devious New York Senator Martin Van Buren, the "Little Magician," the followers of Jackson and Crawford were combining against him in what would later become the Democratic party. Van Buren, a diminutive man, dandified in dress and manner, was chief of the Tammany-based Albany Regency that through its political patronage dominated New York State. Deftly, confidently, he plotted the destruction of Adams through a combination of Southern planters and the "Plain Republicans of the North."

The first active opposition to the President took shape during the congressional debates over his plan to send United States representatives to a Panama mission intended to unite all South

America. Clay urged his country's full cooperation. Adams's eloquent appeal for the United States to support the mission was seen by his enemies as an opportunity to attack him. Van Buren and his Senate associates held up the ratification of the American representatives. Calhoun was particularly incensed at the thought of American participation in a conference where suppression of the slave trade was to be discussed and where Haiti—owing its very existence to a slave revolt—would be represented by a black man. But the most savage and continuing attacks on Adams came from the gaunt, mad John Randolph of Roanoke, who liked to stride into the Senate chamber swinging a riding crop and followed by a small black boy carrying a jug of porter. In one vitriolic speech denouncing Adams and the Panama mission he spoke for six hours in his high-pitched eunuch's voice, rambling, vituperative, at one point referring to Adams and Clay as "the combination unheard of 'til then, of the puritan with the blackleg." Calhoun, presiding over the Senate and increasingly alienated from Adams, made no effort to curb or stop Randolph's outrageous language. Adams never forgave his former friend. Seething at the term "blackleg," Clay challenged Randolph to a duel. The two met on the far side of the Potomac and exchanged shots twice, although the only damage was a bullet hole in Randolph's shirttail.

As spring moved toward summer Adams looked forward more than ever to his Quincy respite. Before he left he received the cheering news that George had just been elected to the Massachusetts legislature. He wrote to congratulate his son, but was unable to avoid a homily on early rising and the avoidance of procrastination. Late in May he heard from the Quincy family doctor that his father was failing fast and wanted to see his son and his daughter-in-law.

Then on July 8 he received the news that his father was dying, and early next morning he left with John for Quincy. But by midday a messenger reached him on the road to tell him that the old ex-President was dead. It was something for which he had long prepared himself, and he was more struck by the conjunction with Jefferson's death than overcome with grief. "The time, the manner, the coincidence with the decease of Jefferson, are visible and palpable marks of Divine favor," he wrote on reaching New York. "For myself, all that I dare ask is, that I may live the remnant of my days in a manner worthy of him from whom I came, and, at the appointed hour of my Maker, die as my father has died, in peace with God and man." It was his fifty-ninth birthday. In Washington, Charles with his mother and her nieces celebrated the day by drinking champagne. Charlie thought their merry little party might have looked dreadful to prudish busybodies, but his grandfather had been very old and failing, and no one, he thought, could too much regret his death.

When John Quincy belatedly arrived home everything seemed the same until he entered his father's bedroom. Then suddenly he was overwhelmed by a sense of loss, of helpless anguish at the passage of time. "That moment was inexpressively painful," he wrote in his diary, "and struck me as if it had been an arrow to the heart. My father and mother have departed. The charm which has always made this house to me an abode of enchantment is dissolved; and yet my attachment to it, and to the whole region round, is stronger than I ever felt it before. I feel it is time for me to begin to set my house in order, and to prepare for the churchyard myself."

Under John Adams's will John Quincy was left the house and about ninety-three acres around it on payment of $10,000 to the other heirs. Here, he determined, was to be his place of retirement that he had long planned, where he could pursue agriculture, letters, and a study of the past. Louisa wrote advising him not to burden himself with too much land, pointing out that this had been the ruin of the Jefferson family. She also warned him against trying to settle the estate himself since he could not do justice both to his own children and to jealous relatives. He in turn advised her not to come to Quincy, and she was more than glad to take his advice since she dreaded family quarrels over the estate settlement.

Several months after his father's death, John Quincy joined his ancestral church, of which he had never been a member even though he attended regularly. But in deciding to make Quincy his home, he determined to make a public profession of faith, for, however rooted in doubt, his faith endured. Each day he read the Bible. Each evening he repeated the child's prayer that his mother had taught him from the New England primer. As a young man he had written of God that "of Him, except that He exists, we know nothing, and consequently our knowledge is nothing." He believed in personal immortality, yet found the idea incomprehensible. He believed in the New Testament's "unparalleled conceptions of the nature of God," but he did not believe in miracles. Of the doctrinal questions between Unitarians and Trinitarians, he confessed that he had no precise belief and no real understanding. Nevertheless, on October 1, 1826, he took communion for the first time.

Political news from Washington indicated that he had little or no hope of re-election in 1828. Apparently reconciled to that bitter fact, he made his preparations for retirement. As the head of the family, he expressed the hope that his sons would follow useful professions and live in or near Quincy so that he could enjoy their constant company in his last years.

He returned to Washington to find renewed complications with England, but was pleased at least to learn that the British government had agreed to pay $1,204,960 in claims for slaves carried away in the War of 1812. The questions of the Canadian boundaries and the British ban on American trade with the West Indies remained. Adams wanted Congress to pass a retaliatory act, but Van Buren stood the Adams bill on its head. Gallatin, on a special mission to England, found his task of reconciling differences most laborious. Adams had told him to insist on the forty-ninth parallel as the final northwestern boundary between the United States and British North America. To Gallatin, as to Jefferson, Monroe, Crawford, Clay, and Madison, the Oregon region was a desert not worth arguing about, although the British considered it essential to the operations of the Hudson's Bay Company. Adams valued it, as he did every inch of what he considered American soil.

At about this time Adams learned that his life was being threatened by a cashiered assistant surgeon in the navy, a Dr. George Todson, who had vainly asked the President to intervene in his courtmartial. In that more casual era nothing was done either to apprehend Todson or to guard Adams. The President continued his solitary early morning walks, merely observing that his life was in the hands of a higher power. He and Todson actually confronted each other, Adams telling the disgruntled doctor that he could not reverse the courtmartial but that he was willing to consider the threat against his life as a momentary alienation of the mind. From that point on, the would-be assassin became a suppliant. Several times he came to the White House asking for money. Once Adams gave him $47 to aid him in his legal expense. When a vessel returning to Africa with 112 Negroes illegally imported into the United States stood in need of a ship's surgeon, the President recommended Todson. In their last interview Adams warned the displaced doctor that his future would depend on his good conduct, and when Todson finally returned from Africa apparently rehabilitated, the President endeavored to send him to a company of displaced Indians.

Although Adams considered Indians an inferior species, he deplored their infamous treatment at the hands of the whites. All his attempts, however, to guarantee their rights and to protect their territory in the South and West were frustrated by Congress. In spite of federal law Georgia's governor was ousting the Creeks from their lands in his state, and when they resisted he ordered out the state militia. Clay advised sending in federal troops as a countermeasure. Adams thought Congress should act, and sent a message to that effect. But before any action could be taken the Creeks had been intimidated into signing a treaty renouncing all their claims.

Congress continued to turn a deaf ear to its nonpolitical President. By the time it adjourned in March none of the national measures Adams had asked for had been enacted. Nor did the opposition let the "corrupt bargain" charge drop, a subject so painful to Adams that he could not bear even to mention it. Isolated, depressed, he found the burden of office at times intolerable. His health suffered, he grew listless, phlegmy, weak, and lost so much weight that his last year's clothes hung on him. Sometimes he was so depressed that he wished himself dead. He sought relief and relaxation in planting trees, and noted that he had planted four rows of Pennsylvania walnuts, nine Quincy walnuts, and eight hazelnuts, oppressive though the thought was that he would not live long enough to see them mature.

In July he left for Quincy, and his health and spirits at once improved. He read, swam, fished, planted seedlings, and took trips in and about the Blue Hills. Louisa, who found no lift of spirit in Quincy, went elsewhere on a holiday with John, as she had the year before with Charles. As the summer progressed, politics and affairs of state began to take over even in Quincy. Adams sent for John, who told him on arriving that things looked dark in regard to the next year's election. Despite this the President still declined to consider any attempts at electioneering, and though his supporters urged him to build up a machine organization to oppose the Jacksonites, he refused, even to the point of tolerating his blatantly disloyal postmaster general. Everywhere as the election neared there were signs of rising hostility to him. It seemed as if he had given up the struggle, consoling himself by planting trees and reflecting that his trees would outlast many Presidents.

In the new Congress, meeting in the autumn of 1827, both House and Senate had an antiadministration majority, something that had never before occurred in the United States. The President seemed preparing to leave office. In his message to Congress he avoided controversy, merely sketching out a review of the past political year. He continued to reappoint all officeholders whose terms expired regardless of their attitude toward him, and as if to seal his fate he refused again to consider building up a political machine. With his own career drawing to a close, he turned to his sons, particularly to Charles, on whom he now pinned most of his family hopes. George, despite his seat in the legislature, remained erratic and depressed. Though his father did not know it, he had formed a liaison with Eliza Dolph, a chambermaid at Dr. Welch's. John Quincy's suggestion that keeping a diary was helpful in moments of great agitation was of no great help to his son. John was another disappointment. He had become engaged to Mary Hellen, Louisa's orphan niece, a handsome, flirtatious young lady with whom George had been in love and to whom Charlie had not been insusceptible. They planned an early wedding. John Quincy disapproved of a man marrying before he was self-supporting and gave no encouragement to the young couple. Falling back on Charles he wrote him at least once a week in spite of interruptions (one night as he was writing Charlie he was interrupted ten times). It was a great relaxation and pleasure for the President in his room late at night to shunt aside the cares of office and recall his own bookish past while commenting on Plato, Cicero, Pliny, Voltaire, Rousseau, Pascal, and Madame de Sévigné for his son's enlightenment. That cold young man noted in his diary that his father's letters sounded more and more like sermons.

Without bothering to consult his parents John decided that he would bring his bride to live in the White House. Louisa was dismayed at the news. She sensed that her immature son was being forced into the wedding by the mature and headstrong Mary, noting that he looked as if he had all the cares of the world on his shoulders. The wedding was to take place on February 25 in the Blue Room. George and Charlie both declined to attend. Although John Quincy had refused to speak to his future daughter-in-law before the wedding, afterward he tried to make the best of the situation, forwarding Charlie a piece of the wedding cake and suggesting that he send the couple his best wishes.

The election year promised to be a bitter one. Members of Congress harassed the President, probing into such remote incidents as his vote on the Louisiana Purchase and his handling of the fishery question at Ghent. Russell Jarvis, a frustrated office seeker and former Adams supporter turned sour, revived the scurrilous story in the antiadministration Washington *Telegraph* that Adams as minister to Russia had made use of "a beautiful girl to seduce the passions of the Emperor Alexander and sway him to political purposes." In spite of this, Jarvis appeared at a public reception at the White House. Seeing him, John remarked loudly within his hearing that "*there* is a man who, if he had any idea of propriety, ought not to show his face in this house." Jarvis stalked out and subsequently sent a challenging note to young Adams, who admitted he had made the remark but refused to give a written reply. A few days later John, while carrying official papers of his father's, encountered Jarvis in the rotunda of the Capitol. Jarvis tweaked John's nose, and Adams struck back with his cane. Bystanders then separated them. As a result of this set-to, the President sent a message to Congress stating that his private secretary had been assaulted while on public business within the Capitol, and he asked whether any further laws or regulations might be necessary to insure the security of official messengers between the President and Congress. He added that no consequence should be attached to the private relationship between himself and his secretary. Congress with no great enthusiasm held a hearing and summoned witnesses. Finally a bare majority voted to censure Jarvis, not so

much because of the insult to the President's messenger but because of Jarvis's contempt for the congressional sanctuary.

Just before the session ended for the summer, Congress passed
the tariff law known as the Tariff of Abominations. Piloted by the
wily Van Buren, it was, through its fantastic schedules, designed
to ruin Adams. If he signed it, the South would damn him as a
protectionist. If he did not, the North would condemn him as a
traitor. He finally signed it, since he held himself obliged to sign
bills that had been constitutionally passed, but he told Charlie that
the bill would burden rather than protect New England. He saw a
majority in both House and Senate animated by a common malice
against him. With time running out for the administration, many
of its officials were preparing to resign. Adams watched their preparations with sour, silent contempt. In his sixty-first year he was
increasingly aware of his own physical decline. His memory was
falling off. Feeling the need for exercise, he took up swimming
again. But where formerly he used to swim an hour or two in the
Potomac, now he could swim only fifteen minutes to half an hour.
Instead of long walks, he rode horseback. Yet he still visited his
seedlings in their pots each morning before breakfast and at the
end of the day, and he found his escape in books on botany.

Before the searing July weather struck Washington he returned
to Massachusetts, this time with John. Again Louisa did not go,
refusing to endure the bickering atmosphere of Quincy. Any
thought of retiring there chilled her. She had long wanted her own
house apart from the Adams tribe, cherishing the thought for the
last decade only to have it end in disappointment. Now she saw
herself destined to complete her days in that comfortless Old House
of bitter memories.

The Quincy air did not this time revive Adams as he had hoped.
His journey had left him in a state of lassitude he had never before
experienced. Charlie, the son from whom he had come to expect
the most, was now adding to his troubles. The boy, almost of age

and determined to marry, asked his father how much of an allowance he could then count on. After an involved statement of his own shaded prospects, John Quincy told his son the present allowance would continue. When Charlie insisted that it was not enough, Adams rebuked him bluntly. From then on father and son remained cool and stiff toward one another. On Charles's twenty-first birthday Adams gave him $1,000 and some time later two shares in the Middlesex Canal Company (worth about $500). Charlie remained unpropitiated. The rebuff still burned "like a rankling sore." He resolved to continue to respect his father and to fulfill his duties, though with a less willing heart.

Louisa was suddenly taken ill with erysipelas and her husband cut short his stay in Quincy to return to Washington early in September. Involving himself in his executive duties to the exclusion of everything else, he refused to campaign for the coming election. For all his restraint, the presidential contest was a vicious one, fought on personalities and regional prejudices rather than issues. "Clay is managing Adams's campaign," the Jacksonian editor of the New Hampshire *Patriot* wrote, "not like a statesman of the Cabinet but like a shyster, pettifogging in a bastard suit before a country squire." The Adamsites' most successful propaganda effort was the Coffin Handbill, a lurid broadside edged with coffin silhouettes recounting Jackson's "Bloody Deeds" of having had six militiamen shot as deserters in the War of 1812. Such accusations fell within the accepted limits of political abuse, but Adams's supporters went beyond those limits when they attacked the general's wife—the plump, unassuming pipe-smoking Rachel, with whom Jackson had eloped after her wretched first marriage had ended in divorce. Now, thirty-seven years later, he was accused of cohabiting with her before their marriage. "Ought a convicted adulteress and her paramour husband to be placed in the highest offices of this free and Christian land?" one Adams pamphlet asked rhetorically. Though cut to the quick by such calumnies, Jackson refused

to countenance any retaliation in kind. "I never war against fe-
males," he told his supporters, "and it is only the base and cow-
ardly that do." Privately he regretted that his position as
presidential candidate kept him from cowhiding the pamphlet's
author. Adams took no part in the slander, but neither did he make
any move to repudiate the slanders. To the Adamsites Jackson was
an adulterer, a gamester, a cockfighter, a bigamist, a slave dealer,
a drunkard, a murderer, a thief, and a liar. Jackson's supporters in
turn accused Adams of padding his expense accounts, of adopting
European manners and habits, and of prescribing gaudy uniforms
for American diplomats. But what hurt Adams as much as Rachel's
maligners did Jackson was the never-stilled taunt of "corrupt bargain."

From the single chrysalis of Jefferson's Democratic-
Republicans two fledgling parties had emerged. Under Van Buren's
astute guidance the "Friends of General Jackson"—organized in
every city, village, and hamlet in the nation—had become the
Democratic party with its chief support in the South and West. The
Clay-Adams faction, forming the National Republicans, drew its
support from the North. There was a certain irony in two slaveholding planters of the South, Jackson and Calhoun, opposing Adams and his vice-presidential running mate, Richard Rush, in the
name of the common man. Jackson was far wealthier than Adams.
Yet he had come to believe in his own image of Old Hickory, the
son of the people, as opposed to the aristocratic Duke of Braintree.
In his own eyes and those of his supporters, Jackson was the man
of the heart as opposed to the man of the head. Adams, an
eighteenth-century man in the tradition of Locke and the Age of
Reason, represented the last of the scholarly Presidents. Jackson
brought the Romantic Movement into politics, replacing reason
and proportion with energy and feeling. Through his violent and
impulsive person he projected the age's leading ideas: that the
unchecked development of the individual was paramount; that for-

mal training and traditional learning were unnecessary; that thought should be subordinate to action.

In the 1828 election only Delaware and South Carolina still held to the appointing of electors by the legislatures. Balloting in the other states took place during the first week in November. Before the votes were counted, Charlie Adams advised his family to be prepared for defeat. Predictably, the results were regional. New England, however sulkily, supported Adams. Jackson carried the South and West except for Clay's Kentucky. Van Buren managed to swing 20 of New York's 36 electoral votes to Jackson. In the popular voting Jackson had 647,276 votes for Adams's 508,064, but in the Electoral College the vote was overwhelmingly in his favor with 178 to only 83 for the President. "The ruin of our cause," Adams called the final tally, "the ruin of our administration." A generation later his grandson Brooks Adams considered the defeat "the tragedy of our grandfather's life because it injected into his mind the first doubts as to whether there were a God, and whether this life had a purpose."

Outwardly Adams put on a bold front, maintaining even to his wife that he was relieved to lay down the cares of office. She in the following weeks continued to entertain, holding a lavish ball just before Christmas with all the wives of the administration present in new Paris gowns. At the last and most elaborate Adams White House levee she consoled herself with the thought that they were taking their leave with all grace imaginable.

Just before the close of the Adams administration Jackson arrived in Washington, taking rooms at Gadsby's Hotel. His beloved Rachel had died only a few weeks before, and at her funeral he had exclaimed in anguish: "In the presence of this dear saint I can and do forgive my enemies. But those vile wretches who have slandered her must look to God for mercy!" He avoided Adams, refusing to make a courtesy call at the White House. The President informed him that the White House would be ready for his occupancy on Inauguration Day. Jackson thanked him and hoped he would not inconvenience himself.

Before leaving the White House Adams reflected bitterly in his diary: "Posterity will scarcely believe it, but so it is, that this combination against me has been formed, and is now exulting in triumph over me, for the devotion of my life and of all the faculties of my soul to the Union, and to the improvement, physical, moral, and intellectual of my country."

On March 3 he informed Congress that he had no further communications to make, and the session adjourned. He walked back to the White House alone. Later he asked the remaining members of his administration whether he should attend Jackson's inaugural next day. They thought he should not, and he agreed. He did not want to return to Quincy until the weather improved enough for Louisa to travel in comfort. Until then he had rented a substantial house on Meridian Hill. Even as he was making his final preparations for leaving the White House, thousands of Jackson supporters were converging on Washington to see Old Hickory installed as President. Daniel Webster thought he had never before seen such a crowd: "Persons have come five hundred miles to see General Jackson, and they really seem to think that the country has been rescued from some dreadful danger."

In the turbulent aftermath of Jackson's inauguration, while the mob took over the White House, Adams rode alone out to the Rockville Turnpike and back to his new house, full of somber reflections on his future, his resources, and his family expenses. When invited to a farewell dinner for Henry Clay, he replied that it was his intention to bury himself in complete retirement.

Louisa was content in the seclusion of Meridian Hill. She thought that her husband, busying himself with self-made tasks, had never been happier—so little did she understand the man she had married thirty-one years before. The Adamses remained completely apart from official Washington. Adams sought escape from brooding by reading Cicero's *Philippics* and writing fables in flat imitation of La Fontaine. Meridian Hill in the soft spring weather was at least more peaceful than Quincy. The peace proved fleeting. Charlie relayed distressing news of George, who was becoming more and more reclusive and had declined renomination to the legislature because he felt unable to represent his townsmen. Nervous, in bad health, falling into debt, he was living in a hovel and had taken to drink. John Quincy wrote his oldest son sternly. Refusing to face the fact that George was deteriorating mentally as well as physically, he advised him to join the Boston Temperance Society, keep a diary, and memorize certain stanzas from Thompson's "Castle of Indolence," and he sent him $1,000 to pay his debts.

In April of 1829 Charlie wrote his mother that George was going to pieces. Louisa urged her ailing son to come to Washington for a respite until they all returned together to Quincy. Finally John Quincy peremptorily sent for him. George set out from Providence on the steamboat *Benjamin Franklin* for New York. That night he kept complaining that other passengers were trying to break into his stateroom, that the ship's engine was talking to him. Next morning he was missing. His hat was found on the upper deck. Not for several days would his body be recovered.

Adams was so shaken by his son's suicide that the handwriting in his diary became a scrawl. He had never known such grief before. Louisa, completely prostrated, took to her room with a high fever. Charlie, left with the task of going through his brother's papers—the more compromising of which he destroyed—first learned of Eliza Dolph. Knowing her pregnant, George had requested in a letter Charlie found addressed to him that after his debts were paid the balance of his estate be given to her.

In spite of John Quincy's grief, family affairs and financial matters forced themselves on his attention. He was needed urgently back at Quincy. The Old House was growing derelict from lack of repairs, the surrounding acres going to weed. Reaching New York on his way to Massachusetts, he learned that George's body had been found in the water at East Chester some seventeen miles away. There Adams received his son's few personal possessions—his watch, penknife, silver pencil case, seal, pocketbook, and trunk key. Louisa, who had been hoping against hope that her missing son might yet turn up alive, now begged God to relieve her of her life of suffering. George's funeral left his father in an agony of mind. Stifling his doubts, he turned to prayer. One afternoon, as he walked in his sorrow, he saw a rainbow and wondered if it might be a sign of the goodness and mercy of God.

Louisa did not accompany her husband to Quincy, and it was well she did not, for the house was bleak, battered, uninhabited, and almost stripped of furniture. Gradually John Quincy transformed it, bringing in his books, some of which had not been unpacked since they arrived from England in 1817. Eventually he planned to have a stone library adjacent to the house. Meanwhile he had bookshelves built round his bedroom. Books remained his passion, and he took pride in the thought that no private library in the United States could equal his. In making the Old House livable again, he gradually recovered his own self. Paying scant attention to the outside world, he sometimes went days without even reading a newspaper. The sixty-two-year-old Adams wanted only to be useful to his family, and he thought much of his two remaining sons. As an exception to his seclusion, he did accept an appointment to the Harvard Board of Overseers.

Charlie married his Abby in September of 1829. Her father had bought the couple a house in Boston. Louisa did not come on for the wedding but remained in Washington with John, who was looking after the flour mill. Not until the late spring of 1830 did she finally arrive at the Quincy house with John's pregnant wife Mary and small daughter Mary Louisa. Charles, in spite of his parents' wishes, preferred staying in his Boston house to enduring the confusion of Quincy, made even more chaotic by John's arrival in July and Mary's giving birth to another daughter in September.

John Quincy, patriarch in his father's stead, now seemed resigned to a retired life of letters, a study of the past, and botanizing. Only the sharp-minded Charles noted the depression lurking beneath the calm exterior. He tried in vain to persuade his father to take up the long-contemplated life history of John Adams. But after a few negligible attempts John Quincy gave it up. Then the Jacksonian Boston *Courier* suggested that the National Republicans run John Quincy Adams in 1830 as Congressman from Plymouth. The scarcely altruistic editor privately thought this might be a good way of avoiding any future political challenge from an ex-President. Adams paid no heed to the suggestion until the incumbent Congressman, the Reverend Joseph Richardson, called with the same suggestion since he himself had decided to return to his pulpit. Richardson was certain that the district would support Adams overwhelmingly. The only question was whether an ex-President might find a seat in Congress degrading.

Adams replied that no one was degraded by serving in Congress or even as a local selectman. His concerns were his health and his age. Otherwise he was willing to serve if the people wanted him. But he would not solicit their votes. Louisa found the political prospect not at all to her taste. The other Adamses were dismayed. For Charlie it was as if an officer should rejoin the army as an enlisted man. He was humiliated at the thought of such a downward step and told his father so. John Quincy, though he spent a sleepless night in consequence, had made up his mind. As a member of Congress he would again be part of the political world in which he had lived since adolescence. Another revolution might be at hand over such issues as the public lands, the Indians, the tariff, the railroads and canals, the dark Southern threat of nullification. If there was to be a second Revolution, he did not want to miss it. His place was in Washington.

To everyone's surprise Louisa announced that she was staying on in Quincy. For her even the bleakness of a New England winter was preferable to Washington. Her mind and nerves had suffered too much from political intrigue, though she realized that for her husband a family was and always must be secondary to his career. Having accepted the uncontested nomination of the National Republicans, Adams in the election faced a Federalist and a Democrat. Yet in his home district, at least, his prestige was so great that he received three out of every four votes—1,814 to 373 for the Democrat and 279 for the Federalist. After the humiliations of his presidential years he found a large satisfaction in these small figures. "No one knows, and few conceive," he wrote two days later in his diary, "the agony of mind that I have suffered from the time that I was made by circumstances, and not by my own volition, a candidate for the Presidency till I was dismissed from that station by the failure of my re-election. They were feelings to be suppressed; and they were suppressed. . . . This call upon me by the people of the district in which I reside, to represent them in Congress, has been spontaneous. . . . My election as President of the United States was not half so gratifying to my inmost soul. No election or appointment conferred upon me ever gave me so much pleasure. I say this to record my sentiments."

Although the Congress elected in November, 1830, would not meet until December, 1831, business affairs—chiefly the flour and meal business, in which he had already lost $15,000 speculating in futures—brought him back to Washington before Christmas. Louisa, pressed both by her family and by financial considerations, was at the last persuaded to return. They stayed the winter with John and Mary. An observer of the passing show, John Quincy watched with a certain malicious satisfaction the estrangement of Jackson and Calhoun, and the "Eaton malaria"—the scandal caused by Jackson's quixotic championship of Peggy Eaton, the somewhat less than virtuous wife of his Secretary of War. By April when

Adams with his family was again en route to the Quincy "plantation," the entire Jackson cabinet had resigned.

During the summer Charlie's wife Abby had a baby girl, Louisa, and spent several weeks in Quincy convalescing. Charlie found living under the parental roof detestable. His mother seemed to be ill all the time, and Mary's small daughter was a nuisance. Financial as well as personal affairs were in turmoil. As the self-appointed family accountant he told his father that the flour business would ruin him. Instead of becoming angry, John Quincy promised to think over the situation. He had much else to think over that summer. Delegates from the Antimasons—the third party organized in 1826—came to offer him their presidential nomination. Though he was sympathetic to their cause, considering Masonry one of the great political evils of the time, he declined. He would, he informed his constituents, be accountable to no party and no section. Before he left he was toying with the idea of buying the Boston *Patriot* and making Charles the editor. Charlie was pleased with the idea, hoping that his father could then be persuaded to give up politics altogether in favor of editorial and literary work.

As the ex-President-turned-Congressman attended the first session of the Twenty-second Congress, he was prepared for slights, insults, and humiliations. Yet he entered the raffish atmosphere of the House with singular enthusiasm, as if he had put his presidential past behind him. "The forms and proceedings of the House;" he wrote, "—the colossal emblem of the union over the Speaker's chair, the historic Muse at the clock, the echoing pillars of the hall, the tripping Mercuries who bear the resolutions and the amendments between the members and the chair, the calls of ayes and noes; with the different intonations of the answers from the different voices, the gobbling manner of the clerk in reading over the names, the tone of the Speaker in announcing the vote, and the various shades of pleasure and pain in the countenances of the members on hearing it, would form a fine subject for a descriptive poem."

For almost two decades Adams would occupy his seat in Congress. A singularity at first, then a fixture, he would in the end become an object of respect even to his enemies. At the age of sixty-four his noblest years lay ahead of him. His entrance into the House of Representatives preceded by a few weeks the centennial of Washington's birth. For that occasion it had been resolved to transfer Washington's body from Mount Vernon to a tomb under the Capitol. Somehow that symbolic act was linked in Adams's mind with the preservation of the Union, and when the Washington relations refused their permission he wrote gloomily: "I did wish that this resolution might have been carried into execution, but this wish was connected with an imagination that this federative Union was to last for ages. I now disbelieve its duration for twenty years, and doubt its continuance for five."

He had hoped to be on the foreign affairs committee and was disappointed to find himself instead chairman of the committee on manufactures, about which he knew little. Clay—recently renominated as the National Republican candidate for President—conferred with him over antiadministration tactics. In particular Clay demanded a tariff reduction, while at the same time retaining protection of his "American system." Nor, he insisted, was there any need to pay off the entire United States debt by March 4, 1833. Adams was not so sure. With Yankee prudence he looked forward to a day when the United States would not owe a dollar in the world.

The ex-President was also appointed to a committee to examine the affairs of the Bank of the United States. While the committee majority condemned the bank, his minority report—reflecting his belief in sound money and private property—supported it. In this as in other congressional duties he was so rigidly conscientious in his preparation that he was rarely in bed before midnight and rose each morning at five. His support of the bank was unpopular even in his Plymouth district, and he told his son John that he expected this would be his last winter in Washington. The flour mill was doing so badly that he told John to close it down and sell the property for what it would bring. He was as always short of funds, his Quincy property heavily mortgaged. In the spring his brother Thomas Boylston died. Adams felt the loss deeply, though the more coldly realistic Charlie had no tears to shed for his dissolute, embittered uncle.

During the winter of 1831 John Quincy had occupied his spare moments writing a long narrative poem in Byronic form, composing the verses during his afternoon walks around the Capital. The rhymed tale, *Dermot MacMorrogh*, set in the Ireland of the twelfth century, was—he explained—written to teach the virtues of marital fidelity, patriotism, and piety. He was very proud of his opus, his pride confirmed when on publication it quickly sold out, and he thought no other man in American public life could have written so poetically. Charlie's opinion, which he kept to himself, was that his father's poem lacked invention, imagination, and melody; and he wished it had never been written.

Prepared for the worst, Adams was surprised at the warmth of his welcome when he returned to his Plymouth district. Charlie thought he was popular enough to remain in Congress as long as he had a mind to. But in the winter of 1833 he suffered much from rheumatism, palsy, running eyes, and colds. At times his hands ached so that he could scarcely hold a pen. He was not sure how long he could endure. That autumn Jackson had overwhelmed Clay, "Harry of the West" winning only 49 electoral votes to Old Hickory's 219. Adams did not attend the inauguration. The following month he went on to Quincy alone. It had become a faster and easier journey, part of it on the new railroad. John Quincy was impressed by being able to travel sixteen miles in fifty minutes by rail, although he was discomforted by the smoke and cinders.

Alone in the echoing Old House until his family arrived, he spent his days reading, walking, occasionally hoeing in the garden. He was much troubled by news of John's failing health and begged him to leave the flour business and come to Quincy to recuperate.

One of Adams's Quincy visitors was Harvard's president, Josiah Quincy, who called to tell him that since President Jackson was coming to Boston Harvard had decided to give the Chief Executive the honorary degree of Doctor of Laws. Adams, even though an overseer of the college, stayed away; "as myself an affectionate child of our Alma Mater, I would not be present to witness her disgrace in conferring her highest literary honors upon a barbarian who could not write a sentence of grammar and hardly could spell his own name."

In the summer Charles and Abby presented him with his first grandson, named after him. On the baby's christening day John Quincy gave Charlie a seal his own father had given to him that had been affixed to the peace treaties with Great Britain. After John Quincy's death the seal was to be given to his namesake if he proved a descendant worthy of it. In July, while still in Quincy, Adams was asked to be the candidate of the new Antimason party for governor of Massachusetts and after some deliberation accepted. He was hurt and angry when the National Republicans refused to adopt him as their candidate as well. By the time the election took place he had returned to Washington. John Davis, the candidate of the National Republicans, topped the list, with Adams second and the Democratic candidate third, but as Davis failed to receive a majority of the votes, the election went to the legislature. Although there was a possibility that the legislature might pick him, Adams decided to withdraw.

John's health continued to deteriorate and the following summer when Adams was in Quincy he received word that his son was dying. Although he left at once for Washington, by the time he arrived John was in a coma and died three days later. The second son's death almost broke the old man's heart, and he blamed himself for having been too hard on him. Louisa shared his guilt. "To my other two I failed," she wrote; "and God Almighty forgive me! I was not worthy to keep them and my Sin was visited on them."

Neither personal domestic tragedy nor ill health would long divert the old man from his official responsibilities. Regularly elected to Congress, he remained one of its most conscientious members. Only the most severe illness could keep him from his desk. During his years in the House the slavery issue came to engross all others. Although he had long ago concluded that slavery was a moral blot, a violation of fundamental American principles, a lifetime's experience had taught him that men could not be changed by fiat. He could not sympathize with the abolitionist disregard for the Constitution and for consequences. His most burning and most enduring concern was for the free right of petition which he considered "the right of prayer, not depending on the condition of the petitioner." Embodied in the Constitution, the right, in Adams's belief, antedated the Constitution. No matter what the substance of a petition, the ex-President Congressman stood ready to sponsor it.

During his first congressional session he had presented fifteen petitions from the Society of Friends, calling for the immediate abolition of the slave trade and of slavery, even though he disagreed with the demands themselves, since "the most salutary medicines, unduly administered, were the most deadly poisons." More important to him than the slavery issue was the preservation of the Union. Yet gradually he came to believe that a temporary division might be the only means of destroying slavery and forming a greater union, even if this meant civil war. As Southern statesmen defended their "peculiar institution" with belligerent eloquence, he realized that the unifying effect of slavery on the slave states was more powerful than the unifying effect of freedom on

the rest of the country. Eventually, he thought, the Southern planters would break away from the Union. The slaves would in the
end revolt and free themselves. What he would do then he did not
know. He assumed that these disruptive events would not take
place in his lifetime.

In 1835 President Jackson was informed that an English sci-
entist and Fellow of the Royal Society, James Smithson, had left
his estate "to the United States of America, to found at Washington, under the name of the Smithsonian Institution, an Establishment for the increase & diffusion of knowledge among men." Why
Smithson had done this for a country unfamiliar to him remains
unknown, but his bitterness at his illegitimate birth may have had
something to do with it. Jackson submitted the offer to Congress,
and a committee was formed under the chairmanship of John
Quincy Adams to consider the offer. Adams was a most enthusiastic advocate of accepting it, and on the advice of his committee
Congress authorized the President to claim the legacy. When after
two years the money arrived in America, it took another eight
before anything was done with the bequest. Van Buren as President refused to concern himself about the matter. For Adams it
offered such possibilities as his long-cherished "light-houses of the
skies." He remained for years the unofficial guardian of the fund,
constantly alert to see it preserved for its original purposes and
not siphoned off in sinecures for political hacks. That the institution did survive the depredations of politicians is due in a large
measure to the Congressman ex-President.

As Adams approached seventy he was indeed becoming a fixture in Congress, a testy, withered man and withal an
unforgettable presence. So unusual was it for him to be away from
the House that the *National Intelligencer* commented on his absence in April, 1836, when he was laid up with an abscessed leg.
After a week, enfeebled and rheumy, he managed to get to the
Capitol by carriage. He came back, strong in mind if weak in body,

to defend a defense appropriations bill against charges by Daniel Webster, a bill that the *National Intelligencer* had so violently opposed that it announced it would rather see a foreign enemy at the wall of the Capitol than support it. When Adams rose creakily to comment on this, everyone sensed it was to be an occasion. Other members left their desks to crowd round the old man's chair.

"Sir," he concluded in a voice surprisingly resonant for his years, "for a man uttering such sentiments, there would be but one step more, a natural and easy one to take, and that would be, with the enemy at the wall of the Capitol; to join him in battering them down."

There was a moment of silence, then a tremendous burst of applause that continued in spite of the rapping of the Speaker's gavel. One enthusiastic Congressman, recalling Milton's sonnet to Lady Margaret Ley, applied its phrase "Old Man Eloquent" to the eloquent old man, and the phrase stuck.

Mondays were petition days in Congress, and inevitably Adams was present with a batch of petitions, mostly from antislavery and abolitionist groups. Southerners and Northern Democrats reacted by passing a "gag rule" that all such petitions and memorials relating to slavery should be laid on the table and no further action taken. Adams accused his colleagues of defying the Constitution by denying the right of petition guaranteed by the First Amendment. Each year the gag rule was reimposed. Each year Adams vainly presented his batches of petitions. One day he reached a peak of 350. In his perennial struggle he moved closer to the abolitionists, although he still felt that their extremism retarded rather than advanced their cause. Southerners came to view him as the Massachusetts Madman, "the hell-hound of abolition." Almost daily he received threats of lynching and assassination, in his opinion a fair index of the morality of slave communities.

The struggle wore him down. In moments of despondency he looked back on his life as a succession of failures. The goals he had set for himself were still unattained, apparently unattainable. He saw himself in his later old age as forsaken by men, with only the consolation of his own rectitude. Unlike most men, he was less devoted to the status quo as he grew older. In earlier years he had feared the mass of unguided or misguided people as a danger to society's stability. But with the years he had grown more sympathetic to ordinary folk, more willing to brave "popular prejudices" from a greater confidence "in the calm and deliberate judgement of the people."

His speeches reflected increasing hatred, scorn, and contempt for slavery. Ironically he presented one petition from the inhabitants of Jeffersonville, Virginia, demanding his own expulsion from Congress as a nuisance. He moved that it be referred to the committee on the judiciary, but it, too, was tabled. When he presented a petition asking the recognition of the black republic of "Hayti," his hate mail from the South doubled.

In February, 1839, Adams set forth his own gradualist antislavery program, although he knew it would neither be received nor even discussed in Congress. He proposed three amendments to the Constitution: that every child born in the United States after July 4, 1842, should be born free; that with the exception of the Territory of Florida, no state whose constitution allowed slavery should thenceforth be admitted to the Union; finally, that after July 4, 1845, neither slavery nor the slave trade should be permitted in the nation's capital. From opposite ends of the political spectrum Southerners and abolitionists reacted with equal anger. Abolitionists were infuriated by Adams's gradualness.

Yet even his most inveterate enemies were compelled at times to give him their grudging admiration. When, in December, 1839, the House of Representatives was unable to organize because of five disputed New Jersey seats, it was Adams who broke the parliamentary deadlock after appealing to his fellow members "in the name of the people, of their country, and of mankind to organize themselves." Carried away, South Carolina's Richard Barnwell Rhett leaped upon his desk to move that Adams be appointed Speaker of the House protem until a speaker could be duly elected. There was a thunderous chorus of ayes, and even his embittered enemy, Virginia's Henry Wise, was among those who rushed forward to congratulate Adams. The old man served through ten tempestuous days but was much relieved when he could finally relinquish his temporary post.

Far more acutely aware than his critics of the limits of the politically possible within the bounds of union, Adams remained alert to any case of conscience. By chance he read in the *National Intelligencer* of the slave woman Dorcas Allen who after being separated from her husband had cut the throats of two of her four children and then tried to kill herself. Now she was advertised for sale with her remaining children. To learn more about the case Adams called at the newspaper office. Dorcas, he discovered, had been freed on the death of her mistress fifteen years before but lacked the papers to prove it. Although she was married to a free Negro, a waiter at Gadsby's Hotel, an enterprising slave dealer had taken possession of her and her children. Now, after her children's death, she was again offered for sale. Adams called on the district attorney, Francis Scott Key, to see what could be done to help her. The author of "The Star-Spangled Banner" advised him to stay out of the case, that it was dangerous to interfere in such matters in a slaveholding town like Washington. Undeterred, Adams talked to Dorcas, to her husband, to the mayor of Washington, and finally to the slave dealer who had bought Dorcas and her children and who now agreed to sell them back for $475. Adams subscribed $50 from his own pinched funds. The affair ended more happily than most such. Dorcas's husband managed to raise the price of his wife's freedom. Together they visited Adams to thank him for his efforts, and his proffered $50 completed the amount needed to free their children. After they had left, Adams, watching them disappear down the street, sensed a greater satisfaction than he had experienced in days.

Most of his time and emotions in 1839 were taken up by the complications resulting from a mutiny on the slave ship *Amistad*. Blacks brought from Africa and transferred to the *Amistad* in Havana had been bound for Puerto Principe when they revolted, killed the captain, and seized control of the ship. For days they sailed erratically in search of free land until finally they anchored off Long Island. Apprehended, they were taken to jail and charged with piracy and murder. The Spanish minister demanded that the *Amistad* be returned to her owners and the mutineers sent back to Havana. Jackson's successor, President Van Buren, was indifferent to their fate; his slaveholding Secretary of State was all for yielding to Spanish demands. Abolitionists and antislavers at once raised a fund and asked Adams to undertake the mutineers' defense. Prudence might have suggested his declining, but his New England conscience was the stronger force, and he accepted. At the trial he argued that, whether pirates or not, these men were not now slaves but masters. The judge finally ruled that the *Amistad* mutineers, whatever bloody deeds they might have been guilty of, had been illegally captured, illegally transported, and illegally enslaved. He ordered them delivered to the President of the United States for transportation back to Africa. Van Buren was unhappy that the judge had failed to consider the larger political aspects of the case. The decision was at once appealed to the Supreme Court as an issue between Spain and the United States.

When the case at last came before the high court, Adams was present as assistant counsel for the defendants. In his summing up, which impressed even the justices as extraordinary, Old Man Eloquent spoke for four and a half hours. In one nostalgic, if irrelevant, aside, the old man in facing the seven justices recalled his first appearance before the Court in 1804 and enumerated those long dead who had then listened to his voice. The high court confirmed the lower court's ruling. The *Amistad* mutineers were to be placed at the disposal of the United States and sent back to Africa.

In session after session Adams made his Monday appearances with a bundle of petitions under his arm. They were years in which the remnant of the National Republicans coalesced with the Antimasons and disaffected Democrats to form the Whig party. In 1840, in their second presidential effort, the Whigs capitalized on the depression of the Van Buren years to elect the aged general and former Federalist William Henry Harrison. Though Adams ran on the Whig ticket in Massachusetts, he took no part in the national election. When Harrison died after a month in office and was succeeded by Vice President John Tyler, Adams remarked of the new President that "no one ever thought of his being placed in the executive chair." The hawk-nosed, slaveholding Virginian President was no favorite of the Massachusetts ex-President. When in 1842 Tyler held his first New Year's reception, the White House doors had to be locked to keep the crowd from storming in. Adams observed sardonically that they must have come to see the house rather than the occupant.

On that same New Year's Day at least five hundred persons called on Adams, twice as many on that date as ever before. In his seventy-fifth year he was indeed becoming a legend, a man still alive who had heard the cannon thunder of Bunker Hill, who had known Washington, Franklin, and Hamilton, whose memory even embraced Louis XVI and Marie Antoinette, Napoleon, George III, and George IV. Bald, watery-eyed, his neck wrinkled like a turtle's, this frock-coated patriarch had been born in the age of the rococo, that incomprehensible time when Americans were still Englishmen and dressed like Meissen figures.

Neither age nor the public's growing veneration daunted him. Among his petitions he presented one from the voters of Habersham County, Georgia, asking for his removal as the chairman of the committee on foreign relations (to which he had been assigned that session) because of his "monomania" about slavery. When Southerners moved to place the petition on the table, Adams demanded the floor to speak in his own defense. Given permission—obligatory under House rules—he denounced slaveholders, slave trading, and slave breeding with such invective that the Southern members left their seats to push toward him, demanding hoarsely that the Speaker "put him down!" and "shut the mouth of that old harlequin!" Adams replied in tones that set them raging. "I see where the shoe pinches, Mr. Speaker," he taunted in his high-pitched voice. "It will pinch *more* yet. I'll deal out to the gentlemen a diet they'll find it hard to digest."

Topping all his other performances, Adams on January 25, 1842, offered a petition from forty-six citizens of Haverhill, Massachusetts—probably instigated by John Greenleaf Whitter—praying for Congress peaceably to dissolve the Union. No such drastic petition had ever before been introduced. The Southerners reacted in fury. A Virginian member at once presented a resolution to censure the Honorable John Quincy Adams, maintaining that he was guilty of high treason and that he merited expulsion for his insult to Congress and the people of the United States. The censure motion caused a great excitement both in Washington and in the country. Whenever the grey little man with the rheumy eyes and trembling hands rose to defend himself, the galleries were packed. By way of initial defense Adams demanded a reading of the Declaration of Independence. When the clerk came to the passage declaring the right of a people to throw off a despotic government and to provide new guards for future security, he insisted that the passage be read again. He had, he explained in his defense, received a petition, and it was his duty to present it. That was the real point at issue. The right of petition was a guarantee that the Southern bloc threatened to destroy.

It seemed as if the long-drawn-out debate would go on for weeks. Wise, one of the most intemperate defenders of slavery—

whom Adams had characterized elsewhere as "a motley compound of eloquence and folly, of braggart impudence and childish vanity, of self-laudation and Virginia narrow-mindedness"—attacked Adams with slashing rhetoric in a speech that lasted five hours. Adams at length said that though he was willing to continue, he was also willing to call a halt and dismiss the whole subject from further consideration. The Southerners had had enough. A Southern Congressman then moved to lay the resolve on the table, and this was carried overwhelmingly. The defiant Adams returned to Quincy at the session's end to find himself something of a hero. He was met with banners, toasts, and speeches. He was given dozens of receptions. Someone had even written a poem in his honor to the tune of "My Country 'Tis of Thee."

The following summer he was asked to be present at the dedication of the Bunker Hill Monument, of which Lafayette had laid the cornerstone in 1825. Webster—no favorite of John Quincy's—was to deliver the address. "His Accidency," President Tyler, would be there. Adams refused to attend. The thought of Webster over-orating, of Tyler's long nose casting a shadow to eclipse the granite obelisk itself, would, he feared, have reduced him to either indignation or laughter. He was proud though on July 4 when Charlie gave the annual oration at Faneuil Hall. Listening to his son, he recalled that his last Independence Day in Boston had been in 1809, and that memory, strangely agitating, underlay the applause of the crowd.

Two days later he began a tour of western New York with his daughter-in-law, her father, and his grandson John Quincy. But what was intended as a tour turned into a triumph. Wherever he went, by boat or train, he was greeted by cheering throngs, processions, militia in uniform, brass bands, bells ringing, cannon firing, nightly torchlight parades, and fireworks. Each city vied with the next in the pomp of its reception, from Buffalo to Rochester to Utica to Albany and all the towns in between. Wherever his train stopped for wood and water, crowds gathered. For the first time in his life he tasted mass popularity. In September he received an invitation to lay the cornerstone of an observatory to be built by the Cincinnati Astronomical Society. Though he had scarcely returned from his New York travels he agreed to go, and summoned all his energies to write an oration for the event. It would be a hard journey for an old man, but in spite of his family's objections, he insisted he must go.

The first snow had already fallen by the time he reached Utica late in October, and the way was bare, the summer crowds vanished. From Cleveland to Columbus he had to endure traveling by canalboat in narrow, stifling quarters and at a speed of two and one half miles an hour. He was received with great enthusiasm at Cleveland, Dayton, Columbus, a cavalcade of carriages accompanying his coach through each city. The actual dedication in Cincinnati was interrupted by torrential rains, and Adams had to postpone his speech until the following day. He spoke for two hours, outlining the development of astronomical studies and sketching the history of European astronomical societies. On this occasion he defiantly resurrected his abused and derided phrase "light-houses of the skies," and congratulated the Cincinnati society on being the first to construct one in the United States.

The receptions waiting for him on his return journey he found extremely wearing, and he thought that he had little life left in him. Louisa was shocked when she saw him. He looked so worn, so old. His chronic cough was worse than it had ever been. "It would be a glorious moment for me to die," he told his wife, "so let it come." It would not come for several years yet. On New Year's Day, 1844, much recovered, he greeted a stream of callers. Each year he renewed his struggle against the gag rule. Each year he came closer to his goal. In 1842 the rule had been sustained by a mere four votes, and in December, 1843, by only three even though the Democrats had a two-thirds majority in the House. At the end of January, 1844, he noted defiantly: "The report on the rules was immediately taken up, and Andrew Johnson, a new member from Tennessee, made an hour's speech in support of the gag rule, and especially abusive upon me. I am compelled not only to endure it with seeming insensibility, but to forbear, so far as I can restrain myself, from all reply." In April a group of his admirers presented him with a silver-knobbed ivory cane inlaid with a golden American eagle bearing a scroll with the motto "Right of Petition Triumphant" and a blank space for the date when the gag rule would be finally abolished. Adams had always refused the smallest gift, and this he turned over to the Patent Office.

The election year 1844 was dominated by the question of Texas. Adams and Clay were sternly opposed to adding such strength to the slave states, Adams fearing that annexation would be followed by the conquest of Mexico and the West Indies. Van Buren also opposed annexing Texas, his opposition costing him the Democratic nomination for the presidency as Southern Democrats and expansionists turned to the first dark-horse candidate in the country's history, James K. Polk.

Following Polk's election the Van Buren Democrats took their revenge by voting against the gag rule. On December 3, 1844, Adams could at last write in his diary: "At the meeting of the House this day ... in pursuance of the notice I had given yesterday, I moved the following resolution: 'Resolved, that the twenty-fifth standing rule for conducting business in this House, in the following words, "No petition, memorial, resolution, or other paper praying the abolition of slavery in the District of Columbia or any State or Territory, or the slave trade between States or Territories in which it now exists, shall be received by this House, or entertained in any way whatever" be, and the same is, hereby rescinded.' I called for the yeas and nays. ... The clerk called the roll, and the motion to lay on the table was rejected—81 to 104. The question was then put on the resolution; and it was carried—

108 to 80. Blessed, forever blessed, be the name of God." Adams then sent to the Patent Office for his ivory cane to have the triumphant date engraved on it.

In January, 1845, House Southerners and expansionists joined to vote for the annexation of Texas, carrying the measure by 120 to 98. The Senate concurred, with two votes to spare. Adams thought it one of the heaviest calamities that had befallen himself and his country. Any further resistance was useless. He knew he must harbor what strength he had left. The previous March he had recorded in his diary: "I approach the term when my daily journal must cease from physical disability to keep it up. I have now struggled for nearly five years, without the interval of a day while mind and body have been wearing away under the daily, silent, but unremitting erosion of time. I rose this morning at four, and with smarting, bloodshot eye and shivering hand, still sat down and wrote to fill up the chasm of the closing days of the last week; but my stern chase after Time is, to borrow a simile from Tom Paine, like the race of a man with a wooden leg after a horse." He could no longer bathe in the river or the sea, and even had to give up his portable shower bath. So beset was he with palsy that he had to use a metal support to steady his hand for writing.

With Texas annexed, Oregon was the next issue, the area occupied jointly for so long by England and the United States. The territory up to 54°40' latitude was now demanded by swarming settlers with their slogan "Fifty-four forty or fight." Adams thought the American title legitimate but predicted the final settlement would be an extension of the forty-ninth parallel to the sea. Although the settlement would be just that—with the minor concession of granting the whole of Vancouver Island to Great Britain—Southerners were not at all anxious to see their Texas gains offset by the absorption of the free Oregon Territory. Congressman Thomas King of Georgia accused Adams of agreeing to joint occupation of Oregon in 1818 and 1827 and now wanting to put an end to it. The old nationalist replied that he wanted the West for the pioneers to settle in and make a great nation.

The Oregon issue was soon overshadowed by the approaching crisis with Mexico. Two days after the Texas annexation the unstable, debt-ridden Mexican government broke off relations with the United States. Border incidents multiplied on both sides, culminating in a Mexican attack across the Rio Grande in which a squadron of American dragoons was annihilated. Polk told both houses of Congress in his message of May 11, 1846, that Mexico had shed American blood and war now existed. The Mexican War began in a wave of popular enthusiasm shared by Democrats and Whigs alike. Only the self-conscious intellectuals dissented at first, although others joined them as the war prolonged itself and the casualty lists grew. Adams was one of the fourteen radical "conscience" Whigs who at the outset voted against what they considered an unrighteous war. At its end the war added half a million square miles of territory to the United States, including the present states of California, Utah, and Nevada, and large parts of Arizona, New Mexico, and Colorado, but at a cost of $100 million and thirteen thousand dead.

Adams was now in his eightieth year. Not until August did Congress adjourn, allowing him to leave for his beloved Quincy. Wrinkled, halting, he shrank physically by the month, but his faculties and his spirit remained intact. "An old man, absorbed in work and public life," his grandson Charles Francis, Jr., recalled him. "He seemed to be always writing—as, indeed, he was ... A very old-looking gentleman, with a bald head and white fringe of hair—writing, writing—with a perpetual ink-stain on the forefinger and thumb of the right hand." In 1846 the Massachusetts Whig convention unanimously nominated him for re-election and this he took to be an endorsement of his stand on the war. A few weeks after his re-election, as he was walking in Boston with his friend Dr. George Parkman to the new medical college, his knees suddenly buckled under him. Although he suffered no pain, his speech and his right side were affected by what the doctor diagnosed as a slight paralytic stroke. His recovery was slow. On New Year's Day, 1847, he went outside for the first time in a carriage, then rode out daily. Later in January he took a short walk. By the end of February he was able to walk to church for both morning and evening services, and thought himself well enough to return to Washington.

As he entered the House of Representatives, frail but determined, all present stood up and business was suspended while he was conducted to his seat. The old man was much moved. He continued to be present at each House sitting, though except for his favorite Library of Congress committee he was no longer burdened with assignments. Outside Congress he seemed to be preparing for the end. To Charlie he now turned over all the trusts in his care, saying he was too old in mind and body to deal with them. Yet he planned to return to Congress in December, although he doubted if he could participate in debates.

On July 27 he celebrated his fiftieth wedding anniversary quietly at home. Louisa at that time, as remembered by her grandson Henry Adams, appeared "singularly peaceful, a vision of silver gray, presiding over her old President and her Queen Anne mahogany; an exotic, like her Sèvres china; an object of deference to every one, and of great affection to her son Charles; but hardly more Bostonian than she had been fifty years before, on her wedding-day, in the shadow of the Tower of London."

The New Year of 1848 seemed to bring the old man renewed vigor. He attended a reception given by the mayor of Washington, and next day conducted a meeting of his Library of Congress committee. That Saturday he and Louisa held open house for a large number of guests. Twice each Sunday he went to church. He planned to attend the Washington's Birthday ball with Louisa, who was a patroness.

On January 21 he rode in his carriage to the Capitol, apparently in good health. There was a debate that day on a resolution to thank certain army officers for their services in the Mexican War. When the Speaker called the question, Adams's strong loud No could be heard above the babble of Ayes. As the clerk read the formal words of praise for these officers, an abolitionist reporter watching the indignant Old Man Eloquent saw his face suddenly redden, saw him move his lips silently, then clutch at the corner of his desk with his right hand as he slumped to the left. A Congressman cried out and caught him in his arms before he reached the floor. The others crowded around the prostrate figure. A sofa was brought in and he was placed on it and carried to the Speaker's chamber. The news spread through Washington like a fire alarm that Adams was dying. The Senate and Supreme Court rose at once. Lying on the sofa the old man rallied a little, called for Clay, who came to clasp his hand, the tears running down his cheeks. Those nearby saw Adams's lips trying to form words. A few minutes later he spoke suddenly and quite clearly: "This is the end of earth, but I am composed." He did not speak again.

# 6

# *Charles Francis Adams*

## VOICE OF HONOR

T HE CHILD'S first memories were of St. Petersburg, that gracious city of imperial vistas set so inappropriately yet so magically in northern Russia. Within the court and diplomatic circles in which his parents moved, everyone spoke French, and this became Charles Francis Adams's first language, the one he would always privately prefer. When his mother spoke to him in English, he answered her in French. In this polyglot cosmopolitan world he also learned German and Russian. It was a world far removed from the brick provinciality of Boston, the homeliness of Quincy. Little Charlie took it for granted that while walking with his father, John Quincy Adams, they might stop to chat with the Czar or some ambassador. At the elaborate children's parties and dress balls to which he was invited he met the children of Europe's nobility. He was just over two when his mother took him to a ball at the Duke of Vicenza's dressed as an Indian chief. The diminutive Noble Savage in his feathered headdress was much applauded, and somewhat to his bewilderment was chosen to lead out a Miss Vlodeck in opening the ball.

Theaters and puppet shows as well as parties occupied the little boy's gayer hours. His father tutored him daily, reading to him in French and English, often from the Bible. At six he went to a school for the children of diplomats where he improved his Russian. Languages came easily to him, numbers less so. When, after six years in Russia, his father was sent on to England, Charlie spent two years at an English boarding school, its rigors somewhat mitigated by his being allowed to spend one or two days a week at home. Because of his slow progress in arithmetic he was considered dull, though his disappointed father thought he had aptitude enough for learning what took his fancy. America was a foreign land to him when he arrived in Quincy in 1817 on his tenth birthday. He was distressed when after three weeks his parents left for Washington without him, nor did he take to the idea of boarding in Boston and attending the Boston Latin School with John. At first he tried to stay in Quincy by pretending he had dysentery, but the sight of his grandmother's bottles of home remedies made him recover at once. Weekends, at least, he and John could spend with their grandparents, who thought them both good boys and a great comfort. Yet even there Uncle Tom's drinking often marred the atmosphere. During the Christmas vacation the boys visited their parents in Washington, and John Quincy took the occasion to test their progress in Greek and Latin. The results were less than satisfying. He recorded gloomily in his diary that in all likelihood none of his children would ever answer his hopes.

When John entered Harvard in 1819, his father took the thirteen-year-old Charlie back to Washington. The unfinished Capital was, to say the least, an inelegant contrast to St. Petersburg, but Charlie was much happier there than in Boston. He was happy to be with his parents again, he preferred his new school to Boston Latin, and he liked his schoolmates. Summer mornings at sunrise he often swam in the Potomac with his father, though John Quincy complained that it was hard to get his son out of bed that early. Frequently he attended debates in Congress. At puberty he seemed a small adult rather than a boy, taciturn, reserved, solemn-faced. His mother regretted his stubbornness, although she took this to be an Adams trait. He had no close friends, and did not seem to want any.

When he was fourteen he entered Harvard, more from lack of an alternative than from any enthusiasm on his part. Conscious of his standing as an Adams, contemptuous of parochial Cambridge, he felt no impulse to excel. At the end of his first term he ranked fifty-first in a class of fifty-nine. Several times during his college years he threatened to leave. John Quincy persuaded him to stay on by pointing out that he would have to determine on some other course of life that might prove less agreeable than Harvard. Unenthusiastically Charlie managed to endure four undergraduate years, his ennui mitigated to a degree by billiards, oyster feeds, champagne, and card parties. He studied what interested him, refused to bother with mathematics and other subjects that did not. His reading was wide, if random, chiefly in history and poetry. Like many an undergraduate he nursed vague literary ambitions. Politics he thought a bore, and daringly maintained that he had no faith in the future of his country. What he really wanted was an unimpeded private career. Yet with a father as Secretary of State, he knew that he was a figure on the public stage in spite of himself. Graduating in absentia in 1825 he left his future in abeyance.

The months that he spent in Washington after graduation were pleasanter than any he had lived through in Cambridge or Boston. Being a President's son kept him in the center of the Capital's society, a position he much enjoyed. Yet, as if shadowed by his Puritan inheritance, he could never really relax in the present for fear of the future, and he had moments when he considered that the happiest parts of his life were already past. Following the Adams family tradition he kept a diary. With his father constantly under political attack, the atmosphere of the White House was tense. His mother seemed chronically ailing, and his father, unable to defend himself against the scurrility of his attackers, was always on edge. Though Charlie's duties were minimal, he occasionally assisted John in performing the President's secretarial tasks. Often the two brothers quarreled.

Fascinated by young women, he was at the same time able to regard his own emotions with cold detachment. Early he recorded that if he should get married he expected to "receive something like pleasure for so disagreable step." As a Harvard junior he wrote in his diary: "There is magic in a Petticoat to a young man. I cannot tell, but my passions and feelings are so affected that I want their society. Of the tendency of this passion I am so well aware, that I make great attempts to keep it on guard." It did not guard him, however, from forming a liaison with a young woman of a social status presumably too low for him to consider marrying her. Whenever he thought of a career he kept coming back reluctantly to the law. It seemed to him a practical, even an inevitable choice, although at heart he thought it a dullish, mechanical profession in which to round out his days. At times he would flee the Capital's social life to bury himself in his law books, but the impulse never lasted long.

In January, 1827, he met Abigail Brooks of Medford, Massachusetts, then in Washington visiting her sister, the wife of Edward Everett. Her father, Peter Chardon Brooks, who had made several million dollars in moneylending, insurance, and commercial ventures during the Napoleonic Wars, was the wealthiest man in eastern Massachusetts. "This young lady has been somewhat in my mind of late," Charlie recorded the meeting in his diary. "I have been somewhat disposed to pay her attentions, which in the first place were paid only from an inability to get rid of them. But latterly I have been thinking more seriously, whether it would not be expedient to pursue the subject. My mind is not yet made up." A week later he was "much struck" with her character. When shortly after this he proposed to her, she told him in embarrassment that she would have to consult her family. The more he thought of marrying into the Brooks family, the more the idea appealed to him. "Whenever I consider the advantages and disadvantages of this connection," he wrote, "so far as they may apply to me in a worldly point of view, I cannot but think that the former outweight the later in such a degree as to throw them out of sight."

She was willing to become engaged to him. He was in love, yet like his forebears he could view his elected with a critical eye. For all her warmheartedness "she has many faults, arising as much from the education she has received as from her natural disposition. She seems to have been looked upon by the family as a darling and her feelings have always atoned for her hasty errors.... She is not handsome but her face is expressive and has made as much impression as a beauty's would have done.... Her temper is high and requires the check of kindness rather than any violent opposition.... On the whole I think her calculated to make a person happy, provided he is aware of the duties that fall on him."

Peter Brooks refused to consider his daughter's marrying a nineteen-year-old and said so to John Quincy, who replied that he would be satisfied with an engagement if Charlie would agree to postpone his marriage until he was twenty-one. Shortly after Abby returned to Massachusetts, Charlie broke off his earlier affair, noting tersely: "In the evening I went through one of those disagreeable scenes which occur sometimes in life. No man of sense will ever keep a Mistress. For if she is valuable, the separation when it comes is terrible, and if she is not, she is more plague than profit. Ever since my engagement, I have been preparing for a close of my licentious intrigues, and this evening I cut the last cord which bound me."

In August Charlie left Washington for Boston where he began to read law in Daniel Webster's office. He spent a fretful two years, brightened chiefly by the moments he passed in Abby's company. Law took up neither his time nor his interest. In 1829 he passed his bar examination and opened a law office in a Court Street building owned by his father but attended his office rarely and had no clients. He grew apathetic, melancholy, and after Abby's brother died of tuberculosis, he began to fancy himself ailing.

At the news of his brother George's death he felt a "chill under the skin which seems to be like it's stagnation." Two days afterward he had recovered enough to write that "George had an extremely amiable disposition, but he was the creature of impulse and frequently gave way to the seductions which an ill regulated imagination excited. My father almost lived in him and the loss will to him indeed be dreadful." Later, when he had learned about Eliza Dolph, his reaction was colder and he concluded that his brother's fate was "melancholy, but on the whole . . . not untimely. He would have lived probably to give much misery to his friends and more to himself, and he died when his fate was not so evident as not to admit of a doubt." As for Eliza with her child of a few weeks, Charles was willing to provide her with a small sum of money, but stood by indifferently when she went back to work as a chambermaid.

George's death softened John Quincy's attitude toward his youngest son. He put Charlie in charge of the Boston affairs that George had previously managed, and hoped that this extra compensation would help his marriage plans. Charles, urgent in his desires, tried to pin down Abby's father as to his intentions. Brooks told him that he allowed and would continue to allow his daughter $1,200 a year. "This, united with mine," Charles thought, "will do to live tolerably well but not more." But Brooks still refused to consider an early marriage. Two months later Charles wrote a stiff letter telling him that it would be years before he earned a more adequate living and that if his prospective father-in-law continued to object to him on financial grounds, "I have already frankly told

Abby that our engagement must cease." Brooks insisted that Charles and Abby must wait at least another year. "The course of Mr. Brooks to me has not been handsome," Charles complained, "intimating as he does that my youth and want of occupation are objections to me, without thinking that such allusions do no good *now* and irritate my feelings besides. These things remain in a tenacious memory and will probably have no very pleasant effect in future life if ever I should surmount my difficulties, either upon his happiness or mine in the relations we may hold to each other. . . . Rolling in wealth as he is, a little well disposed might do much, but with a timid doctrine, the consequence of habits of early years, he delays it while every day takes off something from the value of the gift."

Not until September 3, 1829, some weeks after his twenty-second birthday, was Charlie finally able to marry. The waiting had tried him sorely, and his mood during that time was dark. He felt his days were numbered, that he would never be able to approach the standard set by his father and his grandfather. Although he had looked forward to his wedding for so long, as the actual day approached he was beset by the nagging second thoughts that trouble most men. On the evening before the ceremony he wrote in his journal: "I went to Quincy to dine, it being the last day I shall probably be there in a similar way. In the afternoon I was occupied in packing my things and making the final arrangements here. I regret a little leaving here and this way of life for with many disadvantages it has some pleasures and not a little Independence. But I have views and objects in life other than this loose way allows, and I have affections which are worth cultivating now if ever."

Marriage was to be the turning point in his life. Decades afterward he told his son Brooks that but for his wife he would never have amounted to anything. Settled at last in his own home he became a different person, self-confident, eager, determined to add his own luster to the Adams name. At once he began a program of self-education, reading, and translating Demosthenes to improve his own manner of speaking; laboring over exercises in English composition; studying American history. Each day he felt obliged to spend a few hours at his office in order to appear in Boston as a man of affairs, although he did little after arriving but attend to accounts, receive payments of bills, and read the newspapers.

In his early twenties his personality already was fully formed. Conservative in the tradition of Burke, he described himself to Abby as "grave, sober, formal, precise and reserved," though, he added, "not *naturally* reserved." Such qualities, he well realized, were no passport to popularity, and he decided that his career had to be based on character and accomplishment. Cold rather than arrogant in manner, he had few friends and did not seem to feel the lack. Typical of his personality was his religious outlook. He believed in God as a beneficial and moderate creator, but found Calvinism and evangelical emotionalism equally repellent. Christianity he preferred to accept without too much pondering. May "the most high God . . . guide me in the right path," he wrote just after his marriage, ". . . fit me to perform the part assigned me and lead us through this life to a happier in the succeeding World."

In 1831 Charles Francis's daughter Louisa was born. As a family man his relations with his father grew more cordial. He and Abby usually spent the summer months in Quincy, and during that time he helped catalogue his father's library. He also kept John Quincy's accounts. Though he disapproved of his father's congressional career and considered the old man too impulsive and even self-righteous, he came more and more to respect his mind. Politics was, nevertheless, a field the younger man shunned. His goal was a literary one. He had a mild success in a review he wrote of James Grahame's *History of the United States of America* for the *North American Review*, but he was depressed at the mutilations in the published text. At twenty-five he still had no real standing, and he wondered if he had the capacity. Sorting through his grandfather's papers, he came across his father's letters from Holland, and reflected gloomily how infinitely superior John Quincy had been at the same age. Occasionally he wrote articles for the Boston press on current topics, but to his mortification most of them were rejected. He tried to console himself with the thought that he had done nothing merely to court popularity. But the thought failed to quiet his ambition.

Up until 1832 Charles Francis deliberately avoided public life, although, with his father active in Washington, he was never able to avoid politics. He was much concerned over tariff questions and even more over the South Carolina nullification controversy. Both he and his father applauded President Jackson's firm stand for the Union, although John Quincy continued to doubt the President's sincerity. Charles Francis on the contrary was so impressed by Old Hickory's proclamation that he thought it must either have been written by or cribbed from his father.

It was the Antimason movement that finally brought Charles Francis onto the political stage. Masons had been suspected of doing away with a renegade Mason, William Morgan, who had mysteriously disappeared after threatening to divulge the secrets of the order. Morgan's supposed fate was seen, particularly in rural America, as an elitist challenge to democratic government. John Quincy, who had earlier thought well enough of the Masons, thought twice about them when in 1831 the head of the Antimason party asked him to be its candidate for President. If the National Republicans would also choose him, John Quincy saw in that combination a bright hope of triumphing over Jackson and eradicating the humiliation of 1828. His more realistic son did not want his father subjected to the buffeting of another presidential campaign. To his relief the Antimasons finally passed over John Quincy to nominate William Wirt.

Nevertheless, in the summer of 1832 Charles Francis at last took his own stand against Masonry. Its secret and exclusive character he now openly denounced as a threat to government, morality, ·and religion. By this time the Antimasons had replaced the Democrats as the second largest political party in Massachusetts. Adams began writing a series of newspaper articles on the threat of Masonry. So engrossed in his subject did he become that during Sunday church services he found his thoughts constantly shifting from the divine to the Antimason mundane. He was deeply disappointed by the thin response to his carefully prepared articles.

They did, however, bring him to the attention of party leaders, and in 1833 he was elected a delegate to the state Antimason convention. It was his first experience with practical politics, and he was pleased when the Antimasons nominated him as one of their candidates for state Representative. He was less pleased when the convention nominated his father for governor, as he thought that a "graceful end" to the old man's political life was long overdue.

Since no candidate for the legislature in Charles Francis's district secured the required majority, a runoff election was necessary. Adams asked to have his name withdrawn. In the next few years the strength of the Antimason party declined even as the Whigs emerged. He himself turned his back on politics to relapse into his old monotonous routine. On his twenty-seventh birthday he decided that if by the year's end he had not made his mark, he would accept the obscurity that the Deity had obviously intended for him.

After his brother John's death in 1834, he went to Washington to help put his father's financial affairs in order, though it seemed to him that in so doing he was sacrificing his "great year." John Quincy saw his son's intrusion otherwise. Grieving for his dead son, he was in no mood to discuss investments and mortgages with the living. The latter's cold admonitions angered him and he told Charles Francis sharply to stick to his account keeping. The old man wanted no financial advice. Mere property no longer interested him. There was nothing he owned that he could not easily part with tomorrow. To Charles Francis, his father's outburst was just another indication of how little he really cared for the future of his family. The son was bitter as he left Washington. Yet this would prove their last serious quarrel, and each ensuing year would bring them closer together.

By 1835, still at loose ends, still with vague literary ambitions, Charles Francis thought briefly of writing a life of Francis Bacon, then gave it up. Meanwhile, the political tide closed in around him. In Massachusetts a seat in the United States Senate was vacant, to be filled by the state Senate and the House of Representatives. John Quincy was the choice of the Senate, and Governor John Davis of the House. Adams's support of Jackson in his firm stand against the payment of French claims alienated the now dominant Massachusetts Whigs, and Daniel Webster persuaded enough Senators to switch their votes so that Davis was elected. Charles Francis could not forgive this Webster-inspired reversal. In the 1836 presidential election he came out against Webster and the Whigs and did his best to swing the Antimasons to Van Buren. In spite of Van Buren's victory, Webster's Whigs carried Massachusetts by a large margin. Charles Francis in disgust once more forswore politics and politicians.

For the next three years Adams remained an independent. During the economic depression of the Van Buren years he wrote a number of articles, nonpartisan analyses of current questions. Yet for all his professed nonpartisanship he was moving slowly into the Whig ranks. Slavery was to be the catalyst that would reactivate him politically.

During the first fifty years of the Republic slavery had remained a dormant issue. However much old John Adams may have disapproved of the institution, he had raised no personal objections when during his English mission Jefferson's eight-year-old daughter Polly, accompanied by the little mulatto slave girl Sally Hemings, had stayed with the Adamses for some weeks before going on to her father in Paris. Abigail often took the two little girls shopping. Such tacit acceptance would have been inconceivable in the growing tension of the eras of John Adams's son and grandson. Slavery, the genie bottled up by the Constitution, had been uncorked and like a whirlwind was darkening the political horizon. Charles Francis, as did his father, still held that the South had been given certain constitutional guarantees for its "peculiar institution" that the free states could not go back on. This, of course, cut him off from stentorian abolitionists like William Lloyd Garrison who were ready to see the Union smashed if slavery could be destroyed at the same time.

Nevertheless, Adams was outraged when a Boston mob that included some of the city's wealthiest and most prominent citizens dragged Garrison through the streets with a rope around his body. "Among other things we have had a mob to put down Abolitionists," he wrote in his diary, "as if the Country was not going to pot fast enough without extraordinary help." The murder of the Reverend Elijah Lovejoy in Illinois by a proslavery mob that first burned his printing plant and then shot him seemed to Charles Francis "a shock as of an earthquake throughout this continent."

Disgusted by what he considered Van Buren's yielding to the Calhoun proslavery faction, Adams moved closer to the Whigs in spite of his distrust of them. Politically he remained withdrawn, occupying himself chiefly with sorting out the mass of John Adams's papers and preparing a somewhat expurgated edition of his grandmother Abigail's letters to be finally published in 1840 with his introductory memoir. He wrote a number of miscellaneous articles, including several for the prestigious *North American Review* and—as was common practice among New England intellectuals—delivered occasional public lectures, mostly on the events and personalities of the Revolution.

Unlike his forebears he felt little need for physical exercise, finding no particular charm in nature or the out-of-doors. His daily hour of reading and rereading the classics gave him more pleasure than anything else. He had little sympathy with or feeling for current writers. Social reformers like Robert Owen he considered threats to the time-tested fundamentals of marriage, religion, and property. The transcendentalist belief in the perfectibility of man he thought "mistiness." Like his father and grandfather before him he feared the unrelieved, unstable will of the majority. Above all he feared a President in the role of a tribune of the people, casting aside the checks and balances essential to control fluctuating mob passions. As the democratic principle advanced, his faith in government ebbed. The two most formidable enemies of the state were, in his opinion, pure democracy and slavery. He was content, as he said, to follow the path marked by his fathers. Nevertheless, his path was a lonely one. He claimed that in all Boston he had not a single intimate friend.

In 1838 the Whigs had offered to nominate him for the legislature, but although his father and his father-in-law urged him to accept, he refused. When the Whigs renewed the offer in 1840 he accepted, not—as he explained—because he looked forward to public life, but because of the insistence of his friends. That presidential election year marked the defeat of President Van Buren by General William Henry Harrison. Adams, though he had no great opinion of the aged general, thought that the election at least proved that toadying to the slaveholders was no highroad to political success. He himself won election to the Massachusetts House of Representatives with the highest plurality of any Boston candidate. Yet the pleasure of his success was marred by doubts. He took no satisfaction in becoming a politician, and he wondered if he might not be throwing away his life in political squabbles.

Five years he was to serve in the Massachusetts legislature, three annual terms as Representative and two as Senator. He became one of the state's most emphatic antislavery leaders, and this recognition gave him both confidence and balance. By the time he entered the legislature he had five children. Besides Louisa and John Quincy, there were Charles Francis, Jr., born in 1835, Henry Brooks (who would later drop the Brooks) born in 1838, and Arthur born in 1840. During Charles Francis's legislative terms his father-in-law gave Abby a town house at 57 Mount Vernon Street, and there Adams lived in the winter months until his death. In 1837 he had built his own summer house in Quincy an eighth of a mile from the parental Old House—as it was coming to be called. There, between sessions of the legislature, he stayed from late May to early November, studying, reading, writing, and adding to his already voluminous diary. With the reserve and caution that was his nature he began his legislative career inconspicuously, intent on no Websterian fireworks but rather on building a reputation for "steadiness and general ability." A lukewarm Whig, he regarded himself not as a party man but as a representative of the whole people. After reading President Harrison's Inaugural Address he prayed God to save the country "on this voyage" since her captain was "but half fitted for his duty." When Harrison died in April, 1841, at the end of his first month in office and was succeeded by the Virginia states' rights Whig John Tyler, Adams became even more critical of the administration.

Opposition of the Northern Whigs to Tyler soon split the party. When in 1842 Adams was proffered his third nomination, he accepted only because the possibility of the Whigs losing the state made him feel obligated to run again. The Democrats did in fact win the governorship and the Senate, the Whigs retaining control of the House by only a small majority. At the beginning of the session Adams presented his first antislavery petition and soon after was made a member of a committee to consider all such matters. The highlight of the session was the Latimer petition, one destined to resound far beyond the borders of Massachusetts.

George Latimer, a Virginia slave, had fled to Boston with articles stolen from his master. A Boston lawyer, acting for the owner, had him arrested for larceny and then demanded that he be held as a fugitive. Latimer's jailing stirred up much local indignation. He was finally released in his owner's personal custody, but the latter, fearing that Latimer might be rescued by a mob, sold his claim. Subsequently, Adams presented a petition of over sixty thousand names to the legislature asking for state laws to prevent human beings from being returned to slavery. The petition was referred to Adams's committee. Two weeks later he issued a report in which he requested a law to forbid all Massachusetts officials from aiding in the arrest or detention of fugitives from slavery, and to deny the use of jails and other state property for detaining such fugitives. Although he cautiously disclaimed any intent to oppose the binding nature of the provisions of the Constitution, he and his committee demanded an end to that original constitutional compromise by which three fifths of the slave population were counted in determining the number of Congressmen from the slave states. Adams considered their action perhaps the most memorable event of his life. After this resolve had been adopted by the Massachusetts legislature, John Quincy Adams introduced it in the national House of Representatives. There it was turned down. The Senate, by a vote of two to one, denied even a printing of the proposed amendment.

Charles Francis's final series of resolves that he presented on behalf of his committee related to the annexation of Texas. These resolves stated that the admission of that potential slave state would be regarded in Massachusetts as dangerous to the continuance of the Union in peace and prosperity. Massachusetts Congressmen were instructed to oppose it. Since his state had a Democratic administration, Adams was forced to make common cause with his fellow Whigs. He feared he was becoming a party hack, and decided that he had had enough of politics, that he could contribute more to the world through his writings and historical studies.

Nevertheless, when the Whigs nominated him for the state Senate, his reluctance gave way to the satisfaction of being promoted. In the election the Whigs regained control of Massachusetts and Adams himself was easily elected. A few weeks after election day as he was traveling with his mother by steamer to New York the ship caught fire, and for some minutes he thought he was doomed. His close brush with death brought him face to face with his own basic verities. For fourteen years, he was forced to admit, he had "been swimming in a sea of domestic happiness." What little he had managed to accomplish he had done from vain and trivial motives. His mortal danger, he thought, had purged him of personal ambition. Never in his life had he felt so humble.

The state Senate now seemed to him at best "a species of sleepy hollow." So it might have been but for the reverberations of the Texas question. When petitions against the admission of the Lone Star State began arriving at the State House in increasing numbers, Adams was appointed to a committee to consider them. Subsequently in February, 1844, he presented a report on the effect of slavery on the country's democratic institutions, pointing out that slavery had originally been tolerated in the Constitution as a necessary evil but that now the national government had become an institution for its perpetuation. Massachusetts, he suggested, should separate itself from any responsibility for slavery. He warned that the annexation of Texas might tend to drive the free states into the dissolution of the Union.

As the probability of a Texas annexation increased, opposition grew even among the conservative Massachusetts Whigs although they still hesitated at any direct action. Adams wrote a series of articles on the Texas question for the Boston *Courier* but these were generally disregarded. However, his father in Washington approved highly of them, writing that it was a great comfort to him at the close of his own career to know that at the approach of the most portentous crisis the country had ever known, his son "*had entered the battle.*"

In the presidential campaign of 1844 Adams toured Massachusetts speaking for the Whig nominee, Henry Clay. Candidate for the fourth time, the sixty-seven-year-old nationalist had come out against the Texas annexation. The Democrats, in nominating Speaker of the House James K. Polk, made annexation the campaign's chief issue. Their slogan, "All of Oregon, all of Texas!" summed up the expansionist mood of the country, and the relatively obscure Polk was elected by a small margin over the far more popular Clay. In Massachusetts, at least, the Whigs carried the state and Senator Adams was easily re-elected. One of his first assignments in the new Senate was to consider the action of South Carolina in expelling Massachusetts judge Samuel Hoar, sent south to investigate the imprisonment of Massachusetts Negroes, seamen for the most part. Adams's final report was widely circulated and carefully listened to, much to his satisfaction, and he thought with some exaggeration that his position was the equal of any of his contemporaries in the entire country.

President Tyler and the Democrats took the election as a sign of approval of their Texas course, and two days before Polk's inaugural Congress authorized the annexation. Polk's administration, in Adams's opinion, initiated a policy of subservience to the slaveholding oligarchy. Over the heads of the more conservative Massachusetts Whigs he prepared a new set of Texas resolutions repudiating the annexation as a perversion of republican government and an assault on the compromises of the Constitution. Drastic countermeasures were required even if they should in the end bring about the downfall of slavery. In his final resolution Adams demanded that no further territories be admitted to the Union as slave states. However little force these resolutions might have in

Congress, they were passed by a large majority in the Massachusetts legislature.

Five years beneath the dome of the Massachusetts State House were, to Adams's mind, long enough. He was satisfied with what he had accomplished. He had brought his party to a declaration of policy on slavery. Now he wanted to devote himself to his more personal interests—history, letters, his family, and his property. Though he would continue to write political articles, he kept apart from public life. His closest friends were Charles Summer, Richard Henry Dana, and the historian John Palfrey. With them he spent many pleasant hours in the large library of his Mount Vernon Street house. In February, 1846, his pleasant hours were shattered when his youngest boy, Arthur, died suddenly. Adams was so overcome that he shut himself away with his grief for the next three months. Then, as if to ease his sorrow through work, he joined with Palfrey and Stephen Phillips in buying the Boston *Daily Whig*—a faltering six-month-old paper—and took over as editor. Every day he labored on his paper from nine to two. In issue after issue he attacked the temporizing policy of the state Whig party and those conservatives more concerned about the rights of cotton than the rights of men. Mercantile Massachusetts wanted in no way to disturb the South and Adams's attacks were much resented by the mill-owning Abbots, Lawrences, and Appletons and other Boston financial leaders. The outbreak of the Mexican War brought forth his bitterest opposition. For him it was a war so unjust that no citizen was obliged to support it directly or indirectly. John Quincy, happy at the role his son was playing, encouraged him: "Proceed-Persevere-Never despair—don't give up the ship!"

By the time of the Massachusetts Whig convention of 1846 the party had split into "Conscience" and "Cotton" Whigs. Despite the party's denunciation of the Mexican War and of the expansion of slavery, the Conscience Whigs considered its platform generalized verbiage. After the convention, much bad feeling ensued between the Conscience Whigs and their majority Cotton opponents. Old social as well as political friendships were severed. The Conscience Whigs were ostracized by the business community, though Adams was less affected than many others.

When President Polk submitted a bill to Congress requesting $2 million to induce Mexico to end the war, Congressman David Wilmot of Pennsylvania attached a proviso to the bill prohibiting slavery in any territory acquired from Mexico. The proviso, passed by the House, was talked to death in the Senate. Nevertheless the Wilmot Proviso became a shibboleth for the Conscience Whigs. Adams in his paper declared that the true course of the party lay in strict adherence to it. Nationally the Whigs divided further over the election of Robert Winthrop of Massachusetts as Speaker of the House of Representatives. Palfrey, newly elected to Congress, opposed Winthrop, who, although the choice of the party caucus, refused to commit himself on the questions of the war and slavery extension. Two other Massachusetts Congressmen also withheld their votes. After three ballots Winthrop was finally elected, but only by a single vote. Then it was learned that John Quincy Adams had given the deciding vote for Winthrop. He meant this merely as a gesture of friendship, for long ago Winthrop's father had supported John Quincy when others had deserted him. But in Massachusetts it looked as if the elder Adams had repudiated his son's position. Charles Francis appealed to his mother: "*Don't let my father play into their hands. I don't ask him to help us—All I want is to have him stand aside and see fair play....*" Louisa explained that her husband's health "renders him at times the creature of impulse.... He intended no wrong to you or to *his friends* but the allurements of flattery; and that desire which has ever possessed him, of striking out a new path for *himself* led him to this."

In February, 1848, when Charles Francis and other disenchanted Conscience Whigs were considering combining with the Liberty party and other antislavery groups, John Quincy died. Just before the funeral the son stood alone for some minutes by his father's coffin. What his thoughts were he did not record, but he must have sensed that he was now the political successor as well as the head of the family. Briefly there was a movement to elect him to his father's congressional seat, though he was passed over for Horace Mann. That February also saw the end of the Mexican War. Adams was willing to support the peace treaty since there was nothing in it justifying the war or claiming reparations. He emphasized that the land acquired had been purchased, though he glossed over the fact that if it had not been for the war, the Mexican government would never have agreed to such a purchase.

His father's death, and in that presidential year the almost inevitable nomination by the Whigs of the elderly general and slaveholder Zachary Taylor, broke his last link with the party. He determined to give up the editorship of the *Whig* as soon as he could find a replacement. On June 24, 1848, his son Brooks was born, his last child and for the father a partial recompense for the lost Arthur. That same month the disaffected Conscience Whigs of Massachusetts met in a convention that was really more of a demonstration. They made no nomination proposals but resolved to support only those presidential candidates opposed to the extension of slavery. Charles Francis was one of the speakers. Those who saw the slight bald man on the platform were struck by his singular resemblance to his father and grandfather. As if to emphasize the family continuity, Adams when he spoke used the very words his grandfather had used in signing the Declaration of Independence, avowing that "Sink or Swim, Live or Die, Survive or Perish, to go with the liberties of my country, is my fixed determination."

After the Democrats had nominated the expansionist Lewis Cass, the New York Free-Soil Democrats declared for Van Buren, who in spite of his earlier vacillations on the slavery question had defied his party by coming out against the Texas annexation. In August a Free-Soil convention in Buffalo brought together anti-slavery Democrats, Barnburners, Conscience Whigs, and members of the old Liberty party. After some hesitation Van Buren was chosen as the new party's presidential candidate. Since he was an Eastern Democrat, it was assumed that his running mate would be a Western Whig. The Western delegates, however, insisted that they wanted Adams. Charles Francis was present wearing a black band on his white hat in mourning for his father, and this visible reminder of Old Man Eloquent stirred poignant memories. When Adams's name was finally presented to the convention men stood on chairs, huzzaed, and tossed their hats in the air. Afterward, as parades formed and bands played, he was much moved to hear the old Revolutionary shout of "Adams and Liberty!"

Like most Whig-derived Free-Soilers, Adams found Van Buren an embarrassment. There was no correspondence between the two during the campaign that they both realized they could not possibly win. Yet Adams consoled himself with the thought that as long as he was alive there would still be an Adams ready to defend his country against every foul bargain. The Cotton Whig *Atlas* savaged him as a dilettante living on inherited wealth and reputation whose chief traits were egotism and selfishness.

Although Adams knew the Free-Soilers could not win nationally, he hoped that they would establish a firm base for the future. In Massachusetts he predicted that the party of property would never recover from its defeat. Van Buren and Adams nationally managed to poll a tenth of the votes cast, although they failed to win a single electoral vote. In Massachusetts they won almost a third of the votes, preventing Taylor from gaining the necessary majority. Since the naming of electoral delegates now devolved on the Whig legislature, Taylor became the choice of Massachusetts. Nevertheless, Adams was not displeased with the results. The

Whig leaders in Boston had received a setback. The new party had made a good beginning. In spite of the Whig victory, he sensed that the party was in an irreversible process of disintegration. He himself was satisfied that he had done his honest duty. He could now return to his books and his studies and the organization of his grandfather's papers. He was forty-two years old, and he considered that the best part of his life was over. The thought of past years was painful to him. Though he could not accuse himself of being lazy he had fallen short of his ambitions. On New Year's Day, 1849, Peter Brooks died, leaving an estate of over $2 million. To Charles Francis and each of his other sons-in-law he willed $75,000. The residue was to be divided equally among his seven children. Charles Francis and Abby inherited over $300,000, a handsome fortune in an era when a workman's wage was often no more than a dollar a day. For the first time wealth, that necessary appendage to a dynastic family, came to the Adamses. With the death of his father and of his father-in-law, Charles Francis was financially as well as emotionally independent. Money gave him both assurance and stature.

After John Quincy's death Louisa remained in Washington, a place and an atmosphere less alien to her than New England. Charles Francis, while visiting her in December, 1849, was struck by the intransigence of both sides in the slave controversy. The radical North had bound itself to the Wilmot Proviso; the South threatened disunion if the proviso ever became law. Adams was willing to break the impasse by allowing the slave states to form their own government and so free the national government from their power and influence. When their confederation failed—as he was certain in the long run it would—they would be forced by economic necessity to return to the Union, but with much diminished influence.

To end the bitter differences between North and South, Henry Clay offered his own compromise plan. Under it California was to be admitted as a free state, while the rest of the Mexican land would be divided into the territories of Utah and Mexico without any mention of slavery; the slave trade—though not slavery—would be abolished in the District of Columbia; there would be no restriction on slave trade between slave states; and finally there would be a more effective fugitive slave law. After Taylor's death in 1850, Congress quickly passed Clay's compromise. Adams wanted no part of such a compromise and spoke out against it at a Massachusetts Free-Soil convention. It meant, he pointed out, surrendering the Wilmot Proviso, surrendering the principle of no more slave states—for several slave states might yet be carved from Texas. He foresaw later a possible annexation of Cuba, another Mexican war, the seizure of the West Indies, "and so on until the crack of doom."

Whatever Adams might have thought, in the wake of Clay's compromise both major parties considered the slavery issue settled. All over the country there was a reaction against abolitionist agitation. "The moral tone of the Free States never was more thoroughly broken," Charles Francis wrote. The Whigs—a doomed party—were divided, lacking both leaders and ideas; the proslavery Democrats gained in strength, while the Free-Soilers were fading away. In 1852 the uneasy Whigs again turned to a general, Winfield Scott, as their presidential candidate. The Democrats nominated Franklin Pierce, a Northern man with Southern sympathies. Adams accepted the Free-Soil nomination for Congress. He came out second in a field of four. Though he had not expected to win, he was gratified by the sizable vote he received.

The lassitude following Clay's compromise fell away in 1854 with the passage of the Kansas-Nebraska Act repealing the 1820 Missouri Compromise. Kansas and Nebraska were now to be organized into territories whose inhabitants would decide whether they wished to become free or slave states. The act started a furor in the North. Conservative lawyers, merchants, and professional men who had gone along with the Clay compromise now felt swindled. The issue came to a head in Boston when a stowaway slave, Anthony Burns, was seized and marched to the docks to be shipped south. So threatening were the protesters that a thousand soldiers stood guard on the streets from the courthouse to the waterfront. Adams, angry and dismayed, was by now convinced that the time had come for a new party alignment. Yet personally he hesitated. When the Massachusetts Free-Soilers, trying to renew themselves and expand their appeal, adopted the name Republican, he remained apart from them. Another new political movement, the cabalistic Native American or Know-Nothing party asked him to join. Anti-Catholic, antiforeign, the Know-Nothings battened on the prejudices aroused by the mass arrival of foreigners, particularly the Irish swarms fleeing the potato famine. Adams would have nothing to do with such a party. "Any action," he replied, "which tends to draw distinct lines between foreign-born persons and natives cannot fail to be unfortunate. It will perpetuate instead of expunging, as it ought, the traces of distinction between men equally anxious to become the supports of their common country." Nevertheless, in the next Massachusetts election, capitalizing on the disgust of many former Free-Soilers with both established parties, the Know-Nothings swept the state, garnering almost two-thirds of the votes.

From 1853 to 1856 Adams had little or nothing to do with politics. Yet in that period his stature grew and he came more and more to be recognized as the representative of Adams continuity—though often, to his anger, in a diminished sense. "Constant reference" to his father and his grandfather, his son Charles wrote, "in connection with himself annoyed and at times irritated him. He could not habituate himself to it, nor learn to take it lightly . . . 'sharp decline' was the approved form of speech." He busied himself with his private affairs, served on the boards of banks and schools, and turned for relaxation to the classics and to his coin collection. From 1850 to 1856 he brought out ten volumes of John Adams's papers, and in 1856 completed a life of his grandfather that he considered the equal of the best historical literature produced in the country. To his disappointment, it roused little outside interest either among scholars or the public. He then turned to an editing of his father's papers, which he proposed to round off with a biography—although, after numerous interruptions, this would not be completed until 1877.

The approach of the election of 1856 brought him out of his study as a delegate to the Republican national convention in Philadelphia. That year there were to be no less than six national conventions, three of them held by the Know-Nothings. The Whigs, a sorry remnant of a once triumphant party, followed the Know-Nothings in nominating former President Millard Fillmore. Republicans chose the explorer and conqueror of California, John C. Frémont, as their presidential candidate, he being also endorsed by the antislavery wing of the Know-Nothings. The Democrats named the compromising Northerner James Buchanan. Although losing the election to Buchanan, the Republicans won a surprising 114 electoral votes, and over half a million more popular votes than the Whigs. Like other incipient Republicans Adams was encouraged by defeat, convinced that a combination of groups and forces had been welded together that would eventually control the country.

After the election he continued to live quietly and unpolitically, though he loudly protested the Dred Scott decision and contributed both money and advice to "Bleeding Kansas." To Charles Summer he complained that political leaders never concerned themselves with him except when they wanted money, and of that distinction he was a little weary. For years he had nursed the idea of some day succeeding to his father's old seat in Congress, but that hope had now worn thin. "Sometime or other," he wrote in his diary, "some unexpected accident may do something for me. I am sure nothing else will." The unexpected accident occurred in 1858 when the Republicans nominated him from his father's district. At first he could not believe his good luck. Yet true to his family tradition he refused to campaign actively, merely making a few occasional speeches. The Republicans carried the state. He did even better. In his third district he ran well ahead of the Republican candidate for governor and received almost double the votes of his nearest opponent. To his surprise he found himself momentarily popular. Everywhere in the North the Republicans had gained strength, capitalizing on an economic depression and on popular discontent with the indecisive Buchanan. Of the twenty-one new Republicans in Congress, Adams was outstanding, looked on in advance as a party leader.

As he prepared for his journey south he was filled with misgivings about his new political life, uneasy at the prospect of leaving his ingrown surroundings, worried about not being able to look after his properties and personal affairs. After his father's death he had taken over the Old House in Quincy and was restoring it as his summer residence. All this must now be interrupted.

Adams and his wife, accompanied by their two youngest children, Mary and Brooks, arrived in the Capital in December, 1859, only a week before Congress convened. John Quincy and Charles, in the Adams tradition, had taken up law for want of anything better, and remained in Boston. Henry, on graduating from Harvard in 1858, had gone to Germany, ostensibly to study civil law. Louisa, married to "a severe and bearded gentleman, from Philadelphia, Charles Kuhn," now lived in Italy. Charles Francis had rented the Washington residence formerly owned by the British minister. He enrolled Brooks in a preparatory school, rented a pew in the Unitarian church, and left the details of moving to Abby and the servants. "The governor is doing well," son Charles wrote Henry with muffled cynicism. "Character, ability, wealth and family all rank high in Washington and all of them he has."

The presidential election of 1860, shadowed by the gathering clouds of secession, obscured all other issues in Washington and in Congress. The crisis had been intensified by John Brown's raid, the North coming more and more to consider Brown a martyr, the South castigating him as a villainous madman. Southerners were coming out openly for their own independent republic. Most of Congress's time was consumed by North-South antagonisms. Not until May did Adams make his maiden speech, his only one of the session. He spoke calmly and temperately—in obvious contrast to the abusive language of Sumner and the Radicals—warning the Southerners that secession would solve no problems. They might try independence if they wished, he told them, but it would end in ignominious failure. North and South had too much in common to separate—a common blood, common literature, "social and religious affinities." The violent men advising separation would in the end disappoint the Southerners, and though they might consider him their enemy, he wanted to warn them in time.

Adams's speech was well received. Even the Southerners complimented him. William Seward, the Republican Senator from New York and an old Adams family friend, thought it a great effort. To conservative men of conciliatory temperament like Adams, Seward seemed the most desirable and most probable candidate for the Republican presidential nomination. No other candidate could touch his qualifications. Long ago as a young lawyer he had opposed the Albany Regency in speaking out for "John Quincy Adams—and better government." Slavery he viewed as an irrepressible conflict between North and South, yet he wanted above all to preserve the Union. Viewed through the eyes of young Henry Adams he appeared "a slouching, slender figure; a head like a wise macaw, a beaked nose; shaggy eyebrows; unorderly hair and clothes; hoarse voice; offhand manner; free talk, and perpetual cigar." Henry's brother Charles thought his clothes must have been made twenty years earlier, and by a bad tailor at that.

Seward and Salmon Chase, Ohio governor and a founder of the Free-Soil party, and Governor Edward Bates of Missouri were the three leading Republican candidates for President, with Seward the favorite. Like many in Washington Adams could scarcely believe his ears when he heard that the relatively obscure Lincoln had been nominated on the third ballot. He thought the Illinois lawyer honest and reasonably capable, but lacking in experience. He counted on Seward to play the dominant role in the new administration. Overcoming his ingrained reluctance, he made a political tour with Seward through the Northwest, taking his son Charles with him. There he let Seward know that he wanted no place in any Lincoln administration. His father's congressional seat was the highest post he cared to occupy.

In September the Southerners openly declared that Lincoln's election would end the Union. But they had cried up the wolf of disunion many times before, and the Republicans in their confidence of victory showed little concern over the threat. Four parties competed in the election. The Democrats had split in two, the Northerners endorsing Stephen Douglas, while the dissident Southerners named John Breckinridge. In addition to the Republicans there was a Constitutional Union party with John Ball as its presidential candidate and as his running mate Adams's brother-in-law Edward Everett. If the Democrats had remained united, they could have won easily. As it was, Lincoln was elected with a mere third of the vote. Within Massachusetts, however, the Republicans carried the state almost by two thirds. Though in the third congressional district, Constitutional Unionists, Democrats, and Know-Nothings had united on one Leverett Saltonstall, Adams was overwhelmingly re-elected. When his Quincy townsmen learned of his victory they held a grand torchlight parade in his honor. Watching them in their exuberance pass by the Old House, he felt at last that he had vindicated himself as an Adams.

Of the four-month interlude between Lincoln's election and his inauguration Adams wrote afterward that "our only course in the defenseless position in which we found ourselves was to gain time, and bridge over the chasm made by Mr. Buchanan's weaknesses." Vital for the North were the wavering border states, for a South once unified was capable of destroying the whole fabric of government before Lincoln took office. When the South Carolina legislature called for a secession convention, Adams was ready to let the intransigent slave states go. "Let them secede from Congress," he wrote, "long enough to enable the Republicans to establish their authority in the federal government and the game is played." He was more than willing to make concessions to the Southerners, but felt that their real grievance was that they still wanted to rule. President Buchanan in his State of the Union message declared secession unconstitutional, but at the same time claimed that neither he nor Congress had the power to prevent it. Several members of his cabinet were indeed outright secessionists. Adams considered the President's message weak and vacillating toward the South, insulting to the rest of the country, satisfactory to no one, and of no use in calming the voters.

To calm the waters became the goal of Adams and Seward, in the hope that if the North showed itself restrained and conciliatory, latent Union sentiment in the South would assert itself. Adams became a member of the House Committee of Thirty-three—one member from each state—formed, along with a similar Committee of Thirteen in the Senate, to propose remedies that would keep the Union intact. Though Adams would have preferred to see the end of the Union to the extension of slavery, nevertheless in the interest of conciliation he was ready to support a constitutional amendment forbidding interference with slavery where it already existed, and he was willing to have the territory of New Mexico admitted to statehood with or without slavery in accordance with the Compromise of 1850. This he thought a reasonable concession without any sacrifice of principles. His Massachusetts constituents were not so sure, and his declaration caused surly resentment in the North. In his more depressed moments he felt that his hopelessly divided committee could not accomplish anything, and that there was no way out but the ultimate test of war. Summer and the Radicals might welcome such a test. Adams did not.

The final meeting of the committee could agree neither on measures to be reported out nor on adjourning without making any report at all. As a result seven minority reports were presented to Congress. Adams, in an even-tempered speech in the House, said that Congress's object should be to preserve Republican principles while at the same time bridging over the chasm of a rebellion. He admitted that the South had cause for complaint in the personal liberty laws and the denial of equal rights in the territories. He was again willing to support the New Mexico proposal. But the North would not guarantee in advance the protection of slavery in territory not even possessed by the government, as had been proposed by Southerners. Such, he told them, would repudiate the principles of the Founding Fathers and disgrace the country in the eyes of the world.

While Congress debated, four more Southern states followed seceding South Carolina, but to Adams's relief, the border states did not. When the Virginians asked all the other states to send delegates to a peace convention in February, Adams approved in spite of the objections of radicals on both sides. Though the conference itself proved futile, Adams and Seward continued to press their policy of moderation. Henry, returned from Europe to become his father's secretary, thought the Union was a sentiment but not much more.

Till shortly before Lincoln's inauguration, Adams had been repeatedly mentioned as a possible member of Lincoln's cabinet. Such a post in such company he in no way aspired to, and he thanked his good fortune that the rumors turned out to be no more than rumors. Seward, named Secretary of State, told him, however, that he was being considered as the next minister to England. This, Adams admitted, was something he did want, both for himself and for his family.

It was a post also wanted by his erstwhile friend Summer, who when he heard the news of Adams's appointment used such violent and abusive language that the two men never again resumed their old intimacy. Lincoln's choice for minister to England had not been Adams, and it took considerable arguing on Seward's part to induce him to change his mind. Seward insisted. Adams had returned to Boston when a telegram arrived announcing his appointment. According to his son Charles, the news "fell on our breakfast-table like a veritable bomb-shell, scattering confusion and dismay. . . . My mother at once fell into tears and deep agitation; foreseeing all sorts of evil consequences and absolutely refusing to be comforted; while my father looked dismayed. The younger members of the household were astonished and confounded." Charles blamed the desiccating influence of Boston. "My father and mother had lived there steadily for almost thirty years," he explained in his autobiography. "They had grown into a rut, and begun to entertain a species of religious cult on that head. My mother, in some respects remarkably calculated for social life, took a constitutional and sincere pleasure in the forecast of evil. She delighted in the dark side of anticipation; she did not really think so; but liked to think, and say, she thought so. She indulged in the luxury of woe! . . . As to my father, he had then lived so long in the atmosphere of Boston, that I really think the great opportunity of his life when suddenly thrust upon him caused a sincere feeling of consternation. He really felt that he was being called on to make a great personal and political sacrifice."

Whatever Adams's dubious second thoughts, he left for Washington at once to receive his instructions. Seward accompanied him to the White House, that now remote edifice that had been his home three decades earlier. Lincoln met them, a tall, gaunt, shabbily dressed man wearing carpet slippers. The Secretary of State introduced the new minister, who made the customary brief speech of appreciation. "Very kind of you to say so Mr. Adams," said Lincoln dryly, "but you are not my choice. You are Seward's man." Then, as if he had dismissed the English mission from his mind, he turned to Seward. "Well, governor," he said, "I've this morning decided that Chicago post-office appointment." He seemed indifferent to and uninterested in the problems his new minister would have to face. Adams was shocked. All his earlier doubts about Lincoln's unfitness for office were confirmed.

Such doubts persisted. Adams blamed the drift toward war on the President's indecision, his failure to consult his official advisers. He himself was convinced that the only way for Lincoln to avoid a civil conflict at this time was to recall the federal troops from Fort Sumter. When war finally did come he thought it was mostly Lincoln's fault.

Adams had no more realization than the rest of his countrymen of the grim years that were to follow. At the beginning war seemed an exciting pageant to both North and South, with eager volunteers drilling, equally eager women sewing flags and uniforms, bands playing in bunting-draped streets, and the easy feeling that after a few months of excitement and adventure it would all be over by Christmas. Americans of that generation did not yet know what war really was. And this was to be the first modern war. Adams had postponed his departure for six weeks to attend his son John's wedding, a postponement that led to grave political complications and that his son Charles later judged as discreditable both to him and to Seward. Charles had already enlisted when Adams sailed on the first of May from East Boston on the "wretched old Cunard steamer Niagara," taking with him his wife, Brooks, and Mary, and Henry as his private secretary. Almost half a century later Henry recalled their departure, even as he recalled the previous long April evenings with the regiments forming ranks before the Boston State House:

"Minister Adams, remembered how his grandfather had sailed from Mount Wollaston in midwinter, 1778, on the little frigate Boston, taking his eleven-year-old son John Quincy with him, for secretary, on a diplomacy of adventure that had hardly a parallel for success. He remembered how John Quincy, in 1809, had sailed for Russia, with himself, a baby of two years old, to cope with Napoleon and the Czar Alexander single-handed, almost as much of an adventurer as John Adams before him, and almost as successful. He thought it natural that the Government should send him out as an adventurer also, with a twenty-three-year-old son, and he did not even notice that he left not a friend behind him."

When Adams was not seasick he spent his days at sea reading Macaulay's *History of England*. What lay ahead of him was formidably unknown. He knew at least that Lord Palmerston, the prime minister, was no friend of the United States. Lord John Russell, the head of the Foreign Office, was an uncertain factor, but Adams knew at least that he was antislavery in sentiment. The new American minister's instructions were to make it clear that the federal government did not look on secession as permanent, but expected the logic of events to bring an eventual reconciliation. Meanwhile offers of mediation were unacceptable, and recognition of the Confederacy would be considered an unfriendly act.

Before landing young Henry assumed "that he was going to a friendly Government and people, true to the anti-slavery principles which had been their steadiest profession. . . . Instinctively English, he could not conceive the idea of a hostile England. He supposed himself, as one of the members of a famous anti-slavery family, to be welcome everywhere in the British Islands. . . . He had to learn—the sooner the better—that his ideas were the reverse of truth; that in May, 1861, no one in England—literally no one—doubted that Jefferson Davis had made or would make a nation, and nearly all were glad of it, though not often saying so. They mostly imitated Palmerston, who, according to Mr. Gladstone, 'desired the severance as a diminution of a dangerous power, but prudently held his tongue.' "

Social obligations had not delayed the Confederate envoys, and they reached London several weeks before Charles Francis. In Liverpool he was dismayed to learn that Queen Victoria had already issued a Proclamation of Neutrality in which the Confederates were accorded belligerent rights, regarded as the first step to recognition.

Shortly after his arrival in London Adams was presented at court. In accordance with the directive of an earlier Secretary of State, his two predecessors had appeared in plain black, and the Queen had taken offense at this gesture of moral superiority. After it had been pointed out to Adams that black was the costume of butlers, he decided to revert to the traditional diplomatic uniform of blue coat with gold eagle buttons and embroidered stand-up collar, and white waistcoat and knee breeches. So dressed, he presented the "personal regards" of the American people to Queen Victoria, whom he found gracious and dignified if not handsome and imposing. The Queen remarked afterward of his costume that she was thankful "we shall have no more American funerals."

His English reception at court and in general was cordial. In his first month at the legation five members of the cabinet gave dinners in his honor. A first interview with the foreign secretary, Lord John Russell, was agreeable. The two men took to each other at once. Much alike, they even resembled one another physically. Adams explained his fear that England's "precipitous" recognition of Confederate belligerent rights might lead to formal recognition. Privately Russell, though antislavery in feeling and sympathetic to the North, had concluded that it would be impossible to restore the Union and considered recognition—at an appropriate time—the means of speeding the inevitable. But he let Adams believe that his country had no intention of recognizing the Confederacy. Pressed further, he declined to give any pledge as to future policy. Adams said nothing, but he expected his government to take indignant exception to this equivocal position, and concluded his stay in England would probably be short. Formal recognition, however, was not as close as he had feared. Though Adams distrusted Lord Palmerston and assumed that he would recognize the Confederacy at an opportune moment, the prime minister moved with great caution. England's attitude hung on the military situation in the dis-United States. If the battlefield balance swung decisively toward the Confederacy, British and European recognition could be expected to follow. All Adams could do meanwhile was to display outward imperturbability while awaiting developments. Prudently he took care to rent his London house by the month only.

The American minister sensed that however the prime minister might feel, there was still sympathy for the United States in government circles, and he was relieved when a sharply debated motion in the House of Commons to recognize the Confederacy was indefinitely postponed. At the outbreak of the war English public opinion generally favored the North, but this was an antislavery sentiment that wilted under the federal government's insistence that its war aim was reunion and not abolition. Some English abolitionists even argued that the South should be allowed to secede as the best way to quarantine slavery. The upper and commercial classes tended to be pro-Southern. Aristocratic England felt sympathetic to the South, and hoped to see the democratic presumption founder. Commercial interests saw in an independent South a way of breaking the Northern tariff wall. The cotton spinners wanted a quick, peaceful separation to assure their supplies of raw material.

Engaged in frustrating negotiations with the British government over the question of Confederate privateering, the American minister was speechless with dismay at the news of the Union army's July defeat at Bull Run. His son Henry considered it "a worse diplomatic than military disaster." The Union defeat led to a noticeable shift in English opinion. The London *Times* for the first time displayed open friendliness toward the Confederacy.

The American legation staff was small and bogged down in paperwork. Besides Henry, Adams had a secretary of the legation and an assistant secretary. Most of the minister's time was spent in miscellaneous ephemera—receiving visits from those who wanted to join the Union army; who had run out of money; or, at the other end of the scale, who wished to be presented at court. Always there was the occasional crackpot, such as the eager Englishman who presented his plan for solving all the ills of America by establishing a national church, setting up a monarchy, and doing away with the individual states. In addition to his official duties, Adams was forced to participate to a degree in London social life. He found the rounds of dinners and balls tedious and disagreeable. Though himself civilly treated in society—his son thought him indistinguishable from any upper-class Englishman— he resented the supercilious attitude of the aristocracy toward things American. Daily he took a walk through the city, partly because he felt an obligation to know London better, partly to get away from his office. He did not share his father's and his grandfather's love of walking nor their fascination with the English metropolis. Rarely did he like what he saw, and thought London as crime- and vice-ridden as New York. Particularly was he offended by the blatant prostitution to which official London seemed indifferent.

By the autumn of 1861 Adams had come to think that the most he could hope from the English was continued indifference. The war stalemate weighed him down, and he hoped for a clear-cut

Northern victory that would demonstrate to England and to Europe the North's superior strength. But by now he had little confidence in Lincoln. As he realized all too clearly, any further Union disaster in the field would probably bring European recognition of the Confederacy.

Early in November, 1861, Jefferson Davis appointed two special commissioners, James Mason of Virginia and John Slidell of Louisiana, to take over the functions of Confederate agents abroad. After running the Union blockade they arrived in Havana where they boarded the British mail packet *Trent*. En route to London the *Trent* was stopped by a shot across the bow from the United States sloop of war *San Jacinto*, commanded by Captain Charles Wilkes. Wilkes knew the Confederate agents were aboard but acted on his own without instructions from his government. He took Mason and Slidell prisoner and brought them to Boston. The North acclaimed him. Here was a victory at last, a vindication, an affront to British pride. Henry and the other two secretaries of the legation shouted with delight. Governor John Andrew of Massachusetts gave Wilkes a public banquet. Secretary of the Navy Gideon Welles hastened to congratulate him. Congress voted him a gold medal.

For the sober-minded American minister the news was calamitous. Whatever the legal rights, the incident would, he knew, inflame opinion in England. "The people are frantic with rage," an American in London wrote Seward, "and were the country polled, I fear 999 out of a thousand would declare for war." Palmerston demanded the return of the two prisoners and an official apology. Prince Albert, in his last illness, intervened from his sickbed to soften British demands by adding an expression of hope that Wilkes's act had been unauthorized. A wave of chauvinism swept England. Editorials denounced the American action so persistently and so vehemently that Adams gave up reading them. He deplored the blatant rejoicing in the United States and informed Seward that the present state of British opinion could easily lead to war.

As for his countrymen, he wrote Charles, "they may regard Messrs. Mason and Slidell as more precious than all their worldly possessions. May be so. For my part I would part with them at a cent apiece."

By mid-December both sides were having sober second thoughts. In spite of the public clamor to uphold national honor, neither side wanted war. Much depended on the nature of the American reply to the British note. In a dispatch to Adams Seward declared that Wilkes had acted without the instructions or knowledge of his government. Adams explained to Seward the possible consequences of not meeting British demands. Retreating from his original belligerency, the American Secretary of State agreed to release Mason and Slidell, although he balked at an apology. The British accepted the freeing of the two men as essentially complying with their demands and let the apology drop. Adams was much relieved at the news. Officially he and Russell exchanged congratulations, and the Englishman expressed the hope that nothing further would disturb the peace of the two countries.

When it became clear in England that the United States government wanted to avoid a quarrel, sentiment again swung toward the North. "The Trent affair has proved thus far somewhat in the nature of a sharp thunderstorm which has burst without doing any harm," Adams wrote Charles, now a lieutenant in the Union army, "and the consequence has been a decided improvement of the state of the atmosphere. Our English friends are pleased with themselves and pleased with us for having given them the opportunity to be so. The natural effect is to reduce the apparent dimensions of all other causes of offense. . . . So that I am now quite encouraged to think that the prospect of interference with us is growing more and more remote."

In the period of diplomatic calm that followed, Adams continued to explore the London streets. Systematically he visited the National Gallery, hoping to improve his taste in art. Socially he found a few people, such as the Duke and Duchess of Argyll, whose company he enjoyed. Abby began holding weekly receptions for Americans in London. In May when Adams heard of Farragut's capture of New Orleans he danced across the ministry entry shouting "We've got New Orleans!" Henry wrote his soldier brother that "the effect of the news here has been greater than anything yet. It has acted like a violent blow in the face on a drunken man."

On June 12 Adams received a note from Palmerston violently attacking the Union General Ben Butler, who had responded to what he considered the insulting behavior of the ladies of occupied New Orleans by issuing an order that any women showing discourtesy to his soldiers would be "regarded and treated as common women plying their vocation." No such act, the prime minister concluded, could be found in the whole history of civilized nations. "Palmerston wants a quarrel!" Henry heard his father say on reading the note. Adams feared that it indirectly indicated a change in British policy. Insulting in tone, it seemed to him to mark an end to his own usefulness, for he knew he could never again have friendly relations with the prime minister. After an exchange of several more notes, Palmerston backed away from what had at first appeared a complete rupture. But Adams in his final communication stated that the prime minister's note was the only instance of discourtesy he had yet received in England, and that in the future he would refuse to accept any communications except through Lord Russell. After that Palmerston avoided recognizing Adams in public, and Lady Palmerston stopped inviting the Adamses to her levees.

Adams was shortly faced with the problem of the formidable gunboat known as the *290*, then under construction at Liverpool for the Confederates, one of the fast merchant ships that were armed and fitted out for war only after leaving British ports. It was difficult to find legal grounds for detaining such vessels, although in this case the judge advocate of the fleet admitted that the Americans would have serious ground for complaint if the *290* were launched. Adams requested Russell to have the ministry seize the *290*, but the latter deliberately delayed taking action until the ship had left port. The *290* would become the famous raider *Alabama* that before her own sinking would wreak devastation among Union vessels. Defending his government's inaction, Palmerston to Adams's indignation maintained that the American minister had given no evidence against the *290* on which the English courts could have proceeded.

After Stonewall Jackson's defeat of the Union army at the Second Battle of Bull Run and after Lee's invasion of Maryland, Russell began to revive the always latent idea of intervention, instructing the English ambassador in Paris to sound out the French government on possible joint action. Russell and Palmerston agreed that if the North then refused mediation on the basis of permanent separation, the next step should be recognition of the Confederacy. But opposition within the cabinet to such a change of policy, and the coolness of the French to the British proposals, made the prime minister hesitate. Adams's own instructions were to suspend his functions should the South be recognized.

Lincoln's Emancipation Proclamation, to go into effect on January 1, 1863, led to a sharp rise in sympathy for the North, making it even more difficult for the ministry to intervene. Upper-class England might ridicule the proclamation, pointing out that it would not free a single Negro, but Lincoln's action deeply moved the majority of Englishmen. How the balance would finally swing, as Adams well knew, depended on the military situation. His hopes went glimmering with the defeat of the Union army at Fredericksburg. But Grant's successes in Mississippi were heartening, and when at last the news came that Vicksburg had fallen on July 4,

1863, and that Lee had been repulsed at Gettysburg the day before, Adams sensed that the crisis was over and that any possibility of intervention had ended.

The issue of the rams remained, two ironclads being constructed by the Liverpool shipbuilding concern of the Lairds for the Confederate navy to aid in breaking the Union blockade. Ostensibly ordered by a French agency for the Viceroy of Egypt, the rams—as everyone knew—would, once they were at sea, be transferred to the Confederacy. Yet there was no evidence sustainable in a court of law to prove that they were destined for any other country than Egypt. In September, 1863, as the rams were nearing completion, Adams presented a culminating note to Russell stating that should the rams be permitted to leave England, "it would be superfluous in me to point out to your lordship that this is war."

The foreign secretary at this point had prudently determined to stop the delivery of the rams no matter what their legal status might be. His final decision, in which Palmerston concurred, was made before Adams had written his note. Eventually the British government would settle the problem by purchasing the rams outright for its own use. In America Adams was nevertheless credited with a great diplomatic victory. James Russell Lowell wrote: "None of our generals, nor Grant himself, did us better or more trying service than he in his forlorn outpost of London."

"Minister Adams's success in stopping the rebel rams fixed his position once for all in English society," his son Henry recalled a generation later. "From that moment he could afford to drop the character of diplomatist, and assume what, for an American Minister in London, was an exclusive diplomatic advantage, the character of a kind of American Peer of the Realm. The British never did things by halves. Once they recognized a man's right to social privileges, they accepted him as one of themselves. . . . Minister Adams had a rank of his own as a kind of leader of Her Majesty's American Opposition. Even the *Times* conceded it. The years of struggle were over, and Minister Adams rapidly gained a position which would have caused his father or grandfather to stare with incredulous envy."

For the remainder of the war Adams suffered no further diplomatic controversies of any consequence. Henry wrote his brother Charles in June, 1864, that in England the whole question of America "is now old and familiar to every one, so as to have become actually a bore and a nuisance." With the lightening of his official duties, the American minister was able to spend his weekends at the seaside resort of St. Leonards. Later he toured Wales with his family. Since he was no longer essential, he grew increasingly impatient with a life so little to his liking. Yet to return home, as he was painfully aware, would plunge him into the turbulence of domestic politics. He deplored the program and attitudes of Summer and the Radicals toward the South. For all his and his family's devotion to the antislavery cause, he found it "almost impossible to resist the conviction" that Negroes were an inferior race. In contrast to the Radicals he thought it would be folly to make Negro suffrage an issue in the face of popular opposition. Following Lincoln's re-election in 1864 he had asked Seward to be relieved in the spring, explaining that he did not wish to shrink from public service or embarrass the President, but he had completed his task. Seward delayed any decision.

On receiving the news of Lee's surrender at the end of April, 1865, Adams wrote in his diary: "Thanks be to God this deplorable war seems to have come to an end and the Union is not destroyed and emancipation is undoubtedly obtained." Three days later he was appalled to receive a telegram announcing Lincoln's assassination and the attempt on Seward's life. In spite of his past criticisms of the President he had come to see him as a man who had risen above his own limitations. His loss was, to Adams's mind, irreparable. The possible loss of Seward distressed Adams even more for he saw the Secretary of State as the more indispensable, the real guiding hand behind the Lincoln administration. Andrew Johnson's succession, however, did not dismay him for he appreciated his courageous honesty as the Radicals did not. Of the new President's first message Adams wrote that it "raised the character of the nation immensely in Europe."

Lincoln's death transformed sentiment in England. Magazines like *Punch* that had been reviling him a few months earlier now published their contrite tributes. Lord Russell thought the tragedy brought out the real feeling of the British nation. Adams was carried along in the tide of goodwill. His son Henry wrote a generation later: "Minister Adams became, in 1866, almost a historical monument in London; he held a position altogether his own. His old opponents disappeared.... His personal relations were excellent and his personal weight increased year by year."

Adams's plans to retire were blocked when he learned that he was being considered for Secretary of State in case Seward failed to recover from his wounds. At such a time he thought it would be improper for him to leave his London post. Meanwhile he was occupied with lesser matters: the spate of Americans wanting to return to the United States; the frustrations of the perennial war damage claims; the difficulties with Fenians in Ireland who, when arrested for plotting against the government, asserted that they were American citizens. Adams intervened when he could, secured the release of many Irish-Americans on condition that they leave the country, but refused to assist naturalized Americans who had been caught attempting to overthrow the government. His efforts were disparaged by Irish-Americans in the United States who demanded an investigation of his conduct.

As the year 1868 neared, Adams determined to resign as of April 1. This time Seward agreed, graciously and promptly. News of the American minister's retirement brought forth an extraordinary demonstration of cordiality in England. Newspapers, even his old antagonist the *Times*, praised him. A reference to him in the House of Commons brought forth spontaneous cheers. Prominent Londoners wanted to give him a public banquet, but he declined the honor as likely to prove embarrassing to himself and to other members of the diplomatic corps not so honored. British appreciation finally took the form of a testimonial signed by most of the leading men of England.

In America praise for Adams was more muted. Seward paid him a glowing tribute. So did some newspapers. But the Radical Republicans were out to take their revenge on the minister for his sympathy with beleaguered President Johnson and his coolness to Radical reconstruction demands. At Summer's instigation the Senate rejected the appointment of John Quincy Adams II to the Boston Custom House. With equal mean-mindedness Summer sponsored a bill banning court dress for American diplomats. Irish-Americans organized public demonstrations against Adams. Yet, when he learned that the Democrats were considering nominating him as their presidential candidate, he delayed his sailing in order to arrive in New York *after* the Democratic convention.

He left England with few regrets. His years there, by his own admission, had marked the only really difficult portion of his life. England had never been congenial to him, and he had no feeling of sadness in watching the English coastline recede. He had every reason to be content. In a period of unparalleled crises, he had by his steadiness and caution sustained and strengthened his government's position. When needful he had not hesitated to act without official instructions. He had held Seward's aggressiveness in check, toned down the Secretary of State's demands and accusations, outmaneuvered Palmerston, and prevented a rupture between the two countries that might have altered the course of the war. As he departed England for America, he left both countries in his debt.

When he arrived in New York Harbor aboard the *China* on a stifling summer evening, he was taken by a revenue cutter from his ship to the shore in a sudden drenching rainstorm. No bands were playing, no welcoming committee waited on the dock. Only emptiness and rain. He viewed his nonreception with a certain sardonic amusement. He was not so amused at his indifferent welcome in Massachusetts. The Radicals, who had gained political control of the state, took pains to avoid the man who had expressed the view that Congress had not "the smallest right ... to meddle with the reconstruction of a single state," who opposed giving the vote to Negroes, who sided with President Johnson. Former political intimates wanted nothing more to do with him. At the solitary reception given him, only a few men of any consequence attended. That he might end up a Democrat the Radicals considered a distinct possibility, and some of Summer's friends even thought he was preparing to challenge the Senator for his Senate seat.

Adams, for all their suspicions, avoided any political activity, declining all requests to speak. A rumor—alarming to the Radicals—gained currency that President-elect Grant was planning to take him into his cabinet. But at a public dinner in Boston, Grant received Adams with a marked lack of cordiality. Snubbed by politicians, Adams found a more satisfactory honor when he was asked to become president of Harvard, a position of far more importance to most Bostonians than any mere cabinet post. Though he declined, pleading "no especial fitness," he was flattered by the offer and shortly after did accept the presidency of the Board of Overseers. In the world beyond politics he was at last welcomed into the inner circle of old Boston families, the first Adams to become reconciled with social Boston. Ironically enough it was at a time when the brick colonial town was becoming a festering city under the waves of beaten Irish famine refugees who in the next generation or so would snatch Boston from the faltering hands of the old Yankees.

After Adams's long absence, he saw little change in Quincy. But on his first trip to Boston he was struck by how much things

had changed there. Everywhere business and commercial estab-
lishments were encroaching on the old residential and park areas.
Silas Laphams were rising; the war-rich blatantly obvious. One of
the things that struck him most forcibly was the diminished importance of the clergy. Ministers were now much less in evidence
at public functions. Church attendance had become a polite routine. "Established" Unitarianism seemed to him particularly lifeless,
without warmth in its services or emotion in its liturgy. The Irish
slums appeared menacing in their potential. Adams noticed how
the "ignorant" were more and more taking over in government,
and in his more depressed moments he predicted a future of anarchy and confusion.

It took him some time to re-establish the ordered personal life
that he found so necessary for his well-being. New servants had
to be trained. His neglected affairs had to be straightened out. Both
the Mount Vernon Street house and the Old House needed repairs
and remodeling. In Quincy he at last built the stone library that
his father had dreamed about. It turned out to be a more expensive
and time-consuming project than he had imagined and a constant
source of irritation to him while the work was going on. But after
half a year he had managed to settle down into a quiet, regulated
existence. He resumed his readings in the classics, worked on his
accounts, relaxed with his coin collection, and passed intimate
evenings at his "Wednesday" and "Friday" dining clubs. Earlier he
had found such excluding circles offensive, but now he relaxed in
the social milieu of his own kind. Yet he had no intimate friends
on either side of the Atlantic. Palfrey had been his solitary friend
in America, and he had made no new ones overseas. A year after
his return from England, he had not written a single personal letter
there. He remained an isolated man.

He was aging rapidly and was all too aware of it. Thrown back
for companionship on his family, he felt the loss when his son
Henry, closest to him of all his children, left for Washington in

1868 to make his way as a political journalist. The father admitted in his diary that he would miss him every day and hour for the rest of his life.

In the summer of 1870 Louisa died suddenly in Italy after a carriage accident. Adams had loved her and Henry more than his other children, and the news of her death numbed his mind to the point of emptiness. To ease his grief, as much as it could be eased, he devoted himself to the family papers that he had been sorting out in a desultory way and in some cases destroying ever since he returned home. Before beginning the long-planned editing of his father's diary, he decided to revise his biography of his grandfather.

The years slipped by in habitual sequence. Adams rarely went far from home, took no part in party politics. What he lost in political standing he gained in national reputation—as he was well aware. He thought himself that no one in the country occupied a securer place in public esteem though in his darker moments he wondered whether his fame exceeded his merits.

His prestige remained so unassailable that it was probably inevitable, whatever his own feelings, that he would be brought back into public life. What finally did bring him back were the still-unsettled American Civil War damage claims against the British government. The year 1870, with its renewed war in Europe, seemed appropriate for the settlement of these old and irritating differences. At this time the British and American governments agreed to appoint a commission of five members each to settle all disputes between them. Adams thought his earlier experiences made him a natural choice for one of the commissioners. Grant, who disliked him, thought otherwise. The Treaty of Washington, resulting from the deliberations of the commissioners, did settle a number of lesser questions. But the commissioners felt that the disputed claims for damages wrought on Union shipping by Confederate raiders should be brought before an international tribunal.

Both sides agreed that this tribunal should consist of five arbitrators chosen respectively by the King of Italy, the Emperor of Brazil, the President of the Swiss Confederation, and by the two nations concerned, Great Britain and the United States.

The press and the public generally saw Adams as the most obvious choice for American arbitrator. So did Secretary of State Hamilton Fish. Grant again did not, informing his Secretary of State that he would find more repugnance in appointing Adams than in appointing an out-and-out Democrat. Nevertheless, Fish insisted on Adams, and after he and the President had gone through and discarded a number of alternate names, Grant reluctantly yielded.

Adams was gratified at this official recognition of his past services and present capacities. Yet he hesitated at the prospect of abandoning the easy pattern of his resumed domestic life. Although he complained that he was too old for such discomforting labors he reluctantly agreed to go. He was even more reluctant at this point since Abby's health kept her from going with him. In November, 1871, he sailed once more for Europe, lonely and apprehensive, with only his youngest son Brooks as companion and secretary.

The tribunal met in Geneva, where a room in the Town Hall had been placed at the disposal of the arbitrators. At the first session the only matter at issue was that of the language to be used. The proceedings opened in French, a language that the British arbitrator, the choleric Chief Justice Sir Alexander Cockburn, did not understand. He suggested to Adams that the two of them get together to settle the differences between their countries and let the other three arbitrators resign. Adams, who was more impressed by the other arbitrators than he was by Cockburn, rejected the suggestion.

After the preliminaries had been arranged, the tribunal adjourned until June, leaving Adams high and dry in Europe for the next half year. Disgruntled, he set off with Brooks on a tour of southern France and Italy. On the way he received alarming news about Abby's health, and decided to return to Massachusetts until the tribunal met again. Stopping off in London he discovered unexpected tensions in British and American relations. Portions of the Washington Treaty had been ambiguously phrased. The British commissioners had gone away thinking that the United States no longer intended to press its claims for indirect war damages. These claims, sponsored by Sumner and the egregious Ben Butler, demanded absurdly inflated damages for such matters as Britain's premature recognition of belligerent rights, failure to control departure of ships and supplies for the Confederacy, and prolongation of the war itself. Secretary Fish, though forced to allow such preposterous claims to be presented, privately intended to have them overruled and so disposed of for good. Unfortunately he failed to make this clear. When the American case for the tribunal was published in London in December, the British were outraged. Disraeli as leader of the opposition called the claims "preposterous and wild," the equivalent of demanding "tribute from a conquered people." Men of all parties denounced the United States, and urged the ministry to withdraw from further arbitration. Adams, passing through London on his way home, was reminded of the anti-American feeling of ten years earlier.

Once back in the United States in late February, he went directly to Washington for an interview with Fish, whom he had never seen before. He was much impressed by the sensible, clear-minded Secretary of State, in contrast to the mediocrities cluttering up the rest of Grant's cabinet. Adams told Fish that Europeans generally held that the Americans were being unscrupulous in making demands never contemplated earlier. He asked for a temperate statement of facts to refute such slander. At their second interview Grant was present, suffering from a cold and sitting back in his chair puffing on his inevitable cigar. He broke into the discussion to observe that even if Great Britain should decline to participate, he wished the deliberations of the tribunal to continue. At this fatuity the usually self-controlled Adams could hardly keep a straight face. Fish in his embarrassment stared silently at the fire, then gathering himself together pointed out that if there were no longer two parties to an arbitration, the arbitrators could not act.

Immediately after a cabinet interview, Adams left for Quincy, where he found Abby in much improved health. He spent his days studying the American and English cases at length, although he feared he might be wasting his time. As the date for his return to Europe neared, the impasse remained. The British government refused to allow the indirect claims to be brought before the tribunal; the American government insisted that they must be.

The interval months that Adams spent in the United States were a period of frenetic political activity preliminary to the November presidential election. Reform Republicans, breaking away to form the Liberal Republican splinter party, were determined to defeat Grant the "despot" and his corrupt entourage, and appealed for an "uprising of honest citizens." Liberal Republicans were even willing to consider fusion with the Democrats, still smarting under the label of the "rebel party." Adams was spoken of frequently as the most logical, most impartial, and most distinguished reform candidate. He was particularly favored by the Democrats for his long advocacy of leniency and understanding toward the South. There were those, on the other hand, who considered him too self-centered, too aloof, too antipopular. The Irish were of course against him. Against him also was his refusal to accept any party label or to canvass actively, for he declined even to send his sons to the Liberal Republican convention in Cincinnati. Condescendingly he wrote a letter to the Liberal Republicans saying that although he did not want the nomination, he would consider an "unequivocal call."

He was in mid-Atlantic with Abby when the Liberal Republican convention opened in May. With no effort on his part, and with no headquarters or organization, he still retained the support of a large bloc of independent delegates. New England, however, was for Horace Greeley, the editor of the New York *Tribune*, high-tariff advocate, and old-time Radical. At the outset it was generally assumed that the absent Adams would win. He led Greeley on the first five ballots, and even on the sixth ballot—with Greeleyites pulling all possible strings—he still kept his lead. Then followed a sudden landslide swing to Greeley, though no one could ever determine afterward whether it was the result of fraud, strength, or luck.

Adams heard the news of Greeley's nomination on reaching London when a stranger rushed up on the street to tell him. "Success with such a candidate is out of the question," he wrote. "My first sense is one of great relief in being out of the *mêlée*." He was pleased at his own showing and considered it a tribute to his reputation. No candidate, he realized, would have much chance against General Grant's subrational popularity. Although he preferred Greeley to Grant, he thought there was not much to choose between them, but he preferred to put all thought of the presidential contest behind him.

The international tribunal reconvened on June 15. After the Americans had presented their summary the British agent, Lord Tenterden, stated that he would not present his country's final argument while the question of indirect claims remained open, and he then requested an eight-month adjournment. To Adams another such delay was intolerable. As one way out of the impasse he suggested that they proceed at once to the cases of direct damage and leave the indirect claims until later. Tenterden explained that the inflamed state of feeling in England made this impossible. The dilemma seemed insoluble. Great Britain refused to recognize the jurisdiction of the tribunal over indirect claims. The United States insisted on it. Adams at last broke the deadlock. He admitted that the arbitrators could not decide a question not recognized as legitimate by both parties. But they could, he maintained, at least declare how they would have decided if the question had been legitimate.

Cockburn agreed that an extrajudicial renunciation of indirect claims by the United States might clear the deck. Adams drew up such a proposal, stating that in the unofficial opinion of the arbitrators Great Britain was not, according to the recognized rules of international law, responsible for any indirect claims. Washington agreed to accept the decision as final. The British government withdrew its motion for adjournment and pronounced itself satisfied.

Arbitration of the direct claims that followed, though interrupted by bickering and ill temper between the English and the Americans, was essentially an anticlimax. The arbitrators—even the short-tempered Cockburn—held that Great Britain had not used due diligence in preventing the use of its ports and waters as a base for Confederate naval operations, and had violated the law of nations by not detaining Confederate raiders when they entered British harbors. The damage caused by these raiders, particularly the *Alabama*, was a British responsibility. Cockburn, irascible and impatient, thought that the arbitrators were no longer impartial, as in a sense they were not, for they had already made up their minds to award the United States a sum in gross. All that remained was to decide the individual cases and determine the amount. Cockburn angrily accused the Americans of having padded their demands. Adams rebuked him for questioning the integrity of the United States. The American and the Swiss arbitrators fixed on $18 million as the gross sum for damages. The Italian decided on $16 million, the Brazilian on $15 million, while Cockburn considered that $4 million was sufficient. Reluctantly the Englishman finally raised his sights to $15 million and Adams lowered his by

$2 million. At last the arbitrators reached a compromise of $15.5 million. Cockburn, in a rage, recorded his dissent and stalked off without so much as bidding goodbye to the others. Lord Tenterden on the other hand remained cordial. He thought that the award was moderate and that the arbitration might in the end be a good thing for both countries.

Many in England grumbled at an indemnity that their American counterparts found meager. But the issue of claims had at last been laid to rest. The tribunal was formally dissolved and the city of Geneva celebrated by firing a twenty-two-gun salute. Adams stood out as the hero of the event. Even the London *Times* recognized that he had singlehandedly saved the negotiations. Lord Tenterden paid tribute to the "perfect and dignified impartiality with which, throughout the proceedings, Mr. Adams maintained himself as a judge between the two contending nations."

During his weeks in Geneva Adams had grown fond of the city on the lake with its mountain vistas. On one of his last evenings there he walked toward Lake Geneva at sunset for a glimpse of Mont Blanc in the serene fading air, an impression that remained for him an ineradicable memory. On the way back to America he stopped briefly in London where he paid a courtesy visit to Lord and Lady Russell. In departing Europe he was leaving his greatest triumphs behind him. At the peak of his fame, he wanted now to shed his life of travel and the burden of public affairs. He had no regrets for the old world as he saw the English coastline recede.

Adams's status in America was now that of an elder statesman, considered capable of any responsibility, listened to respectfully on any subject, yet free at last of any duties. He thought his position was the most desirable in the whole country. Yet, perplexingly, he found it hard to resume his old routine. Small matters irritated him beyond reason. He dreaded even trivial tasks. The bother of looking after repairs on the Old House so upset him that he came to hate the place. Part of his state of mind was no doubt a result of the tensions of Geneva but part—as he knew with grim awareness—was the approach of old age. At sixty-five, though he remained reasonably fit in body, his memory was failing. Turning to the long-postponed task of editing his father's diary, he did the work almost mechanically, without enthusiasm. As he leafed through the yellow pages, reviewing the old issues, he was overwhelmed by the enigma of time's passage and by the realization that he was nearing the end of his own road. He spent his days quietly at home—he could do little else—leaving there only to attend the meetings of the Historical Society, the Harvard Board of Overseers, or going once a month to his dining club that included Longfellow, Howells, and Emerson. Rumors circulated that Grant would appoint him Secretary of State to replace Fish, but he took no stock or interest in them. In 1874 there was some talk of his being selected as Republican candidate for the United States Senate. He wanted no such burdensome duties. The following year some of his more enthusiastic supporters campaigned to elect him governor as a prelude to running him for President in 1876. The idea repelled him as being even more distasteful to him than the Senate. In spite of his negative attitude a quarter of the delegates to the Massachusetts Republican convention voted for him as their candidate for governor. Hamilton Fish sardonically noted the "annually returning periodical demand for a pure, an exemplary statesman in the person of Charles Francis Adams—Governor, President—Town Clerk or something."

Reformist groups in 1876 were eager for a presidential candidate of stature and dignity for the centennial year. Adams seemed a most proper choice. Carl Schurz in his independent reformist zeal even hoped that the people in a burst of moral enthusiasm would take the matter out of the hands of the politicians and make Adams the candidate of both parties. Adams, although he did not want the nomination, still did not flatly decline it. His candidacy was in any case an impossible one. He did not have the personal magnetism for mass appeal, and his crusty independence had long alienated the professional politicians. When the Republicans after much frustrating debate picked Rutherford Hayes, Adams considered him a nonentity and let it be known that he would vote for the Democratic candidate, Samuel Tilden.

Following this apostasy the Massachusetts Democrats named Adams for governor by acclamation. The perennial candidate had at last been nominated: He was surprised, flattered, and beyond that content, since he knew that he had no chance of election in Republican Massachusetts. He took no part in the campaign, made not a single speech, attended no rallies. Briefly he worried that he *might* be elected. He need not have. Not only did he fail to win, but because of Irish opposition he received fewer votes in the state than Tilden.

Although Adams visited Tilden and expressed his sympathy and support for the Democrat, he took no part in the hectic disputes of that contested election. When less than twenty-four hours before Hayes took the oath of office the electoral commission declared that the Republican was elected, Adams expressed his dismay and wondered whether the American democratic experiment could survive its centennial year.

The year did mark Charles Francis's seventieth year and the end of his career. All that he had left him in life was to finish the editing of his father's diary. In August, 1877, he completed the twelfth and final volume. There were tears in his eyes when he held the bound copy in his hand, tears of gratitude that he had been able to complete it and that justice would at length be done to those who endured injustice while alive. "I am now perfectly willing to go myself," he wrote. "My mission is ended."

He lived nine more years, years of quiet, accelerating decline. Occasionally he would write a short piece for the Historical Society or the obituary of a friend. He still attended the meetings of the Harvard Board of Overseers, kept up his accounts, relaxed with his coin collection, re-read the classics. Rarely did he leave home except when Abby's poor health took them on trips to New York for medical consultation. His memory grew steadily worse. In 1880 while preparing an address for the American Academy, he found he could not complete it. This he took as a sign. He resigned from the Board of Overseers and even gave up the diary that he had kept daily for fifty-five years. "Age takes all things, even the mind," he had read long ago in Virgil's *Ninth Eclogue*, and now it took his. For before his body yielded, his mind went—the thing he had dreaded most—a descent into silence and isolation until he was unaware even of his surroundings. Abby alone he still recognized, never failing to totter to his feet whenever she entered his room. His countrymen scarcely remembered him when he died on November 21, 1886.

# 7

## Charles Francis Adams
## Henry Adams

A FAMILY of turbulent children, Henry Adams called his brothers and sisters in his *Education of Henry Adams*. But "by some happy chance," as he put it, and indeed in happy contrast to the preceding two generations, the children of Charles Francis and Abby all grew up to be "decent citizens." "Almost every large family in those days," Henry wrote, "produced at least one black sheep, and if this generation of Adamses escaped, it was as much a matter of surprise to them as to their neighbors." Three of them, Charles Francis, Jr., Henry, and Brooks, would make their mark in the United States, and Henry and Brooks more than their mark. The star of the eldest son, John Quincy, whom Henry thought "the most brilliant of the family and the most certain of high distinction," never glittered beyond Massachusetts. A gentleman farmer, he became the leader of the Democratic party in a Republican state and five times an unsuccessful candidate for governor. Less perhaps is remembered of him because he deplored the "vile family habit of keeping papers," and kept none. Charles in the gross postwar era would make a fortune larger than his grandfather Brooks's but would eschew any political career. "He had all he wanted," Henry explained, "wealth, children, society, consideration, and he laughed at the idea of sacrificing himself to adorn a Cleveland cabinet or get cheers from an Irish mob."

Henry loved his father, and in a measured way admired him. "Charles Francis Adams's memory was hardly above the average," he thought. "His mind was not bold like his grandfather's or restless like his father's, or imaginative or oratorical—still less mathematical; but it worked with singular perfection, admirable self-restraint, and instinctive mastery of form. Within its range it was a model." Charles Francis, Jr.'s, opinion was more astringent. He concluded bluntly that he did not like his father. "He was never the companion of our sports and holidays," he wrote in his autobiography. "To us, it would, as I now see, have made all the difference conceivable had he loved the woods and the water—walked and rode and sailed a boat; been, in short, our companion as well as instructor. The Puritan was in him and he didn't know how." In later years Charles shivered at the memory of Boston's "winter gloom" and of his bedraggled schooldays. His mother he dismissed as negligible. He had not one pleasant memory of the Mount Vernon Street house. At thirteen he had entered the Boston Latin School and at the direction of his parents begun a diary. Later he burned it. He would have liked to burn the school as well, "a conventional, mechanical, low-standard day-school and classical grind-mill." "I have not a good word to say of it," he wrote sixty years later; "and like John Randolph and the sheep, I would go a long distance out of my way to give it a kick."

Harvard College, which he entered as a sophomore in 1853, he managed to enjoy in spite of a fusty curriculum relatively unchanged since his grandfather's student days. By this time the college had become an Adams birthright. John Adams in 1755 had ranked fourteenth socially among the twenty-five members of his class. Charles Francis, of the class of 1856, "belonged easily and of right, to all the clubs and all the societies, literary and social."

He did find his classmates rather run-of-the-mill, observing in after years that their "chief distinction . . . was contributing two inmates to the State's prison." Though his studies were routine he had time for "infinite reading and much writing." His writing, prose and verse, he later destroyed. He graduated in the lower half of his class, yet he conceded that "the nutriment, and there was lots of it, passed into my system." Lacking any special aptitudes he drifted—the Adams drift—into reading law. After twenty months in the office of Francis Parker and Richard Henry Dana—the author of *Two Years Before the Mast*—at times wondering why he bothered, he passed his bar examinations before a Quincy neighbor and family friend Judge Bigelow. "I was no more fit to be admitted than a child," he recalled. "Bigelow's personal knowledge of me had something to do with it." As a fledged lawyer he shared an office briefly with his brother John, then moved his quarters to "a gloomy, dirty den in my father's building, 23 Court Street" where he waited for clients surely who would have disappointed him if they had appeared.

The mild dissipations of his contemporaries held more interest for him than his law books. In 1859 he confided to Henry, then in Germany: "Never since I have been in society have I seen a winter go off with such a sort of shriek & howl, so drunk with wine & excitement, so ram full of canvas-back duck & oysters, so slop up in jollity, so jam down in fatigue." With an ample allowance, he did not need to worry about earning a living.

In gloomier moments Charles, Jr., worried about his future, fearful that he might yield to that "fatal magnetic risk for us, the knowledge that our family is wealthy and that for us there is no real object in labor." As an antidote to the musty torpor of his office, he speculated in real estate and read history, a passion of his since he had first discovered Macaulay. The outbreak of the Civil War coincided with the publishing of his article "The Reign of King Cotton" in the *Atlantic* in which he predicted the ultimate though peaceful destruction of the slave economy through internal stress. Before this, writing as "Conciliator" in the Boston *Transcript*, he had deplored the talk of war and acclaimed the rumored surrender of Fort Sumter as "a wise, statesmanlike and judicious move."

At the war's outbreak he did not at first consider volunteering, though for five weeks he served with a militia unit garrisoning Fort Independence on Boston's Castle Island. "War is no plaything," he wrote just after the attack on Sumter, "and, God knows, I have no wish to trifle with it. I therefore shall not now volunteer, or expose myself to unnecessary service. But I can, and will, obey orders at any sacrifice, and, if called upon, shall go into active service." He saw his friends off with a resigned wistfulness at the thought of staying behind to manage his father's affairs, "scolding tenants, auditing bills, discussing repairs, rendering accounts, and so on—doing my duty!—Psh!" But in October while riding through Braintree woods he experienced a change of mind as sudden as a conversion. "Why do I stay at home?" he asked himself, and in a moment he was "all aglow." He applied for a captaincy, settled for a commission as a first lieutenant in the First Regiment of Massachusetts Cavalry. "Even now," he recalled in his autobiography, "though more than fifty years have since passed on, I look back on that ride as at the moment of an inspiration—the time when I resolved to burst the bonds, and strike out into the light from the depth of darkness. No wiser determination did I ever reach." It was, he maintained, his duty. Could the most "American" of families, the antislavery Adamses, be "wholly unrepresented in the field?" he asked rhetorically. To which his father had dryly remarked that none of his ancestors had been soldiers, and why should he? The elder Adams concluded that his son had so far made little use of his abilities. In any case his talents were scarcely military, and his joining the colors was a dilettante gesture.

Late in December Charles learned that his name had been sent in for the commission of first lieutenant. "Well, at last my commission!" he exulted in his diary. "Within the next four days I shall leave this room, and my native city. My office will know me no more, and to my profession I shall bid a long farewell. A new existence opens before me; and, when I return to old haunts, I hope it will at least be in more prosperous times and with more sanguine feelings."

He found a congenial group of officers in the First Cavalry, many of them (three of the ten majors, seven of the twenty-eight captains) Harvard graduates. Compared to the trudging routine and bloody conclusions of the infantry, the cavalry proved a pleasant if at times rather boring life. In April, 1862, he wrote his brother Henry from Milne Plantation on Port Royal Island in South Carolina: "Here I am surrounded by troopers, missionaries, contrabands, cotton fields and serpents, in a summer climate, riding immensely every day, dreadfully sick of the monotony of my present existence, disgusted with all things military and fighting off malaria with whiskey and tobacco. So far, the island of Port Royal is a small Paradise.... Our privations have been next to nothing and our career has been more of a winter picnic than anything else. The future I fear has less agreeable things in store for us." His first action, at James Island, elated him. "The excitement of a battle-field is grand," he wrote. Two months later, at "that veritable charnel-house, Antietam," his regiment was held in reserve and during the action he "dropped quietly asleep—asleep in the height of the battle and between the contending armies!" The same thing happened to him at Gettysburg where his much-reduced regiment saw no direct action. As in all wars, long periods of tedious routine dwarfed the battle moments. Adams, made adjutant, soon groaned under his burden of paperwork.

During the winter of 1863 when his enlistment ran out, he sailed to England to visit his family and even made a quick trip to Paris before returning to re-enlist. Through a college friend he managed to have himself transferred to the headquarters of the Army of the Potomac where for the first time he was able to see some of the large operations of the war and observe the generals in high command. He was not impressed. In the autumn of 1864 he transferred as a lieutenant colonel to the black Fifth Massachusetts Cavalry, a regiment made up chiefly of freed slaves and Negroes smuggled from Canada. To the dismounted Fifth was assigned the task of guarding prisoners at Point Lookout in Maryland. "The Post here," Adams wrote his father, "is established on a low, sandy, malarious, fever-smitten, wind-blown, God-forsaken tongue of land. . . . It is remarkably well adapted for a depot of prisoners, as it is not only notoriously unhealthy, but most easily guarded." Adams, already disabled by dysentery, contracted jaundice and malaria. Between bouts of illness he managed to secure mounts for his troops and had them assigned to active service—a mistake, he thought, after he had observed his troopers' ineptitudes. Nevertheless, as colonel of the regiment, he led his men into burning Richmond the day after Lee abandoned it, "the one event which I should most have desired as the culmination of my life in the army. That honor has been mine and now I feel as if my record in this war was rounded and completely filled out."

Prematurely bald like the rest of the Adams males and shattered in health, Charles Francis, Jr., weighed only 130 pounds and looked old enough to be his own father when he left the army in August, 1865, with the brevet of brigadier general. He had long since grown weary of soldiering, but if army life had become "a Dead Sea apple," the law had always been one. He knew he would never go back to the Court Street office.

Just before sailing for England on leave, he had visited his married sister in Newport. There he met Mary Hone Ogden, of whom he wrote: "I thought I had never met so charming and attractive a person." After that meeting, she—the "Minnie" of his renewed diary—ran through his head night and day. He met her again on sick leave at the year's end, became engaged to her the following February, and in November, 1865, they were married. A marriage of love, it also had solid financial underpinnings, for Minnie's father was a staid New Yorker of colonial descent and inherited wealth. On Charles's engagement, his father had written from London that he would allow him $3,000 a year on his marriage, as he had planned to do for all his sons. He wished he could do more, he explained, but most of his capital was locked up in trusts or land.

The young couple spent eleven desultory months in Paris and Rome. Where should he go, what should he do now, the renegade lawyer asked himself on his return. "Surveying the whole field," he wrote in his autobiography, "—instinctively recognizing my unfitness for the law—I fixed on the railroad system as the most developing force and largest field of the day, and determined to attach myself to it. I now stand amazed at my own inexperience and audacity; but, having made up my mind, within a fortnight of my dreary homecoming, and, in perfect good faith, evolving my facts from my inner consciousness, I proceeded to write an article on 'Railroads' for the *North American Review!*"

He followed this first article—often aided by his brother Henry—with a steady flow of pieces on railroads and railroad law that soon established him as an authority in the field. When Charles Francis returned from London, Charles and Minnie moved to a little house on the Neponset road to Quincy. There during the winter "with infinite pains, sparing no labor" he wrote *A Chapter of Erie*, a bitterly worded exposure of the corruption and graft reaching deep into the Grant administration during the piratical Commodore Vanderbilt's attempt to snatch the Erie Railroad from the manipulative hands of "Uncle" Daniel Drew, the ferret-eyed Jay Gould, and "Jubilee Jim" Fisk.

In July, 1869, he was appointed one of the three members of the Massachusetts Board of Railroad Commissioners that had been established mainly at his insistence. For ten years he served on the board, becoming its chairman in 1872. His innovative reports on the need of reform and control in railroad operations and on accidents and arbitration had an influence that extended far beyond Massachusetts. With a solid reputation as a railroad reformer, he was in 1878 appointed chairman of the Board of Government Directors of the Union Pacific Railroad, a position that he saw as a means of shaping railroad legislation and a national railroad policy. The Union Pacific was something of an enigma to him as a commissioner from the beginning. He admired the relentlessly energetic men who had forced it to completion and spanned the continent, yet at the same time he was repelled by the secrecy of the Union Pacific's financial arrangements. After a year he resigned from the board at about the same time he resigned from the Massachusetts board, but the Union Pacific remained in his mind. So convinced was he of its future that he bought twenty-five hundred Union Pacific shares for himself, additional shares for his various trustee accounts, and urged others to invest in what he believed would be "the Broadway or Washington Street of this continent."

Thus began Adams's transition from a railroad reformer to a railroad executive, from the little house on the Neponset turnpike where he had done his own plumbing and upholstery to a mock castle in Boston's newly filled Back Bay area. In 1883 he became one of the directors of the Union Pacific and the following year he was elected its president.

"I took the position advisedly," he wrote, "and from purely selfish considerations. I was then only forty-nine, and ambitious. With a good deal of natural confidence in myself, I looked upon assuming the management of a great railway system, and correctly enough, as the legitimate outcome of what had, in my case, gone before. I was simply playing my game to a finish. I was not yet fifty, and I did not want to break off, and go into retirement, in mid-career. So I assumed charge of the Union Pacific, quite regardless of the fact that, in so doing, I took the chances heavily against myself; for the concern was in bad repute, heavily loaded with obligations, odious in the territory it served; and, moreover, though I had no realizing sense of the fact, a day of general financial reckoning was at hand."

He planned to stay five years as president. During that time he put the Union Pacific's finances in order, re-established its credit and paid off its floating debt, and improved the service and relations with the communities the railroad served. If he had left according to plan he would have been considered a success in every way. Unfortunately for himself he stayed an additional year and a half, a time during which the Union Pacific's financial position deteriorated to the point of bankruptcy. Unable to obtain financial help from Boston or New York, Adams was forced to turn to the rapacious Jay Gould, "the little wizard," whom he had once excoriated and who had long been plotting his downfall. At a meeting in his office Gould told the cornered Adams that he was ready to take over the railroad as soon as the board of directors could meet and give their approval. After this brief humiliating encounter in Gould's office, Adams reluctantly shook hands and Gould showed him out. "The little man," Adams recalled, "seemed to look smaller, meaner, more haggard and livid in the face and more shrivelled up and ashamed of himself than usual;—his clothes seemed too big for him, and, his eyes did not seek mine, but were fixed on the upper buttonhole of my waist-coat. I felt as if in my hour of defeat, I was overawing him,—and, as if he felt so, too."

Adams's railroad days were over. His further career would be that of investor and speculator. He acquired stock in mines, railroads, nascent electrical concerns like the Westinghouse Company, and, judging shrewdly by what he had seen on his railroad trips, bought land from Massachusetts to Texas and Oregon that he correctly perceived would rise in value as the country grew. Sometimes, as in the Back Bay, he and his brother John made joint speculations. His most profitable venture was the Kansas City Stockyard Company which in the four decades after he became president grew from a small concern with a capital of $100,000 and earnings of $26,000 to the largest of its kind in the world, with $10 million capital and annual earnings of $1.2 million. Most of his fortune was made in real estate deals in and about Kansas City. Many of his speculations were made on borrowed money, and sometimes he would run as much as a million dollars into debt. Yet, though his ventures flourished and he grew rich, he lacked the iron nerves of the born gambler. "Here I stop! Cash or nothing," he had written uneasily in 1874. Ten years later he was still accusing himself of not getting out of the borrowing habit.

In 1869, he had told the American Social Science Association, admonishingly, that the accumulation of wealth was not the loftiest end of human effort. Two decades later he had so absorbed the acquisitive time-spirit of the seventies and eighties that he would write with self-satisfaction: "They may say what they please, but today wealth is the [standard] in America. . . . [With wealth] I become a power to be considered. Whenever I choose to come forward, I am received with deference and listened to with acceptance;—I can dictate my own terms. . . . I could do more for my own success by getting rich than by slaving my life away in mere political action. This I failed to appreciate twenty years ago."

In 1870 Adams had built himself a house on what would be called later President's Hill—land given him by his father across the street from the Old House. Built in the style of those houses afterward labeled the "atrocities of '72," with mansard roof, porches, and plateglass windows, it loomed as pretentious as the original Adams homestead was unpretentious, as graceless as the Old House was graceful. Sixteen years Adams lived there, his family increased by three daughters, and finally to his unutterable relief twin sons. "In Quincy," he wrote in his autobiography, "I was very active as a worker, and was an influential citizen. My record too was creditable. I left a mark on the town government— on its schools, on its Public Library, on its Park system. . . . I worked with and through my brother, J. Q. Adams. I never was sympathetic or popular; he, somehow, was."

By 1887 Adams had begun to feel the pull of Boston, particularly on his adolescent daughters, and with money to spare built himself a brick town house in the Back Bay at the corner of Gloucester Street and Commonwealth Avenue, castellated, turreted, and with stained glass by La Farge. It was, Adams was pleased to admit to his friends, very handsome. There he lived winters, in the mild weather returning to Quincy. But Quincy itself was changing from a rural community to a dormitory suburb of Boston, its fields cut up into little streets, its hills eroded by granite quarries. The town meeting, he complained, was being taken over by low types, vulgar, loudmouthed, and pugnacious. He and his brother John thought that it was about time to go. In May, 1893, he bought an estate, Birnham Wood, in Lincoln twelve miles west of Boston, from a friend who had intended to be a country squire there but soon thought the place too lonely. Adams found just what he wanted in the 320 verdant acres along the Sudbury River where it opened into Fairhaven Bay. He planned to occupy it in a not too distant future when Quincy had become impossible.

The Great Panic of that same year saw Adams overextended, perilously in debt. He later wrote: "When in those June days of 1893 the collapse came, I was then carrying a large amount of sail—far more than was prudent; for, my head turned by long and considerable success, I had become reckless. . . . With much canvas spread, I was loaded down with a cargo I had never intended to take on.

"The storm broke! There was the misadventure of my life. I was fifty-eight when the crash came. The fury of the gale was weathered; but its results were felt continuously through five long, precious years. They were for me years of simple Hell—years during which I had to throw everything aside, and devote myself to rehabilitating a wreck. It made no sort of difference that the wreck was the result of my own improvidence; there it was right under me, and the question of again reaching a port was the only one to consider. The dislocation this event caused—coming just when it did—shattered my whole scheme of life. Breaking in upon it, it broke it up. I was sixty-three years old, and a tired man, when at last the effects of the 1893 convulsion wore themselves out, and my mind was once more at ease so that I could return to my calling."

In his retrenchment Adams gave up his town house and the house on President's Hill and moved to Lincoln. "Quincy was bone of my bone—flesh of the Adams flesh," he wrote of his going. "There I had lived vicariously or in person since 1640; there on my return from the war I made my home, and later [1870] built my house; there I had fought my fight, not unsuccessfully, through the best years of my life; there my children were born; in fact, I felt as if I owned the town, for every part of it was familiar to me...." Nevertheless, early one Monday morning in November, 1893, "I mounted my horse at the door of my house on the hill at Quincy—the sun being hardly above the horizon of the distant sea-line in the nipping atmosphere—and rode over to Lincoln. I have not passed a night at Quincy since."

Prosperity returned to Adams as well as to the country and by the opening of the new century he had recouped much of his fortune. In 1905 he was richer than he had ever been. Two years later, turning his back on "provincial" Boston, he bought a town house in Washington and spent most of his remaining winters there. "For two hundred years," his brother Henry would write, "every Adams, from father to son, had lived within sight of State Street, and sometimes had lived in it, yet none had ever taken kindly to the town, or been taken kindly by it." Charles, in his leave-taking, was even blunter. Boston, in his opinion, tended to "stagnate." Its society seemed to have to pass through "a long period of cold storage." "I have summered and wintered it," he declared, "tried it drunk and tried it sober; and, drunk or sober, there's nothing in it—save Boston!"

In Lincoln, and within the limits of Massachusetts, he served on a number of advisory committees, including a state committee to devise a system of parks and reservations within the Boston area. He was particularly pleased that he was able to preserve the Blue Hills section, that haunt of his ancestors, from the speculative builder. But he concluded that current politics had no place for men of his type. Nevertheless, the Spanish-American War and its imperialist aftermath stirred him to angry and active opposition. "We are blood guilty," he wrote, "and we are doing to others . . . what we have protested against when attempted on us or doing elsewhere." For twenty-five years Charles served on the Harvard Board of Overseers, causing some stir but achieving little in his effort to have Greek abolished as an entrance requirement. At his fiftieth Harvard class reunion he regretted that he had not acquired "tens and scores of millions" to give to Harvard. "I would like," he told those surviving classmates who were present, "to be the nineteenth-century John Harvard—the John Harvard-of-the-Money-Bags, if you will. I would rather be that than be Historian or General or President."

In his sixtieth year, Adams in taking stock of himself decided that he had but ten years left and that he must be up and doing. His future course seemed well marked out—biography, history, European travel. In the remaining twenty years of his life he would achieve a minor reputation as a historian, becoming first the president of the Massachusetts Historical Society, then president of the American Historical Society, and a popular lecturer whose career would culminate in four lectures given at Oxford in 1913 under the auspices of the Rhodes Scholarship Foundation on "Trans-Atlantic Historical Solidarity."

Although history had intrigued him ever since he had read Macaulay as a boy of thirteen, his debut as a historian was accidental. In 1874 he had accepted an invitation to deliver a historical address for the 250th anniversary of the settlement of neighboring Weymouth. Though he did not then realize it, the event marked a turning point in his life. That address together with a sketch of Quincy for a history of Norfolk County formed the nucleus of *Three Episodes in Massachusetts History* (published in 1892), an expanded history of Quincy, one of the most original town histories ever written in the United States. The year before, he had concluded a biography of Richard Henry Dana over which he had been working off and on since 1882 at the request of the Dana family. Locally, at least, the Dana book was a best seller.

Writing history and exploring the past became the pleasures of Adams's later life. He next turned his attention to the vast material that his father had left behind, prepared to devote five years to writing his father's definitive biography. He soon discovered the material overwhelming, his father's diary of six decades alone being longer than Gibbon's *Decline and Fall.* In his lifetime he did manage to write a compact single-volume life of Charles Francis Adams for the American Statesmen series, but the larger task he never finished.

Although he looked to culminating his career with his father's biography, he meanwhile wrote his own autobiography—in a pen often dipped in acid—completing it in 1912. The following year he left for Europe to search out primary materials on his father's diplomatic years located there. The outbreak of the First World War scarcely interrupted his self-imposed task. "To the last he was working over his material," wrote Worthington Ford, editor of the Massachusetts Historical Society publications, "recasting his sentences and moulding his opinion, and thus to the last his mind remained active, potent and creative. Exposure to cold overtaxed his body, and after a few days of illness the end came on March 20, 1915, in Washington."

As a historian Charles Adams's most enduring accomplishment was his stand against the ancestor worship of the earlier American historians, of whom only Parkman escaped his censure. His model remained the coldly detached Gibbon. With the number of his own days thinning, he looked back with some scorn at the associates of his business years. In his autobiography he confessed that he was "more than a little puzzled to account for the instances I have seen of business success—money-getting. It comes from a rather low instinct. Certainly, so far as my observation goes, it is rarely met with in combination with the finer or more interesting traits of character. I have known, and known tolerably well, a good many 'successful' men—'Big' financially—men famous during the last half-century; and a less interesting crowd I do not care to encounter. Not one that I have ever known would I care to meet again, either in this world or the next; nor is one of them associated in my mind with the idea of humor, thought or refinement. A set of mere money-getters and traders, they were essentially unattractive and uninteresting. The fact is that money-getting, like everything else, calls for a special aptitude and great concentration; and for it, I did not have the first in any marked degree, while to it I never gave the last. So, in now summing up, I may account myself fortunate in having got out of my ventures as well as I did. Running at times great risks, I emerged, not ruined."

For Charles's brother Henry, a career in the jostling, thrusting financial world seemed as alien as it would have to his grandfather John Quincy. Far earlier than Charles, Henry Adams sensed that Boston was not for him. To the child Henry, Quincy and Boston were like summer and winter. Quincy was the "smell of hot pine-woods and sweet-fern in the scorching summer noon; of new-mown hay; of ploughed earth; . . . of salt water and low tide on the marshes. . . . The intense blue of the sea, as he saw it a mile or two away, from the Quincy hills; the cumuli in a June afternoon sky." Boston was "the cold grays of November evenings, and the thick, muddy thaws of . . . winter. . . . Winter was always the effort to live; summer was tropical license. . . . Summer was the multiplicity of nature; winter was school."

When Henry was six or seven his mother took him for a stay in Quincy long enough so that he went to school there. One of his sharper memories was of an early summer morning when he stood at the bottom of the long staircase leading to his grandfather's library announcing vehemently to his mother that he was not going to school. Then, as she stood by perplexed, "the door opened, and the old man slowly came down. Putting on his hat, he took the boy's hand without a word, and walked with him, paralyzed by awe, up the road to the town. After the first moments of consternation at this interference in a domestic dispute, the boy reflected that an old gentleman close on eighty would never trouble himself to walk near a mile on a hot summer morning over a shadeless road to take a boy to school, and that it would be strange if a lad imbued with the passion of freedom could not find a corner to dodge around, somewhere before reaching the school door. Then and always, the boy insisted that this reasoning justified his apparent submission; but the old man did not stop, and the boy saw all his strategical points turned, one after another, until he found himself seated inside the school, and obviously the centre of curious if not malevolent criticism. Not till then did the President release his hand and depart."

It is a poignant glimpse; the bright summer morning, the small boy and the old man walking down the dusty road. As an equally small boy, the old man had walked with his mother to watch the cannon smoke billowing up from Bunker Hill. And when the second small boy became an old man he would see his country engaged in the first of the World Wars. On that Quincy morning, captured from time in the pages of Henry's third-person autobiography, the grandfather "had shown no temper, no irritation, no personal feeling, and had made no display of force. Above all, he had held his tongue. . . . Neither party to this momentary disagreement can have felt rancor, for during these three or four summers the old President's relations with the boy were friendly and almost intimate."

Sundays as Henry sat in the Quincy church behind his President grandfather he could read above the bald head in front of him the tablet in memory of his President great-grandfather. All during his growing up he went to church twice each Sunday. He read his Bible and learned religious poetry by heart, he prayed, he observed the inherited ritual. But for him and his brothers and sisters, religion was no longer real. "Even the mild discipline of the Unitarian Church was so irksome that they all threw it off at the first possible moment, and never afterwards entered a church."

Old John Adams had predicted that his grandchildren would be free to study the arts. His prediction would become most fully realized in his great-grandson Henry, professor, historian, and esthetician. As a boy Henry in no way fitted into the still-eighteenth-century Boston world into which he had been born. Even at the age of ten he began to ask himself what he was, where he was going. "He felt that something was wrong, but he concluded that it must be Boston."

The Boston Latin School had been for two hundred years the automatic prelude to Harvard for upper-class Boston boys. But Henry did not follow his brother's path there, being barred by an economy-minded school committee because of his father's legal residence in Quincy. Also barred was Boston Latin's outstanding master, Epes Sargent Dixwell, who refused the committee's demand that he become a Boston resident. Sargent then founded his own Latin School at Boylston Place. Sent there from a small private school held in the basement of the Park Street Church, Henry liked it no better than his brother Charles had liked the old Latin School. In after years he maintained that his schooling from the age of ten to sixteen was time thrown away. Undersized, he was too frail to take an active part in the more enjoyable side of school life that he referred to as Blackguard Boston in which the Common became the scene of snowball fights between the Latin School boys and the tough Irish urchins led by the "terrible Conky Daniels." Henry could only participate ineffectually behind his sturdier brother. Looking back he concluded that if violence was part of a complete education, in this respect Boston was not incomplete.

More enduring for him than his schooldays were the hours he spent in an alcove of his father's Mount Vernon Street library with its eighteen thousand volumes. There the boy read at random, at times correcting proofs of his great-grandfather's writings that his father was editing. There from his alcove he heard Palfrey and Dana and Sumner discuss current politics, oblivious to his small presence. There his father in free moments tutored him in French and corrected his pronunciation. The alcove was his true school.

After three generations of Adamses had gone to Harvard, it would have been unthinkable for the fourth generation not to have continued there. Henry entered on the last day of August, 1854. Looking back half a century later he regretted, as do most men of any intellectual capacity, the time he had squandered, the subjects he might have learned. He concluded that his college experience had been negative and in some ways mischievous. Harvard "taught little and that little ill," was his later opinion, even though "it left the mind open, free from bias, ignorant of facts, but docile." From his classmates "he got less than nothing, a result common enough in education." Yet, "if the student got little from his mates, he got little more from his masters. The four years passed at college were, for his purposes, wasted. . . . The only teaching that appealed to his imagination was a course of lectures by Louis Agassiz on the Glacial Period and Palaeontology, which had more influence on his curiosity than the rest of the college instruction altogether. The entire work of the four years could have been easily put into the work of any four months in after life. . . . He wanted to be done with it, and stood watching vaguely for a path and a direction."

The direction was furnished by James Russell Lowell, who came to Harvard fresh from Germany in 1856 to succeed Longfellow as professor of modern literature. It was under Lowell's influence, in the informal seminars he introduced at Harvard, that Henry seized on the idea of himself going to Germany. His reading list, which he prepared as a senior for an article, "Reading in College," that appeared in the *Harvard Magazine*, included Scott, Bulwer-Lytton, Cooper, Dickens, G.P.R. James, *Vanity Fair, Pendennis, The Book of Snobs*, Dumas, Eugène Sue, George Sand, Paul de Kock, *Sartor Resartus*, Emerson, Humboldt, Ruskin, Macaulay, Prescott, Niebuhr, Grote, Theodore Parker's sermons, De Quincey, Irving, Gibbon, Shakespeare, *The Spectator, Paradise Lost, The Divine Comedy*, Homer, Euripides, Aeschylus, Demosthenes, and Cicero.

Socially Henry was active, at times convivial. The talks he gave at the Institute of 1770, a literary society, were well received. He acted in Hasty Pudding Club plays, was elected librarian of the club, its "Krokodeilos," and finally its club orator. Even as a freshman he was contributing to the newly founded *Harvard Magazine*. In an article at the end of his sophomore year entitled "My Old Room," he described his room in Hollis as "the coldest, dirtiest, and gloomiest in Cambridge," yet for him it would always be haunted by the books he had read there, and "by a laughing group of bright, fresh faces, that have rendered it sunny in my eyes forever."

In his last year he submitted a literary essay for the Bowdoin Prize that his brother Charles had won a few years earlier, but came in only second. He was popular and esteemed enough to be named class orator. As his contribution to the *Life-Book* of the class of 1858, he wrote of his Harvard years that he did not think it possible to pass four pleasanter ones. His election as class orator, he admitted, was the most gratifying compliment that he had ever or probably ever would receive. Now, with his college years at end, and since there was no immediate need of his earning a living, he proposed to go to Europe and master languages. Ultimately he expected to study and practice law, although his deepest wish was for a quiet literary life, "as I believe that to be the happiest and in this country not the least useful." Germany was his goal.

The most plausible reason that he could think of for going there was to study civil law—although he later admitted that neither he nor his parents knew what civil law was nor any reason for studying it. He planned first to study in Berlin, then in Heidelberg, and possibly in Paris. Late in September, 1858, he sailed from New York to Liverpool with several college classmates on the Cunard side-wheeler *Persia*, "the newest, largest and fastest steamship afloat." After a rough eleven-day passage, a passing glimpse of England verdant with literary associations, and a few days in London, he left for Berlin by way of Antwerp. In Berlin he found a scattering of Americans. "Within a day or two he was running about with the rest to beer-cellars and music-halls and dance-rooms, smoking bad tobacco, drinking poor beer, and eating sauerkraut and sausages as though he knew no better." Civil law was another matter. The first lecture he attended at the university was his last. It would take months of study before he could begin to follow what the lecturer was talking about. Frustrated by the language barrier, he quit the university to enroll as an "Ober-tertia," a sophomore, in the Friedrich-Wilhelm-Werdesches Gymnasium. There he sat in a foul-aired classroom among twelve- and thirteen-year-old sons of "small tradesmen or *bourgeoisie* of the neighborhood" and recited in turn. It seemed a ridiculous, not to say demeaning, position for a Harvard graduate, a class orator, the Hasty Pudding Krokodeilos. Above all it was a poor way to learn a foreign language. He soon realized that he could not go back ten years in his life. Later he concluded that the gymnasium interlude was the most foolish thing he had ever done, yet he stayed on until spring.

Then in April with four American friends he took a brief walking trip through the Thuringian Forest, ending up in Dresden. Never could he really explain why he had come to Germany. He stayed "because he did not want to go home, and he had fears that his father's patience might be exhausted if he asked to waste time elsewhere." There was nothing, he thought, worth studying in Dresden, but it was pleasanter than Berlin, the theater and the opera were often excellent, there were the art galleries, and if he did nothing else he could at least learn the language. "For the next eighteen months the young man pursued accidental education, since he could pursue no other; and by great good fortune, Europe and America were too busy with their own affairs to give much attention to his."

In the summer of 1859 he met his sister Louisa in Bern. She had come to see him from her home in Italy, a country and climate she much preferred to New England. The most rebellious of the Adams children, she had amused the others long ago by her remark that she "would marry a blackamoor to get away from Quincy." After traveling in Italy with her, Henry joined his friend Ben Crowninshield for a tour down the Rhine to Antwerp, Rotterdam, and then back into Germany. Berlin on a return visit seemed so depressing that they left at once. At Hildesheim, that most perfect of small medieval towns, he and Crowninshield sat drinking one evening in the wine cellar of the Domschenke until the room spun. Henry wandered off into the darkness and into a strange house where, over the astonished protests of several young women, he insisted on sleeping on top of a trunk until the next morning.

The following winter he spent in Dresden. His mornings he divided equally between riding and fencing lessons. In the evening, operas, the theater, and more casual entertainments occupied him. His chief task being to learn German, he dabbled in books on constitutional history before turning with relief to lighter reading. His father, now in Congress, had begun to wonder what his son was doing, while Charles had already concluded that his brother was doing nothing at all. By April, 1860, Henry admitted himself that his plans had disintegrated and that he had become "a mere tourist, and nothing else."

The month of May he spent in Rome, caught up in the enchantment of that still-medieval city. "One looked idly enough at the Forum or at St. Peter's," the elderly Henry recalled, "but one never forgot the look, and it never ceased reacting." From Rome he went to Naples and then Salerno where through the American minister he met Garibaldi. His impressions he sent back as a "pleasant series of letters" to Charles, who published them in the proslavery Boston *Courier*. "The month of May, 1860, was divine. . . . So it ended;" he was to conclude, "the happiest month of May that life had yet offered, fading behind the present, and probably beyond the past, somewhere into abstract time, grotesquely out of place with the Berlin scheme or a Boston future." The next three months he passed in Paris, where his accidental education went far, even though he admitted he studied nothing and met no one. "Therewith, after staying as long as he could and spending all the money he dared, he started with mixed emotions but no education, for home."

He arrived back in Quincy in time to see the torchlight parade in honor of his father's local victory in the 1860 election. Election day marked his formal introduction to the study of law in the office of Judge Horace Gray. But within three weeks he had cast off common law, as easily as he had shed civil law, to go to Washington as his father's secretary for the final session of the Thirty-sixth Congress. "It's a great life," he wrote his brother Charles from Washington, "just what I wanted." Before he left Boston he had managed to get himself appointed Washington correspondent of the *Advertiser*, the Massachusetts capital's leading Republican paper. He also planned to write Charles a series of letters on the country's most momentous period since the Revolution. In the middle of March, 1861, he returned to Boston, and again sat down with his law books, but only for a few days, for on March 19 came the news of his father's appointment as minister to England.

Henry was twenty-three when he arrived with his father in London, a provincial from Quincy-Boston-Cambridge. In the seven years he was to spend in England he would become a cosmopolite, British in appearance, manner, and accent, however American he remained at heart. During the previous winter in Washington he had come to know Henry Raymond, the editor of *The New York Times*, and arranged with him to act as the *Times*'s London correspondent. This had to be kept a secret even from Charles Francis, as the State Department prohibited "all communications with the press." The young secretary's first months at the legation were isolating, occupied with trivial tasks in frustrating contrast to his friends across the Atlantic now in uniform. English society disregarded him. He suffered, in his isolation, from chronic dyspepsia. Each Saturday afternoon he retired to his room on the fourth floor of the legation to write out his account of the week's political and diplomatic affairs for the *Times*. These reports were duly published as was then customary without a by-line. At one point he decided to learn firsthand about the situation and sentiments of the cotton-spinning North by making a trip to Manchester. There he spent five days interviewing industrialists and inspecting factories. To his somewhat technical report he added a few reflections on the society of Manchester as opposed to that of London, in which he relieved himself rather trivially of his stored-up resentment at London hauteur. "In Manchester," he wrote, "one is usually allowed a dressing room at an evening party. In London a gentleman has to take his chances of going into the ball room with his hair on end or his cravat untied. In Manchester it is still the fashion to finish balls with showy suppers, which form the great test of the evening. In London one is regaled with thimblefuls of ice cream and hard seed cakes."

He sent the finished manuscript to Charles in Boston for publication in the *Atlantic*. Since it arrived too late for the January issue, Charles reluctantly handed it to the *Courier* where it appeared under the title of "A Visit to Manchester—Extracts from a Private Diary." Unfortunately the editor in his enthusiasm violated his instructions by revealing that the diary was written by "Mr. Henry Adams, the son of our Minister to Great Britain."

When London newspapers became aware of the article, they reacted with condescending mockery. "The Courier in putting my name to my 'Diary' has completely used me up," Henry wrote Charles. "To my immense astonishment and dismay I found myself this morning sarsed through a whole column of the Times, and am laughed at by all England. You can imagine my sensations. . . . The Examiner scalped me with considerable savageness."

Hurt, humiliated, he resolved to give up journalism altogether. He thought himself of no further use in London and envied his brother's active life in the army. "It worries me all the time," he told Charles, "to be leading this thoroughly useless life abroad while you are acting such grand parts at home." Yet by spring the temporary successes of the Union armies had buoyed his spirits to the point that he could write: "I feel like a King now, I assert my nationality with a quiet pugnacity that tells. No one treads on our coattails any longer, and I do not expect ever to see again the old days of anxiety and humiliation."

Gradually Adams's isolation in the London world gave way to a measure of acceptance, but he was impatient and resented the snubs along the way. In his first months his acquaintances were limited to influential friends of the Union, unaristocratic liberals and radical reformers who received him as his father's son, even as his father and his grandfather had formerly been received. Again and again he wrote to Charles complaining of the exclusiveness of London society. After the Union forces' capture of New Orleans, the strength of the North became apparent, and the English aristocracy began to take a second and more critical look at the Confederacy. The young man eager to be accepted grew more acceptable, and more and more doors opened to him. His appointment book from 1861 to 1868 is a running succession of interviews, calls, breakfasts, dinners, balls, teas, "at homes." Life in a great world capital, once he was taken in, suited his temperament as Boston had never done. From his early association with John Bright, Monckton Milnes (Lord Houghton), Thomas Hughes, Richard Cobden, and Robert Browning, he moved outward into London's more hierarchical circles. In 1862 Minister Adams sent him as a special messenger to the King of Denmark, and the next year in Paris Henry was presented to Napoleon III. In March Monckton Milnes put him up for the St. James Club. The following month marked the beginning of his lifelong friendship with Charles Milnes Gaskell, the son of the member of Parliament for Wenlock in Yorkshire. Through Gaskell he was introduced to a circle that included Francis Turner Palgrave, Gaskell's brother-in-law and the compiler of *The Golden Treasury*, who had just finished editing the poetry of Arthur Hugh Clough. He felt himself much at home with this group of young intellectuals whose literary tastes and inclinations he shared so readily and whose companionship he cherished. Looking back in the nineties to this period of his life he told a young American diplomat that it was a golden time.

It was also a time of unprecedented scientific expansion, of the great debate touched off by Darwin's *Origin of Species*, of revolutions in the natural sciences, physics, and mathematics. No realm of knowledge was exempt. The new science seemed about to produce the key to the universe. Henry was caught up in the intellectual ferment. "I tell you these are great times," he wrote prophetically to Charles. "Man has mounted science, and is now run away with. I firmly believe that before many centuries more, science will be the master of man. The engines he will have invented will be beyond his strength to control. Some day science may have the existence of mankind in its power, and the human race commit suicide by blowing up the world. Not only shall we be able to cruize in space, but I see no reason why some future generation shouldn't walk off like a beetle with the world on its back...."

Exploring the new scientific world set him to thinking of ultimates. The laws that ruled inanimate things, he was convinced, would eventually be found to govern all life. Through science he was drawn to the positivism of Auguste Comte and his goal of reconstructing society according to rational and scientific principles. Comte, Herbert Spencer with his identification of the social and physical processes, and the scientific historian Henry Buckle became Adams's guides in forming a systematic conception of life. From history he turned to political economy, particularly the writings of John Stuart Mill, and then from Mill to contemporary French thinkers. Alexis de Tocqueville's *Democracy in America* gave him profound if dubious reflections on the American political system. Through his friend Thomas Hughes he became acquainted with the political counterparts in England of the scientific revolution, though he was far from accepting Hughes's Christian socialism. By his twenty-sixth birthday it was clear to him that he had abandoned law forever.

Yet if he abandoned law, what could he do? The friends and acquaintances of his own age in England were going ahead in their careers—law, politics, literature, art. He, already growing grey and bald, had no apparent prospects. The political situation in the United States caused him additional uneasiness. "We are now under any circumstances within four or five months of our departure from this country," he wrote Charles shortly before the 1864 presidential election. "I am looking about with a sort of vague curiosity for the current which is to direct my course after I am blown aside by this one. If McClellan were elected, I do not know what the deuce I should do. Certainly I should not go into the army. Anyway I'm not fit for it. . . . I do not think McClellan's election can much change the political results of things, and although it may exercise a great influence on us personally, I believe a little waiting will set matters straight again. So a withdrawal to the shades of private life for a year or two, will perhaps do us all good. . . . But if Lincoln is elected by a mere majority of electors voting, not by a majority of the whole electoral college; if Grant fails to drive Lee out of Richmond; if the Chief is called to Washington to enter a Cabinet with a species of anarchy in the North and no probability of an end of the war—then, indeed, I shall think the devil himself has got hold of us and shall resign my soul to the inevitable. This letter will reach you just on the election. My present impression is that we are in considerable danger of all going to Hell together. You can tell me if I am right."

After the reassuring election, the war's end, and then the shock of Lincoln's assassination, a period of calm followed. Henry had two more years to spend in London, a time he divided between his social life and writing. In November, 1865, Charles had arrived with his bride, and the brothers talked over various literary projects, finally settling on two that Henry determined to undertake: the puncturing of the Captain John Smith-Pocahontas legend; and a study of British finance at the close of the Napoleonic Wars. In dealing with Captain Smith, Henry examined the discrepancies in the four accounts Smith had written of his captivity and concluded that the story of his rescue by Pocahontas was a fabrication, possibly concocted by Smith himself to secure public employment. The article, appearing in the *North American Review*, caused a sensation and was particularly resented in Virginia. Adams followed this up with two weighty articles on England's experience with a nonconvertible currency, an apt theme in the current state of greenback financing in the United States. The articles brought him recognition on both sides of the Atlantic, and he seemed at last to be moving beyond his father's shadow. But the effort exhausted him. Nevertheless, when Sir Charles Lyell, England's leading geologist and one of the earliest and staunchest supporters of the North, asked him if he would help draw American attention to the recently revised tenth edition of Lyell's *Principles of Geology*, Adams agreed to review it for the *North American*. It was a formidable task for an amateur with no more than a dilettante's knowledge of geology, and Adams would be back in Quincy before he had completed his thirty-five closely reasoned pages. But by the time he returned to America he had proved his ability to deal with problems of history, finance, and science, and his writings had demonstrated his right to be heard.

In October, 1868, he set out for Washington to make a career as a journalist, stopping en route in New York where he arranged to contribute articles to the *Post* and to the recently founded *Nation*. "The great step is taken and here I am, settled for years, and perhaps for life," he wrote from the Capital to his friend Gaskell in England shortly after General Grant's election to the presidency. "In about five years I expect to have conquered a reputation. But what it may be worth when got is more than I can tell. The sad truth is that I want nothing and life seems to have no purpose."

Shortly after arriving in Washington he visited President Johnson who received him cordially. Adams was never to see him again. Seward he would see often. But the old Secretary of State, although he talked freely and received the young journalist with his customary kindness, was already a survivor from another era. "He appeared to have closed his account with the public;" Adams observed sadly, "he no longer seemed to care; he asked nothing, gave nothing, and invited no support; he talked little of himself or of others, and waited only for his discharge."

Adams was drawn to a group of newspaper men whom the *Nation* called "working practical reformers." His contacts were large and varied, from statesmen and high officials to Congressmen and lobbyists. Each week he wrote his father on the state of political affairs. Charles, absorbed in his railroad studies, kept at him for documents, especially about railroad matters and new details of corruption. Before Grant's inauguration he had moderate if not high hopes of the new President, though the hope soon withered. His own journalistic success limited him. He soon realized he could not contain his ambition within the bounds of an anonymous correspondent and lobbyist for revenue and tariff reform. He wrote Charles: "I am very hard at work and care very little for the new administration, as I find I can get on without it. What do you say to this? Our labored work does not gain us all it ought. I want to be advertised and the easiest way is to do something obnoxious and to do it well."

He wrote a scathing indictment of the fraud and corruption in the tariff and revenue systems for the *Edinburgh Review*. This he followed with a sardonic article describing in biting phrases the last congressional session. The article, much to his satisfaction, made him talked about, a recognized figure at last in the Adams dynasty. With President Grant he kept his distance. When someone asked him if he had been at the White House lately, he said he had not, that he preferred to remember the house as Lincoln had left it.

Washington he found lacking in a theater, art, music, cultivated parks, drives, clubs, and even good dinners, a raw contrast to the London he had known. Yet it had its advantages. The Capital, he recalled a generation later, enjoyed "the easiest society he had ever seen, and even the Bostonian became simple, good-natured, almost genial, in the softness of a Washington spring. Society went on excellently well without houses, or carriages, or jewels, or toilettes, or pavements, or shops, or *grandezza* of any sort; and the market was excellent as well as cheap. One could not stay there a month without loving the shabby town. . . . Therefore, behind all the processes of political or financial or newspaper training, the social side of Washington was to be taken for granted as three-fourths of existence. . . . He could have spared a world of superannuated history, science, or politics, to have reversed better in waltzing. . . . In such an atmosphere, one made no great pretence of hard work."

The summer of 1869 he spent in Quincy casually reading Gibbon. But for all his boyhood memories he was restless in that limited environment. During the summer months Jay Gould and Jim Fisk made their gamblers' attempt to corner the gold market, counting on the support of Grant's brother-in-law and on the passivity of Secretary of the Treasury Boutwell to keep the government inactive. September's Black Friday saw the ruin of many before Grant finally ordered Boutwell to sell enough Treasury gold to break the Gould-Fisk conspiracy. "That Grant should have fallen within six months, into such a morass," the Henry Adams of the *Education* concluded, "—or should have let Boutwell drop him into it—rendered the outlook. . . . mysterious or frankly opaque, to a young man who had hitched his wagon . . . to the star of reform. . . . The worst scandals of the eighteenth century were relatively harmless by the side of this, which smirched executive, judiciary, banks, corporate systems, professions, and people . . . in one dirty cesspool of vulgar corruption."

On his return to Washington he at once began consulting his private sources of information in preparation for an article on the gold conspiracy which he intended for the *Edinburgh Review*. At the same time he wrote various more fugitive political pieces. His observations were sharp, but nowhere else did he speak out with as much sustained venom as in his "Gold Conspiracy" article. Gould, president and treasurer of the Erie, he here described as a spider who "spun huge webs, in corners and in the dark. . . . It is scarcely necessary to say that he had not a conception of a moral principle." Fisk was "coarse, noisy, boastful, ignorant; the type of young butcher in appearance and mind. . . . In respect to honesty as between Gould and Fisk, the latter was, perhaps, if possible less deserving of trust than the former." Adams concluded ironically that it was "worth while for the public to see how dramatic and artistically admirable a conspiracy in real life may be, when slowly elaborated from the subtle mind of a clever intriguer, and carried into execution by a band of unshrinking scoundrels." After completing another bitter article on the current session of Congress for the *North American Review*, he left Washington in June, 1870, for England.

This visit of nostalgia and friendship was cut short by news of his sister Louisa's illness in Italy. She died shortly after he reached her bedside, and there was no more joy left in his European journey. A week after France had declared war on Prussia, he passed through Paris en route to England disheartened and dismayed, wishing only that both sides might be defeated simultaneously.

Yet, in spite of its burden of sorrow, the summer of 1870 turned out to be a memorable one for Adams. First he received an offer from the recently appointed dean of faculty at Harvard, Ephraim Gurney, of Gurney's old post as editor of the *North American Review*. He turned it down, explaining that he did not wish to leave Washington, although if Gurney wished he would act as political editor. Meanwhile, two letters had been following him across Europe from the new president of Harvard, Charles W. Eliot, offering him the post of assistant professor of medieval history. Eliot, determined to shake up Harvard and appoint "young men and men who never grow old," had been much impressed by the brilliant young journalist with a flair for history. Adams, though highly flattered, declined. Two years before, he replied to Eliot, he might have considered teaching, but now he wanted to follow his journalistic career as far as it would take him. When he disembarked in Boston he thought the matter was settled. In his *Education* he declared that he "knew nothing about history, and much less about teaching, while he knew more than enough about Harvard College."

Neither Dean Gurney nor President Eliot was prepared to take Adams's No for an answer. Father and mother and brothers, as well as dean and president, united in their determination to make Henry change his mind. As he wrote to Gaskell in England, at the end of September, 1870: "Not only the President of the College and the Dean made a very strong personal appeal to me, but my brothers were earnest about it and my father leaned the same way. I hesitated a week, and then yielded. Now I am, I believe, assistant professor of history at Harvard College with a salary of £400 a year, and two hundred students, the oldest in the college, to whom I am to teach medieval history, of which, as you are aware, I am utterly and grossly ignorant. Do you imagine I am appalled at this prospect? Not a bit of it! . . . I gave the college fair warning of my ignorance, and the answer was that I knew just as much as anyone else in America knew on the subject and I could teach better than anyone that could be had. So there I am. My duties begin in a fortnight. . . . I should add that what with one thing and another my income is about doubled, and I have about £1,200 a year. With the professorship I take the *North American Review* and become its avowed editor."

In an interview with President Eliot, Adams reiterated his lack of knowledge. "With the courteous manner and bland smile so familiar for the next generation of Americans, Mr. Eliot mildly but firmly replied, 'If you will point out to me anyone who knows more, Mr. Adams, I will appoint him.' "

Adams soon found his dual role of professor and editor more demanding than he had expected. His teaching schedule took up nine hours a week, while each evening he had to go through three or four ponderous German texts. Resenting large classes and lectures, he set up seminars on medieval institutions, sending his students out to examine sources, documents. "The boys worked like rabbits," he noted, "and dug holes all over the field of archaic society; no difficulty stopped them; unknown languages yielded before their attack, and customary law became familiar as the police court; undoubtedly they learned, after a fashion, to chase an idea, like a hare, through as dense a thicket of obscure facts as they were likely to meet at the bar." Professor Adams was a provocative teacher, probing, questioning, criticizing—"robust and virile," according to one of his students, rather than "subtle"—far more a student than any of his students. His classes were exciting, and the students regarded him with a mixture of respect and awe. The bald, elegant, waspish little man in the Vandyke beard led them through the maze of Anglo-Saxon law to history itself. For history, he maintained, should be a science like any other science.

At faculty meetings he sat in the back of the room and wrote letters while others droned on about questions of discipline. After two years he gave up attending altogether. Almost on arrival in Cambridge he had become a Harvard character, looming large for all his five feet three inches. "There was no closing of eyes in slumber when Henry Adams was in command," one of his students recalled. "All was wholly unacademic; no formality, no rigidity, no professional pose. . . ." He was "a friendly disposed gentleman . . . whose every feature, every line of his body, his clothes, his bearing, his speech were well-bred to a degree."

Among his colleagues were James Russell Lowell and William Dean Howells. In 1871 John La Farge was appointed a tutor. Adams became one of the group of younger men who made up The Club, such convivial diners as Oliver Wendell Holmes, Jr., John Fiske, and Henry and William James. He had few contacts with the older generation. Gurney's home was almost the only one he visited. At the dean's often-frequented fireside he met Gurney's sister-in-law, the twenty-eight-year-old Marian Hooper whom Gurney was tutoring in Greek. A little woman—an inch shorter than Henry—"Clover" Hooper, though no beauty, was poised, quick-witted, sharp-tongued, and amusing. The perennial bachelor was drawn to her at once. In February, 1872, he and Clover became engaged. Both families approved the match. The Hoopers were of as ancient Yankee lineage as the Adamses. Only Charles was alarmed upon learning of his brother's engagement, bursting out "Heavens!—No!—they're all crazy as coots. She'll kill herself, just like her aunt."

In taking over the *North American Review* Adams had hoped to salvage much of his political journalism, to quicken the magazine as an organ of political reform. Lowell commented approvingly that Adams was out to make the old teakettle think it was a steam engine. But before his wedding, in preparation for an extended trip abroad, Adams resigned the editorship. Like the earlier Adamses he was able to take a singularly detached view of a wife-to-be. She "belongs to a sort of clan, as all Bostonians do," he confided to Gaskell. "Socially the match is supposed to be unexceptionable. One of my congratulatory letters describes my 'fiancée' to me as 'a charming blue.' She is certainly not handsome; nor would she be quite called plain, I think. . . . She knows her own mind uncommonly well. She does not talk *very* American. Her manners are quiet. She reads German—also Latin—also, I fear, a little Greek, but very little. She talks garrulously, but on the whole pretty sensibly. She is very open to instruction. *We* shall improve her. She dresses badly. She decidedly has humor and will appreciate *our* wit. She has money enough to be quite independent. She rules me as only American women rule men, and I cower before her. Lord! how she would lash me if she read the above description of her!"

Henry and Clover were married in June, 1872. Though they were both agnostics, indifferent to the religion of their ancestors, they had a conventionally formal church wedding. "For twelve years I had everything I most wanted on earth," he wrote privately of his marriage, destined to end tragically. In his *Education* he never mentions his wife, making only the barest reference to the Saint-Gaudens sculpture on her grave. On their wedding trip to Europe he was as usual seasick. A joint travel letter written on shipboard recorded the voyage with queasy humor. On landing, the newlyweds first visited Henry's father, still in Geneva as a member of the international tribunal. From Geneva they went to Berlin where George Bancroft, Clover's cousin and now American minister to Prussia, gave two dinner parties for them to which he invited the most eminent German scholars in history and public law. Adams left Germany with several cases of books. He and Clover read Schiller's *History of the Thirty Years' War* as they traveled south to Egypt by way of Italy. Henry had brought the most modern photographic equipment with him for a long Nile cruise. They went as far as Philae, above the First Cataract of the Nile. He was entranced with his first view of that most ancient of civilizations. With Clover beside him his customary cynical self faded away. "Henry is utterly devoted and tender," she wrote in her weekly letter to her father. Yet somewhere on that Nile cruise she suffered a brief neurasthenic collapse, a portent that at the time they managed to disregard.

By May, 1873, they were staying in London in Gaskell's Park Lane house that he had placed at their disposal. From London they went to Oxford and Cambridge, meeting historians and scholars from Sir Henry Maine to Benjamin Jowett. England was for Henry a renewal of old scenes and old friendships, though sometimes Clover remained unimpressed. Yet she as well as Henry expanded under the spell of London.

In early August the Adamses returned to Boston and the house at 29 Marlborough Street, a more convenient distance from his students, to which Henry had moved from his rooms in Wadsworth House in the Harvard Yard. He now held his seminars in his own library. There, formally informal, he would sit after dinner with his students before an open fire, smoking a cigar and sipping sherry—a liberty in no way allowed the others—as the talk flowed and, led by him, they questioned all authority, challenged all assumptions, tracked effects to their causes. "Life is so pleasant," Clover lamented when they first moved in, "I wish death and old age were only myths." Once again Adams assumed the editorship of the *North American Review*, keeping it under his autocratic control but delegating most of the day-to-day tasks to the twenty-four-year-old Henry Cabot Lodge as his assistant editor. James Russell Lowell, Henry James, and William Dean Howells, among others, contributed articles and reviews. Adams's Harvard schedule was more exacting than ever, demanding twelve hours a week in the lecture rooms. He suffered under the pedantic burden of examination books and Division Returns. Eliot gladly agreed to his proposal to establish a class of doctoral candidates, and Professor Adams then turned over his more elementary and popular courses to one of his graduate students. In 1874 he was working hard on a new course in colonial history. The next year, at the end of his five-year term, he accepted an appointment for another five years. After two more years of extended reading in the colonial period, he moved on to the period in which his great-grandfather and grandfather had played such important roles. His new course, History VI, dealt with the history of the United States from 1789 to 1840. Out of this course grew his most extended work, his nine-volume *History of the United States during the Administrations of Jefferson and Madison*, as well as his biographies of John Randolph and Albert Gallatin, and his *Documents Relating to New England Federalism*.

By 1876 he had baked his first batch of doctors of philosophy and believed that they would compare favorably with any in Europe. His scholars now took over the courses in which he himself had lost interest. For his new course he immersed himself in a sea of state papers. But even as he planned his course he was growing weary of the academic world, fretful at the provinciality of Boston. "It would bore you to extinction," he wrote Gaskell, now a member of Parliament, "to follow me through my daily struggle to find out how boys who have no minds can be made to understand that they had better be contented without the education of a Newton, and how boys who have minds can be made to understand that all knowledge has not yet been exhausted by Newton and such. This effort to get rid of rubbish and to utilize good material is one of my labors. I am preaching a crusade against Culture with a big C. I hope to excite the hatred of my entire community, every soul of whom adores that big C. I mean to irritate every one about me to a frenzy by ridiculing all the idols of the University and declaring a university education to be a swindle. I have hopes of being turned out of my place in consequence, in which case I shall become a reformer and my fortune is made." To a friend he admitted that the instruction of boys was mean work, weakening to both parties. As the presidential election of 1876 neared, promising at least the elimination of Grant and his hangers-on, Adams pined again for Washington. He considered his university work essentially finished. To one of his more brilliant students he remarked that he had been a professor as long as he ought.

His independent-reformist editing of the *North American Review* finally brought on a quarrel with the publishers, and he resigned, leaving behind a volcanic October, 1877, issue in which he and his contributors attacked all their political enemies. As editor and as teacher he had had enough. President Eliot was puzzled and a little annoyed at the resignation of his extraordinary assistant professor (although he made no move to offer him a full professorship). But Adams's departure was no surprise to his Harvard circle to whom he had freely expressed his contempt for the college establishment. His decision lifted his spirits, and he wrote almost gaily to Gaskell from the Capital in November, 1877: "We have made a great leap in the world, cut loose at once from all that has occupied us since our return from Europe, and caught new ties and occupations here. The fact is I gravitate to a capital by a primary law of nature. This is the only place in America where society amuses me, or where life offers variety. Here, too, I can fancy that we are of use in the world, for we distinctly occupy niches which ought to be filled. We have taken a large house in which we seem lost. Our water-colors and drawings go with us wherever we go, and here are our great evidence of individuality, and our title to authority. As I am intimate with many of the people in power and out of power, I am readily allowed or aided to do all the historical work I please; and as I am avowedly out of politics, there will, it is to be hoped, be no animosities to meet. Literary and non-partisan people are rare here, and highly appreciated. And yet society in its way is fairly complete, almost as choice, if not as large, as in London or Rome.

"One of these days this will be a very great city if nothing happens to it. Even now it is a beautiful one, and its situation is superb. As I belong to the class of people who have great faith in this country and who believe that in another century it will be saying in its turn the last word of civilization, I enjoy the expectation of the coming day, and try to imagine that I am myself, with my fellow *gelehrte* here, the first faint rays of that great light which is to dazzle and set the world on fire hereafter. Our duties are perhaps only those of twinkling, and many people here, like little Alice, wonder what we're at. But twinkle for twinkle, I prefer our kind to that of the small politician. . . ."

He had indeed outgrown Boston without ever really having grown into it. But the eighteenth-century town of his boyhood had become a city threatened by the rise of the Famine Irish—"the low and socialistic elements," Parkman called them—to political power. Within seven years of Adams's departure, Boston would elect its first Irish mayor even as the old Yankees retreated to their Beacon Hill-Back Bay enclave. After Boston's threatened provinciality, Washington was to Adams a relief. Since the Civil War, the Capital—that had seemed an overgrown Southern village when he first saw it—had achieved an outward elegance typified by paved streets, wide sidewalks, and horse-cars gliding smoothly along Pennsylvania Avenue. With only half the population of Boston, Washington had an air of spaciousness, of great vistas, that the older city warped in its narrow peninsula lacked. And only a short canter away were the enchanting wooded ravines of Rock Creek.

The Adamses had rented the old yellow Corcoran house at 1501 H Street, a short block from elm-bordered Lafayette Square. With their prized possessions, their bales of oriental rugs, their furniture, their pictures, their Japanese bronzes and vases, they were able to banish the drab Washington congressional look. Lafayette Square reminded them of London's gracious squares. Three hundred yards away, across lawns and flower beds, the White House itself loomed up, bristling with memories for an Adams. Clover was as relieved to get away from the opinionated Adams clan as was Henry to leave Boston. She took charge of the social life. The elegant household ran smoothly with four, later six, servants. Each day at five o'clock a small inner circle of political leaders gathered around Clover's Japanese tea table—Secretary of State William Evarts; Carl Schurz, now Secretary of the Interior in Hayes's cabinet; Attorney General Charles Devens; Baron Yoshida, the Japanese minister; the Turkish minister Aristarchi Bey; the more engaging Southerners now appearing for the first time since Reconstruction. General Richard Taylor, the son of President Zachary Taylor, would come almost every day promptly at five. John Hay, Assistant Secretary of State and author of the casual *Pike County Ballads*, whom Henry had met when Hay came to Washington from Ohio in 1861 as one of Lincoln's secretaries, became an Adams intimate, as did an earlier acquaintance, Clarence King, the geologist with whom Adams had spent the summer of 1871 in Wyoming and Colorado on a geological exploration trip. "Since 1879," Adams was to write in his *Education*, "King, Hay and Adams had been inseparable." With its celebrated teas and its small convivial dinners the yellow house on H Street soon became envied and sought after in Washington society. Clover was a resolute excluder. Neither money nor office nor even intellectual achievement gained entry to her salon if social grace and charm were lacking. Those of doubtful reputation waited in vain.

At first Adams had worried about the twin problems of a new house and a new career. But soon he relaxed in an agreeable pattern of daily life. After breakfast, often with some of his more intimate friends, he and Clover rode for two hours when the weather allowed, usually accompanied by their two Skye terriers, Boojum and Pollywog. The Secretary of State had lent Adams a desk on the fourth floor of the new State Department Building and there he secreted himself from 11 A.M. to 5 P.M. poring through the documents of the Jefferson period. Each day at five he broke off for tea. Then came an evening round of dinners, receptions, balls, and entertainments, of which he never tired. Driven by an inner restlessness he would sometimes go alone when Clover was fatigued. The days slipped by, he wrote Gaskell, "like a dream of the golden age." Life passed so quickly that he sometimes wondered if the remaining days were worth exerting oneself about. The scarcely mentioned shadow darkening their sunniest hours was Clover's childlessness, as much a cause of sorrow for Adams with his dynastic family feeling as for his wife.

In spite of her marriage, Clover remained very close to her father. Each Sunday she wrote him a long letter on her week's activities, little barbed vignettes about what she had seen and heard. "We all adjourned to pay our respects to Mr. and Mrs. Hayes," she wrote, following a visit to the new President. "She is quite nice-looking—dark with smooth black hair combed low over her ears—and a high comb behind . . . no jewelry. . . . The Hayes suffer much from rats in the White House who run over their bed and nibble the President's toes." Or in a more malicious mood she observed: "General Buchanan was a colonel in the regular army many years ago when a young lieutenant rode drunk into the mess and tried to get on the table. The colonel naturally requested the dismissal of that lieutenant whose name was Ulysses S. Grant—the wheel went round and somehow or other General Buchanan didn't get to the top."

Soon after Adams had begun his new Harvard lectures on the history of the United States, Albert Gallatin's only surviving son asked him to edit his father's papers and write his biography. Adams admired Jefferson's Secretary of the Treasury, his grandfather's old colleague at Ghent, and agreed to this, his first major literary undertaking. For him it was a labor of love, convinced as he was that in ability, integrity, and knowledge, Gallatin had no equal. Through two seasons, Adams at his unofficial desk in the State Department worked on the Gallatin papers. To whet his style he reread Macaulay. The Gallatin biography, innovative in its cool detachment, would endure for the next two generations as the definitive study. Yet in finishing it, he felt another and more compelling impulse stirring in him. Years ago in Berlin he had toyed with the idea of writing fiction. Now with compulsive speed he turned aside to write a novel of the Grant era that he called *Democracy*, with cutting satire exposing the secret strings by which the puppets of public life were made to dance. Influenced by the novels of Disraeli, and less directly by Thackeray, he was more concerned with holding up a mirror to his times than with telling a tale. The plot of *Democracy* is slight. Mrs. Lightfoot Lee, a discerning widow of means, comes to Washington and Lafayette Square to get "to the heart of the great American mystery of democracy and government." What she discovers is the moral disintegration of the Gilded Age.

The disintegration is personified in the forceful venal party dictator, Senator Silas P. Ratcliffe of Peonia, Illinois, the man behind the President, who falls in love with Mrs. Lee. When *Democracy* was anonymously published, Ratcliffe was immediately recognized—even to his physical appearance—as James G. Blaine. Mrs. Lee was superficially modeled on Mrs. Bigelow Lawrence, a summer neighbor of the Adamses and a woman to whom Blaine was devoted. But her fundamental traits derived from Clover. Other characters were apparent: Nathan Gore, the "self-appointed Massachusetts poet historian," being the historian and former minister John Lothrop Motley; Baron Jacobi, the thinly disguised Turkish minister; and so on. The President was an amalgam of Grant and Hayes. His wife, "Lemonade Lucy," who refused to serve wine at the White House, was satirized more directly. On publication *Democracy* was an immediate success, and an immediate scandal. Blaine, recognizing himself and supposing Clarence King the author, cut him dead on the street. Others conjectured that the author was an Englishman, a Southern sympathizer, a member of an antebellum Washington family, a Washington society woman. Years later Adams told his brother Brooks that with its publication he bade good-by to politics, but at the time not even his brothers knew he had written it. Charles sent Henry a copy, calling it—to Henry's delight—a "very 'coarse' novel," although he was pleased with the portrayal of the leading character as an example of Western venality. *Democracy* made an equal hit in England where some compared it to Trollope's political novels. Others clearly took great enjoyment in looking down their noses at the coarse, crude, dishonest Americans portrayed with such detached malice.

While the Gallatin biography was going through the press and the *Democracy* manuscript was still on the way to the publisher, Adams and his wife in May of 1879 left for Europe where he now planned to embark on the major project of his career, his *History of the United States During the Administrations of Jefferson and Madison*, that vital period when the republic took shape. Working in the State Department, he had become increasingly aware of the lack of counterparts to the reports sent by American envoys during the period. To complete his researches he decided needed several months in the archives in London, Paris, and Madrid studying the diplomatic correspondence in regard to America during the Napoleonic era.

In London he was welcomed by Charles Milnes Gaskell and other old friends. At a Foreign Office reception he managed to talk with the foreign secretary about the regulations blocking access to government documents after 1802. Adams asked that the ban be lifted to 1810, or, if possible, even to 1815. Within a week he received his permission.

France presented him with more formidable bureaucratic obstacles. Although the French Premier promised him access to the secret papers in the Office of Foreign Affairs and the Ministry of the Marine, official permission was so slow in coming that in exasperation he left to try his luck in Madrid. But Spain was to prove more bureaucratic, more dilatory, more obstructed by red tape even than France. The Spanish foreign secretary finally decided that the papers Adams wanted to see were still too sensitive to be shown. Luckily Adams encountered the grandson of the Spanish minister to the United States during Jefferson's administration, the young Marquess de Casa, who in spite of the foreign secretary was able to open the locked archives for him.

After two months in Spain Adams returned to France. There a new government more subject to the influence of his Parisian friends at last made the needed documents available. He thought he had never better employed six weeks. Faced with such formidable masses of paper and books he was off every morning at ten, home at twelve for breakfast—as he called it—then off again from one until dark. Evenings he read at home. When the time came for him to go to London, he quit his Paris archives with regret.

For the Adamses London was again the magic city. They rented a house in Queen Anne's Gate. Three or four times a week they were invited to dinner, and visitors flocked to them. Henry James was at Queen Anne's Gate almost every day. Sometimes he and Adams talked until midnight, although Clover refused to keep them company after 10:30. She came to think it was time Henry James was summoned home by his family. "He is too good a fellow to be spoiled by injudicious old ladies in London—and in the long run they would like him all the better for knowing and loving his own country. He had better go to Cheyenne and run a hog ranch."

Adams's work went smoothly. By May, 1880, he had finished with the record office, completed his search through newspapers in the British Museum, collected most of his pamphlets, and gone through the essential private collections. Copyists were at work for him in Paris and Madrid. Given health and leisure, he predicted a good history in the next five years. Two months later he wrote Henry Cabot Lodge: "My work is done, at least so far as it ever will be done. I have made a careful study of English politics from 1801 to 1815, and have got my authorities in order. My Spanish papers have mostly arrived. The French documents are, I hope, coming, although I am still nervous about them. My material is enormous, and now I fear that the task of compression will be painful. . . . We are very weary of our London season, which has now lasted six months, but luckily the weather is cool and wet. I suppose we shall stay in Scotland till near September, and reach New York on October 5th or thereabouts, whence we must go directly to Washington to furnish our new house. We have taken Corcoran's White House, next his own, on President's [Lafayette] Square, and I fear there is a great deal to be done before we can get in. . . . I look forward placidly to recurring winters and summers in Washington and Beverly, until a cheery tomb shall provide us with a permanent abode for all seasons."

On their arrival in Washington the Adamses had to stay for a time at Wormley's Hotel, since the Corcoran house was still being renovated. Adams often walked over to the square to supervise the work and direct the workmen, who found his fussy and meticulous orders at times unendurable. He was at last rather shaken when a cornicemaker whom he had repeatedly upbraided broke down and went home and murdered his wife.

By December the Adamses were at last able to settle into what seemed a serene future. Their gracious house with its antiques, its Japanese bronzes, oriental rarities, sketches by Watteau, Tiepolo, Rembrandt, and Michelangelo, paintings of Turner and Constable, and collections of English water colors was again an enviable social center. Adams devoted his days to research and writing until teatime intruded. During the long days Clover took up portrait photography as a hobby and soon became very skilled at it.

A few weeks after the Adamses' return to Washington, their friend James Garfield was elected President. But on taking office Garfield felt himself obliged to appoint Blaine Secretary of State. This was too much for Adams, who on Blaine's arrival gave up his desk in the State Department. Among their new friends were their Lafayette Square neighbors, the commonplace though extremely rich Pennsylvania politician Senator James Donald Cameron, and his very young, astonishingly beautiful second wife. For the wife's sake they were willing to put up with the pedestrian husband. With the amused toleration of his wife, the very proper Adams indulged in an arch intellectual courtship of Elizabeth Cameron. "I adore her," he wrote Hay, "and respect the way she has kept out of scandal and mud, and done her duty by the lump of clay she promised to love and respect."

Henry James, visiting the United States under an alias in 1882 to escape publicity in the press, again enjoyed the intimacy of the Adams household. Yet even he sensed the flaw in his friends' salon that Clover kept so fussily exclusive. After his return from Europe in 1881 Adams had renewed his intimacy with Clarence King and John Hay. With them and Hay's wife, the Adamses now formed a more intimate circle among their circle of intimates to which they gave the name of Five of Hearts and even had notepaper so engraved. Adams thought that he and King and Hay were as close as friends could be.

Approaching his history that he believed destined to be the great work of his life, Adams was mindful of Gibbon, who just over a century before, while musing amidst the ruins of Rome's capital, had first conceived of writing his *Decline and Fall*. Adams determined to write something as massive and enduring on the theme of the rise of a new nation on the sprawling American continent during that critical period between 1800 and 1815 when the American character was still being formed. He saw his work as scientific, paralleling Darwin in the natural sciences, an explication of the deterministic laws that governed historical development and that the leading statesmen were powerless to control. His would be the first sustained attempt at writing American social history, as the German historian Leopold von Ranke had demanded, history "as it really was"—or as near as possible. It had taken him more than half his lifetime to start his real career. "Just at present," he wrote, "life seems as real and enjoyable as ever. Indeed, if I felt a perfect confidence that my history would be what I would like to make it, this part of life—from forty to fifty—would be all I want. There is a summer-like repose about it; a self-contained, irresponsible, devil-may-care indifference to the future as it looks to younger eyes; a feeling that one's bed is made, and one can rest on it till it becomes necessary to go to bed forever."

Only a few months after he had set to work, his friend John Morse, editor of the American Statesmen series, asked him to do a volume on John Randolph of Roanoke, the bizarre, insolent, half-mad Virginian who had so viciously attacked both the Presidents Adams. For their descendant to write a life of their maligner was a labor that he eagerly undertook, completing the task in three months. From Randolph, Adams moved on to a biography of

Aaron Burr which he completed with equal speed. Clover liked it better than Randolph, but Morse refused it for his series because Burr was not a "statesman." Adams observed that Morse ought to live in Washington awhile and get to know some *real* statesmen! After two other publishers declined the manuscript, he put it aside. It has never been found, and it seems probable that Henry cannibalized it for the account of Burr in his history.

With these two malevolent figures behind him, he turned back to his magnum opus. At forty-four he felt the years creeping up on him inexorably and feared that he might not have enough time left to finish his task. Taking his father as an example, he thought he could count on his brain for another twenty years if his body held out. Every evanescent hour now seemed golden to him. Summers the Adamses escaped Washington's oppressive heat at Beverly Farms on the coast north of Boston, in a many-gabled house on a hill in the midst of twenty-five woodland acres that he and Clover had built next to her father's estate in 1876. There at the end of the path of forty steps Adams worked in a playhouse in the woods that Clover had had made for her nieces. He took to using a newfangled typewriter, extended his working hours from nine to five each day.

When Hay—who had inherited several million dollars on the death of his father-in-law—learned that Adams was upset at the prospect of a seven-story apartment house next door to his Washington house, he bought an entire corner tract on Lafayette Square directly opposite the White House and suggested that he and Adams build adjoining houses on it. Adams was delighted with the idea. He and Hay engaged Adams's Harvard classmate H. H. Richardson, reviver of the Romanesque and architect of Boston's Trinity Church, to design their houses. While Richardson set to work on the plans, Adams finished the first section of his history, a large volume—later to be revised and published in two volumes—six copies of which were to be printed and sent to his friends for criticism and recommendations, Then, wearied from the straitness of his task, he turned inward to write another novel, *Esther*, through which he debated within his agnostic self those ultimate and unanswerable questions about the meaning of life and the grounds of belief, scientific or religious.

*Esther* reflects and refines the intimate discussions of Adams's own circle. Esther herself, lovingly modeled after Clover, is a free-thinking, strong-willed young painter who lives with her father. The antagonists are her cousin George Strong, a high-spirited skeptic, obviously modeled on Clarence King, and the Episcopalian clergyman Stephen Hazard, a thinly disguised portrait of Adams's second cousin Phillips Brooks, who was then making such dev-astating inroads on the inherited Unitarianism of Boston old ladies. Endlessly they discuss the struggle between science and religion. The remaining two characters are derived from Elizabeth Cameron and John La Farge with La Farge given certain features of Clover's cousin William Sturgis Bigelow, who after a desultory Bohemian existence ended up in Japan as a convert to Buddhism. Catherine Brooke (Elizabeth), Adams describes cloyingly as a beautiful "child of nature," "fresh as a summer's morning," and so on. The artist Wharton (La Farge) is engaged in painting murals on the transept wall of Hazard's church. Esther leaves her own art work to paint one of the murals. After she has finished it she finds she cannot go back to her own trivial work. So, without art, and following the death of her father, she is left to face life alone. She must now emancipate herself both from her art and from her father's shadow. Although she has come to love Hazard, she cannot accept his faith. Before her final interview with him she asks her cousin Strong to state his own religious views. These represent Adams's own cau-tious agnosticism: a disbelief in a personal God and in old wives' tales of future rewards and punishments. All that Strong could bring himself to say in reply to Esther was that there was a "strong probability of the existence of two things . . . mind and matter."

Adams finished *Esther* in March, 1884, and Holt published it under a pseudonym. Adams guaranteed expenses, but insisted that it be published without advertising or comment, that no review copies should be distributed, that it should make its way by word of mouth as did the books of the previous century. Its appearance roused little interest. Adams expressed the mocking doubt that any man, woman, or child had ever read or even heard of *Esther*. Yet it was a book to which he remained emotionally attached. Five years later he would write to Elizabeth Cameron that he cared more for a dozen pages of *Esther* than for his whole history.

Following *Esther* he again resumed the history, a labor that at times seemed to him interminable. By the late spring of 1884 his new house became his most pressing concern. He had planned on a square, functional building. But the ebullient Richardson was not to be restrained from his Romanesque, and the twin houses rose with steeply gabled roofs, dark-red brick façades of massive solidarity, and Richardsonesque arches. Adams's correspondence for those months is full of the house. A dozen times a day he would leave his desk to see what the workmen were doing. The building proved a constant distraction to him. Yet shortly before the end of 1884 he was able to announce that he had half completed his history, with two volumes already in type.

After bringing his history to the halfway mark, after producing two novels and three biographies, he was overcome by a sense of languor. Yet with Cleveland's election he expected that his history would go on as quietly as it had before. Then in 1885 he was struck by the crisis he had intimated in *Esther*. After a lingering illness Clover's seventy-four-year-old father died. Her first stoical reaction was followed by a nervous collapse, and Adams had to interrupt his history for two months to take her to Old Sweet Springs in West Virginia. By the summer's end she seemed on the way to recovery, but during the autumn she lapsed into an unrelieved depression. Watching her deteriorate, Adams found it almost impossible to resume his historical work. What he had called "history" he now felt as a mere mechanical fitting together of quotations.

On Sunday, December 6, Clover sat at her desk where for so many years she had written her weekly encompassing letters to her father. She now penned a note to her sister, one that was never sent. "If I had one single point of character or goodness I would stand on that and grow back to life," she wrote in her despair. "Henry is more patient and loving than words can express . . . tenderer and better than all of you even." Breaking off her writing, she went to her photographic darkroom for a jar of potassium cyanide that she kept there, came back with it and swallowed a handful of the crystals. Adams was taking his usual Sunday walk. When he returned he found her lying dead on the hearth rug.

His first impulse was to hide, to see no one. As the weeks passed, his Lafayette Square neighbors had occasional glimpses of him standing and staring fixedly out the window. If he wanted anything he wanted to be quit of that haunted house, to be in the new one before the first of the year. He told Hay that he was getting through the days somehow or other. After he moved into his Richardsonesque house at the very end of 1885, Elizabeth Cameron and other women friends sustained him through the dark months. More and more he came to rely on them, on his nieces, on an atmosphere of femininity. He himself said he had only a bystander's interest in life.

Once he had finished the first half of his history he had planned a trip to Japan with Clover. After her death he felt it a kind of duty to her memory to make the trip. Dreading to travel alone, he looked for a companion. But King had gone to England, while Hay was occupied with his extended life of Lincoln. Finally he found La Farge, frustrated in working out his design for an Ascension painting in New York's Tenth Street Church and more than willing to go as Adams's guest. They left Boston in June, 1886, Charles supplying them with the director's private car of the Union Pacific, to take ship at San Francisco. In their two months in Japan, the Buddhist William Sturgis Bigelow acted as their guide. "The only practical result of my trip," Adams wrote Gaskell on his return, "has been to make me earnest to close up everything here, finish history, cut society, forswear strong drink and politics, and start in about three years for China, never to return. China is the great unknown country of the world. Sooner or later, if health holds out, I shall drift there; and once there, I shall not soon drift back. You may find me there with a false pig-tail, and a button on the top of my head as a mandarin of the new class."

He arrived back in the United States to find his father dying and postponed his return to Washington to share the deathbed watch with his invalid mother. Winding up family affairs after the funeral depressed him almost beyond endurance. How he felt about his father's death he never revealed in his letters. His one determination now was to complete his history as soon as possible. The following summer he took his work with him to Quincy to be near his mother, remaining longer at his desk than he had ever done before. "I write history as though it were serious, five hours a day;" he told John Hay, "and when my hand and head get tired I step out into the rose-beds and watch my favorite roses. For lack of thought I have taken to learning roses and talk of them as though I had the slightest acquaintance with the subject." At summer's end, instead of returning to Washington alone, he brought his eldest niece, the twenty-year-old Mary Adams, back with him, the first of a series of "nieces-in-residence."

When Elizabeth Cameron's daughter Martha was born in June, 1887, the child released all Adams's frustrated paternity. In 1888 his diary recorded: "I am almost alone except for an occasional visit from Martha and her mother, and I have been sad, sad, sad. Three years!" He continued doggedly on with his history, seized at the last, as he admitted, with a frenzy to bring it to an end.

Finally, while visiting his mother in the Old House where his grandfather and great-grandfather had come back "to eat out their hearts in disappointment and disgust," on Sunday, September 23, 1888, he finished his ninth and final volume. On reaching the last page, he remembered how Gibbon on finishing his *Decline and Fall* had walked under an arbor of acacias, thinking that whatever might be the fate of his history, "the life of the historian must be short and precarious." That same Sunday he wrote Hay: "I have composed the last page of my history, and the weather is so wet that for a week I've been in vain trying to do Gibbon and walk up and down my garden. I wish Gibbon had been subjected to twelve inches of rain in six weeks, in which case he would not have waited to hear the bare-footed monks sing in the Temple of Jupiter, and would have avoided arbors as he would rheumatics. I am sodden with cold and damp, and hunger for a change." The great work of his maturity, for which all else had been merely a preparation, was completed. Yet the history, he knew, belonged to the Henry Adams of 1870, a strangely different person from the Adams of 1888.

# 8

## *Brooks Adams*

### THE CONTINUING DYNASTY

I N THE remaining autumn weeks Henry Adams continued to leaf through and burn his old diary although, on the chance that he might some day need it for reference, he hesitated to destroy much of what he had written after 1862. For a long time he had been concerned with a fitting monument for Clover's grave in Rock Creek Cemetery. In Japan he had conceived of a figure of Buddhalike detachment. Now at the "haunting anniversary" of December 6, he engaged his sculptor friend, Augustus Saint-Gaudens, to model a statue that would fuse the art and thought of East and West. Saint-Gaudens agreed to undertake the work, but, after many discussions with Adams, struck out on his own, discarding philosophic abstractions to create, in his own adaptation of *art nouveau*, the hooded, enigmatic figure that would become recognized as one of his greatest works.

With the completion of his history Adams had at last freed himself for his long-promised pilgrimage to China. But before he could leave, he was faced with the unavoidable preliminaries of getting his history through the printers, correcting the first drafts, revising, and rewriting. His brother Charles took over as his se-

verest critic, pruning the lusher passages from the proof sheets—
"Macaulay flowers" he called them—caustically striking out whole
paragraphs. In the midst of the editing Adams's mother died. Grief,
he maintained, was irrelevant. Stoically he thrust his personal feelings aside to carry on with his emendations. However empty he
might feel, he consoled himself with the thought that his history
was worthy to be set beside those of Gibbon and Macaulay, Froude
and Green, Parkman and Bancroft. In October, 1889, the two volumes on Jefferson's first administration were published.

During Adams's last months in Washington he formed the habit
of taking his daily mint julep before dinner with Elizabeth Cameron across the square. More and more he became dependent on
her. Though she was only a few steps away, he constantly wrote
her little notes, sent her poems he had composed for her. For all
his prim correctness, his persistent attentions to his charming
young neighbor eventually made tongues wag. And beneath his
formality, there lurked deeper and more demanding emotions that
Elizabeth could not disregard. In the end she decided that she must
send him away. She herself sailed for Europe. Leaving the proof
sheets of his next volume behind him, he headed for the West
Coast, again taking the eager but impecunious La Farge as his
traveling companion. "Here goes then, for Polynesia!" he pro-
claimed bravely.

For Adams the South Seas seemed the track by which the
course of civilization might be traced back to China, his ultimate
if barely acknowledged goal. Although Elizabeth had banished
him, she had not forbidden his corresponding with her, and from
the very beginning of his travels he wrote her long diary-letters
to which she replied with lighthearted gossip. He received her first
letter just as he embarked on the *Zealandia* at San Francisco, but
even before he reached the Golden Gate, seasickness laid him so
low that for a whole day he lay on his bunk unable to read a word.

Bustling Americanized Hawaii proved a far cry from his imagined palm-fringed island where "old-gold girls"—as King had called them—swam out in the crystal water from the long sunny beaches. If such girls had ever existed, they were long since gone. In Samoa, however, he did encounter the archaic world he had dreamed about. For him at least the eternal feminine formed the core of such dreams. He even saw the Siva, the sensuous legendary dance of Polynesia that the missionaries had done their best to suppress and that he described in a letter to Hay: "You would rush for the next steamer if you could realize the beauty of some parts of the Siva. There are figures stupid and grotesque as you please; but there are others which would make you gasp with delight, and movements which I do not exaggerate in calling unsurpassable. The *pai-pai* is a figure taboo by the missionaries . . . but it is still danced in the late hours of the night, though we have seen it only once. Two or three women are the dancers, and they should be the best, especially in figure. They dance at first with the same movements, as far as I could see, that they use in many other figures, and as I did not know what they were dancing I paid no special attention. Presently I noticed that the chief dancer's waist-cloth seemed to be getting loose. This is their only dress, and it is nothing but a strip of cotton or *tapa* about eighteen inches wide wrapped round the waist, with the end or corner tucked inside to hold it. Of course it constantly works loose, but the natives are so well used to it that they always tighten it, and I never yet have seen either man, woman or child let it fall by accident. In the *pai-pai* the women let their *lava-lavas*, as they are called, or *siapas*, seem about to fall. The dancer pretends to tighten it, but only opens it to show a little more thigh, and fastens it again so low as to show a little more hip. Always turning about and moving with the chorus, she repeats this process again and again, showing more legs and hips every time, until the *siapa* barely hangs on her, and would fall except that she holds it. At last it falls; she turns once or twice more in full view; then snatches up the *siapa* and runs away.

"You must imagine these dances in a native house, lighted by the ruddy flame of a palm-leaf fire in the centre, and filled, except where the dancing is done, by old-gold men and women applauding, laughing, smoking, and smelling of cocoanut oil."

Every day Adams sat with his writing board and inkstand just as if he were in Washington, his pen gliding quickly over the paper, page following fluttering page, as he described the landscape, the geology, the chiefs, the military receptions, the dances, and the food. Over and above his innately flirtatious self, he remained the primly correct New Englander. He might find the dancers charming, record it as delightful to be kissed by one, yet never was he tempted further. He did admit, though, that thirty years earlier he probably would have behaved quite differently.

As the anniversary of Clover's death neared, his spirits, as always, sank. In his depression he wrote a poem on the wretchedness of human existence. On the actual day of her death he reflected that since he had been able to endure five years, he could probably stand ten. Whenever Elizabeth's letters arrived he gloated over them, read and reread them. In reply to her apology for their being so trivial he assured her that they gave him a famished castaway's delight. She now lifted her ban and urged him to come home.

In Samoa he met Robert Louis Stevenson. Neither was impressed by the other. Adams described Stevenson as "so thin and emaciated he looked like a bundle of sticks in a bag." Stevenson for his part could not even remember Adams's name the next day. Subsequently they saw enough of each other to become friendly, and when Adams was about to leave for Tahiti Stevenson gave him a letter of introduction to Tati Salmon, the ruling head of the Tevas, whose father had been Alexander Salmon, a London Jew who had married Arii Taimi, the heiress of the dispossessed Teva clan. Adams at first found Tahiti dull and empty. But the boredom of his early weeks—worse than "in the worst wilds of Beacon Street"—was soon relieved by the overwhelming hospitality of Tati Salmon in his old French house at Papana. Tati, a heavily built high-spirited man, became Adams's fast friend. "Hebrew and Polynesian mix rather well," Adams noted, "when the Hebrew does not get the better." The old chiefess, Tati's mother, adopted the two Americans—a not uncommon Tahitian gesture of friendship—and Adams was renamed Taura-atua—"Bird Perch of God." With his adoption Adams took a proprietary interest in the island and its history, so much so that La Farge accused him of becoming more Teva than the Tevas. Adams now suggested that Tati's sister Marau, the divorced Queen of the King of Tahiti, record her memoirs. He himself volunteered to put them into literary shape. When she agreed, he buried himself once more in his self-imposed trade, working out a complicated genealogy that was in a larger sense the history of the island. He urged Marau to add all the scandal she could remember. "The devil knows," he wrote hopefully, "she can put in plenty." Her memoirs indeed recorded the passing of a heroic age, the decay of a once numerous people.

Their completion ended his stay in Tahiti, and after affectionate farewells to his adopted family, he left for Fiji in June of 1891 to conclude his exploration of the archaic South Seas. From there he and La Farge moved on to Australia, Batavia, Singapore, Ceylon, and then by way of Suez once more across the Mediterranean. His longed-for China remained a land apart. At Marseilles he found letters from Elizabeth, who had gone to London with Martha, leaving her husband at home in the slime of Pennsylvania politics. "Fourteen months!" she wrote. "It is almost a life." And she hurried to Paris to await his arrival. She had counted the days till their meeting, yet for all the anticipation the actuality was disillusioning. The two weeks they spent together to end his banishment turned out to be constrained, fragmented.

Once more in London they found a temporarily more cheering atmosphere. La Farge had returned to the United States with portfolios of South Seas paintings. Elizabeth soon followed him. Adams stayed on, traveling north to Gaskell at Wenlock Abbey in Yorkshire, where he and Clover had visited long ago. On lowering November days he walked alone toward Wenlock Edge, the sodden, melancholy landscape reflecting his own mood as he thought of his parting from Elizabeth in London. Days passed in grey succession, moving relentlessly toward the anniversary of Clover's death. He maintained that he was dead himself and only waiting to be buried. Elizabeth wrote him from Washington that his friends were furious with him for his prolonged absence. Still he hesitated, not knowing what to do next, dreading to resume the old pattern of Lafayette Square. Sometimes he wondered if his friends were nothing but phantasms or if he himself was one.

When he finally did sail for his annual winter in America, he kept mulling over his idea of a tour or perhaps a stay in Central Asia. Aboard ship he discovered that Rudyard Kipling and his new American wife were among the fellow passengers, and although from his first acquaintance with the Indian stories he had considered Kipling vulgar, he became very friendly with him during the voyage. Back in Washington, he was able at last to see the brooding, enigmatic figure over Clover's grave. From that first encounter, the plot in Rock Creek Cemetery became his favorite retreat where he would remain by the hour, almost as enigmatic a figure as the hooded bronze above him. "It is good," he said in a rare moment of breaking silence. "It is not commonplace. I shall be glad to be buried under it some day instead of in that dreary place in Boston with my ancestors."

In 1892 Harvard offered him an honorary degree, but to President Eliot's annoyed surprise he refused it, saying that no work of his warranted it, and that in any case he could not bear the thought of facing a commencement crowd. His brother Charles was furious at this arch refusal, accusing him of having quite outgrown his family under the "etherealized" influence of the Hoopers, La Farge, and Elizabeth Cameron. But even as Henry drifted farther apart from Charles, he grew closer to his brother-in-law Edward Hooper. Not only did Hooper's five daughters succeed each other as nieces in residence at Lafayette Square, but Hooper himself became Adams's financial agent and guide. Adams, after declining his Harvard degree, set out with Hooper and the girls for a three-month tour of Scotland—the first of many such expeditions.

His next return to America left him nervous and depressed, wondering why he was there, why he even existed. John Hay, out of office following Cleveland's election, was equally depressed, equally at loose ends. They were both cheered and enlivened by the emphatic presence of Theodore Roosevelt, recently arrived in Washington as a civil service commissioner. Roosevelt became a frequent visitor on H Street. Adams continued his now celebrated "breakfasts," as he in the French manner called his 12:30 luncheons. Travel became a compulsion for him, and the slightest reason, or none at all, would see him off to Cuba or Mexico or the East, if not to Europe. Between bouts of travel he finished his Tahitian book, *Memoirs of Marau Taaroa, Last Queen of Tahiti*, which he had printed in an edition of ten copies. Some years later he would expand this slim book to encompass the whole rise and fall of the Teva clan—a "South Sea Idyll," he considered it.

In May of 1893 he joined the Camerons in their private railway car for a two-day visit to the Chicago World's Fair before sailing with them for Europe. What he found at the fair astonished him: "As a scenic display, Paris had never approached it, but the inconceivable scenic display consisted in its being there at all—more surprising, as it was, than anything else on the continent, Niagara Falls, the Yellowstone Geysers, and the whole railway system thrown in, since these were all natural products in their place;

while, since Noah's Ark, no such Babel of loose and ill-joined, such vague and ill-defined and unrelated thoughts and half-thoughts and experimental outcries as the Exposition, had ever ruffled the surface of the Lakes."

A financial storm of menacing proportions had been blowing up since May, but to this Adams was all but indifferent as he and the Camerons embarked early in June. They went on to the Continent while he lingered in Scotland, spent a few days at Wenlock Abbey, and then traveled to London for a visit with Henry James. By the time he joined the Camerons in Switzerland the Great Panic of 1893 could no longer be overlooked even by such a detached *rentier* as Henry Adams. There he received word from Charles that the Adams finances were in serious trouble. His brother John, directing the family trust, had been so affected that he had gone into a nervous collapse that would see him dead within the year. Charles told Henry to come home at once. When he reached London he was overwhelmed by the news of the spreading panic: the wave of business failures, the bankruptcies, the stock market collapse, unemployed tramping the streets, and the ominous bread-lines in the cities.

By the time he arrived in Boston, Charles and Brooks were distraught to the point of paralysis at the overextended state of the Adams investments. Unlike his brothers, Henry could keep calm, since he had no notes to meet and had plenty of cash on hand. In spite of his professed disdain for the world of business and finance, he had developed an expert knowledge of stocks and bonds, and he now took the family affairs from the hands of his unnerved brothers. Later Brooks admitted that Henry's decisive action saved them from ruin. Brooks now replaced the expansive and free-spending Charles as manager of the family trust and in a few years restored it to health. Henry could report by mid-September of 1893 that the Adamses had survived the crisis "with our colors flying and have defied all Hell and State Street." Others were not as fortunate. Clarence King's affairs so overwhelmed him that he ended in a mental hospital.

Henry and Brooks spent most of that summer together in Quincy, talking endlessly through the hot August evenings of the Panic, of their hopes and fears, and of Brooks's historical and economic theories that Henry found as exciting as he did enlightening. Brooks showed his brother the manuscript of a book that had long occupied him, his *Law of Civilization and Decay*. It would have much influence on Henry's later views. Anticipating Spengler and Toynbee by a generation, Brooks saw the course of history as cyclical and governed by the same physical laws as the material universe, each period flourishing and fading, to end finally in inevitable decay and death.

As he explained: "Probably the velocity of the social movement of any community is proportionate to its energy and mass, and its centralization is proportionate to its velocity. Therefore, as a human movement is accelerated, societies centralize. In the earlier stages of concentration, fear appears to be the channel through which energy finds the readiest outlet; accordingly, in primitive and scattered communities, the imagination is vivid, and the mental types produced are religious, military, artistic. As consolidation advances, fear yields to greed, and the economic organism tends to supersede the emotional and martial."

Animal life, he maintained, was merely one of the outlets through which solar energy, the original vital source, was dissipated. History moved in cycles as energy was expended. Each civilization was destined to run its course. The religious-artistic stage was fated to give way to the economic-scientific stage, the priest and the warrior to the usurer. The decline of the modern age, he concluded, could be measured from the Gothic culmination when the cathedrals of Paris, Bourges, Chartres, and Rheims were built. That the decline was preordained gave small consolation to either brother. Brooks longed for the days of the priest and the soldier. Henry admitted that he detested his own age and wished only that he could see the end of it. His pessimism intensified by the collapse of 1893, fortified by Marx in his deterministic belief that historical processes could not be altered, he took a certain malicious pleasure in the thought that the velocity of financial concentration would be so great that the system would break down completely within the next century.

On returning from the South Seas Henry had made several casual trips to Cuba, finding the lush tropical scenery there almost as enchanting as that of Samoa and Tahiti. In the spring of 1894 he visited the Caribbean island again with the recuperating Clarence King. The next year, after drifting across America and through Mexico and the West Indies and traveling almost twenty thousand miles, he ended up again in Cuba. When later that year a Cuban revolt broke out, he supported the insurgents, a number of whose leaders he and King had met earlier. His Lafayette Square house became a center of Cuban intrigue where émigré conspirators made arrangements for smuggling arms and supplies to the rebels. Since old Senator John Sherman, Elizabeth's uncle and chairman of the Senate foreign relations committee, was sympathetic to the insurrectionists, Adams was asked to write the committee's report on the Cuban question. His document in substance demanded American intervention. A Cuban historian has called it one of the great state papers of the controversy. His interest in Cuba was diverted, however, when President McKinley appointed Hay ambassador to England. Adams decided to sail with him. But after only a brief stay in London he went on to Paris in May of 1897 to wait for Elizabeth, who had suffered some sort of mental breakdown.

In Paris Adams rented a villa for himself and his five Hooper nieces in the fashionable suburb of Saint-Germain-en-Laye, and one for Elizabeth and Martha a few squares away. Here he retired again into his study—when he was not interrupted by feminine visitors. His studies ranged from Byzantine history to the old French epics, though he was still vague as to any definite literary plans. Yet even as he wondered what he might do next, a new and encompassing project was gradually taking shape in his mind, the genesis of his *Mont-Saint-Michel and Chartres.*

Among his visitors that summer was the volatile Brooks, whose incessant emphatic talk of finance, economics, politics, art, and the course of history, literature, and society wore down his responses, leaving him depressed and exhausted. During Brooks's visit the agitation over the Dreyfus case was reaching its peak. Influenced by their old friend Aristarchi Bey, now in exile and linked with the military and the Catholic reactionaries, the Adams brothers sided with the army and the Church. Dreyfus, Bey assured them, was guilty, and his case was being used to undermine the established order. Henry, with the provincial hauteur of a Boston Brahmin, retained an anti-Semitic bias, in spite of his sister's marriage to a Jew and the Hebrew origins of his Palgrave friends. About the Dreyfus affair, he told Elizabeth, "the current of opinion is running tremendously strong, now that the whole extent of the Jew scandal is realised. For no one doubts now that the whole campaign has been one of money and intrigue." The more passionately prejudiced Brooks wrote: "Here are all the most distinguished officers in France, day after day brought up by a gang of dirty Jews, and badgered and insulted, and held up to contempt with the connivance of the government."

After Brooks's exhausting visit Henry was glad to relax with Hay on a trip to Egypt. At Aswan on the Upper Nile they received the news of the blowing up of the *Maine* in Havana Harbor. This, they knew, meant war, and Adams welcomed it. At last the country would take its stand on his Cuban report. War would give the young men something to live for, even in Boston, even if they died! When Hay's duties forced him to return to London, Adams stayed on. He thought the war might mark a turning point in history, but he did not intend to let it interrupt his travels that now took him from Egypt to Constantinople, Greece, the Balkans, Vienna, and finally London.

The Camerons, in England, had taken a country house in Kent, Surrenden Dering, "about the size of Versailles." Hay made it his unofficial summer embassy and here Adams stayed. During his visit the news came that Hay had been offered the office of Secretary of State, and he suggested that Adams succeed him as ambassador. It was a post that Adams would have much liked, that he might even have had if he had been willing to condescend to the hurly-burly of politicking. This he would or could not do. In his family tradition, he wanted the office without any canvassing on his part, an unsolicited offer. As the chance, or semi-chance, passed him by he pretended not to care. En route to America in November, 1898, he convinced himself that as a nonpolitical figure he could not have been considered, and that in any case he would have been miserable in such a post.

Once more ensconced in Lafayette Square, Adams became almost a second self to his friend Hay. Each fair day at four the two walked briskly for an hour through narrow back streets to Sixteenth Street, talking of the world's finances, America's insolent prosperity, and the course of history itself before returning to the Hays's for tea. As Hay's confidant, Adams was increasingly sought out by foreign diplomats. His midday breakfasts, with six places always set in advance for self-invited guests, became an informal gathering of the diplomatic corps. His house itself was niece-infested. One resident niece, John's daughter Abigail, recalled in her old age how he liked to speak of himself as a cardinal. When he dined alone he reread Saint-Simon's memoirs, washing them down with a pint of champagne. At the end of each evening he would relax by playing a game of solitaire. Abigail particularly remembered the pictures scattered all over the house: "There were many examples of English eighteenth and nineteenth century watercolors—De Wints, Cotmans, Coxes and Girtins—while the dining room held two notable Turner oils—an early one of Norwich cathedral over the fireplace and on the opposite wall a later one of a characteristically luminous whaling ship. In his study were many drawings including a weird and repulsive Blake oil of Nebuchadnezzar on all fours eating grass, a picture that had a grisly fascination for me."

Always as the anniversary of Clover's death neared, his spirits declined to a point where he saw little hope for himself and only catastrophe ahead for the world. It was a feeling that came back to him every November and culminated in December. "I have to get over it as I can, and hide, for fear of being sent to an asylum," he told Brooks.

Spring found him discontented, restless, wanting to be off again on his travels yet not knowing where he wanted to go. Globe-trotting at sixty-one, he admitted, was an imbecility. He complained that he spent the income from more than a million dollars yet lived like a troglodyte. Finally he was rescued from his indecision and his feeling of being trapped by the young and charming wife of Henry Cabot Lodge, who insisted that he join the Lodge party on a tour of Italy. Relieved to have his mind made up for him, he sailed in March, 1899.

The trip through Italy and Sicily renewed him. At Monreale "looking down over forests of orange and lemon on Palermo and the Sicilian seas," he was overwhelmed by the immediacy of the past that had so haunted him during the long hours he had spent at his desk translating *Chansons de Geste* and poring over the literature of the twelfth and thirteenth centuries. Several years earlier on a tour of the cathedral towns from Mont-Saint-Michel to Chartres he had experienced something in the nature of a conversion when confronted with the "great glass Gods" at Chartres. He came to see himself as a reincarnation of his ancestors, those anonymous men who had helped build Chartres, Caen, Bayeux, Saint-Lô, Coutance, and Mont-Saint-Michel. After repeated visits to Chartres, after afternoons of meditation under the lapidary glass of the great windows, he, the unbeliever, pleaded in his enigmatic "Prayer to the Virgin":

> You, who remember all, remember me;
> An English scholar of a Norman name,
> I was a thousand who then crossed the sea
> To wrangle in the Paris schools for fame.

By a process of osmosis he by degrees absorbed into himself the age in which he would most have liked to live, the age of the Chartres glass and cathedral sculptures, of the *Dies Irae* and Nicolette and the *Song of Roland* and the Arthurian legends, of Abelard and Aquinas and St. Francis. In his evolving *Mont-Saint-Michel and Chartres* he would struggle with words to make those years come alive again, "the Church, the Way, and the Life of the twelfth century that we have undertaken to feel if not to understand."

Long before, John Adams as delegate to the Continental Congress in Philadelphia had against all his Puritan inheritance been moved to fascination by a Catholic service he attended. In his great-grandson that fascination would become all-enveloping. Henry Adams came to haunt Chartres, physically and spiritually, for all his unbelief, worshiping the vital force from which all else derived, the eternal womanly, "Astarte, Isis, Demeter, Aphrodite, and the last and greatest deity of all, the Virgin." "Mary," he wrote, "concentrated in herself the whole rebellion of man against fate; the whole protest against divine law; the whole contempt for human law as its outcome; the whole unutterable force of human nature beating itself against the wall of its prison house, and suddenly seized by a hope that in the Virgin man had found a door of escape."

On a superficial level Adams's *Mont-Saint-Michel and Chartres* is a vade mecum, a guidebook that the author pretends to have written for a party of nieces traveling in France, but this is no more than a convention such as Adams's use of the third person in his autobiography. What he really succeeds in accomplishing is the almost impossible task of re-creating an age. Disarmingly he claims that it is easy. To grasp that age one need only go to Chartres on a sunny afternoon with a child's awareness, "your mind held in the grasp of the strong lines and shadows of the architecture; your eyes flooded with the autumn tones of glass; your ears drowned with the purity of the voices; one sense reacting upon another until sensation reaches the limit of its range."

The religion of the twelfth century with its enshrined Virgin was so creative a force, so touchingly beautiful a myth, that he felt it *should* have been true. For him, emotionally at least, it was true. Yet what he had come so to love, his rational self could only see as being dead as Demeter, its art alone surviving. At the end of his Chartres chapters he made his own sombre summing up: "For seven hundred years Chartres has seen pilgrims coming and going more or less like us, and will perhaps see them for another seven hundred years; but we shall see it no more, and can safely leave the Virgin in her majesty, with three great prophets on either hand, as calm and confident in their own strength and in God's providence as they were when Saint Louis was born, but looking down from a deserted heaven, into an empty church, on a dead faith."

When Elizabeth was not in Paris, Adams occupied comfortable attic quarters in her house in the Bois de Boulogne. There he worked at his *Chartres* in monklike seclusion, surrounded by mounds of photographs, books, and manuscripts. On a pleasant afternoon he liked to walk to the Paris Exposition, fascinated by the dynamos there, which in their relentless humming came to seem to him the modern energy equivalent of the Virgin. After Elizabeth returned in September of 1900, he moved up the avenue nearer the Arc de Triomphe, but her household remained the center of his social existence. She had become Balzac's "woman of forty," mature, self-assured, still beautiful. With the years she had increasingly moved apart from her husband, without rancor, as if the two had merely lost interest in each other. Joseph Trumbull Stickney, a Harvard poet young enough to be Adams's grandson, had become one of her fervent admirers. She took open pleasure in his affections, although Stickney's fellow poet, Bay Lodge, was regretfully certain that there was nothing in it but an innocent flirtation. Nevertheless, the young man's presence bothered Adams, reminding him oppressively of the weight of his own years.

In January he returned to Washington with his first draft of *Mont-Saint-Michel and Chartres.* Temporarily he put it aside to resume the scientific and technical studies that so engrossed him in connection with his and Brooks's theories of history. By summer he was again in Europe where he now spent seven months of each year, in spite of his chronic seasickness, crossing and recrossing the Atlantic as if it were a kind of ferry trip. He was having breakfast in a Stockholm restaurant when he learned of McKinley's assassination. "What is the moral of all this for our Theodore?" he asked Hay in dumfounded amazement. "You shall have twenty guesses,—more if you like, for I don't know the answer and can't see through the muck." Adams did not return to Washington until the year's end, and when he arrived he was dismayed to learn that his friend King had just died in wretched circumstances. The years were slipping by with increasing momentum, as they do to those over sixty. Hay's son had been killed in an accident that autumn.

Earlier in the year Edward Hooper, whom he had come more and more to rely on, had followed the family pattern and in a fit of depression killed himself.

Though Adams's friends were dwindling, his patterned existence in Lafayette Square remained unchanged, surrounded as he was by his bodyguard of Hooper nieces. Roosevelt of course invited him at once to the White House. Adams was apprehensive about going to a place so bristling with memories that went back a century to his great-grandfather's shattered days there. Nor could he cross the threshold to endure Roosevelt's too-hearty greeting without remembering the happy times when he had gone there with Clover to dinner. The new President's abounding zest, his unashamed courting of popular favor, his tactlessness, and his self-assertion dismayed his old friend who concluded that he was no longer a friend.

In spite of a constant succession of guests Adams managed to seclude himself in his study six hours each day for what he called his communion with the Virgin. "Four weeks at home, in the very heart of the world," he wrote Elizabeth, "with my fingers close to the valves, and I pass my time entirely in the 12th century, as far away as mind can get. . . . I've seen no one and glad of it." As he bent over his desk, the present receded. Sentences and paragraphs took shape; epigrammatic, ironic, unique in style and imagery. By the spring he had rewritten and completed the whole volume. "I'm perfectly square with the Virgin Mary," he told Elizabeth. "I've sent Tahiti in Tati's name to half a dozen public libraries, and have started a historical romance of the year 1200." This companion piece to *Chartres* taking shape in his mind would emerge as his third-person autobiography, to demonstrate with infinite subtlety that he had been born in the wrong century.

Each spring saw him bound for Paris to keep himself from "mental extinction"; each winter found him back in Washington. In 1904 he at last arranged for a private printing of *Chartres*, his

"Miracles" as he sometimes called it, in an edition of a hundred copies but with his own name withheld. Brooks considered the book the crowning achievement of the Adams family and begged him to publish a regular trade edition.

Long ago in writing his history Henry had concluded that society was at the mercy of impersonal forces beyond the control of man. To explain them he searched for a law akin to the laws of physics. Spurred by Brooks's theories he worked out logarithms and graphs and mathematical formulas, yet always the ultimate answer escaped him. What he was really seeking was the philosopher's stone to reveal the unity underlying the multiplicity of his century. Men had found such a unity once, as he saw it, in the thirteenth century in the symbol of the Virgin. As he wrote in his autobiographic chapter, "The Dynamo and the Virgin": "Symbol or energy, the Virgin had acted as the greatest force the Western world ever felt, and had drawn man's activities to herself more strongly than any other power, natural or supernatural, had ever done; the historian's business was to follow the track of the energy; to find where it came from and where it went to; its complex source and shifting channels; its values, equivalents, conversions. It could scarcely be more complex than radium; it could hardly be deflected, diverted, polarized, absorbed more perplexingly than other radiant matter. Adams knew nothing about any of them, but as a mathematical problem of influence on human progress, though all were occult, all reacted on his mind, and he rather inclined to think the Virgin easiest to handle."

He told his friend Henry Osborn Taylor in 1905 that he had at last formulated the ratio of development in energy. "The ratio for thought is not so easy to fix. I can get a time-ratio only in philosophy. The assumption of unity which was the mark of human thought in the middle-ages has yielded very slowly to the proofs of complexity.... Yet it is quite sure, according to my score of ratios and curves, that, at the accelerated rate of progression shown since 1600, it will not need another century or half-century to tip thought upside down. Law, in that case, would disappear as a theory or *a priori* principle and give place to force. Morality would become police. Explosives would reach cosmic violence. Disintegration would overcome integration. This was the point that leads me back to the twelfth century as the fixed element of the equation."

In Spenglerian terms Henry's twelfth and thirteenth centuries were the springtime of Western civilization, the technological age was the autumn, and after that came the immobility of winter. A generation after Adams had written *The Education of Henry Adams*, Henry Seidel Canby thought that a truer title might have been: "How I Educated Myself in the Nature of the Nineteenth Century; and Learning what it was Like in Reference to Me, went on and tried to Discover where it was Going; Made some brilliant Guesses, but could see no Final Solution hopeful for Man; and so Resolved that my use of Education had led only to a Demonstration of the Extent of Human Ignorance."

Adams's alter ego, the Henry Adams of his autobiography, he maintained in his preface, was an unreal "manikin" that nevertheless "must be taken for real; must be treated as though it had life. Who knows? Possibly it had!" Whether the "manikin" of the *Education* was real or not, Adams considered the book his "last will and testament." Of its composition he wrote: "Every man with self-respect enough to become effective, if only as a machine, has had to account to himself for himself somehow, and to invent a formula of his own for his universe, if the standard formulas failed. There, whether finished or not, education stopped. The formula, once made, could be but verified.

"The effort must begin at once, for time pressed. The old formulas had failed, and a new one had to be made, but, after all, the object was not extravagant or eccentric. One sought no absolute truth. One sought only a spool on which to wind the thread of history without breaking it. . . . As term of a nineteenth-century education, one sought a common factor for certain definite historical fractions. Any schoolboy could work out the problem if he were given the right to state it in his own terms.

"Therefore, when the fogs and frosts stopped his slaughter of the centuries, and shut him up again in his garret, he sat down as though he were again a boy at school to shape after his own needs the values of a Dynamic Theory of History."

A dynamic law, he wrote a few pages later, "requires that two masses—nature and man—must go on, reacting upon each other, without stop, as the sun and a comet react on each other, and that any appearance of stoppage is illusive." Science as he conceived it was the philosophical search for the ultimate reality, although in the end he would have to conclude that this reality was a riddle.

Adams's *Education* is divided by a gap of twenty years that includes his happy married years of 1872 to 1885 which he passes over in silence. The first twenty of the thirty-five chapters take him from his childhood—the idyll of Cambridge and the chill of Boston—through the Civil War period in London. Deftly, urbanely, he pays off old scores, from Harvard to the British diplomats who harassed his father. As a picture of the times, for all its Adams self-image, it is unrivaled. His brother Charles on reading the early reminiscent chapters thought himself a boy again in Quincy. Brooks was more critical, considering it a comedown after *Chartres*, an overextended attempt to mix science with society. The chapters after the twenty-year gap were more philosophical, less personal—his interpretation, largely measured in Darwinist terms, of the transformation science had brought about in America since the Civil War. Adams himself thought that the two chapters "A Dynamic Theory of History" and "A Law of Acceleration" were the heart of the book.

At the conclusion of his *History* Adams had asked if the American democratic experiment would be as successful in moral as it had been in material progress. By the time he wrote his *Education* he decided that it had not been, could not have been. In December, 1905, he brought the manuscript with him from Paris when he returned to Lafayette Square. This time he did not even bother to visit Roosevelt, finding the President's rambunctious personality by now merely offensive. The following year he had a hundred copies of his *Education* privately printed to distribute to his friends for their comments. The book was bound in the same format as *Chartres*, and Adams dated the preface February 16, 1907, his sixty-ninth birthday. He made his annual trip to Paris that year in the midst of another business depression. Now, disregarding politics and the present, he had become engrossed in his projected essay "The Rule of Phase Applied to History," based on the hypothesis of the new physics, that would not be published until after his death. Seeking to enlarge on his dynamic theory of history, his law of acceleration, he spent eight hours a day in his Paris apartment working out mathematical formulas, ratios of foreign exchange and coal resources, military comparisons of the great powers, the later developments in physics and chemistry. He admitted that he was more of a schoolboy at seventy than ever he had been at seven. The atom, the electron, electricity—what were they, he asked himself, searching for the key to the real nature of matter, energy, force, and radiation. His involved pseudomathematical calculations had no lasting value in themselves, however much they may have aided a more scientific approach to history. But for the future of civilization he saw three possibilities: an indefinitely prolonged stagnation; the power of the dynamo running away with itself until it finally exploded; a ruling elite capable of managing the forces which the scientific elite had developed. In the end, of course, would come nothingness, for the universe as well as for man.

Age in its withering lent a distinguished cast to Adams's features. To the nieces and would-be nieces who arrived in Paris to have him show them the cathedrals he appeared a boulevardier, primly dapper in immaculate white suit, his hawk nose ranged above his clipped pointed beard, gracious as he was elegant. Paris was part of him, and he part of Paris. He was a familiar figure in the best restaurants, deferred to by headwaiters. Yet he lived in a kind of anonymity, making no effort, showing no desire to mix in the Proustian world of the Faubourg Saint-Germain. At this time he began a friendship with Bernard Berenson, then emerging as the premier connoisseur of Europe. It was a friendship that in spite of Adams's polite anti-Semitism would flourish and endure to the end of his life. "We had much in common," Berenson commented, "but he could not forget that he was an Adams and was always more embarrassed than I was that I happened to be a Jew." Adams introduced Berenson to Edith Wharton's salon—that Adams liked to call a "saloon"—where the older generation of American ex-patriates met with the old French families of the Faubourg.

In July, 1908, Adams while visiting a Paris antique shop suddenly began babbling in incomprehensible French. Though he quickly recovered, he knew that a cog had slipped in his brain, that this was a sign that the mechanism was wearing thin. He hoped for at least two more fruitful years before his father's fate overtook him. In November he had his last will and testament drawn up with the instructions that he was to be buried beside Clover, but with no inscription on his grave, not even his name. The following spring he was again in Paris. There was an air of uneasiness about the city, of uncertainty, the pall of that fateful July of five years later. One of his more casual visitors on his return to Washington was the Southern biographer and historian Frederick Bancroft. Bancroft's first impression of his small bearded host was of "a very small and superior watch: his tick and movements are hardly noticeable." When his visitor inquired about his health, Adams replied: "I am growing old fast. After 70 one ages rapidly, and then one realizes how little is left and how little has been done." A year later when Bancroft met him again in Lafayette Square at luncheon his face seemed fuller, his eyes inflamed. It was a simple but elegant meal—milk soup, wild duck, rice, peas, sweet potatoes, apple pie, nuts, chocolate creams, and coffee. Adams ate lightly, and drank only water. "He lives," Bancroft noted, "in the most *perfect* but not the greatest luxury that I have anywhere seen. There is not a sign of display, but everything is rich, artistic and in perfect taste."

In April, 1912, while having dinner in his Lafayette Square dining room he had another seizure and toppled out of his chair. Put to bed, he soon improved, then suddenly suffered a relapse from which few expected him to recover. For extended periods he was delirious, talking of those long dead as if they were alive, particularly of his mother whom he imagined to have been lost on the *Titantic*. Then, when least expected, he rapidly began to recover. Moved to a cottage on his brother Charles's Lincoln, Massachusetts, estate, he improved still further. Elizabeth took charge of his Paris affairs, closing his apartment and shipping the furniture back, then taking passage herself, determined to dedicate the rest of her life to looking after her devoted invalid. She was a little discomposed to discover that he needed no looking after, that he was again quite capable of looking after himself. However, she established herself in Boston, visiting him each day to his delight, though Charles was less than delighted. Ralph Adams Cram, the architect of the New Gothic, was now finally able to persuade him to allow the American Institute of Architects to publish *Mont-Saint-Michel and Chartres*, Adams telling him they could do as they pleased so long as they did not bother him with details.

By the spring of 1913 he was well enough to return to Paris. There in Elizabeth's apartment he was able to renew old ties, to resume his medieval studies, particularly medieval music, in which he had recently become engrossed. In the summer he drove through the countryside searching out obscure twelfth-century buildings. He still felt the effects of his stroke, however, complaining to Brooks that he had only one hand, one foot, one eye, and half a brain.

In May of 1914 Bancroft met Adams in Paris. Two months before the catastrophe, Adams had become convinced that there would soon be a general war, and he complained about the inconsideration of the European nations in disturbing his peace. He was staying in the country when he heard the bells ringing late in July to call up the reservists. The actuality of the war declaration so upset him that when he had to register for a visitor's visa he could not remember his mother's name. Two weeks later he had regained his composure sufficiently to write Gaskell: "The weather is too hot for comfort, but we are otherwise at ease except for being kept poor and confined in Paris. All the world is worse off. We are at least awfully interested and absorbed. It is an appropriate ending to my life which has of late seemed flat. To you, of course, it is even more personal, but to me the crumbling of worlds is always fun." He left for England, writing more soberly to Sir Ronald Lindsay the day after his arrival: "It was an escape from what verged on Hell, and no slouch of a bad one. We got out of Paris just in time. . . . I own that the war has been rather too much for me. . . . When one's universe goes to pieces just on one's head, one has to scramble. I see no way out of it. For the first time in my life, I am quite staggered."

The following month Adams sailed for home. He was not to see Europe again. Most of his friends had disappeared or were fast disappearing. Elizabeth remained in Paris, usefully engaged at last in running the Foyer for Refugees. "I think of my reckless wasted life with you as the only redeeming thing running through it," she confessed to him. "Whatever I have or am is due to you." Then his brother Charles died, a shock to him to have the blood tie dissolved, even though the brothers had not been close for many years. The death of Henry James the following year was an even greater shock; he had been Adams's friend for forty years, Clover's friend even before her husband had known him. Weighed down by melancholy, Adams wrote Elizabeth that he had been living all day in the seventies. He told Gaskell he was horrified to be still alive. "Farewell!" he wrote. "Every letter I write I consider—for convenience my last." Two years yet remained ahead of him. After thirty-two years he returned for the summer to the house at Beverly Farms that he and Clover had built in 1876 and that he had thought he never wanted to see again. So feeble was he now that he had to dictate his letters, but his mind remained agile. He still took his daily walk, yet daily he seemed to shrink. He still managed to have guests for luncheon or for dinner. What he feared most was another stroke that might leave him mindless.

Three days after his eightieth birthday he wrote to Gaskell from Washington: "I am inclined to say now that the man who has attained 80 years has achieved the most stupendous failure possible, because he has, at least in my case, seemed to have got to the bottom of everything, and has left no experience that has not failed. . . . I have buried all my contemporaries except you, and have nothing more to ask from them. . . . The various horizons which you and I have passed through since the '40's are now as remote as though we had existed in the time of Marcus Aurelius, and, in fact, I rather think that we should have been more at home among the Stoics. . . . Really I have nothing whatever here to remind you that we had common friends fifty years ago. I can send you no news of anybody you ever saw or heard of. I doubt a little whether you have anybody whom I ever knew, to talk about. . . . Perhaps our next letters will grow more cheerful with the improvement of the world."

There would be no next letter. Seven weeks later, on the evening of March 26, 1918, Henry Adams died peacefully in his sleep.

Following the Adams family pattern, Henry reached eighty when he died. His brother Charles and his father had died in their eightieth year, John Quincy at eighty, and only John had passed the eighties barrier. In four generations their average life span was eighty-one years. Brooks, born in 1848 ten years after Henry, had the probability of another decade stretching ahead of him. Henry's death had been a great blow. Brooks told his friend, the Harvard professor Barrett Wendell, that his brother had been closer to him than any other man. "As long as Henry lived it was the same old world," he wrote. "Now he is gone. Say what I will, the oldest relation in my life is closed. I too must go very soon, and small loss provided there be no great pain."

Henry is still a presence today, his books and letters still read, his thoughts explored, while Brooks lurks in his shadow. *Chartres* remains an inner guidebook to the twelfth century. *The Education of Henry Adams*, published in a trade edition after its author's death, was awarded the Pulitzer prize. That account of twentieth-century displacement, with its moving evocation of the previous century in its charm as well as its chicanery, its sense of the end of things, its confession of failure, fitted the disillusioned mood of the post-World War I intellectual. Though Adams's pseudomathematical, pseudoscientific formula predicting the end of our civilization proved invalid, the prediction itself still has an ominous ring. For a time Henry Adams became a cult. Yet Brooks, in the shadow, had more significance than he is usually given credit for. As his biographer, Arthur Beringause, wrote: "His was probably the first comprehensive attempt of any American to develop a scientific formula for explaining history. Before J. Allen Smith and Charles A. Beard, Adams had described the class bias of our Constitution. He anticipated Spengler's theory of the decline of the West, as well as his concept of the movement of power. Adams was among the first to recognize the effect of geography on politics. And Adams, while agreeing with Karl Marx in many respects, nevertheless offers correctives to the German's philosophy, notably in the field of finance and economics."

Sharp-tongued, moody, irascible in his old age, he was commonly regarded—and often avoided—as a cross-grained eccentric. Until he was over forty he lived with his mother in the Old House in Quincy, to which of all the brothers he alone was emotionally attached. After his mother's death he decided to look for a proper wife and hostess. Rumor had it that the first young lady to whom he proposed turned him down, and he by way of reply told her he had always known she was a damned fool. Equally characteristic, if better vouched for, was his reply to Harvard's President Eliot who, when Brooks was a guest lecturer at the Harvard Law School, mildly remarked that Adams seemed to have little respect for democracy. "Do you think I'm a damned fool?" Brooks snorted at him.

Of the six children of Charles Francis Adams who reached maturity, Brooks, named Peter Chardon Brooks and the youngest, was by far the oddest, a misfit from the time he could toddle, irrepressibly talkative and assertive, rebellious at school, prone to accidents. His two older brothers detested him. Henry alone showed himself kind and indulgent to the irritating small boy. When his father took him to England on his diplomatic mission in 1861, the twelve-year-old Brooks was considered backward. He was sent to Wellesley House, a school about a dozen miles from London, where he remained a student for the next four years, his father hoping against hope that he would somehow learn enough to enter Harvard. As he attained his bodily growth, his mind also seemed to mature. Before he left Wellesley House in 1865 to return to America, he had won prizes in English, history, geography, and mathematics, while growing indistinguishable in manner, appearance, and accent from an English schoolboy. Despite his English schooling he still lacked the knowledge of Latin and Greek necessary to pass the Harvard entrance examinations, and he was forced to spend a year tutoring privately with Harvard's Professor Gurney. In September, 1866—somewhat to the surprise of both himself and

Gurney—he passed the examinations and was admitted as a freshman with the class of 1870.

Harvard was still little more than a continuation of a preparatory school, scarcely altered since Henry Adams had fretted there. Brooks did not fret. He showed himself more interested in enjoying himself than in his studies. Charles, who now and then dropped in to have a critical look at his younger brother, thought him fat, sleepy, and lazy. At the end of his freshman year he was admonished for cribbing in a Latin examination. A sunny, blond, good-natured boy, he was popular among his classmates. He rowed on the freshman and sophomore crews. He turned convivial, running up bills at the local wine merchant's and charging them to his brother Charles. In his senior year he was asked to join Harvard's most exclusive undergraduate club, Porcellian, the first of his family to be a member. The curriculum he considered stupid, pigheaded. His father wrote admonishingly from London that he did not seem to be developing much enthusiasm for intellectual pursuits. Yet, little as the college courses appealed to this young man-about-town, the course that Professor Gurney gave on the fall of Rome made a deep impression on him, one that would help shape his life. Admitting that he had known nothing about the period, he wrote his father that it was more interesting by far than anything else he had studied at Harvard.

After a summer's trip west with two Harvard friends, Brooks—like so many Adamses before him—decided to study law. That September he enrolled at the Harvard Law School, occupying rooms in Wadsworth House where his brother Henry had already set up bachelor quarters. But social life continued to engross him. With not too great effort he still maintained "gentleman's C's" in his studies. At the year's end his father took him to Geneva as his secretary on the Alabama Claims Commission. When after several months in Geneva Charles Francis returned briefly to Quincy because of his wife's health, Brooks chose to stay on in Paris where, while waiting for his father's return, he led a modified Bohemian existence on the Left Bank. The next winter he spent in Geneva, then in September, 1872, returned with his father to America, determined to study law on his own. Though his preparation was superficial, he managed to pass his bar examination. Unlike the other law-trained Adamses he started an actual practice, opening an office with a Harvard classmate, Edward Jackson Lowell, in Pemberton Square, Boston. Of independent means, both young lawyers were more interested in public service than in making money. The following year Lowell decided to give up the law in favor of a writing career. Brooks, not overly occupied with the law, contributed reviews to his brother Henry's *North American Review*, wrote articles on taxation for the *Atlantic Monthly*, and became deeply involved in the reform movement in Boston. In 1877 he ran for the state legislature, failing the election by only two votes. To his fury he discovered that his two Brooks uncles had voted against him.

It was about this time that his acquaintances began to notice that the genial undergraduate of a few years back was beginning to develop crotchets. Whatever Brooks did, he did too vigorously, using up all his mental and physical energies in the process. Political life, to which he was drawn, left him exhausted, his nerves on edge. He wrote more articles, concerned himself more with politics. Then in 1880 he broke down completely. Unable to stay still, he could not bear to move. A walk of half a mile exhausted him. He could write nothing, and all he could read were the novels of Scott. Though he went south as far as Florida to try to regain his health, his broken state of mind and body persisted. On his return he visited Henry, now married to Clover and living in Washington. So depressed was he at this point that he declared he wished he were dead. Henry took him aside and sternly ordered him to get well. By the time he arrived back in Massachusetts he was again in good physical condition. But he had had enough of the law. His father's mind was now all too obviously failing, and his seventy-four-year-old mother had grown crippled with rheumatism. It became Brooks's self-imposed duty to look after them.

Ever since he had listened to Professor Gurney lecture on the fall of Rome, Brooks had concerned himself with the pattern of history. He came to see as his life's work the formulation of a philosophy of history, the elucidation of a law moving along predictable lines that would clarify both the past and the present. While Henry was in Polynesia, Brooks began by writing what he considered a scientific study of Puritan New England, *The Emancipation of Massachusetts*, the struggle of the laity against the dominant Puritan theocracy to obtain intellectual freedom and equality before the law. As he explained to Henry Cabot Lodge, "It is really not a history of Massachusetts but a meta-physical and philosophical inquiry as to the actions of the human mind in the progress of civilization; illustrated by the history of a small community isolated and allowed to work itself free. This is not an attempt to break down the Puritans or to abuse the clergy, but to follow out the action of the human mind as we do of the human body. *I believe that we and they are subject to the same laws.*"

Darwinist in concept, the *Emancipation* is shaped to a thesis. As history it is often faulty, but its insights are occasionally brilliant and its attack on the Puritan clergy—indirectly on the ancestor-worshiping school of New England historians—is devastating. The book stirred up much interest, much resentment. After its appearance New England history would never seem the same.

While Brooks was writing his *Emancipation* his father had died, an event long anticipated and in a sense discounted by the slow fading of Charles Francis's mind. But the death of Brooks's mother in 1889, the person to whom for all her feebleness he had been most attached in the world, overwhelmed him. Without her presence the Old House seemed unbearably empty. In his isolation he told Henry Cabot Lodge's wife that if he could find another woman like her he would marry her at once. She suggested her sister, Evelyn "Daisy" Davis. He is said to have proposed to her while taking her on a buggy ride, he expostulating as he held the reins that he was a mad eccentric and that if she married him it would be on her own responsibility and at her own risk. A gentle, gracious, witty young woman with everything but money, and delighted that Brooks could supply that deficiency, she agreed to accept him for all his limitations. The Daisy nickname, he told her, would have to go. He would not have her treated like a cow. She must be Evelyn. She later called him Brook, because, as she explained, "Brooks" was plural and he was singular. His brother Charles, going to call on her for the first time, announced that he was going to pay his respects "to the unfortunate lady who says she is going to marry my brother Brooks."

A few months after their marriage the coupled sailed for Europe. Brooks was already mulling over his next book, *The Law of Civilization and Decay.* Years later he pinpointed the moment when the initial inspiration came to him, although this may owe more to Gibbon than to fact. Gibbon had written that the idea of his *Decline and Fall* first came to him as he was musing among the ruins of Rome's Capitol while the barefoot friars were singing in the Temple of Jupiter. Brooks, after Henry's death, wrote in an introduction to his brother's philosophic writings: "I can see myself now as I stood one day amidst the ruins of Baalbek, and I can feel the shock of surprise I then felt, when the conviction dawned upon me ... that the fall of Rome came about by a competition between slave and free labor and an inferiority in Roman industry."

Brooks's law, reduced to its simplest terms, postulated that thought is a form of human energy manifesting itself in two phases: fear and greed. Man in his first or primitive phase is governed by fear of the unknown that stimulates his imagination to create a belief in an other world. Human society, constantly in motion, constantly seeking outlet for its energy, expands, coalesces, moves into the second phase as the velocity of social movement increases. The economic and scientific mentality flourishes at the expense of the martial, the imaginative, and the religious. More specifically, according to Brooks's neo-Marxist definition, as the government becomes centralized currency becomes restricted. Financiers manipulate prices and wages. Competition of the traders and the lagging salaries of the workers sap the nation's energies. Society decays. A cycle of history ends.

Critics might raise objections to many of his points, many of his details. Yet whatever their objections, Brooks's remains a significant and durable achievement. He was one of the first to expound the effect of economic forces on history. In an age of fragmented national histories, he saw history as a whole. Finally with pungent insight he underlined the rule that history is not merely the relation of what happened, but the elucidation of why it happened. Henry on reading Brooks's *Law* concluded that his brother was indeed a genius. "He has done...what only the greatest men do," he wrote Elizabeth; "he has created a startling generalization which reduces all history to a scientific formula, and which is yet so simple and obvious that one cannot believe it to be new. My admiration for it is much too great to be told."

The first edition sold out in a few months. Among those whose interest it stirred was Theodore Roosevelt, then police commissioner in New York. Not long afterward Roosevelt would come to Washington as McKinley's Assistant Secretary of the Navy and become one of Brooks's intimates, having lunch with him almost daily, absorbing and later radiating his views. Brooks saw Darwinian struggles ahead, with the United States either accepting its decline or emerging through war as a superpower, an empire. Adams, a militarist at heart, was excited at the latter prospect. In the years to come he, Roosevelt, and Lodge would be the proponents of military preparedness, expansion, and the New Nationalism. He was in France when he heard of the blowing up of the *Maine* in Havana Harbor, and headed at once for home. For him the Spanish-American War marked the beginning of a great Western empire under his country's leadership and control. He thought the war was the opening salvo in the struggle for the world. His view of the future was grimly exciting—total war, an elitist state socialism at home, imperialism abroad in which the United States would control much of Asia. He told reporters he believed in war and the policy of expansion it forced on the nation. In the end, country and world and universe would lapse into eternal nothingness, even the past ceasing to have existed, but in the immediate future he saw the glittering prospect of America as mistress of the world.

Brooks and Evelyn were at Beverly Farms when the news arrived of McKinley's death. Brooks was so elated that he could not stop talking, could not even sit down. Elizabeth Cameron, who also happened to be there, remarked that she had never seen him so agreeable, so animated. With Roosevelt's accidental accession, Brooks became the President's confidential adviser, consulted almost daily on all manner of affairs. Behind the Square Deal was Brooks Adams, reiterating to Roosevelt the need for the control of capital, the control of labor, in preparation for expansion and war. His influence is traceable in Roosevelt's seizure of the Panama Canal Zone, his response to Russia's threat to Manchuria, his mediation in the Russo-Japanese War, and in much else that is otherwise puzzling in the Roosevelt foreign policies. Domestically Adams played a leading legal role in the attempt of the administration to regulate and control the railroads. "We are having our little day now," he wrote Henry. "Let us thank God and enjoy it. Those who follow will pay. We may skim through."

In 1903 Dean Melville Bigelow of the Boston University Law School appointed Brooks lecturer on constitutional law. Brooks also kept in constant contact with Oliver Wendell Holmes, Jr., whose relativistic humanist approach to the law had much influenced him and whose appointment to the Supreme Court he had strongly endorsed. Roosevelt, Lodge, Holmes, and Bigelow were the four men with whom Brooks was most intimate during the two Roosevelt administrations. When Taft succeeded Roosevelt, the Washington scene changed for Adams beyond recognition. Closeness to the power centrum had been heady for him. Now he was left alone. He and Henry had diverged to the point of coldness over Brooks's militarism. Both brothers were, nevertheless, convinced that the fall of Western civilization was in the offing, although they could not agree as to what protective steps the United States should take. Brooks saw Roosevelt as the country's only hope against disaster. Henry considered Roosevelt a mis-leader, a neurotic who would probably end up in mental collapse or in a state of acute mania.

In July, 1914, Brooks was in Bad Kissingen taking a water cure. By the time he reached Paris, mobilization was in full swing. He thought the sudden appearance of the soldier swarm the most impressive sight he had ever seen. Whichever side might win, he knew that the world would never again be the same. When a young friend asked him how long he thought the European war would last, he replied presciently that, allowing for temporary truces, it would probably go on for thirty years.

By October he was back in Quincy. That month the pastor of the First Parish Church—the church of his ancestors, where John and John Quincy and their wives lay buried in the crypt—asked him to bear testimony to his faith. It was an odd position for an unbeliever to be in, and he accepted with reluctance. Yet, though God might be for him, a mirage, he recognized that human standards were only relative, that right and wrong could not be defined except by the standards of a revealed religion. Standing in his pew, he told the congregation that any appeal to reason was an appeal to private judgment, and an appeal to private judgment was an appeal to chaos. The universe remained a mystery that neither philosophy nor science could begin to explain. Only the Church could furnish an answer to the riddle of existence. Enigmatically the unbeliever ended with the despairing cry: "Lord, I believe; help thou mine unbelief!" In a revised edition of his *Emancipation*, published that same year, Brooks wrote a more detached confession of faith, concluding that "each day I live I am less able to withstand the suspicion that the universe, far from being an expression of law originating in a single primary cause, is a chaos which admits of reaching no equilibrium, with which man is doomed eternally and hopelessly to contend."

His writings in his later years were voluminous but for the most part ephemeral—magazine articles and essays, speeches and addresses, letters to the various editors, the occasional book. He had little new to add to his beliefs which, when assembled, contained many of the ingredients of the later corporative states. He accepted race theories and the class division of society; he detested the feminist movement, and the mere mention of woman suffrage made the veins start out on his forehead; bankers were for him subversives, "gold-bugs"; war became the test of a nation and the test of manhood; he believed in a governing elite superimposed on both capital and labor, a strong executive ruling without legislative hindrance. Before America entered the war he joined with Roosevelt and Leonard Wood in the preparedness movement and agitated for compulsory military training. The first Plattsburg volunteer training camp stirred all his enthusiasm. On a visit to Plattsburg he remarked that the martial atmosphere was congenial to him, "much more so than that of State Street." The testy, bald little man, cantankerous and dyspeptic, became fearsome to cross as he grew older. Even his relatives tended to avoid him, referring to "that crank Brooks." "Kill Wilson!" he shouted in a rage to Lodge, after the President had returned from Paris with his peace treaty. At

Christmas, 1919, he announced that he disliked everyone, but that he hated Lloyd George more than the rest.

Brooks Adams saw himself as the last of the Adams dynasty. "I too must go very soon," he wrote Barrett Wendell the week after Henry's death, "and small loss provided there be no great pain." In 1919, in his introduction to several of Henry's philosophical essays that he published under the title *The Degradation of the Democratic Dogma*, he wrote: "It is now full four generations since John Adams wrote the constitution of Massachusetts. It is time that we perished. The world is tired of us. We have only survived because our ancestors lived in time of revolution."

Summers he went abroad. Winters he spent in Boston in the house he had bought on Chestnut Street. His springs he passed in the Old House. He alone among the living Adamses remained attached to the ancestral home in now suburbanized Quincy. After the war he formed the Adams Memorial Society to preserve and administer the house, which he wanted kept as a museum after his death. He collected all the furniture and fittings he could get hold of, restoring the interior and the formal gardens as closely as possible to their condition in John Adams's day. Age exaggerated his cantankerousness. Even his wife irritated him. She in turn went into a mental decline and finally had to be put into a sanitarium.

In spite of his agnosticism Brooks was drawn emotionally toward the Catholic Church. In 1921 he made a retreat with the Benedictines on the Isle of Wight. Later, in America, he stayed at Portsmouth Priory, the Benedictine school and monastery at Portsmouth, Rhode Island, explaining that he merely went there to get peace in his last days. "I have no real belief," he told the prior as if he wished he had.

As his health deteriorated, his temper grew worse. Increasingly suspicious, he kept a loaded pistol at his bedside. He intimidated a succession of nurses. His bills and expenses, he announced belligerently, were altogether too high, and he ordered his servants to economize. His coachman suggested putting Adams's twenty-year-old horse, Beauty, to sleep. Adams in turn suggested that this might equally be done to elderly servants. For all his querulous egotism his servants remained devoted to him, and he provided for them handsomely in his will. In January, 1927, Evelyn died in her sanitarium. Brooks knew that his own end was near. He wanted to die in the Old House, but this last wish was not to be granted him. On February 13 he died in Boston. He was buried from Quincy's Old Temple, the Church in which he could not believe.

Brooks, ending the fourth generation, was the last Adams to live in the Old House, the last to live in Quincy. The Adamses would continue and flourish, but it was as if in abandoning their native earth they had lost their primal strength. Or it may have been that the Boylston blood, that in John Adams's opinion transformed a line of obscure farmers into a dynasty, had become too diluted to remake its mark. Yet even in the fifth and sixth generations the Adams look persisted: long-nosed with a prim narrow mouth; the males short of stature, prematurely bald, and with a characteristic hunch of the shoulders. But the Adamses' traditional opposition to State Street was buried with Brooks. In the twentieth century the sixth, seventh, and eighth generations have become indistinguishable from the other upper-class families of long descent scattered in intrenched estates west and north of Boston; Harvard overseers, directors of innumerable firms and banks, pillars of historical societies, public-spirited, and scarcely known beyond Massachusetts.

Charles Francis of the fifth generation, who died in 1954 at the Adams age of eighty-seven, was the last Adams to be brought up in Quincy. After attending the eponymous Adams Academy in Quincy, he entered Harvard in 1878, becoming president of his class and acquiring the nickname "Deacon" that he would bear the rest of his life. Like his father and his uncle, after whom he was named, he became an impassioned amateur sailor. After graduating from Harvard he went abroad for a year, chiefly to observe English yacht racing. Returning to Boston he studied law with the goal of specializing in trusteeships and the administration of estates. In his early career he kept his legal residence in Quincy, and in 1896 and 1897 was elected mayor on the Democratic ticket. He refused to run again, claiming that he could not afford to continue in office. He became director or controlling head of a number of banks and an officer in forty-three corporations. For thirty years he was treasurer of Harvard, and also served as president of the Board of Overseers and of the Alumni Association. He was a trustee of a wide variety of charitable institutions and public agencies, and a member of the Unitarian Church.

His epitaph might well have been "His name was writ in water," for his greatest successes were on the sea. In 1920 he steered America's cup defender *Resolute* to victory over Sir Thomas Lipton's *Shamrock IV*. Eight years later he piloted the yacht *Atlantic* in a race from America to Spain. When he was seventy-three he won the King's, Astor, and Puritan cups, the first time that the three most-coveted domestic racing trophies had been won by the same person in a single season.

By 1929 Charles Francis had converted to the Republican party, and President Hoover appointed him Secretary of the Navy, a post he held for the next four years. He and Hoover did not always hit it off, according to rumor. However, in his memoirs Hoover wrote: "Secretary Adams was our generation's distinguished representative of that great family which has contributed so much to American life. In personal appearance he was the image of his great ancestor, John Quincy Adams. He was a man of high cultivation, fine integrity, full knowledge of American life, and was able in the conduct of public affairs. Had I known him better earlier, I should have made him Secretary of State."

His son Charles Francis lives today in the rural seclusion of

Dover not too far from Boston. A Harvard graduate of the class of 1932, he took the naval officers' training course as an undergraduate. Before the end of World War II he commanded a destroyer-escort. His hobbies, by his own admission, are shooting and sailing. For the last twenty-eight years he has been connected with Raytheon, the electronics company, and from 1964 until his retirement in 1975 was board chairman. In a symposium at his twenty-fifth Harvard class reunion he was chosen to represent business.

More in line with the pious hopes John Adams expressed for his descendants is the career of Thomas Boylston Adams, son of the fifth-generation John Adams and the same age as his second cousin, the Raytheon board chairman. After graduating from Harvard in 1933, Thomas Boylston wrote editorials for several years for the Boston *Herald*. During World War II he served as a captain in the army air corps, then for seventeen years was connected with the Sheraton Hotel Corporation. He lives in rural Lincoln in a barn converted to a rambling house overflowing with books, the walls covered by his wife's paintings and some of his own and by those of his son, who is also an artist in stained glass. Three of his four sons live communally with their families in a large old-fashioned house nearby.

Thomas Boylston has become the unofficial sixth-generation representative of the family. Until late 1975 he was president of the Massachusetts Historical Society, and he is a trustee of a number of institutions and libraries as well as fellow and treasurer of the American Academy of Arts and Sciences. Politically he is a liberal Democrat, in religion a Unitarian. Opposed to the Vietnam War, he ran as a peace candidate in 1966 for the Democratic nomination for United States Senator. At a Harvard demonstration, he took part in a "Read-in for Peace," reciting a poem he had written on the day of President Kennedy's funeral. Yet in spite of a lusty campaign and massive publicity he received a mere 8 percent of the vote. Two years later he supported Robert Kennedy as the presidential candidate most likely to bring his own dreams of peace and justice to fruition. A few weeks before the bicentennial of the Battle of Concord and Lexington in 1975, he told reporters: "I kept thinking about John Adams on the right of revolution. When government becomes corrupt there is an absolute right of revolution. The fight never stops. There'll always be the establishment and the rebels. I hope our family will always be on the side of the rebels."

His elder brother, John Quincy Adams of the Harvard class of 1931, lives on the Birnham Wood acres—shrunk now to about half their size—that his grandfather moved to from Quincy in 1893. With an inherited passion for the sea and sailing, he is by profession an architect, limiting his public activities to serving as director of Lincoln's De Cordova Museum. Some confusion is caused by two other living John Quincys, second cousins of the first one. The second John Quincy, another great-grandson of the Civil War minister to England and a nephew of Hoover's Secretary of the Navy, graduated from Harvard in 1945 as did his son, John Quincy, in 1974.

The most brilliant member of the Adams sixth generation, George Caspar Homans, does not bear the family name. He is the grandson of the post-Civil War John Quincy Adams and the son of Abigail Adams Homans. Starting out in life to be a poet, he ended as professor of sociology at Harvard. He describes himself as a Republican, a "hardboiled egghead." His mother in her eighties wrote a charming little book, a period piece mostly concerned with her memories of Henry and Brooks, which she called *Education by Uncles*. She, dying in 1974 at the age of ninety-four, was the last of Henry's "resident nieces."

In her book Abigail Homans called Quincy a city of historic ghosts. To an Adams it would have to be that. But to an outsider walking through the crowded, commercial half-city half-suburb it is more the vestige of a dynasty that in its passing recalls the fate of all dynasties. There are the two Adams farmhouses stranded beside the stoplights near the main traffic artery. There is the Old House with its stone library and formal garden and abundant relics, carefully manicured by the National Park Service. The grey granite bulk of the Old Stone Temple perches on a lozenge of land in the middle of Quincy Square. A tablet in the now-Unitarian church reads "till the last trump shall sound," and beneath in the crypt the two Adams Presidents and their wives lie in their granite sarcophagi awaiting that summons. Across the street is the cemetery where the first six generations of Adamses are buried, Point 5 on the Quincy Historic Trail. Half a mile beyond the square, Penn's Hill lurks furtively beneath the bungalows and two-deckers of suburbia. The cairn marking the spot where Abigail and her little son watched the smoke of burning Charlestown and heard the cannon thunder is overshadowed by a cylindrical water tower. Still visible from where they stood is the saddleback line of the Blue Hills that John Adams loved so well, but one can no longer see Charlestown or Boston. Or even the sea.